DANTE'S DIVINE COMEDY

DANTE'S
IVINE OMEDY

A Guide for the Spiritual Journey

MARK VERNON

Angelico Press

First published in the USA
by Angelico Press 2021
Copyright © Mark Vernon 2021

For information, address:
Angelico Press, Ltd.
169 Monitor St.
Brooklyn, NY 11222
www.angelicopress.com

paper 978-1-62138-748-0
cloth 978-1-62138-749-7

Book and cover design
by Michael Schrauzer

For Phoebe, Josh, and Sam,
and the discovery of life in all its fullness

CONTENTS

LIST OF ILLUSTRATIONS

Contents

INTRODUCTION

THE DIVINE COMEDY CHANGES LIVES. READERS of Dante Alighieri's masterpiece have found so ever since copies began circulating in the early fourteenth century. However, there have also always been readers left unsure how to reckon with its genius. This is the challenge of labyrinthine texts that can reveal more of life each time they are read, once a way into them is found.

That difficulty is compounded today because most contemporary commentaries, introductions, and translations of Dante are not interested in The Divine Comedy as a work that catalyzes spiritual transformation. Similarly, it is relatively common for The Inferno to be celebrated, and for The Purgatorio to be respected, but for The Paradiso to be declared redundant, notwithstanding its tremendous displays of literary inventiveness when it comes to portraying light and love. The upshot is that it is easy to find guides to the brilliance of Dante's poetry, the history of his turbulent times, and the significance of his theological innovations. It is hard to find a companion to the journey as a revelation.

And yet Dante himself was adamant that his poem should lead people to perceptions of the divine comparable to his own. He felt charged by heaven to write so as to open hearts and minds to the most basic truth of existence: that our lives and God's life is one life. I hope to help rectify the contemporary dearth by following Dante's advice, which is to track his every step, to feel into each encounter, to ponder his insights and allusions, and thereby descend and ascend with him. His book changed my life when, at least in some measure, I realized what he might be asking of me. I hope to share that here.

This book can be read on its own, as a narrative retelling and interpretation of Dante's journey, or as a commentary that maintains a focus on what is happening to him as he travels, first with Virgil, down the circles of the Inferno and up the terraces of Mount Purgatory, and then with Beatrice, through the heavens of the Paradiso. To use the interpretative schema that Dante suggested: my aim is to stay not only with the literal meaning of the poem, which looks at who he meets and how he captures the encounters in wonderful verse; or with an allegorical reading of the text, which is drawn to the moral implications and religious meaning of the pilgrimage; but also to actively seek out the revolutionary transformations that happen along the way, and the manner in which he describes these perceptual shifts. I am fascinated by how Dante undergoes a process of realization, which is described by the technical term "tropological," after the Greek word "tropos," or "turn." Such changes require an unflinching and, at times, brutal assessment of his life and times, though only so as to discover the ever-present origin that draws him back to itself.

This way of reading The Divine Comedy is crucial for understanding its full significance. The journey is not a Grand Tour of reality, from fiery Inferno to blazing Empyrean, but a total reformation of Dante's ability to know reality, and thereby experience the fullness of its being, without reserve. It's why I think the considered implication of the epic is that Christianity is a universal creed: it reveals that God wills all people to be saved by coming to knowledge of the truth, to recall the words of the First Letter to Timothy in the New Testament. At first, Dante descends into hell presuming that poor moral conduct condemns souls to its dark alleys and inventive tortures, but he gradually realizes that actively participating in God's life is about being free, desirous, comprehending, and aware: in short, having all that we are consciously aligned with all that God is. Ultimately, nothing can separate people from the divine, because that would be to fall out of existence altogether and, conversely, awakening to the fullness of divine life is a matter of complete perception, not perfected behavior. That's our destiny: Dante invites his readers to learn its wisdom and truth.

The year 2021 marks the 700th anniversary of Dante's death in 1321, a year after he completed The Paradiso. The poem is many things: a critique and celebration of human qualities, a warning that this life matters, a path of awakening, an odyssey, a diatribe against the Church and deadly political foes. But it was born of a crisis. Dante begins his journey when waking up in a dark wood. The air tastes bitter. He is fearful. The way forward is utterly obscure.

His predicament resonates with where we find ourselves now, in the middle of various emergencies, a spiritual crisis underlying them all, in my view. Individually and collectively, we must see the world afresh and find ways to reorient ourselves. Alongside other inspired texts, Dante can help us discover how. He called his epic The Commedia, meaning a story with a good ending, for a reason.

Another element that is key, Dante insists, and which is often sidelined, is the crucial role of erotic love in relation to spiritual enlightenment. The figure of Beatrice, Dante's muse, whom he first saw when they were both minors, in 1274, is of course central to any appreciation of The Divine Comedy. What is trickier is understanding how a youthful infatuation morphed into an ascent to God. Christianity, in particular, tends to be averse to the erotic, when not disciplined by marriage. Dante can help us remedy that.

One figure in particular has helped me: Owen Barfield. He was one of the Oxford Inklings, and greatly inspired C. S. Lewis and J. R. R. Tolkien. Lewis drew on Dante not only in individual books like *The Great Divorce*, but right across the *Chronicles of Narnia*, structuring them according to the realms of the seven heavens Dante traverses in *The Paradiso*. Another from the group, Charles Williams, advanced an understanding of Beatrice illuminated by his romantic theology, and I think Barfield's insights can help too. They cast fresh light on the inner workings of *The Divine Comedy*. I pick this up as the cantos unfold.

When it comes to translations, I would recommend the one by Mark Musa published by Penguin Classics. It keeps the *terza rima* form for which Dante is famous without attempting to find rhymes (aba, bcb, cdc), and uses language that is as transparent as possible. The accompanying notes offer continually useful assistance. I have also found invaluable a second translation, by Robert and Jean Hollander. Their scholarship enables secondary questions to be pursued and also discusses the insights of other commentators, medieval and modern. Online, I have often turned to Digital Dante (https://digitaldante.columbia.edu).

The main drawback with these rich resources is that they are not interested in the transformation of Dante — his perceptual development that I consider so key. Two books in particular helped me with that. The first, *Dark Wood to White Rose: Journey and Transformation in Dante's Divine Comedy* by Helen M. Luke, provides an explicitly Jungian interpretation, and a second, *Dante the Maker* by William Anderson, frequently takes the discussion to visionary and mystical traditions that Dante has either influenced, or was influenced by. In addition to her commentary, Helen Luke uses quotes from the translation by Dorothy L. Sayers, which is probably the best English attempt to follow the *terza rima* schema with rhymes.

A final, crucial source to thank is The Temenos Academy. Lectures by Andrew Frisardi, and a reading group led by Jeremy Naydler, were revelatory.

Dante was a realist about his vision. He knew it to be authentic, not in the limited sense that Christianity is the one true religion, but in the sense understood by all great visionaries: their path is one path to the common goal of human life. It demands all that we are and promises all that we can be. Improbable though it seems when we are caught in the thickets, our origin and end is in the love that moves the sun and the other stars.

I
Inferno

Dante, frightened by his plight and terrorized by strange beasts, discovers a guide.

INFERNO I
Lost

D ANTE'S THE DIVINE COMEDY BEGINS WITH
famous words. Halfway through the journey of life, he wakes up.
He is in a dark wood, having wandered from the path.

We have begun. The year is 1300. The day is Good Friday. Dante is
thirty-five years old, at the midpoint of his three score years and ten. He
is already a famous poet and politician. He is married, a father, and has been
in love. However, fortune has turned against him. Florence is being ruined
by a civil war between the groups known as the Guelphs and Ghibellines.
Dante has found himself on the wrong side, with the faction known as the
White Guelphs. He is soon to be expelled from his beloved city, on pain
of being burnt alive.

3

What is life really about? He is midway through it and finds himself far from the path that he thought was navigable. The dark wood is confusing and bitter, as is his life. Both fill him with fear. Has everything that he stood for been lost? He had thought he was a success and is wondering if he has been simply and thoroughly deluded.

The journey beginning is of far greater significance than he could have possibly imagined. It will be an odyssey, full of strange encounters, in a cosmos that is far odder than it has so far seemed. It will be labyrinthine, in the sense that although full of twists and turns, and often seeming to take him away from the center, there will prove to be no wrong turnings, no matter how dark and difficult it gets. This journey is willed and held by barely imaginable forces.

These realizations are not his at the moment. He wakes to a living nightmare, akin to a lucid dream. There is a forest around him, and it looks strange and uncanny. It is dark and full of twisted roots. The place feels slippery. It renders any direction of travel unclear. Maybe this is the first real step: to wake up to where he actually is. Lost.

Casting his eyes this way and that, he spots a hill and some sunshine. They give him hope. He knows that with the sun can be found the light of reason and direction, and an orientation toward the divine. If you can see the stars or the sun, then you can never go too far wrong. Maybe this waking up is no more than an everyday depression or difficulty.

He tries to ascend the slope, seeking a short cut from the darkness, but the way is blocked. Standing before him are three powerful beasts: a dancing leopard, a strong lion, and a hungry she-wolf. They taunt and intimidate him in the gloom. Every move Dante makes is met with threat and a snarl. It seems there is no way to escape them. They are too wily, too fast. His hopes for a speedy return to normal life fade as a gnawing panic sets in.

Commentators discuss what the creatures stand for, and I think they represent three capacities or skills that Dante thought he had and fears he hasn't: the three character traits of wisdom, of love, and of virtue.

The dancing leopard, I suspect, is the embodiment of a reduced or even perverted wisdom. He thinks he knows how to respond to whatever life throws at him, though it turns out he doesn't and he never did.

My sense is that the strong, proud lion who strides deliberately toward him, represents desire and love. Only, with the rising sense that he is way off course, the qualities that might guide him terrify him.

He backs off and moves down the slope, to be confronted by the lean she-wolf. To my mind, this beast stands for virtue, misused. Good traits

4

have become possessive, envious, hungry in him. They have morphed into calculation and vice, and they scare him.

To see the beasts off, Dante must understand them, but he is worlds away from such a conception. That said, his panic indicates something to us about the nature of this journey.

His great poem is populated by the characters and crimes that he has encountered and witnessed during his life, as well as by demons, angels, and unexpectedly great-souled saints. But it is simultaneously an inner journey. One of the things Dante will learn is how to navigate his interiority.

Moreover, something similar is required of us, if we are fully to follow him. The poet's opening remark is midway along the journey of *our* life. Dante the poet invites us to accompany him as he retells the time he was a pilgrim. We can read about what happens to him but must also peer more closely to see how he was transformed. The hope is that, following him aright, we will be transformed too.

It might be thought of as an initiation: a process by which an inner eye opens and everything in life finds its place because we participate in its vitality in a wholly new way. We change. To do so, we must experience all that exists in the deepest darkness as well as the brightest light because it is only when we know about hate that we can really know about love, only when we know about fear that we can really know about hope, only when we have confronted the impossible that we wake up to what is possible. The poem is full of tragedy but is more completely understood as a comedy: a story that ends well. That comes because all has been faced and seen. There is no short cut, no backing off.

It is an ascent that starts with a descent, and this is the thrill of reading *The Divine Comedy*. It's not just a travelogue or biography. It is far more active than that. It can work on you and extend your consciousness, if you take the time to dwell with and reflect on it.

Dante has written a guide to life in all its fullness, and he has a guide too. As he is spinning around in the woods, the beasts of his personal failures hunting him down, a human figure appears. It is Virgil and he is going to become a tremendous, life-changing blessing. Virgil was Dante's great poetic teacher. There's something irreplaceable about the person who prompts undreamt glimpses of what's possible, which extend to and reach over horizons.

Virgil is the author of another odyssey, *The Aeneid*. It features the journey of Aeneas, through light and darkness. It includes a trip to the underworld, which is to say that Virgil has been to the land of the dead before. He has undertaken a similar journey and Dante needs someone like that, someone who can keep faith when hope ebbs, can reach for the practical wisdom that knows the way down is often the way up.

Virgil is not alongside Dante by chance, of course. He is here at the request of the great love of Dante's mortal life, the lady, Beatrice. Dante barely spoke to her before she died too young and rarely saw her on the streets of Florence when she was alive, but the sight of her stirred love in him. It was an infatuation at first, though it lit a flame that grew. It became the one reliable feature of his life. It gave him energy and, still reliable, gives him energy again in the dark wood. Youthful, seemingly mad, immature love. It might yet save him.

Only Virgil's presence prompts a question in Dante's mind. It's another key feature of this undertaking, for with questioning comes awareness. His question is this. Virgil is a pagan. He was born under false and lying gods, Dante presumes, the gods before Christianity. So, how can Virgil guide him? Why has Beatrice sent him?

It seems a bit harsh. But it is an honest expression. Dante is still naïve. He is on the threshold of hell, a zone of crude views that conceal as much as they reveal. He must express what he feels truly to change. He must ask questions. Inner states of mind trap people, unless they are brought to the light of day. Assumptions must be understood in all their stark ferocity, which is to say Dante must travel to the domains where confusion rules.

The first canto concludes with Virgil offering Dante a summary of what lies ahead: they will go to the desperate, before coming to the transforming, and continuing to the rejoicing. *Inferno* comes before *Purgatorio* and *Paradiso*. Only, Dante can't take it in. He's still terrified in this forest, midway through the journey of our life. He has woken in this unpleasant, unwanted reality. All he can do is cling close to his guide. What else, who else has he got? They set off.

Dante wavers and Virgil reveals why he is here.

INFERNO 2
Afraid

ANTE IS WALKING DIRECTLY BEHIND HIS NEW-found guide. The day is ending. The night is beginning as the shadows lengthen and darkness comes down. The creatures of the light disappear.

Then, he addresses his readers, us. I will relate what happened with an unerring memory, he insists. It is the first of many times that he directly attests to having experienced what he describes. Not that it is remotely straightforward to do so. Dante also calls on the muses and all the gods. He needs all the intelligence and insight they can offer, which as a poet he knows is considerable. It is just as well.

A prayer is one thing, feeling empowered is something else. Doubts press in on him, and he turns to Virgil and asks whether he is, in fact, up to the task. Will he complete the journey, let alone be able to wrestle with its meaning and find ways of communicating that to others? He asks, why me? Surely there is someone else who is better equipped? Fear chills his soul.

They are the anxieties of the prophet who is sensing what they are called to undertake. It's the Jonah complex: it might be better to be lost in the belly of a whale. It happens when stepping into the unknown. Trepidation is a consequence, and, at times, that is terrifying. It means letting go of what he trusts, thinks, knows.

The extent of his journey is captured in two figures who come to mind: Aeneas and Paul. They travelled to other worlds too: Aeneas to Hades in Virgil's great poem; Paul into the third heaven, an experience he relates in the Second Letter to the Corinthians. Aeneas was a hero. Moral courage drove him. Paul was a saint. Spiritual sight transformed his life. They inspired renewal, Aeneas's journey refreshing Roman paganism, Paul's vision revolutionizing the world, as is remembered in the millennia turning from BC to AD. Which raises a question: is Dante an Aeneas or Paul? The extent of what might be involved as he travels is dawning on him, as he feels the trembling and self-doubt.

Further, Dante must want this new sight, he must collaborate with it, he must will it. This is not about will in the sense that is often meant today, when it means little more than the freedom to choose. It's more about considering the direction he wants his life to turn toward, what he wants to be aligned with. He doesn't know what that entails or what lies ahead. He cannot. But he does have to agree to what may come.

It is hard for Dante to cultivate this will. He wants to turn away out of a deepening sense of dread. So, Virgil makes a powerful intervention. He cuts right across what Dante is feeling and points out that it is not modesty that is making him doubt, as if he is not worthy. The problem is timidity, pusillanimity. Humility is a cover story.

In effect, Virgil tells Dante off. It's the first of several times he will do so, as will Beatrice further along the line. It's shocking to read as it seems to be the opposite of the compassion we might expect in a Christian story. But Dante needs to realize that he is a human being, and human beings are capable of much, if they want much. Dante is being invited to want it all. This is his chance, midway through the journey of his life. He could continue to engage with the life he knows, and stay where he feels safest, in spite of its traumas. Or he can step out.

Virgil puts it another way. He says that human beings have a river that runs through their souls, but unlike a natural river that readily finds its way to the sea, the human stream can become blocked or diverted. It may flood or become polluted before reaching the fullness of the ocean, which is to say it may be ruined before it finds the divine, though it never stops having the capability to do so. It needs tending and maintaining to ensure that it flows as richly as it can, guided by the broadest vision.

This exhortation makes Dante more nervous. Oh, for the quiet life! Oh, for the peace of the Arno and the beauty of Florence! Virgil tries again. He tells Dante the reason they are walking side by side. It is because he has been called by Beatrice to guide Dante.

Virgil describes what it is like to meet her. She is beautiful. Her eyes are brighter than stars. She shines with a spiritual light that the daylight only mirrors and reflects. The sight was so powerful that immediately Virgil responded wholeheartedly to her request to seek out Dante and save him. She knew that Fortune had not been kind to him, that his earthly life is slowly being destroyed by the brutal Italian wars. But she heard his cry. His desperation is perceived in heaven, where he has friends. Does that not give him courage?

There is more. It turns out that Beatrice is not the only friend Dante has in paradise. No less a saint than the Virgin Mary has been moved by his dire straits, she who in the medieval Christian imaginary sits closest to God. Further, Mary has spoken with Lucia, the saint of light, who had then spoken with Beatrice. There has been a cascade of attention toward Dante from the heights.

Maybe the three saints are a counterpart to the three beasts of the first canto, with Mary, Lucia, and Beatrice being personifications of true wisdom, love, and virtue. Mary knew how to respond wisely when the angel Gabriel appeared to her, unlike the dancing leopard. Lucia moves with the light of love, unlike the shadowy lion. Beatrice fills hearts with the beauty of her virtue: she is full of God, unlike the she-wolf who is perpetually hungry. Dante could know these qualities himself. He has called on all the muses and the gods and, in a way, they have already responded to him, if only he has the eyes to see. Virgil's presence testifies to that.

Virgil is inviting Dante imaginatively to catch sight of just a fragment of this celestial activity, here in the dark woods. The courage it can instill is not about a hero's might but a heart's sense: that which is beautiful can draw us with its promise of so much more. We can choose to follow it, when we don't know where it leads.

It is the common human experience called falling in love. It can lead not just to another person but to divine life, by learning to discern what's beautiful more deeply. It can address him, guide him, if he exercises his freedom to turn toward it. It will carry him into larger worlds. There are deep purposes at work in his life, and ours, even when luck seems to have run out. It's another intimation that a descent is also an ascent: fate can make people capable of more.

Then again, this is not to say he doesn't feel the panic and know the suffering. Virgil tells Dante that Beatrice had wondered if it were too late for him already. Maybe he can't be rescued.

I appreciate these moments in the poem. Dante's account reminds us that his struggle is genuine. Life is fragile. Every moment, and what we do, really counts. The happy ending is not automatic, though strangely it is also guaranteed. The paradox arises because human beings are not puppets of the divine, led to the light like moths to a flame. God must be approached consciously, freely, desirously.

The second canto ends with a beautiful image in which Dante describes the effect that Virgil's words have upon him. They lift his mood, a shift that he compares to a small flower that has become closed and limp on a frosty night and which, warmed by the rising sun, stands up again and opens.

It's a typically Dantean metaphor. Nature herself offers encouragement. Strength blooms within him. He gathers his desire. He regains contact with his longing to know what is good, beautiful, and true. His outer guide, Virgil, has touched his inner guide, his heart, with the remembrance of Beatrice. They take further steps along the rugged road to what lies ahead.

Dante and Virgil enter the gate of hell to find lost souls and a river.

INFERNO 3
Overwhelmed

ANTE AND VIRGIL STAND BEFORE THE GATE OF hell. Words are inscribed above the dark archway. "Through me is the way into the city of sorrow. Through me is the way into fixed grief. Through me is the way to the forsaken. Abandon every hope, all who enter."

The repetition of the phrase "Through me is" echoes the saying of Jesus in John's Gospel. "I am the way, the truth, and the life" (Jn 14:6). Abandon hope, yes. But there is also something strange about the entrance to hell. Is it part of the way? What might that mean? It is clearly the way that Dante must follow.

There is always more going on than meets the eye in *The Divine Comedy*, which is underlined by further lines in the shadowy vestibule: "Justice moved my maker, omnipotence forged me, high wisdom coupled to ancient love."

Hell is telling of its origins and we might expect justice to be part of it, if we have the assumption that hell's punishment is for those who justly deserve it. But what about high wisdom and ancient love? How could they make hell?

I think a clue can be found in Aristotle, the ancient Greek philosopher who profoundly influenced Dante. Aristotle considered justice to be failed love. It's what happens when people have to resort to the law to settle their differences rather than being able to draw on their relationship to work things out. The implication is that justice is not an ideal, as it is often taken today. Rather, it is a necessary failure. Maybe hell is somehow a necessary failure.

Dante asks Virgil about the words. Upon first sight, he thinks they seem cruel. Virgil replies that those in hell have lost touch with the good of the intellect. He doesn't mean dry, logical reason, as intellect can imply. Rather, it's the part of the human soul that resonates with divine understanding, that can see and contemplate the living dynamics of the created world. Virgil is saying that those in hell have lost sight of the inner meaning of things: the soulful, spirited, divine current in life.

They've lost touch with it because they've lost touch with the side of themselves that can appreciate it. And so, in losing touch, they find themselves trapped in a world without that light, without that understanding. It's a literal world where the punishment fits the crime, and indeed, for many of the souls they encounter in hell, that is their understanding of their predicament. It keeps them trapped.

Dante and Virgil pass through the gateway, underneath the confusing words, and immediately hear what they would expect: sighs and cries and shrieks of lamentation. The air itself blows like a sandstorm of black grains. It makes Dante weep. By the end of the canto, he will be swooning, overwhelmed.

The occasions on which he collapses are important. A sight makes him temporarily lose his mind. It shows that he has not been able to understand what he is witnessing, with the implication that keeping a clear mind is a crucial skill to learn during the descent because, as he slowly, gradually gains the ability to do so — even as he witnesses greater and more terrible woes — he gains the ability to see more than what immediately meets the eye.

It's another indicator that all is not as it seems in this domain. It's a sign that there is hidden meaning in its grey existence.

That said, on the inside of the gate, Dante fails to see it. In the early parts of his descent, he draws on the crude understanding of hell that he has gained from the cruder teachings of the Church. It will take him time to change and so detect reality's subtleties.

They encounter their first group of lost souls. They are people who, in their mortal lives, couldn't decide whether they had faith or not, whether they were going to stand for what's good or what's bad. In eternity, their dominant state of mind exposed, they mindlessly follow a banner. They are one of a crowd. They are led by another's will, having lost their own will, their own intuition, their own freedom.

There are very many of these undecideds indeed. Dante is amazed at the number. Their punishment is in one way a repetition, ad infinitum, of the way they lived their mortal lives.

They are surrounded by flies, hornets, and wasps that sting them. The souls are stung so badly that they bleed and red blood drips down their bodies and falls on the ground, where it turns into pus and is eaten by worms. This is the first of the vivid images of suffering in The Inferno. Dante the poet is asking us whether we can tolerate the sight. Can we bear it and so seek a deeper meaning?

Sigmund Freud might say that these souls are caught in a repetition compulsion. They have become so preoccupied with the minutiae of everyday life that they have lost sight of the bigger picture, with the upshot that trivialities repeatedly sting them. It happens. There are people, perhaps many people, for whom the slightest inconvenience prompts rage, and the smallest unease generates panic.

The swarming flies are also the first example of what is called the contrapasso. The word is normally translated as "the appropriate punishment," one that reflects the sin. That said, Dante only uses the term once and, right from the get-go, I think he encourages us to see beyond Hell 101. To my mind, the implication is these individuals' suffering is not a punishment but is to do with what they are capable of experiencing. The currents that shaped their mortal lives have caught up with them. Their habits are made explicit and become amplified. They are haunted individuals. As is sometimes said of ghosts on earth, they have become stuck because they can't see where else they might go, or how else they might live.

It's not that hell is a place of your own making. That's too crude. It's more like hell is the reality you see when your inner eye, your imagination, has grown cloudy or myopic. It's a state of tunnel vision. The same thing can happen in this life. People only see what they are capable of seeing, and the contrary — expanded vision — is a key aim of The Divine Comedy. Dante's message to us readers is: begin this growth without delay.

Dante looks again at the souls and something happens that is going to happen many times on this journey. He recognizes one of them. Given how many are milling before them, this is quite a coincidence — only it's not, of course. This is a world where you see what you can, which is simultaneously to see what you need to, if you can reflect on the sight. He encounters them for a reason: to learn more about their state of mind, and his.

On this occasion he doesn't name the figure he recognizes. I wonder if it's because his eyes are still adjusting. He can't yet name a soul because he is learning how to see them in their stark, naked state. He does intuit that this soul refused something momentous in his earthly life. Commentators wonder who it could be. It might be Pontius Pilate, who refused to decide who Jesus was and, instead, turned him over to the crowds. I suspect the meaning of the moment matters more than the identity of the character. If the soul he spots refused to engage in the most important decision of his life, Dante hasn't. He has embarked upon the odyssey.

Dante looks up, away from the undecideds, and there is a second crowd. They are queuing to cross a river, the Acheron. This is the river that, according to ancient myth, encircles the underworld. To cross it, you have to ask the boatman, Charon. He is a terrifying figure, though he is smart. He does something that will, hereon, happen frequently. He notices that Dante is mortal, having not yet passed on. That is exceptional in the afterlife.

The boatman is outraged. He makes a prophecy, as people sometimes do in altered states of consciousness. He tells Dante that he must enter the afterlife by another port and cross another river on another boat. He's saying that when he dies, Dante will enter the afterlife via another river, that of the Tiber. It is the river that leads to purgatory, not to hell.

That, though, is a long way off. Dante must continue on the path in front of him. There are no short cuts.

And he notices something odd. The souls who are queuing to cross the Acheron are eager to do so. Have they become masochistic? Do they desire their punishment? Or maybe it's not quite punishment, though it certainly looks like it. Maybe somewhere, deep in their jumbled minds, these souls sense that hope has not abandoned them, even if they have abandoned hope. They might yet learn to see more than what ruined them in life.

It is too soon to rush to such conclusions. Patience produces insight, not neat answers, particularly those that attempt to circumvent unpalatable truths. Dante keeps looking at the souls and discerns their wretchedness. They curse their birth, their parents, their time, their lives. They weep bitterly. The force of their suffering hits him. Canto 3 ends with Dante collapsing in a dead faint.

Virgil leads Dante into the first circle of hell.

INFERNO 4
Limbo

ANTE WAKES FROM HIS FAINT. STRANGELY, HE is on the other side of the Acheron and is not sure how he got there.

The mysterious crossing sets up an air of expectation in canto 4. Dante begins to show how his journey promotes new understandings of the Christian worldview that has shaped him. His perception is greatly expanded by his pilgrimage. He is led far beyond what his contemporaries, and many Christians today, might presume.

But illumination cannot be rushed, and what he sees as he recovers is not comforting. Virgil is looking pale and Dante frets. What has happened? If his guide is afraid, what hope does he have? He cries out: how can I not fear if you fear?

However, Virgil is not pale with terror, but pity. He is consumed by compassion for those trapped in hell. He knows what sights lie ahead of them. And yet, at the same time, he feels the uncertainty around them as they journey. What is this place about? What is its meaning, its mystery? For us readers, such touching interactions between Dante and Virgil make us want to know more too.

They are about to enter the first circle of hell. They have been on its threshold, in the vestibule inhabited by the undecided. Now they walk into limbo.

Virgil explains that this is the place for those who were not baptized and so died without hope. It's not a very good account of limbo and, in fact, the Catholic Church officially abandoned the explanation, if only in 2007. I think Dante the poet has Virgil offer the official line of medieval times to challenge it himself, which is implied because the one group of souls Dante would expect to see here, the infants who died before they could be baptized, are absent. Dante's medieval readers would have wondered where they might be.

Dante can revise the received wisdom because he has been to the afterlife and taken a look. Not that this is much encouragement to Dante the pilgrim right now. It's one thing to question a received understanding. It's another to be confronted with the reality that it was supposed to explain, and to realize that it doesn't. The unfamiliarity frightens Dante. Virgil should know about these things. Dante is heavily reliant on his teacher, who said he was sent by Beatrice, Lucia, and Mary. Have the saints in high heaven made a mistake?

They haven't, but Dante's journey is about his inner transformation as much as his external progress. The uncertainty is an opportunity to grow. He might begin to realize something of the tension that has made hell.

It has to do with respecting an individual's freedom. This is experienced particularly in the freedom of will, which is about how we choose to orient our lives. It's crucial because it makes us who we are; it forges our individuality. Human beings are made for much. We can imaginatively travel through the whole cosmos, if we become capable of seeing the whole cosmos. That is our freedom, but it rests on taking responsibility for our lives: what are we going to do with them? And that creates the tension: we might not do much with them.

The Divine Comedy takes seriously Dante's freedom to make much of his life that, in turn, has a lot to do with what he can understand about life. For example, in this canto, Dante asks about the existence of limbo.

Who is it for? And although Virgil replies that it's for those who were not baptized, the implication is that it is not just about being baptized, but knowing what baptism signifies. Someone might be baptized and not understand its ramifications and possibilities, as is the case for those who were baptized and find themselves in hell. In short, baptism is a sign, but what really matters is insight.

It is something that Virgil must learn, as much as Dante. Virgil was born before Christianity, which is to say before a new kind of wisdom or insight came into the world. In his own odyssey, *The Aeneid*, Virgil had respected the virtues of the old world. His heroes were those who were morally courageous, particularly in the face of great calamity. This is what won them admiration from the gods.

But with Christianity came a different appreciation of reality. It's not primarily about morality but comprehension. As Saint Paul discovered, the individual becomes capable of sharing divine life not because of what he does, but because of who he is. An expanded consciousness matters, not just a noble life.

At the moment, Virgil doesn't understand the difference. He tells Dante that he will spend eternity in hell because, in life, he had followed the old insights, never having had the opportunity to know the new ones. The confession devastates Dante as much as it depresses Virgil. It also evokes the long debate among readers of *The Divine Comedy* about what happens to Virgil. Many commentators take the old poet's remarks at face value: he says he is damned and so must be. But, for me, that misses one of the main thrusts of Dante's journey and the joys of reading *The Divine Comedy*. People change as their understanding grows. They become capable of absorbing divine light and so finding unexpected release. Why wouldn't that happen to Virgil, in spite of what he says?

Even at the very early stages of the journey, here in limbo, Dante realizes that there is something objectionable to Virgil's seeming fatalism. Don't people get out of here, he asks? After all, he knows that people have been released from limbo. That came with the harrowing of hell when, after dying on the Cross and before rising on Easter Sunday, Jesus descended into hell and saved souls. Dante puts this to Virgil — incidentally, without using the name of Jesus or God, which are not spoken in hell, I think out of fear of misusing the power that the names carry.

Dante might also be thinking that he was on the edge of hell, lost in the dark wood, and yet seems to have been saved, or at least given a second chance. Doesn't that happen to others? Mightn't it for Virgil? I think that

The Divine Comedy gradually reveals it does, though the hope initially eludes Virgil. First, he must know that he is lost, as Dante does. Only then might he understand more.

Then, as if to underline the need to expect the unexpected, a hemisphere of light comes toward them. It is striking because in hell there is supposed to be no light.

It can't be the light of the stars or the sun. Hell is subterranean. It must be the light of the intellect, a higher light, radiated by divine souls and angels. It must have a spiritual source that, it seems, can radiate in hell. Those who have it must be able to contemplate something of God and so bring illumination to this dark place. Who are they?

The glow reveals a group of walking poets. They are the great bards of the ancient world, led by Homer. Virgil is one of them and they welcome back their friend, as well as Dante, spotting that he is another poet of genius. They share the same spirit, the same charism of understanding, the same ability to use words to disclose truths.

Dante is seeing a limbo that is very different from the one he had been told existed. He is already moving on from Hell 101. It is a place that honors the wisdom of poetry and poets. For example, Homer is described by Dante as soaring like an eagle. This is no idle reference. The eagle is a very important creature in *The Divine Comedy* because, according to the mythology, it can soar so high in the sky, with eyes so steady and piercing, that it can gaze into the sun, which is to say it can bear the blazing light of God. The implication is that Homer could do the same. I think you can say that Dante is recognizing that Homer's poetry incarnated something of the divine, many centuries before Christ.

The inference is left hanging. It's too soon to say anything definitively. Instead, the poets simply enjoy their communion. They discuss many things although, Dante adds, what they talked about is best kept silent. It's a teasing, enticing comment. What did they consider? What did they conclude? I think for us readers it implies that some things can only be understood with the appropriate experience, after a shift of consciousness. It reminds us of the tensions between human freedom and opportunity, between the eras before and after the Christian dispensation. They can only properly be resolved on the journey that Dante has begun.

They keep walking. Dante sees a beautiful castle with many walls. They walk through its gates into a garden, adorned with golden, green grass. It's a very pleasant place, reminding readers of the Bible of the garden of Eden. This too is no idle allusion. The aboriginal garden will be a very important arrival point for Dante, at the end of purgatory. Might this garden in limbo be implying that something of heaven exists in hell?

More figures arrive, including Muslim divines and Greek philosophers. Are they going to be saved? They appear to be sharing in the divine light. Hell is starting to look porous. Maybe the light still pierces its gloom, harrowing it, as Christ did. Could what matters be whether you have the eyes to see?

The question is not answered. It's a canny move because it leaves us unsure. We must wrestle. It is as if Dante is saying: dear readers, your salvation depends upon deeper insight too. Don't expect me to tell you everything. I won't. You must uncover the secrets for yourselves to know them yourselves.

The canto ends. They can't linger in the garden for long in spite of its loveliness. They must continue.

Virgil and Dante enter the second circle and meet those whose love in life imprisoned them.

INFERNO 5

Windswept

HE VOYAGERS ARRIVE IN THE SECOND CIRCLE of hell. It is the first devoted to the theme of love, the central preoccupation of Dante's life and his odyssey. It contains a much-celebrated encounter with the figure of Francesca da Rimini, the precise meaning of which has been puzzled over for centuries. The canto certainly poses a question. You think you know what love is: it is all you need; makes the world go round; is good, maybe the greatest good. The origins of such sentiments reach back to Dante's time and the birth of courtly love, the predecessor to our romantic love. But do we understand what we mean when we say such things about love?

Before meeting Francesca, Dante and Virgil see Minos. He was a mythical king of Crete, known as a wise judge. He understands the hearts and souls of men and women, which is why, in eternity, he has the task of showing lost souls their place in hell. He does so in a grotesque way. The king has sprouted

20

a tail in the afterlife, which he wraps around himself as a soul approaches. The number of wraps equals the circle of hell that is the damned soul's lot.

It is horrendous but perversely comical as well. It is as if Minos judges with a limited kind of wisdom. It's fatalistic, as if his swinging tail is like the casting of dice. The action lacks the wisdom of love.

Virgil and Minos talk in a discussion that exemplifies this dead spirit. It is shouty, harsh. What is Dante doing here, Minos bellows? He has spotted that Dante is a mortal soul. Step aside, Virgil commands! You must obey the will that comes from above. A combative mood sets in. If we know this canto has something to do with love, we are left asking, where will it be felt?

The souls of this round appear next. Dante and Virgil hear them before they see them. These hapless shades are caught in an infernal storm. A relentless wind tosses them up and down, around and about. They loved in life, only it was blind love. It swept them along then; it sweeps them along now. It led nowhere before; it leads nowhere in the afterlife.

It looks like a murmuration of starlings of unsettling beauty. Dante finds himself entranced by the sight, which is to say that the love these souls are caught by is a love that he could well be snared by as well.

It's the state of mind described as reason being the slave of passion. The individual's appetites are so strong that they cannot develop their desires. There's no will. There's no negotiation. There's no freedom. They are just swept along.

"Reason" is meant in this richer sense of resonance, meaning, and being in harmony with something wider than immediate concerns. When coupled to love, it should enable becoming consciously attuned to the patterns of the cosmos, and the way life moves. It can link souls with the divine. A life that goes well is integrated love and reason. It knows how these capacities are part and parcel of the same perception.

Conversely, when love and reason become disconnected, souls grow lost. Dante sees such figures in the swirling cloud before them. There are many, and Dante the poet names some of them. They include historical and mythological figures, some well-known, some obscure.

Such lists of figures can be confusing to readers. It is one of the features of *The Divine Comedy* that puts people off. However, I think what Dante is doing is stressing that he is talking about real lives. His poem is not about abstract problems. Naming people is like naming diseases. It enables what's happened to be seen and, in so far as is possible, diagnosed and understood.

The approach makes sense to me as a psychotherapist. Someone may ask for help because, say, they report suffering from anxiety. But that one word covers many troubles. The first thing to do is ascertain what lies within the anxiety. Is it trauma, fear, anger, regret? Finding the right word is the first step to finding a way beyond the complaint. We can do the same when we examine love, and Dante sees various types of it as he names souls.

There is Semiramis, the Babylonian empress. You might say that she had such a lust for life that when she restored Babylon, she inadvertently turned it into a monstrous, manic place.

There is Dido, the lover of Aeneas. We will hear her name many times throughout *The Divine Comedy*, and she tends to embody the person who loved another too much. In Dido's case, when Aeneas left, she killed herself. Love is supposed to enlarge life by making you desire more and more of it. For Dido, though, it was too focused, too narrow, and so it closed life down. Incidentally, it's striking that she is in this circle of hell and not in the lower circle that holds others who committed suicide. Dante is implying that suicide itself is not the difficulty. It's what the suicide means that counts. Insight is all.

Dante spots Achilles, the tempestuous hero of Homer's *Iliad*. I think Achilles's problem is that his love, particularly for his companion, Patroclus, took him into a death spiral. When Patroclus was killed by Hector, Achilles went on a killing spree, slaying Hector and then abusing the corpse. A higher love wouldn't do that.

There is another insight worth contemplating as we imagine these souls tumbling before Dante and Virgil. They have arrived in the second circle of hell. It has a slightly smaller circumference than the first one, which is to say that the space has become more constricted. Dante imagines hell as a kind of wormhole. The closer you get to the center, the more individuals get sucked in. It's a brilliant imaginative device because it depicts an accurate psychological truth. Outer and inner space grows more confined as they descend. Hell's pain is as much to do with the lack of freedom as anything else.

That said, when conditions are named, space is created. It can be a relief to realize that an anxiety is actually about trauma, fear, anger, or regret. In other words, though Dante is descending, naming the souls before him is a kind of antidote. He is beginning to learn how to tolerate what he sees and so ensure that his mind stays open. To see is to understand, is to be free, which is crucial for any ascent.

Then again, the process cannot be hurried. It is hard to discern when love is taking us away from life because its heat can easily feel it is taking us into life. This was the challenge for Dante. He is drawn to the cloud of circling souls in canto 5 because he must be thinking about his love of Beatrice. At least at first, that love was an infatuation. It supercharged his young life but could have destroyed it. He must discern the difference for himself, which is perhaps why he meets Francesca.

She is eternally swirling with her beloved in life, Paolo, who was her brother-in-law. Dante asks to speak with them.

Francesca obliges by saying that their only crime was to respond to courtly love. One day, she explains, they were reading the tale of Lancelot and Guinevere. It was a classic of medieval love and proved so powerful on that day that it propelled them into having an affair. They were seized by love. The thought of it possessed them, excluding all else, which is their condemnation.

Dante listens carefully to her story. Francesca is charming. You gain the sense that she is still possessed, not so much by her love for Paolo, who is never actually named by her, but more so, by the idea of love. She is in love with being in love. That is the deeper trouble. It's not that she had an affair with her brother-in-law. It is that her love story has become her only story.

Dante the pilgrim starts to feel troubled by what Francesca says. He becomes confused about whether what he is hearing is true or not. In fact, she is lying about what actually happened, as Dante's original readers would have known, or perhaps she is not deliberately lying but has thoroughly deluded herself. Love made her lose touch with what's true and what's false. She blames the poetry and the story, a sign that she has lost her will, her reason, her freedom.

It's love without understanding or insight. It detects no currents other than its own obsession. It's love become anguish.

Dante can't tell the difference. Perhaps it's all too close to his young love for Beatrice. He swoons once more and, at the end of the canto, collapses, dropping as if dead on the floor of the second round of hell.

He is overwhelmed once again. The descent is growing steeper and he can't grasp the nuances and subtleties of what he is seeing. It's coming too soon, too fast. There is a long way to go.

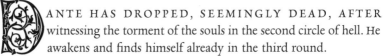

In the third circle, they encounter Cerberus and the disfigured Ciacco.

INFERNO 6

Weight

ANTE HAS DROPPED, SEEMINGLY DEAD, AFTER witnessing the torment of the souls in the second circle of hell. He awakens and finds himself already in the third round.

Suddenly he is here. It's an important detail. Dante the poet implies that, as a pilgrim, he descended through hell not so much by walking as by perceiving. Where you are connects directly with what you can see. This dynamic is carrying him down.

The next stage of infernal reality, which is revealing itself to be as much psychological as physical, is immediately reflected in the poetry of this canto. The verses of canto 5 had mirrored the elegant poetry of courtly love. The verses of canto 6 are visceral, guttural, short, sharp. He has woken up in a different world.

There is relentless rain. It's like being in a daytime storm when the atmosphere goes grey, and the light fades. You can't tell what's near or far

24

away. It's hard to tell the time because the sun has disappeared. And the rain is soaking. It's greasy, falling in a thick deluge that drenches you so that you're not quite sure where you end and the rest of the world begins.

Everything is flowing, dashed by foul water. They are in a state of being where everything becomes a mushy, undifferentiated whole. There is no pleasure, no capacity to know how to receive pleasure, as pleasure dissolves into sludge.

The third circle is often labelled the round of the gluttons, though the word is misleading. The souls they meet don't gorge and eat a lot. They are stuck here for more subtle reasons, which Dante must take on board as he begins to push into this state of things.

I think what this round is really about is greed and, in a specific sense, materialism. Its spirit is the conviction that life can only be satisfied by more and more stuff. Paradoxically, though, this leaves life feeling formless and soulless because matter actually gains its shape, beauty, value, and place through its soul. A tree has a certain vitality, and a rock another, because they have different souls. The sun feels very different from the moon. Rain can be deadening or refreshing.

It's deadening the third round. It's as if life is draining away, which makes sense because the irony of materialism is that it drains life out of the material world. It's a bit like walking through the shopping precinct of an airport terminal. Everything is dressed in gold and red, lit up with bright lights. And everything looks empty and dead, as it yells at you with the same shallow intensity. There is little good in all the goods.

Dante and Virgil meet the fantastic beast, Cerberus. He is a three-headed dog-like creature in mythology, guarding the entrance to the underworld. He has human qualities as well as canine, although as he appears to Dante and Virgil, the bestial dominate. He mauls and growls before them, though it becomes clear that he doesn't really know what he's snarling for. He's a monster acting out of pure instinct. Dante describes his muscles twitching, his heads writhing. He's tearing at things without purpose so, when Virgil approaches, the poet simply throws the beast some dirt from the ground. Cerberus lunges at the muck unthinkingly, and Dante and he walk past.

They then see the souls of this domain. The shades are lying down. Further, it turns out that Dante can step on these souls, which is interesting because while he has a body, as a still mortal person, these souls presumably don't, being dead. He shouldn't be able to tread on them, though he can.

I think it might be that these souls are so wedded to material reality that they don't quite realize they are dead. They are still imaginatively living with physicality and, in the afterlife, that gives them faux physicality because they inhabit that delusion. Dante can step on them because they put so much faith in material reality. It's a bit like the ghosts who are the souls of individuals who have died and yet haven't realized their own passing.

I suspect this is why they're lying down, too. They lack what in the medieval understanding was known as levity: the spiritual force that rises to the heavens. It's the spirited nature of things. It's the energy of the soul. Like a flame, it reaches up. It was thought to be the opposite of gravity, which causes things to sink and lie down. For these individuals, flat on the ground, it's as if their gravity has overwhelmed them. They have forgotten about levity. They lack inner vitality.

One does manage to sit up. He asks Dante to identify him. Dante can't tell, seeing only a formless figure before him, so the soul says that they shared the city of Florence. They lived at the same time. Still, Dante says, you are too disfigured for me to see you. The soul has to name himself.

He is called Ciacco, which is alliterative, sounding in Italian like "pig" or "filth." He wants to be remembered by Dante, perhaps because he can hardly remember himself, and he is the first of many souls to make this request of Dante. The souls might have a vague recollection that prayers can help them, even in hell, though I think it's more likely that they are preoccupied with their past lives, and the details that obsess them. They ask to be remembered because they have grown incapable of experiencing anything novel. They can only go over old ground.

Ciacco leverages himself up and they start talking about the politics of troubled Florence. Much as where you are is related to what you can see, what you talk about is related to where you are, and so it's appropriate that Florence comes up. It's as if Florence's trouble was that it had become overwhelmingly preoccupied with material matters. It was dragged down by civic gravity into bloody wars. It forgot its levity, the spirit that first enlivened it.

Gripped by the conversation, Ciacco becomes prophetic. He speaks of pride, envy, and avarice, as well as more mysterious allusions, referring to "three suns" and "two men" and "three sparks." Commentators have interpreted the symbols in various ways though their significance seems to be that Ciacco doesn't understand them, given they are symbols. Confusion captures his state of mind, much as it had the state of Florence: neither can envisage the future because neither can make sense of the present. Pride is the desire to possess, not live and let live. Envy interrupts the flow of life because it wants what others have, to the point of destroying what can't be had by the envious. Avarice is the desire to accumulate, coupled to the mistaken belief that life is enriched by having more and more.

All of a sudden, Ciacco squints at Dante, and falls back to the ground. He grows suddenly exhausted, overcome by gravity, though the squint is an interesting detail. Did he, for a split second, recognize that he had seen something novel standing before him: a mortal soul, in hell? Did he, momentarily, sense the levity that energizes Dante? Did he half remember what that was like?

If so, he couldn't fix on it, couldn't take it in, couldn't understand. He is stuck and so collapses, overwhelmed by the creature he has become. This is his condemnation. Virgil remarks coolly that this will be his fate, and the fate of those around him, until the day of judgment.

It is not all Virgil says. He adds that on the day of judgment, they will be given their material bodies back, and their pain will increase accordingly. It's a harsh, nasty afterthought, though it fits in with the darkness of hell and, like much of what is said here, contains some truth, though not the whole truth. The whole truth could turn out to be very different indeed, because, of course, the final judge will be a loving judge. That could make a lot of difference.

Dante and Virgil fall into conversation. What they discuss, Dante the poet informs us, will not be revealed at this time. Secrets stay secrets until they can be understood. Though what we can observe is that, at the end of the canto, Dante is not weeping or swooning. He says that he felt like crying but doesn't actually do so. He is beginning to come to grips with what this descent is about. He is adjusting to it. Maybe his awareness is shifting because of it, and he is starting to see things more clearly.

The canto ends with another abrupt detail, the appearance of another mythical creature, the figure of Plutus, who is called humankind's arch-enemy. Why the god of wealth is so dangerous, we are not told or invited to ask. But Dante the poet implies that we might ask something else, because the end of this canto merges with the beginning of the next. Poetically, this is a first in The Divine Comedy. It suggests that Dante may be beginning to join things up, and he asks: are we?

Virgil and Dante are in the fourth and fifth circles meeting those held by money and anger.

INFERNO 7

Rage

HO IS PLUTUS, THE DEITY AT THE EDGE OF THE fourth circle of hell? His parents were agricultural gods, and, in classical mythology, he's often shown holding a cornucopia, a horn of plenty. He gives from the goods of the earth freely and in celebration, during festivities. So, what is he doing in hell?

In his illustration for this canto, William Blake shows Plutus holding a moneybag rather than a cornucopia. It's a smart substitution. The horn that should be giving has become the sack that tries to withhold.

His presence could be a comment on Dante's times. The poet lived during the period when mercantilism was beginning to grip the European economy. It was an age in which the first sweatshops appeared, supporting the mass production of textiles and cloth. Property was becoming important in the modern sense: increasingly, it could be traded rather than inherited. Life was beginning to center around financial markets.

Plutus who once gave freely has become an omen — he now withholds unless you pay — although Virgil tells Dante not to worry about him. He has nothing with which to entice them. Material stuff is not their concern, and they leave him muttering strange words, "*Pape Satàn, pape Satàn aleppe!*," which have caused some debate among commentators. Do they refer to Satan? Do they refer to the pope? It doesn't much matter because, like sails emptying of wind, Dante's fear of Plutus quickly calms. The old god disappears, chuntering, hanging, drooping.

Souls surround Dante and Virgil. They are obsessed by the desire for money. Dante remarks that there were more people in this circle than he had seen in the circles before.

They are depicted manhandling great weights, like Sisyphus pushing his boulder up the hill. The image conveys the sense of the pointlessness of a life spent lugging the great weight of money around. The futility is depicted in a telling way. Dante sees the souls pushing the weights in two semicircles: one group works one arc, the second the other, and they meet as if forming a circle, at which point they clash. "Why hoard?" one group cries. "Why waste?" the other responds. The pattern is repeated time and again.

Their predicament captures the meaninglessness of a life spent pursuing financial wealth. When you serve money, there are only two questions to be asked: am I hoarding, or am I wasting? These souls ask it in eternity. They are caught by the repetition because they have forgotten that life can be about something else. The warning is clear.

The message is underlined because in canto 7, Dante doesn't name any individual souls. He sees a lot of priests, recognizable by their tonsures, who have become addicted to the worldly splendors of the medieval Church, which were substantial. But he can't discern specific souls, just the collective, so he and Virgil don't talk to anyone. The real world has been lost to these figures, lost to a virtual world of money. The tangible qualities of things that might give them distinctiveness, differentiation, a place, and presence in the physical world are gone. With that, their individuality dissolves.

Dante is not against materiality itself. Quite the opposite. It can reveal the glorious life of its divine origin and source, shining within it. But that does raise a further question, which the two travelers discuss: if these souls have got wealth wrong, what is the nature of true wealth and fortune?

The question was already an ancient one in Dante's time. The leading philosopher of true wealth was Boethius, author of the medieval bestseller, *The Consolation of Philosophy*. It features the goddess, Fortuna, turning her wheel. It was a wheel to which Boethius himself had realized he was strapped. He wrote his discourse while in prison, having lost all that he had gathered across an otherwise hugely successful career.

The wheel has often been interpreted as luck. For a while, it spins well for you, and your luck is in. Then it turns against you and your fortune fails. The wheel of fortune never ceases moving. But Boethius interpreted it more subtly. He saw it not as a fable merely to warn people off wasting and hoarding. He realized that Fortuna is a goddess close to divine reality. It's a lead that Dante takes up.

Virgil explains that Fortuna sees God. She knows the bliss of heaven and understands the wisdom of infinity as fully as the highest of the angels. This is the true wealth that she wants to reveal to the world. She is not against worldly splendor but does seek to foster a right attitude toward it. The aim is to see silver and gold as screens within which can be detected deeper treasures. Like sunlight, gold can communicate divine light. Splendor can light up mortal life like a candelabra; true light brightens a life like the stars. It rays everywhere, bounces off everything, spreads goodness to all.

Nothing can diminish this wealth. It is abundant. The more you see it the more you see it has to offer, unlike material wealth which is hoarded out of scarcity. Fortuna spins her wheel to remind us of this fact, which means that the coming and going of worldly goods is a blessing. It teaches us that permanent heavenly goods are the ones to pursue. When that lesson is forgotten or denied, she will take away even the goods you have.

It's a timely, painful lesson for Dante. At the midpoint of his life, he is losing everything. It seems that Fortuna's wheel has turned against him. Only, he may be sensing, here in the fourth circle, that hapless events are revealing deeper truths. The process brings suffering but in the midst of that descent, the earliest traces of an ascent might be detected, if he can bear to look and see. The wheel turns. Fortuna can bring everlasting gifts; it is just that they are not the ones you first thought she was bringing.

The two pilgrims move on quickly. Why wouldn't they? It is an unpleasant world, bounded by tumbling banks of rank mud. And they encounter the source of the wet swamp. The River Styx appears before them.

They leave the hoarders and the wasters behind to contemplate the second river in hell. It marks the boundary of the fifth circle, within which they spot another group of souls. Again, they are in two clusters, one with heads above the water of the Styx, and a second buried in the foul riverbed.

The individuals above the water are locked in battle. Their whole persons are involved in the combat: mouths, chests, legs. They fly and collide in a rage. By contrast, the individuals beneath the water lie in the mud, held still on their backs, though Dante senses that they are angry as well. He realizes that they are trying to yell out but, instead, suck in the sediment, which chokes them. A torrent of bubbles rises to the surface.

The souls are trapped by two types of anger. One is the kind that is projected onto another, promoting uncontrollable hate and violent fights. The other turns in on the person who carries it, leaving him bound by internal battles. The internal rage is quite as ferocious as the actual fights and, being unexpressed, renders the individual rigid. You see people like this from time to time, so angry inside that they are frozen. The life drains out of them, much as a fight can be exhausting, and not that the pain stops the rage.

It's worth saying that Dante is not against anger per se. Anger will be found in purgatory and paradise. A subtler point is being made that anger is a bit like wealth: it is fine when it doesn't become an end in itself. If it can flow and be released, it can facilitate a deeper life because it prompts change. Much as material goods can invite us to yearn for heavenly splendors, so human anger can fire us to desire a better world.

But hellish anger does not do this. It is convinced life is a zero-sum game: if I lose you win, so I must ensure you lose. The upshot is self-defeating. In this canto, we have a chance to consider how money can turn life into a hellish mess, and anger can turn life into a living hell. In terms of their effects, money and anger go together. Both destroy the capacity to see more.

Dante and Virgil press on. They leave the money-obsessed and the perpetually angry. It's a messy sight, distressing, unlovely. And as they turn to look farther down, they catch sight of something else. In the distance is a tremendous tower. Having found some momentum, having gained some ability to learn from these sights, Dante's descent is about to steepen.

Still in the fifth circle, they face the river Styx and the terror of Dis.

INFERNO 8
Blocked

DANTE HAS SPOTTED A TOWER IN THE DISTANCE. It marks the boundaries of the city of Dis, which is another name for Lucifer or Satan. What he and Virgil have seen so far was bad enough. From here on, the situation is about to become far worse. Dante signals as much poetically by breaking the pattern of one circle per canto. It creates a mood of unravelling and falling.

This imparts a sense of feeling unsettled in us readers. We thought we were getting the hang of it. In truth, though, just eight cantos in, reality is shifting again. The land is slipping beneath our feet. Where are we? What is going on? Dante is asking the same questions.

They see signals passing between the tower and another one that emerges from the gloom. We will learn that they are manned by demons, devils, and fallen angels. A hellish communication is underway. Is it to do with the travelers? Have they been spotted?

Then, skimming across the filthy water of the Styx, a boat appears. It flies at supernatural speed, cutting the dank air like an arrow. The pace itself is worth contemplating: the vessel is moving at the speed of thought. This zone blurs the distinctions between the psychological and the physical.

It is driven by Phlegyas, a mythological king who was remembered for his rage. It makes sense that he is in a boat charging across the marsh. But what are his intentions?

He does not sound friendly, because he calls out to Dante: "I've got you, wretched soul!" Like Minos and Plutus, it seems that part of the role of these ghastly guards is to man boundaries. But, as with Minos and Plutus, Virgil knows how to command Phlegyas. He tells the dead king that his shouting is in vain. This living soul is here by divine blessing. With that, Virgil calmly steps onto the skiff.

Dante climbs aboard too, noting that his weight causes the bows to dip beneath the waves. As they move off, the boat ploughs through the water. Dante's presence brings a different quality of experience to the realm. In hell, it's as if he momentarily disrupts the delusions that blind the souls — his weight is like a reality check — though few souls prove able to respond to the intervention, beyond staring.

The trip is not comfortable. As they travel, an angry individual emerges from beneath the waves and tries to grab the craft. Dante addresses the slimy creature, asking who he is. The soul replies that he weeps. It sounds pathetic. It might sound sad, as if Dante should respond with compassion and empathy. In fact, Dante barks back that this damned soul should stay stuck here forever.

The anger of the place is getting inside him, though it is colored by a type of anger that is at least partly justified, because he has recognized who this person is. It is Filippo Argenti, whom the commentators have identified as the brother of one of Dante's main persecutors. Argenti's sibling confiscated Dante's earthly goods when he was banished from Florence. Argenti himself may well have been a beneficiary of Dante's loss. Little wonder Dante loathes him when he sees him.

The brothers lived by seizing things: in life, whatever they could steal; in death, whatever passes by. Argenti's soul is gripped by the habit and, while Dante's anger is no doubt boiling, it can serve a higher purpose. It could just possibly shake Argenti up. It could be his salvation. Only, it's not. Virgil pushes Argenti back into the slime.

Then, something extraordinary happens. Having attacked the angry soul, Virgil turns to Dante and hugs him. It's a startling gesture compounded by

Virgil calling Dante blessed, in arrestingly pious words: "Blessed is she in whose womb you were conceived," he says.

The phrase echoes words from the Gospel of Luke spoken of Jesus. It is high praise for Dante and makes you think further because the thought has come from Virgil, a pagan. He is quoting the Bible and referencing Jesus. Is he starting to see something of the Christian dispensation? Is this journey the beginning of his transformation? Might it offer him a way out of limbo?

The possibility is reinforced, I think, because Virgil actually gets the quote slightly wrong. It is as if he is trying it on for size. It is not a perfect fit for his mind, as yet, though he might become capable of a more Christian way of seeing things, in time.

It is a clue when trying to discern how the descent might be changing them, so it is worth contemplating, via the related question of why Virgil considers Dante worthy of such praise. It seems that his rage at Argenti did arise from righteous anger. He is learning not to swoon at the sight of damaged souls but recognize why they are here. However, Dante's insight is not pure. It lacks maturity and so is tainted by the ugly spirit of this circle. In fact, Dante next continues his rant and says that he would love to see Argenti dunked in the mud again, a wish that is granted. Dante the poet tells us that he thanked God for the sight for the rest of his earthly life.

It's uncomfortable to read about. Dante is changing but he is in dangerous territory. We sense he might be overcome by the demonic elements in the air and rendered as raging as the souls around him.

The atmosphere of evil and risk becomes more explicit when a sound of wailing makes them sit up. Dante strains to see the source of the howls. It is as if a sheet of terror falls upon them. He says he had never felt such a powerful disturbance. He wonders if he might lose his mind. Unsteadied by the appearance of Argenti, he is struggling to keep his grip on reality.

The looming towers of Dis have become more visible, closer to the city. Walls are clearly discernible, and they see fires burning in the place. Structures look like minarets, Dante remarks, remembering that Islam was perceived to be the great enemy of Christianity at the time. Muslim armies had taken land right across Eastern Europe. The followers of Mohammad represented an existential threat, which Dante draws on as he tries to make sense of the city that arises before them. An analogy might be the fear that communism could rouse in Europeans and Americans during the Cold War. It's as if Dante sees nuclear missiles lined up, ready to launch.

Closer still, he notices that the walls are made of iron. This metal had particular meaning in the medieval period as the hardest material with which to build. Forging high walls from it must, therefore, be the devil's work. Foul powers and forces are at play.

An infernal light fills the air. It tumbles over the steely walls. Dante the poet is signaling that they were approaching a new zone. A further aspect of reality is looming before them. The boatman gives them plenty of time to contemplate the shadows because he has to travel some way on the water, circumnavigating the towers, before arriving at the landing place. They have seen quite a lot of Dis, and its gloom, before Phlegyas commands them to disembark.

They do and, instantly, a thousand fallen angels appear on the turrets nearby. They look down from the ramparts, every red eye focused on Dante. They know he is a mortal soul. They want to know what he is doing here. It's as if he is the focus of a perverse miracle. His presence shouts as loudly as a spontaneous healing. Only he shouldn't be here, his journey shouldn't be allowed, though somehow it is. The force of their horror, cursing, and hate pours down. Dante is terrified. He has nowhere to hide. He reports that he believed he was about to be lost to hell forever.

Then again, he notices that Virgil is not worried. His guide tries to calm him by saying that their journey is meant, and he will not be left in the underworld. Their way has the highest sanction. No one can stop them. Virgil counsels Dante to stay still while he walks forward. He knows how to address the fiends.

Whatever Virgil thought he would say, it fails. The devils slam the heavy gates in his face. Returning to Dante, Virgil does look worried. He walks back at a slowed pace.

Dante realizes something is profoundly wrong and comes close to collapse. He asks us readers to imagine the fear felt. We are brought to the moment with this direct address and it is tremendous and terrifying. We are invited to stand alongside Dante in this dire predicament. It is almost as if we are at the foot of the iron walls ourselves, wondering what is going to happen, what it all means, what will be required of them next.

Virgil is not yet at his wits' end. He has another idea. Like the entrance to hell itself, this door cannot be permanently locked, he remarks. He has been assured that they will be allowed to pass into Dis, much as they had been allowed to enter hell. The canto ends with Dante petrified and Virgil prophesying that a power is coming by which the gates will be opened.

Terrified by the demons that block their path, Dante and Virgil must wait for an angel.

INFERNO 9

Help

ANTE AND VIRGIL STAND BEFORE THE GATE OF
Dis. Dante is petrified. Virgil is thrown by his failure because the
demons have not responded to his demand. Embarrassed, he
returns to Dante, muttering about winning the fight. He is expecting help,
only help doesn't seem to be coming.

They are in the grip of a spiritual emergency. It's a living sense of death,
in which you don't disappear into nothingness, but remain unbearably
conscious of how precipitous things are. It feels like being stranded up a
one-way street. There is no turning back, and apparently an insurmountable
block on the way forward. Are they in a cosmic zone where God's power
doesn't reach? Or does God turn a blind eye to what goes on down here?

Dante asks whether anyone has made a trip like theirs before. Virgil says
they have. In fact, he has. He made the journey at the behest of Erichtho.
She is a necromancer who can recall spirits to their bodies. Once upon a

36

time, in another dark adventure, she had asked Virgil to assist her, and he had obliged.

It's not much encouragement to Dante. Necromancers might be allies of devils. Maybe that is why Virgil had managed to open the gates before and is failing this time around.

Furies appear on the ramparts. They are the handmaids of hell, sent straight from Satan to taunt and intimidate Dante and Virgil. Dante once more faces the horrible experience of all the red eyes in front of them falling upon him. He can smell their hatred of his presence. Is there a more unnatural place for him to be?

The furies enjoy themselves. They call on the equivalent of their nuclear weapon, the Gorgon, Medusa. Anyone who sees her and her hair of snakes is immediately turned to stone, even Hercules the hero. Virgil reads the situation, warns Dante, and turns them both around. He covers Dante's eyes just to make sure. He is not taking any chances.

Then, in the depths of desperation, they sense a presence. Rushing across the water comes a power that far exceeds the fearsome forces of Dis. It is like a tornado that, ripping a path, turns everything it touches to matchwood. The fiends become aware of it and, like startled frogs leaping into a pond, jump from the parapets. It is an angel.

Commentators have asked which angel. I imagine this magnificent being as a cross between the Archangel Michael and Mercury, the messenger god from Zeus, because it is carrying a wand like Mercury and not a sword, as Michael is known to possess.

This is the first time in *The Divine Comedy* that Dante and Virgil have been directly exposed to divine energy. They bow their heads, though Dante snatches a look and sees the living intelligence from God brushing the foul atmosphere from before its face. The angel looks faintly irritated.

Without hesitation, it approaches the gate, touches the great doors with its wand, and instantly they fall open. The angel addresses the demons, calling them idiots for having presumed that they could thwart God's will. They have not begun to learn their lesson. They imprison themselves in hell.

Mission accomplished, the angel turns about, and flies straight back across the Styx. It doesn't acknowledge Dante or Virgil, let alone greet them in blessing. That is what great angels must be like. They perform their tasks and leave.

The crisis is over as quickly as it began. The canto concludes with Virgil and Dante stepping through the gates, and into Dis. The taunting demons have fled and, instead, they encounter a countryside of anguish and pain, cluttered with a patchwork of graves. Many of the tombstones are dislodged, revealing fiery furnaces beneath. It's where the heretics lie, Virgil informs Dante. They will talk with them in the next canto.

Before that, it's worth reflecting on what has just happened. Why, for example, did Virgil fail to open the gates?

An answer to that question comes with considering why the walls of Dis exist. What is their purpose? It might be thought that they are the walls of a prison, to keep the damned in. But what if they are battlements to keep enemies out? This makes sense because, on his first trip, Virgil could have presented himself as an ally of the demons. He was on a necromancer's errand. They would let him in. This time, though, they couldn't trust him. They saw Dante from a long way off, the mortal soul, presumably blessed by God. Virgil had become an enemy. They would do anything to fend off such divine missions — which is perhaps why the angel sniffed at them.

It says something about Virgil. He knows he has permission from above to traverse hell. But he doesn't fully understand what it is to be God's ambassador. Perhaps he is still in the old heroic mode of adventuring, as if his courage were the important thing. It is not. He is learning. For me, this adds to the possibility that the pilgrimage has become Virgil's quite as much as Dante's. There is more than one person's salvation at stake.

For Dante, the experience is about facing existential terror. It's significant that, unlike his earlier swoons, he doesn't pass out at Dis. He was scared, on the edge of losing hope. He felt his darkest fears. But he kept his mind. He remained aware. This ability is one he will need in order to descend farther, so the walls of Dis are, for him, a test. It was more about him being ready to pass through them, than about them letting him pass.

That's important. The journey is an inner one as well as outer. Dis is like a trial of initiation. He has found a way through the test. His near breakdown is a breakthrough. Descent and ascent are intimately linked. They have been helped by the angel and this must be part of the lesson as well: they have collaborated with divine power. It was not magic that opened the gates, as perhaps was the nature of Virgil's previous passport. Far more powerful is knowing how to align with angelic intelligences. I think that's why the angel says nothing to them. As far as it is concerned, it was in their service. It was there to assist.

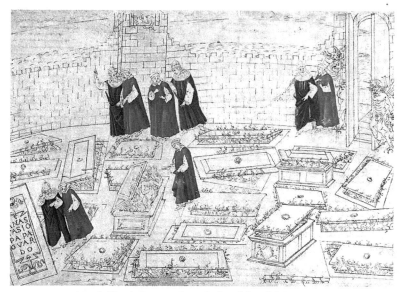

Now inside Dis, they meet those who have followed their own way.

INFERNO 10
Nastiness

THE WALLS OF DIS ARE BEHIND THEM. AHEAD
lies a grey countryside, its undifferentiated monotony interrupted
by flames that shoot out of the ground. Dante sees tombstones
scattered and smashed. He is intrigued. He wants to know what is going
on in this further domain of hell.

Seeing requires understanding, and what that involves is, in fact, signaled
at the end of canto 9. The indicator is concealed in a small detail that is
easy to miss, though is of great significance. Dante the poet reports that,
having passed through the gateway, they turned right.

There is only one other time in hell that they don't follow the usual pattern, which is to keep turning left. Leftward is the divinely sanctioned way
through the labyrinth of hell. If you follow that direction, terrible things
can happen, but ultimately nothing can go wrong. So, it is significant that
they traverse to the right, an adjustment that must have something to do

39

with the circle in which they have arrived.

The place is infected with powerful spirits, as well as housing lost souls. The atmosphere is inclined to affect them, as it must, because Dante's task is not just to see hell, but know hell. That can only happen if he confronts himself as he confronts lost souls, and experiences something of their confusions.

The round of canto 10 is that of the heretics, the sixth circle. These are individuals whose beliefs are erroneous, which matters because if you follow your own sense of things, you can lose track of God's way, which is to become lost in reality. The figures they encounter are those who not only turned from God's way but became incapable of finding a way back.

And yet, there is a catch. Souls must also follow a path that they can call their own. Humans are not puppets, manipulated by God. We are desiring and free creatures, with wills that can learn. Making mistakes and creating your own path must therefore, to some degree, be part of a godly life. Further, the novelty of human paths is part of the expansion of divine life in the cosmos.

Discerning your volition. Testing things out. Going off-piste, if not entirely off track. Being something of a heretic. This is what enables us to find the true path and own it. I think this is the deeper meaning of the right turn on the inside walls of Dis. The domain of the heretics is an opportunity for them. They can benefit from its spirit, so long as they are not consumed by it.

Virgil senses Dante's desire to learn. It's a touching moment: like friends on earth sometimes can, companions in eternity know what is going on in nearby minds. Dante protests that he doesn't want to keep what is on his heart from Virgil. He says that Virgil had told him off for speaking too quickly before, so he is being careful now, though he protests a little too much. There is something guarded in his response. He is a bit cagey. The defensiveness of heresy is in the air. "I did it my way."

As they jostle, they come to the first group, who are Epicureans. These philosophers, whose school was formed by Hellenistic Greeks, are located in a private cemetery, Dante informs us, which is apposite. Epicureans didn't believe in the immortality of the soul but rather that, when people die, their souls, like rotting plants, return to a great mulch in the sky, for recycling. The conviction means they are blind to the survival of individuality beyond death. This must be the meaning of the private cemetery. Surprised to be in eternity, they conclude that they are the only ones there.

The myopia had ramifications in life because the assertion that there is no individual immortality tended to amplify the value of the individual life they did have, as mortals. Sure enough, their way of life was built around self-sufficiency. In one of the surviving letters of Epicurus, the founder of the school, he tells a friend not to rely on others but to cultivate self-reliance: if the cosmos is indifferent to your demise, maybe the world is too. But if you write off divine love, you block off divine love. That is their fate.

Dante and Virgil move on, and a human figure rises from one of the half-open tombs as they pass. Dante the poet paints a picture of this emergence that would have made his early readers immediately think of Jesus rising from the tomb. Only, this soul just manages to sit up, appearing from the waist up. It is a mock resurrection, which is telling. As the soul looks out, it scans the countryside scornfully. Though not an Epicurean, he shares some of the old philosophers' self-reliance, and the separation from God.

This proud soul has heard Dante speaking and recognizes his Tuscan accent, which at first startles Dante. The pilgrim steps back, closer to Virgil, though Virgil encourages Dante to talk with his compatriot, adding a word of warning: choose your words carefully. Dante must find his own way of talking, much as he must find his own way of walking, though consciously, discerningly, with care.

The figure is Farinata. He was a leading figure in the Florentine wars a generation before Dante, and sided with the Ghibellines, the opposite group to Dante's Guelphs. Farinata begins the conversation with a blunt question about Dante's ancestors and, quickly, they launch into a verbal fight about the significance of various conflicts and the outcome of battles. It's nasty and prompts Farinata to toss a painful prophecy Dante's way about his coming expulsion and fate.

With the unpleasantness in full swing, another soul appears from the same tomb, though only his head emerges. It seems that souls are stacked in these burning pits.

He is called Cavalcanti and was the father of a poet called Guido Cavalcanti, who was a contemporary of Dante. Dante and Guido had been poetic and personal friends, though separated following a falling out. Not that his father is concerned about the loss of their friendship. He is worried about his son. Having heard Dante passing overhead, he had feared that if Dante were in hell, his son might be as well. He pops up to find out.

There is a lot going on in this moment. It wasn't just that Dante and Guido fell out. Subsequently, Dante was to cause Guido to be exiled from Florence to a place likely to lead to his death, which it did. Seeing his former friend's father confronts him with a sense of shame that anticipates his future actions: as Dante the pilgrim stands before Cavalcanti, Dante the poet knows of his guilt.

Although Guido's father's concern for his son sounds touching, it turns out that Cavalcanti is more alarmed about how his own reputation would be harmed if his son were damned. He had imagined his son to be a genius and had lived basking in reflected glory. But geniuses shouldn't end up condemned. In short, Cavalcanti is a proud man, though in a different way to Farinata. If the former soul's problem was self-sufficiency, the latter soul's trouble is living his life through the life of another. That can get you into as much trouble as pride in the afterlife, if it leaves you incapable of heavenly life.

Cavalcanti disappears again, distressed. Dante has been unable to reassure him. At which point Farinata continues sparring about Florence. He doesn't skip a beat. He shares the same tomb as Cavalcanti and is not remotely interested in the other.

Farinata's pride becomes more evident when he confesses that a damaged reputation would pain him more than the flames of hell which surround him. What he fails to recognize is that the flames of hell are his preoccupation with his reputation. They scorch any life that comes near, mortal and immortal. They hurt Dante.

Dante, though, is not lost. He recognizes the feelings of guilt the appearance of Cavalcanti prompted and becomes concerned that he has not comforted Cavalcanti adequately. He asks Farinata to tell the doting father that his son is not in hell, so far as he knows. We presume Farinata does not.

Dante's anxiety escalates, and it increases further when Virgil scolds him for being fixated on someone else's future. It sounds harsh. It's in the spirit of this round. But it will turn out to be an important lesson as they descend deeper into hell. The souls they meet are increasingly gripped with worry about the past and future. Dante must learn that the present matters because it is only in the present that you can exercise your freedom, change, and gradually redirect your desires.

The canto nears its end. They turn left again. They had ventured along their own path. It brought distasteful experiences and hostility. But it taught them things they might not have grasped in any other way, in particular it has taught them to want to follow God's way.

Then, like a cliffhanger, in the last sentence of canto 10, Dante the poet tells us that the two were assaulted by a terrible stench. It was so foul that it forced them to stand stock-still.

A hideous smell prompts consideration of lower hell's subtler evils.

INFERNO 11
Stench

A TERRIBLE REEK HAS STOPPED DANTE AND VIR-
gil in their tracks. It's too much to bear. It is wafting up from the
pit of hell and is a further indicator to Dante of just how far the
descent will require him to go. He must navigate a world in which the very
atmosphere stinks with rank odors.

They crouch beneath an imposing tomb, which is worth commenting on
in itself: tombs are found only in hell, not purgatory or heaven. It makes
you think again about what tombs on earth display — perhaps a mix of
vanity, confusion, and misplaced hope, for all that they may also console
those who are mourning. There is an inscription on the side of this one,
which implies it belonged to a pope who was lured from the narrow path,
a move they have just experimented with themselves. This pope is far from
the only prelate Dante will encounter in the dark zone.

43

Virgil starts to speak and spends this canto explaining the layout of hell to Dante. A lot has happened in the time since they set out, although very much more is to come, and it is important to keep thinking. Worse evils are not necessarily simpler evils, but subtler evils.

What Virgil says is, therefore, fascinating for a number of reasons, and a first detail to flag is that it is Virgil who is speaking. He knows a lot, but far from everything. The gates of Dis showed that. I think what he offers Dante is his best sense of things and, while valuable, it is not the final knowledge that Dante will eventually gain. Only a journey from here to heaven can secure that full awareness.

Dante's guide deploys the ethics of Aristotle to cast light on the arrangement of souls. This is not surprising for Virgil who, as an educated Roman, would have regarded Aristotle as worth hearing. It is more surprising that Dante gives such prominence to what Virgil told him when they were travelling together.

Aristotle was a thinker new to Christian Europe in the thirteenth century. His work had been preserved, explored, and developed in the Islamic world, where he had been highly respected for centuries. Its arrival in the West caused much controversy. The theologian whom Dante respects more than any other, Thomas Aquinas, spent his life reconciling Aristotelian and Christian insights, in the process greatly enriching both. However, his writings were banned for periods of time and he was canonized only after Dante's death, as his genius was reluctantly acknowledged by the Church. At the beginning of the fourteenth century, the time of The Divine Comedy, he was at the vanguard of knowledge. He was a source of controversy and inspiration. It is appropriate that Dante should turn to him, therefore, as the poet clearly realized that his own journey and great work were in the same league. The unofficial understanding of reality was growing in Dante's time, and amplifying that unfolding is definitely on his agenda.

He is most overtly against the assumption that Christianity has received a deposit of doctrine that is sure for all time, and that the Church's task is simply to articulate and preserve it. Doctrine only matters when it lives. If it doesn't live it traps you, perhaps in hell, but when it serves as a launchpad for the human mind and powers an imagination that can reach across the cosmos, it can adapt before the insights of divine wisdom. Much may change with that expansion. How could it be otherwise?

The key insight that Virgil offers Dante is that the souls they have encountered so far have been gripped by their desires. The lovers had fallen in love with love itself. The greedy sought only material delights and splendor. The raging had become hooked on anger.

That relatively straightforward analysis of the predicament of souls in hell is going to grow more complicated, he continues. The souls deeper down will be seen to have turned increasingly overtly against God, against nature, against others, and against themselves. This leads to more profound types of violence and fraudulence that imprisons souls more securely. The more calculated they were in their attitudes and actions while on earth, the farther they fell from God, which is to say the farther they fall from light and life in eternity.

Aristotle facilitates this kind of insight because he didn't simply examine the surface of human faults and errors but sought to understand human psychology. He made windows into people's souls. Such perception brings a better understanding of human virtue and vice than a simple list of sins. And while Aristotle's conclusions are not definitive, and Virgil's understanding is limited, the approach that the philosopher developed, and which Virgil communicates well, is crucial for Dante's education at this point.

We readers must constantly look beneath any formulaic explanation of immorality as well. We will be encouraged to consider what we are actually seeing in the souls farther down. Only then will we truly develop an understanding of why they are where they are. Only then will our minds reach that bit farther across the cosmos.

As Virgil talks, Dante struggles to understand. He displays another insight about winning this type of knowledge. It is only really gained when it has been witnessed and, to some degree, experienced. Lists of sins tell you little about living souls, and probably conceal more than they pretend to reveal.

In fact, Virgil makes three attempts at explaining things to Dante. The first is a straightforward description of the circles lower down. It fails to illuminate. The second resorts to Aristotle, and the distinctions he developed to explain human psychology. It helps a bit. However, it is only at the third pass that Dante feels he has got the hang of things, and that happens because Virgil turns to a specific sin to which Dante can relate.

It's an alarming sin for readers of The Divine Comedy 700 years on because the sin Virgil cites is usury. Usury was contained in the medieval world by heavy taboos against making money by lending money. Dante immediately gets why usury is so damaging because when money is used in this way, it becomes its own mini-creator, building its own mini-creations. The double trouble is that many of the things it builds are helpful, pleasurable, and good. Only it's a world that becomes increasingly detached from God. To recall Oscar Wilde's phrase, it leads to knowing the price of everything and the value of nothing, which is to say it fosters meaninglessness amidst material abundance, and blindness of the image of God in nature and human beings.

It is to become increasingly disconnected from the divine. Instead of working creatively with the pulse of nature, which carries the divine pulse, human beings increasingly work against nature, feeling they have the power to force nature in ways that they chose. This way was beginning to emerge in the Europe of Dante's day with the birth of mercantilism, which is presumably why Dante understands the example. It has become the dominant way of organizing society since, which is why usury has lost its taboos. Few can see why making money from money matters anymore, which makes you wonder just how profoundly blind we have become to the divine presence around us. It makes you wonder just how incapable of heaven our society has become.

It is a distressing thought, though simultaneously indicates something of the scope of The Divine Comedy. Dante is aiming not just at individual illumination but civilizational renewal. There is a deep understanding of the world that his poem might foster within us, personally and culturally.

By the end of canto 11, Dante feels more ready to face how bad things can become. He can tolerate the stench. They move away from the shelter of the tomb and begin to descend some more.

Descending a steep slope, they see the Minotaur, centaurs, and a river of boiling blood.

INFERNO 12

Boiling

IRGIL AND DANTE DESCEND INTO THE SEVENTH circle of hell. It is the first of the rounds of lower hell and, in some ways, their first steps in this darker domain are relatively straightforward. What they see they understand, and Dante stays calm during this canto.

The central feature they discover is a river of hot blood, the Phlegethon, within which are boiling those souls whose blood boiled in life. They were violent against their neighbors, their hot bloodedness leading to the spilling of blood. It's grim but hardly unfamiliar to Dante and so quickly comprehendible.

This isn't a trouble that grips his soul. He is not inclined to such violence. However, there are other things he can learn in the seemingly extraneous details of the canto. Such nuances can matter as much as the brute facts of a round. When Dante is doing well on his journey, it is often

47

because he is curious and seeking to understand the subtleties.

They begin by clambering down a steep slope, which is littered with displaced rocks. They realize they are descending a landslide. Dante has to be careful because his weight can move the smaller boulders, and it reminds him of a massive landslide he once saw in northern Italy. The implication is that what they are traversing is no trivial rockfall, though what caused it is not immediately clear.

As they reach its base, they see another monster. It is the Minotaur, the child of Parsiphaë, the Queen to Crete. She had dressed herself in a wooden box that looked like a cow and was mounted by a beautiful white bull. She gave birth to the Minotaur, who is half-bull, half-human. It was locked in a labyrinth that became a device for punishing people. Victims were sent into the maze to meet a brutal end.

The Minotaur's presence is appropriate for this region of hell. When the blood boils, animal instincts take over, which also explains why Virgil and Dante are able to pass the Minotaur without difficulty. They have access to their human wits. Virgil notices that the Minotaur is raging at the sight of the mortal Dante and deduces it is because the beast assumes Dante is Theseus, returning to slay him again. Theseus killed the monster and found a way out of the labyrinth by following the thread that he had been given by Ariadne. So, Virgil yells at the bull-man that it is wrong. The thought confuses it and they run past.

The method deployed by Virgil is instructive. In The Divine Comedy, nothing is incidental. In life, everything carries meaning, if it can be grasped. Dante is relating what happened to him in order imaginatively to prompt further awareness of reality and its ways. In this case, the implication is that the violence of the Minotaur is clearly deadly, but also stupid. It is focused on itself and its one end. Violence can be like that.

Further, the Minotaur is perpetually obsessed with the fact that it was outwitted and defeated. The thought is stuck in its heart, quite as vividly as on the day it died. It blinds. The beast can't see that Dante is not Theseus and, when it is told that the Athenian hero is not approaching, it doesn't know what else to do. Its delusion is their opportunity. They seize it.

It reflects quite a common theme in spiritual texts, namely that the mood which grips the soul at the moment of death is the mood that forges the soul's first steps in the afterlife. More generally, it bolsters the theme that the purpose of mortal life is to become more capable of life in the hereafter.

What is doubly tragic for the Minotaur is that its place in hell is at the foot of the landslide. Its rage means that it hasn't stopped to consider why boulders lie scattered. The signs that a different, transformed future might be possible are all around it. Which takes us back to the cause of the landslide.

It is thought by some commentators to have occurred at the moment of Jesus's death. The Gospel of Matthew reports that this cosmic event prompted a terrestrial earthquake. Maybe it was felt in hell too. Other commentators argue that the landslide happened when Jesus descended into hell after his death to harrow it. I think Dante prefers this latter explanation because he recalls Virgil's remark about the cause. The landslide happened, Virgil believes, when the universe experienced love. That idea comes from the ancient Greek philosopher, Empedocles, who had explained that the cosmos is shaped by two contrary forces: enmity and amity. Enmity brings disarray and chaos. Amity brings harmony and purpose. As an explanation for the landslide, it is limited by Virgil's perspective, but it contains the truth, in fact, as someone with knowledge of the Christian story could see. Love does bring hope, though it may do so through moments of disruption and chaos. Descent and ascent are linked.

I prefer this interpretation because it implies that, even in hell, things change. What grace makes possible is possible everywhere. But while there is no limit to the reach of grace, and it leaves indicators of its presence all around, it needs a response. It is grace, not command.

The Minotaur cannot see the signs. Its predicament reflects that of other souls in hell. They cannot reach out. Their condemnation is self-inflicted.

Sure enough, when the Minotaur realizes that it has been tricked, and that Dante and Virgil have passed by, it falls into another rage. This time it turns on itself, gnawing its bestial body.

They leave the Minotaur in torment and come to some centaurs who are guarding the boiling river with bows and arrows. In myth, there are several stories explaining their origins, revolving around gods tricking humans into sexual congress, but the central message is that they have superhuman strength, which they deploy effectively on the banks of the Phlegethon.

They see Virgil and Dante approaching. One of them calls out. He is Chiron, who is said to be the wisest of the centaurs, as the son of the old god, Saturn. Virgil replies that they will explain their presence when they are at his side, and proceeds to name some of the other centaurs that Dante can see.

There is Nessus, who tricked the wife of Hercules and caused the hero's death. The centaur gave a poison to Hercules's wife, telling her it was a love potion. She soaked her husband's cloak with it when Hercules's eye was drawn to another woman. Hoping to win him back, she killed him. Violence can take many forms.

Another one is Pholus. He was known for the rages he flew into when drunk. Unlike Nessus, he had been a friend of Hercules, though he died one day when he accidently dropped one of Hercules's poisoned arrows on himself. It pierced his skin. His was a careless violence.

They come nearer to the river and Dante sees souls tumbling in its gory waves. There are tyrants and murderers, ranging from dictators such as Alexander the Great to despots from Dante's own time.

Dante and Virgil learn why the centaurs are guarding the river. They run up and down the banks and use their bows and arrows to ensure that those in the river stay immersed in their crime. There may be another symbolic meaning to this. Could their arrows be perverse versions of the arrows of Cupid? Whereas a dart from the son of Venus would make you fall in love, the darts of the centaurs make the bloody souls fall back again into violence.

Now at his side, Virgil talks with Chiron who, in passing, makes a gesture that Dante the poet felt worth recording. The centaur took an arrow and instead of firing it, used it to part his beard to clear his mouth. It's little more than a tick or habit, but it suggests Chiron is thinking. He is prompted to do so because he has noticed how the boulders moved when Dante touched them. He turns to his fellow creatures and points out the detail. What's interesting is that Chiron doesn't fly into a rage at the sight, as the monsters they had met so far were inclined to do. Chiron is considering what it might mean. Maybe he is not so stuck in this state of being, this low circle of reality. Maybe a different future could open up for him.

Realizing he can be reasoned with, Virgil asks Chiron to give them a ride through a ford, farther up the river, explaining that one of the implications of Dante having a heavy, mortal body is that he can't fly. Chiron grants the request and commands Nessus to carry them.

It's another one of these details I love because it implies that there is a physics to hell. It is not just a random assortment of events and encounters, as if a product of Dante's fantasy. It is his imaginative retelling of a time he was taken to another dimension of space and time.

It's a grisly ride. They have to traverse half the river's length, which flows along the circumference of this round. Violent souls bubble up along the way. Some are identified, including Guy de Montfort, an English noble who killed one of his countrymen to avenge a death, while his victim was in church, at Mass. De Montfort is boiling in blood because he disrespected human and divine blood, present in the sacrament.

They reach the ford. Nessus carries them across. They dismount, and the centaur trots back. They are left on the far bank.

They enter an ugly wood filled with wailing and those who killed themselves.

INFERNO 13
Suicide

DANTE AND VIRGIL ARE ON THE FAR BANK OF the Phlegethon river and turn to what faces them next. They are on the edge of a wood without a path. Its gnarled and twisted trunks and branches sprout black leaves and thorns for flowers. It looks ominous. The place brings to mind the wood in which Dante found himself midway through his life.

In fact, there is a sense from the start of canto 13 that Dante will struggle to cope with what this place contains. Unlike the violence of the last round, the souls of this ring, which is still in the seventh circle of hell, suffer from afflictions closer to his own. This is the so-called circle of the suicides, and it's a tricky one for us as well. Suicide feels like an act about which to be compassionate and understanding, not condemning.

Why are these souls here? What holds them? The first thing to remember is Dante's realization that appearances can be deceiving when it comes to assessing human psychology. What seemed obvious to the Church of Dante's day, and remained so until relatively recently, is not necessarily right. Individuals who committed suicide were denied burial in consecrated land. They faced ecclesiastical condemnation. Might Dante be challenging that assumption, rather than affirming it?

The possibility chimes with insights from modern psychotherapy, which has highlighted that there are many different types of suicidality. Having a sense of the kind with which someone is suffering is crucial to offering them the right help. There is the person for whom suicide is a gesture or cry for help because he doesn't know how else to speak about his torment. There is another kind, which is exemplified by Dido. She loved Aeneas too much and killed herself, the love being more determinative than the killing. Hence, she is not in this wood.

A third type of suicide is found in those who deliberately seek to do a violence against themselves. They may want to exact revenge on a hated figure and imagine that killing themselves will hurt the other. Or they may want to kill someone else, realize they can't, and out of frustration kill themselves. Others again approach suicide in the fantasy that they can kill a part of themselves. They may have good reason for their loathing, their suffering, their hate. However, there is a deep tragedy in their decision. As it curtails their mortal lives, maybe it may freeze them in eternity.

Dante wants to explore such nuance. He has already set an agenda of debunking clunky doctrine, though he is still open to the possibility that there are types of suicide that do risk ensnaring individuals. The Church was onto something. Clearly, it's a demonstrative act. It's narrow, confining, constrained. It takes people away from life. It needs thinking about, to discover what it might say about the condition of the soul.

They peer into the woods and spot more bestial creatures. These are the Harpies. They have heads and necks like a woman's, round distended bodies covered with feathers, large wings, and claws for feet, with which they grip the branches of trees. They glower at the travelers, uttering occasional shrieks. If that were all they saw here, it would be pretty terrifying.

Virgil invites Dante to look farther, and the pilgrim notices that the wood echoes with wails of grief, though he can't identify the source of the sounds. Virgil suggests that Dante snaps off a nearby twig. In this place, he will need his guide's advice. He would struggle to keep his mind and work it out for himself if he were alone.

Dante follows Virgil's suggestion, and pulls a stem from one of the bushes. Immediately, the shrub itself wails and moans. Blood oozes from the twig. It sounds like a green log thrown onto a fire. It hisses and spits as if complaining. Dante grasps what is happening. There are souls who have morphed into trees.

They have arboreal bodies and, when branches are snapped, they cry out and speak. These poor souls discarded their bodies in life, in the act of suicide. They have substitute ones now, a replacement that underlies the violence of suicide, whatever its causes. Breaking the body is always a terrible act and a ferocious virtual cry, be it from desperation or deliberation.

The thorny shrub that Dante has inadvertently injured continues to speak. Have you no pity, it cries, to which Virgil replies that he is the one responsible for the seeming attack, and it is done for a purpose: understanding. It is as if the lesser violence of Dante's act might reveal insights into the greater violence of the suicidal act. In the living world, this is akin to therapy, which at times may help people to bear their suffering by exposing them to their suffering, with care and support.

The shrub finds some comfort in Virgil's response, and tells its story. He is Pier delle Vigne and he was a minister in the court of Frederick II. The emperor grew to trust Vigne, a fact about which Vigne is immensely proud, as Dante detects in the way he speaks. He could turn Frederick's heart like a key turns a lock, he explains. Further, he continues, he gained use of what he describes as the two keys of Frederick's power. This is an allusion to the two keys Saint Peter holds in heaven: one is for mercy, the other for judgment. Vigne saw himself as an earthly Peter, as if he controlled the doors that allowed his fellow citizens into the benefits of courtly life.

As he grew to be trusted by the emperor, he grew to love the power. That prompted envy in others, who plotted against him. His enemies dripped poison into Frederick's ear, so to speak, and in time it worked. Vigne was locked up in prison. There he killed himself. He wanted to hurt his former benefactor out of revenge for his loss of position. He could not bear that Frederick had listened to others, as he had become so used to the monarch listening to him.

His suicide was, in a way, the culminating act of his life. It revealed a definitive part of his soul, only it's futile. He harms only himself.

Dante is deeply shocked by the story. He is choked with pity and struggles to speak. The inference is that he understands Vigne's action because a similar suicidality had crossed his mind at some point. Perhaps he knew of the desire for revenge at any cost. Virgil must step in and he asks the tree to say more. As a teacher, he recognizes this is an important moment.

Vigne explains that when he arrived at the entrance to hell, and approached Minos, he was thrown down to this seventh circle like so much trash. He sprouted into a sapling, became the tree, and lives with the consequences.

Dante listens, gripped by the details. The terrible mistakes of Vigne seem to cast light on ones he himself might, or may, make — only the more reflective mood is interrupted.

Suddenly, a hunt springs from a deeper part of the forest. Two black bitches are chasing two naked souls. One of them falls into a nearby shrub, breaking branches and tearing leaves. The hounds leap onto this poor individual and rip him to shreds. Dante tells us that they carried his limbs off in all directions.

The soul doesn't die, of course, and Virgil grabs Dante's hand and leads him over to the broken body in the crushed vegetation. He was a wealthy young man called Lano, who killed himself not by his own hand, but by recklessly throwing himself into the middle of a battle, knowing he would die. It's another type of suicide. He had lost his fortune and thought that he didn't have anything to live for. He is still unable to see what else life might be for and is perpetually hunted by the hounds of hell.

It is brutal. Dante struggles as Virgil converses with the souls, though he doesn't back off from what he sees, and looks at suicide without flinching, which actually brings some marginal compassion to the place, and more understanding of it. And there is an indicator, in the last lines of this canto, that there may yet be hope.

The shrub into which Lano had fallen asks that his torn leaves and broken twigs be gathered up and placed underneath him. The soul is showing some concern for his arboreal body. Maybe he is developing some regret for what he did to his human body.

By burning sands and falling fire, they speak with a soul cursing Jupiter and see a vision.

INFERNO 14

Decay

THE SOUL-TURNED-SHRUB IN THE WOOD OF despair had asked that its broken leaves be gathered and placed underneath it. Canto 14 opens with a moment of tenderness as Dante obliges. Then events move on.

They are now on the far edge of the middle ring of this seventh circle of hell. They have walked through the bleak wood and find themselves at another border. Before them lies a wasteland. It is a dry expanse of burning sand. The wood stops abruptly because no roots can sink into its dust.

Gazing across the landscape, Dante sees flames falling like scorching rain. He notices different groups of souls, some lying flat on the hot surface, some sitting on it, and more wandering, meandering, or running across the parched desert.

Dante has heard about such a place before. There is a reference to a land of burning sand and falling flames in a letter, purportedly written by

Alexander the Great to his tutor, Aristotle. He has recently seen Alexander, flaying around in the bloody river due to his mania to conquer. Joining the dots, developing his perception of hell, Dante fills with dread at the realization that, whether or not Alexander saw such a place during his travels, one exists. What does it mean that there is this zone? What does its eerie weather say about God? Hell looks to be about wider concerns than just fallen Christian souls. It is about pre-Christian times and more.

They see a soul who is lying flat on the ground. Oddly, he seems unconcerned by the fiery flames that fall upon him. Dante turns to Virgil and asks for help. What is going on with this figure? Is he tormented or not? It is not immediately obvious, an uncertainty that Dante expresses by reminding Virgil about his doubt when he failed to open the gates of Dis. What knowledge do they need here to understand things? Does Virgil have it?

The question isn't answered because the prostrate figure speaks unprompted. He is Capaneus, another figure from ancient Greek history. He came to the aid of Polynices, one of the sons of Oedipus, by joining a famous assault on Thebes. His state in hell tells of the lasting confidence he has in himself, marked by a pride that has become vainglory. "What I was once, alive, I still am, dead," he brags. It's as if he can't really see the state of his immortal soul.

The boasting continues. He curses Jupiter, the name by which he knows the supreme deity. All the thunderbolts in Jove's armory could not touch me, he declares.

The falling flames are not thunderbolts and he couldn't stop them if he tried. He seems pathetic in his denial. And then there's a further thought: why would a god care about him? He is blaspheming, yes, but doing so while pinned to burning sand, rained on by fire. That highlights the real problem with blasphemy. It is not cursing the divine. It is centering a life around the delusion that a human individual *could* curse the divine. Capaneus has pinned himself down by foolhardy bloody-mindedness.

Virgil addresses Capaneus, more harshly than any soul he has spoken to yet. Virgil calls out his pride as blustering and bedeviled. Then, turning calmly to Dante, he speaks with his charge.

Capaneus's words pierce him himself more than they pierce heaven, Virgil explains. His pride in life caused him trouble, for sure. His pride in the afterlife causes him more trouble, stabbing him as if the flames were from Jupiter. Oddly enough, Capaneus is right that his torment does not come from God. Jupiter's thunderbolts don't reach him because they don't need to. He is quite capable of self-tormenting.

It's worth adding that Virgil is probably able to identify Capaneus's state of mind so precisely because he is, on occasion, capable of something similar. Maybe this is what deluded him before the walls of Dis. He edged toward a similar vainglory and it could have been his undoing. It suits him to help Dante by implicitly saying that Capaneus is the one with the problem, not him. It eases his own distress, which had been uncomfortably raised by Dante's reminder about the trouble Virgil had before the walls of Dis.

Further insights about the nature of blasphemy follow. The trouble with cursing God is that when a soul does so, it curses itself, because God is its divine source. Blasphemy blocks wellsprings. It leaves souls unable to move, incapable of receiving refreshment, pinned to hot sand. Capaneus certainly looks isolated and out of reach. Maybe that is why Virgil speaks so harshly, though Capaneus seems entirely unperturbed.

They walk on, tracking the boundary between the wood and the sand, and come across a new feature in the landscape. It is a stream, and the sight of it does not bring hope.

It flows red and, moreover, seems to be trickling in an unnatural direction. It doesn't follow the curving sweeps of hell, like the bloody Phlegethon, but instead cuts across the wasteland in front of them like a ghastly arterial vein. Dante's curiosity is piqued, which is a good sign, and Virgil tells him about the extraordinary origins of the waters.

Its source is in an old man who stands beneath the mountain of Crete, called Ida. The old man is a towering, statuesque figure. His head is made of gold, his chest and arms and torso are made of silver. It sounds grand, only the silver is cracked and from the metals flows corruption. Farther down the figure are his legs and feet made of broken brass and fractured iron. He is leaning on his right foot, which is made of terracotta and is crumbling.

It is an image of decay, not just of social or ecclesiastical decay, but civilizational decay. The figure stands looking at Rome with his back to Egypt, halfway between the two centers of Mediterranean civilization, Egypt being the origin of the old, Rome the new. The old man has turned from the ancient world to the Christian world, and now the Christian world is cracked as well.

The culture is not feeding his mind. Its gold and silver are not reflecting the divine. He is leaning on the least valuable part of himself, his terracotta foot, which is disintegrating. It's an awesome metaphor, a terrible image of what happens when civilizations become exhausted. They lose touch with their source. They confuse the valuable with the less valuable. The spirit that flows, which should refresh and revive, poisons and erodes.

The image amplifies the themes of this canto and the previous one and sets a theme that will run throughout The Divine Comedy. When a civilization becomes degenerate, it throws up figures like Capaneus and Farinata. Gods old and new are blasphemed against as people curse the source of their life and, unwittingly, their access to its wellsprings. The most vulnerable and fragile parts of the civilization become exposed. They break and tumble under the weight of their decaying traditions.

Dante felt it in his time, with the corruption of the medieval Church and the internecine struggles of Italian city-states. Today, it makes you wonder whether the old man of Crete represents a culture that relies on the terracotta of the material realm and barely knows of the silver and gold of the spiritual.

The red stream before them brings the deepest troubles of the world into the picture. That said, echoes of hope are sounded here too. Cato is mentioned as Dante and Virgil talk about older times. He is an honorable man and will cross their path not in hell but purgatory. A river of paradise comes to their minds too, the Lethe. When its name is heard in hell, it lifts the mood of dread, momentarily.

They are standing on the edge of the burning sands, still in the shadow of the wood, and Virgil tells Dante it is time to step out, staying close to the edge of the stream. If they walk on the walls that contain it, which rise a little above the desert floor, the flames will not touch them. But stay close, Virgil warns. Resist the spirit of the place, with its fear, cursing, delusion, and pride.

Walking alongside the red stream, avoiding the burning sands, they are approached by a gaggle of souls.

INFERNO 15

Fame

ANTE AND VIRGIL ARE WALKING ABOVE THE sand on the walls that contain the polluted red stream. It reminds Dante of traversing the dikes and water barriers of the low countries and northern Italy, though the banks in hell feel less robust. They are low and thin. The travelers are vulnerable. They are exposed to the whims of this desert.

The mood portends the possibility that the next encounter will be a tricky one for Dante. Souls laboring under travails close to his own are nearby, though what happens may be an opportunity for him to see more, much as the revelations about the old man of Crete have widened his horizons.

Soon, the vegetation of the wood is left behind and they see a crowd of men running toward them. They are a chaotic bunch. Closer in, they look the pilgrims up and down, squinting at them, ogling. Dante describes it as the way men look at each other as they're walking through the dark nights of a medieval city.

It's not clear why they are staring in this way. Commentators tend to make the assumption that the gaze is lustful and lecherous, although for me it carries a distinctly competitive air. It is as if the running souls are asking, who are you, what are you doing here, have you succeeded where we haven't?

The scene raises the big question of the canto, which is why these souls are on the sands? What has gripped their hearts and minds so firmly that it holds them in this bleak place? The common answer of the commentators, drawing on Virgil's description of hell in canto 11, is that this is the circle of hell for those who indulged sodomy. But the label raises more questions than it answers. What if Dante is asking us to enquire more deeply into the state of mind of these souls, as he has done in previous rounds. Relying too closely on the schema Virgil has provided may miss the deeper dynamics, which are only discerned by observing how souls behave and making an attempt to feel into their predicament.

That has just happened with Capaneus the so-called blasphemer. His problem is not really cursing God. Why would that bother God? It's rather how he cuts himself off from God.

One of the gawping onlookers calls out. "How marvelous," he says. Dante looks down and recognizes the individual through the burnt crusts on his face. It is Brunetto Latini. He was a poet and became an important teacher to Dante because he penned allegorical poems from which Dante worked out the art of poetic epic. A few commentators go further and explain that Latini introduced Dante to initiation rites conducted by the Knights Templar. I don't doubt that patterns of initiation can be detected in The Divine Comedy but do doubt Latini's involvement with Dante in that way. After all, the two meet here, in lower hell. That undermines the claim that Latini introduced Dante to the secrets of eternal life.

Like Dante, Latini was a public figure and a Guelph. He was also exiled from Florence. So, there is a real joy in Dante meeting him, for all that it is in this scorching place. However, it prompts an inner tussle. Dante is glad to encounter Latini. He identifies with him, and yet Latini has somehow found himself trapped in hell. As one famous poet looks at another, questions come thick and fast. What does it mean to be so well known? What is it that drives the desire for fame? Might the taste of glory that cursed Latini curse Dante as well? This is certainly what the two discuss during the canto. There is no reference to sodomy.

They converse at great length on the issue of fame and the impulse to spread your name, for reasons good and ill. I imagine that the way Latini greeted Dante sparked a cascade of thoughts in Dante's mind. It must have been lovely to have been greeted with, "How marvelous!" But the delight must have quickly gathered shadows as the possible ramifications of being marvelous dawned on him as he looked upon another marvelous poet, now burnt to a cinder, dodging falling flames.

Latini asks whether he can stay and talk with Dante, which Dante says he would be delighted to do. The request is in marked contrast to Capaneus who, unprompted, blurts out statements about himself. The meeting is respectful and affectionate. Latini touches the hem of Dante's cloak and Dante looks down in reverence, while he stays perched on the wall above his teacher. If this canto is about sodomy, there are grounds for assuming it is about reforming attitudes toward sodomy. Dante implies that affection between men can be shaped by virtue as much as vice. Quick judgments cloud what such exchanges mean. Further, we are going to meet overtly same-sex lovers, when we reach the levels of the saved in purgatory. They are on the threshold of entering paradise. I think there is no question that Dante across *The Divine Comedy*, even if not here, tackles official ecclesiastical attitudes toward homosexuality. He was thoroughly revising them, along with much else.

Dante and Latini walk and talk together. Virgil slips behind them for a while. Latini stresses he must keep walking. If he pauses just for a moment, he will have to lie down like Capaneus for one hundred years. He must live down here as he lived up above: always on the move, always jostling for position, always reaching up for more.

Dante explains how he comes to be traversing the sands, offering a short speech in which he describes the way Virgil, his guide, received a word from heaven and, together, they embarked on descent. Dante describes it poignantly: Virgil is leading him home, he says; the descent will become an ascent, leading to heaven. Dante is displaying clarity of mind.

His true home is a place of glory, he continues. The implication is that, if you are to be remembered on earth, then ensure you are remembered in heaven too, which is to say, become famous for communicating, elaborating, and revealing divine glories. These greater glories are the ones to magnify because they are the glories of eternal life. The poet who becomes hooked on lesser glories, such as his own genius and fame, reduces his appreciation for all that life can be, and so risks rendering himself incapable of heaven.

Dante doesn't put it as explicitly as that, though together, they riff on such themes. For example, Latini comments that all anyone needs to do is follow his star and he will find the way to his heavenly home. It's an ambiguous remark because while Latini is right, and Dante is going to follow the stars through paradise, Latini affirms it in hell. That suggests he doesn't fully understand what he is saying. Maybe another part of Latini's problem is that he has become very good with words, as poets do, but that very art has uncoupled him from their inner significance and meaning. It's an old worry that reaches back at least to Plato, who argued that poets can confuse the images they conjure for the truths those images are supposed to reflect, thereby losing touch with the truths.

Another way of interpreting Latini's comment about the stars is to reflect on its astrological significance. He might mean "follow your constellation," which in Dante's case is Gemini. However, as Dante has already implied, stars are signs not destinations. It is easy to become so absorbed by the meaning of a star sign that the goal to which it points, dips below the horizon.

All the way through their lovely conversation, we readers are encouraged to tease out just what is being said. Compounding the air of delight, as well as things unknown, Latini moves into prophetic mode, as the souls in these altered states of mind can do. His words are about Dante's future. They build on the remarks of others that Dante has already heard. Latini tells him that Florence will be swamped by infamous men who are arrogant and envious and proud. The competitive side of the Florentine spirit will dominate, an insight fitting to this area of hell. It makes sense that it should come to Latini's mind. He is wrestling in the afterlife with these same risks and dangers. They are in the air, falling as flames.

Latini warns Dante not to become locked in disputes. It's a version of the wisdom of choosing your enemies carefully because you become like them in battles with them. Dante replies graciously that he is learning how to seek higher things, partly through the writings of Latini. It is a homage to the older man. They speak like teacher and student, master and disciple, though there is a faint edge of flattery in Dante's reply, another temptation the famous must manage.

And yet, his gift cannot be denied. The reason this conversation is so important to Dante is that he does strive to speak of eternal things. It is his vocation. The Divine Comedy is the great product of his efforts. If he had not wrestled with the desire for earthly glory, he would not have been able to pen his poem. The trick is to stay open to the glories that don't belong to anyone, to ensure the credit is given to God, for all that the individual must shine to channel divine beauty and wonder. Human beings are not the originators of delight and grandeur, though they can share in them fully.

Fortune comes up in their discussion, following on from Latini's prophecy. Dante is perhaps rehearsing in his mind what he learned from Boethius:

a tempestuous life on earth may be a blessing because it is Fortuna's way of reminding mortals to focus on lasting splendors rather than temporary fineries. The latter will be taken away.

Suddenly, Virgil speaks, for the only time in the canto, emphasizing what he says. It's a cryptic remark: "He listens well who notes well what he hears." It asks Dante if he really knows what he is saying, a central issue for a poet. Or maybe Virgil is underlining that when fortune's wheel turns against you, it may be painfully purgative: it is a way of saying, be prepared.

Dante remembered the remark because he includes it in canto 15. However, at the time, it seems it almost passed him by, because he and Latini carry on talking, now turning to other distinguished figures who are running on the sand. Dante wants to learn more about this struggle with talent and fame by naming them. How have others failed to keep their life and God's vitality in proper proportion? How much is he like them?

It adds another inflection on the reason the souls around Dante and Virgil must keep running. They are jogging and scampering as if they were still engaged in the race of life, only they are not. The tragedy is underlined when, at the end of the canto, Latini runs off to rejoin his gaggle. He explains that he can't stay with Dante any longer because, with their walking and talking, they have been approaching the next ring of hell, into which Latini can't cross.

The older poet speeds off. He appears to be running like a winner with lasting fame. He is not. If it weren't for Dante's encounter with him in hell, he would be all but forgotten, known only to a handful of specialists in medieval Italian verse.

Hearing waters tumbling, they meet three more souls before stranger things occur.

INFERNO 16

Reputation

ATINI IS LEFT BEHIND BY DANTE AND VIRGIL.
They carry on, above the sand, walking on the walled banks of
the red stream. As they proceed, they catch a new sound on the
air, of water tumbling in the distance. It is humming and buzzing. Another
step change in hell seems close.

While talking with Latini, Dante had been drawn to another group of souls
dancing and dodging through the heat and flames. He had wondered what
further distinguished individuals it might contain. The group is nearby now.

From it, three break loose and approach the travelers balanced above
them. They look up carefully and notice Dante's clothes. He is a Florentine
wearing Florentine dress. The clothing has drawn them to him.

They must keep moving and in order to do so and talk with Dante,
they perform a strange maneuver. They adopt a circular motion, spinning
around, while keeping their heads still, as if held at the hub of a wheel,

their bodies become spokes. They can keep moving, while staring at Dante and studying him.

The humans-become-turnstile is described precisely by Dante. He is indicating a deviousness in the movement, indicating the state they might be in. The souls look distorted, uncomfortable, but they are prepared to bear the distress in order to turn the situation to their advantage. They want to look and look they will.

It is a type of lust, and one with which Dante is in part familiar. The clue is in the dance and the interest in dress. If Latini's downfall had been self-satisfaction with his ability, I think this group of souls have become fascinated with the allure of what today would be called celebrity. They are drawn by the aura that surrounds Dante. It transfixes them. Their strange maneuver is a symptom of what has taken hold of them. Their bodies twist as their eyes lock on the new arrival as he has become their obsession.

Virgil unwittingly adds flattery to the mix, telling Dante that these souls deserve Dante's respect, not he theirs. Virgil and Dante should be running across the sand to bow down and honor them. Dante confirms he is privileged to meet the three as he knows of their greatness.

It's all very odd. Virgil and Dante speak reverently. We, as readers, wonder what's going on, not least as we also have Dante's description of their nakedness, their burnt bodies, their humiliating contortions. Dante feels a deep grief in his heart, which took a time to pass, he reports, because these noble people are clearly lost in the wasteland, though he is simultaneously wooed by their fame.

The spirit of celebrity is like that. It clouds your view. It conceals. It fails to comprehend the object of devotion. It shines brightly, though unlike the light of the stars and the sun, it distracts from the true light of life.

One of the souls speaks. He is Jacopo Rusticucci and was an enormously wealthy merchant. He made his name in trade. He is keen to preserve his name and its glamour in death. The other two are identified as worldly and successful Guelphs, which is presumably why they impress Dante. Not only were they from noble families, but they won significant victories in the civil wars for Dante's side.

But the knowledge makes us unsure. What kind of nobility is preserved in fighting a civil war? What kind of honor accrues with amassing wealth? Ironically enough, the ambivalence is written into the name of one of them. He is called Borsiere, which means purse-maker.

Borsiere is a relatively recent arrival in hell and he has informed his compatriots that Florence is in a bad state. The old habits of courtesy and valor have ceased. The streets are filled with weeping faces. It sounds like a noble concern, but Dante starts to see through the veneer. He realizes that their display of honor is a pretense. It is really the money that is speaking, the money that ruled these individuals' lives, the money that fomented the envy and avarice of the Florentine conflicts.

He is also starting to realize that the turning souls are not actually that interested in him. They approached and asked who he was, but then didn't listen to his reply. They were drawn to look at him because they needed to measure themselves by the novel presence. That's why they were interested in his clothes. They wore clothes like that once though, having seen Dante close up, they have concluded that they wore them better. Their initial interest has turned to scorn, while he continues reverencing them. They surveyed him, summed him up, and dismissed him, falling back to their self-regard. Standing above them starts to feel, to Dante, a bit like being at a party when the person in front of you is feigning interest in you, while continually glancing over your shoulder.

Dante has had enough. He stands erect, his head looking up. He has remembered his proper nobility. He will speak the truth. What a breed are you, he declares! Where is your restraint? You are the reason Florence weeps!

They have no reason to be proud and yet are. They were rich and powerful on earth, but poor and corrupt in spirit. They did not use their wealth and largesse for the greater good of the city. They caused trouble and waged war. The same attitudes have cut them off from God. They think they won the race of life in terms of status and recognition. They were deluded.

Dante and Virgil start to move on, leaving the three behind, who call out, asking to be remembered. They know Dante is on his way to the stars. Maybe a small part of them knows that there is more to life than the life they led and asking Dante to remember them is akin to asking for prayers. Alternatively, and perhaps more likely, they may hope to feed their empty celebrity and fame when Dante comes to write this canto.

We are left uncertain whether they have a hope in hell because they run off. Dante tells us that their legs beat on the sand like wings might beat in the air. The sight of them receding is deranged, though they must run back because, like Latini, they are unable to leave the region ruled by the spirit of obsession.

Dante and Virgil continue on, and their attention turns to the sound of the water, plunging much more closely. It has grown deafening and, with the end of canto 16, comes a marked change. It prepares us for the remarkable thing that will happen next. The water is so loud that they can hardly hear each other speak. They are at the edge over which it rushes. It reminds Dante of spring floods caused by melting snow, crashing from the mountains. Then, Dante and Virgil perform two peculiar actions.

First, Dante takes off the cord that has been wrapped around his waist as a belt for his clothing. He knows that Virgil is going to ask him to do so, and he does. Second, Virgil draws the cord into a loop and throws it over the precipice down which the waters are tumbling.

The symbolism of these gestures has provoked much comment. Dante tells us that he previously thought the cord might be useful for catching the dancing leopard in the dark wood at the beginning of his story. I think the leopard stood for ill-considered faux-wisdom, erratic and dangerous because it was not sure what to do next. The contrast now is that Dante does know what to do.

His act is also in marked contrast with the wealthy merchants they have just met, who had an obsession with clothing. They dressed themselves up and concealed their vices with seeming virtues. Dante is loosening his clothes. He is relying less on how he looks and turning more to who he is. I think he intuitively knows that this is what is required of him. He has learned the lesson of the sands, that he must open himself to divine influence and glory. He has learned before the gates of Dis that he needs higher powers.

It is a brave act. When approaching danger, a natural response is to wrap yourself up, to keep what you have about you, as if it might offer protection. Dante is doing the opposite. That is real wisdom.

Virgil is alert to the insight as well. He and Dante are working in tandem, connected because they are in tune with the moment.

Not that Dante knows what is going to happen next. He is working from trust not knowledge. In fact, he can hardly believe what occurs. He swears on *The Divine Comedy* itself that what happened was strange, but that he reports it right.

This is a serious oath, swearing on his life's work and revelation. Nothing could be more important, and Dante is prepared to stake his reputation on it. His description will seem like a lie, he tells us. It will make you think the worse of me, he implies, though he is not bothered by reputation as the souls on the sands had been. He will speak of mysterious things regardless. That is what awakening to wider realities requires.

The canto ends with them on the cliff edge, as from the pit into which the waterfall plunges appears a creature who seems to swim through the air. It is a preternatural being, beyond imagining. It rises up to their level like an anchor emerging from murky depths. It spreads out its arms and doubles up its legs.

At the cliffs of deeper hell, they confront the monster Geryon and souls disfigured by usury.

Dive

ANTE CALLS ON OUR IMAGINATION IN CANTO
17. He himself doesn't speak. The action mostly focuses on Virgil.
We have to muse on what unfolds and contemplate what they
experience.

It's another transitional moment in the journey as they descend into
the deeper pits of hell. Dante the poet is, in effect, asking us to shift gear.
As they travelled farther into dark reality, we must sink to an appropriate
level of perception too.

Virgil speaks to Dante, though he could equally be speaking to us. Look
at this beast, he says, as the creature with a pointed tail, who can break
walls and destroy weapons, and infect the world with its reek, floats from
the canyon before them.

The monster is a manifestation of fraud. It's as if the power of fake,
deceitful, and corrupt ways of being in the world were so tangible that

they had assumed a living form. Fraud is not just meant in the way people can deceive themselves and others. It's meant in the way that it percolates throughout nature, as human beings attempt to turn all things to their ends, uncoupled from what's good, beautiful, and true. People so lose their way in this state that they don't even know others exist. All they might see is the monster their fantasy has brought into being. It's the soul without love of others, locked into a state of mind that can only authentically reference itself.

The monster has a name, indicative of its reality. Virgil calls it Geryon. In ancient mythology, he was a giant who lived in nature. In Dante, he has become a beast who lives among us.

Dante discerns its three parts. Its head is a charming human face, appearing benign. Its serpentine body is decorated with arabesques and curlicues, a facsimile of a rainbow-colored fabric or rug. Arachne could not have spun a more gorgeous web, Dante says, only the reference is alarming because Arachne was hubristic, loving her art more than the gods. Then there is the creature's tail. It is in the form of a sting: there is a sting in its tail. The beast becomes a scorpion in this part of itself and is armed with poison. Fraud is like Geryon, at first charming, promising riches, then deadly.

The beast appears, and they turn right, not left, to meet it. They have to break from the left-trekking pathway again, the unnatural move that strains divine blessing. I suppose that no way shaped by God could lead directly to such purity of fraud.

As they turn, Dante is distracted. He notices another group of souls, on the sand close to the vertiginous edge. Virgil says that Dante should go to see them, to complete his knowledge of this round. He has to take only ten steps, which is a physical and psychological measure, the two completely merged in this zone. These souls are not far away from them in space, but also mentally, because it turns out that these souls are the usurers and, as we have already learned, Dante has a good understanding of the peril embraced by them. His familiarity with the issue also means he is not concerned about leaving Virgil's side. The risk they might pose to him is neutralized.

They look like dogs in the summertime, he sees, tormented by bites and fleas. They sit on the ground, and so complete the sets of souls they had seen from the far side of the sand by the wood, when they had noticed some were lying down, some were running, and some were sitting on the ground. Dante doesn't recognize their faces, so disfigured have they become, but he sees each is wearing a greying pouch around the neck. They are purses, decorated with heraldic emblems of animals against faded color backgrounds. As they sit, they stare at the money sacks.

If Latini was preoccupied with his art, and the second group of fellows were obsessed with their fame, then these individuals have dived farther into the vice, hence being closer to hell's heart. They are concerned with money for its own sake. They are not concerned with what it can support or what it can buy. This is usury: money making money, even if it rapes the earth.

Their fanaticism perverts even heraldry, which should be a badge of nobility. They achieve nothing, besides preying upon their victims, who are drawn to borrow or lend out of need or greed. They create a kind of motion in the world, though it's a perversion of the divine motion powered by love. Money makes the modern world go round and here, in hell, Dante sees that it is in ever decreasing circles, terminating in perpetual stasis. The usurers display a horrible diminution of life, a terribly twisted version of divine ways. God showers gifts. God gives. These people make you pay, taking away the little you have.

Dante doesn't speak to them, though one of the number calls out. He is called Reginaldo degli Scrovegni and history relates how his son was so horrified by his father's exploitation of people that he built a church as penance. It is the chapel in which Giotto painted some of his best-known frescoes and has been called one of the most beautiful interiors in the whole of Christendom. The son was trying to redeem the sins of his father, and succeeded in a way, though not so as to turn his father's heart.

Scrovegni sits scratching and hitting himself like the others. As Dante is about to turn back and rejoin Virgil, he notices Scrovegni sticking out his tongue. It protrudes so far that he simultaneously licks his nose and looks like an ox.

Virgil, meanwhile, has been taking control of the situation. He is already seated on Geryon's back. He knows what he is doing, which is in part treating Geryon with respect. He asks the beast to let them ride. He speaks gently to the creature throughout. He reminds it that he carries a mortal soul, and so should move with care, slowly.

Dante mounts, sitting in front of Virgil as instructed, so as to keep out of reach of the tail. Unlike his guide, Dante is terrified. The description of them lifting off and going down likens the ride to a boat trip, with Geryon a navigator. The beast turns around and descends in great circles. During these maneuvers, Dante clutches tightly. Mostly, he buries his face in Geryon's back. When he ventures to look down, he sees the walls of hell closing in. He hears screams, sees flames. It terrifies him all the more. Virgil remains composed.

Maybe Dante's guide understands fraud. He is a model of quiet steadiness that keeps focused, although all around is deceit and poison. Maybe Virgil has seen through Geryon, and Geryon is quietened like the bully who has been outed as a coward.

This could explain why, when they reach the end of the descent, and the two souls have disembarked, Geryon shoots off like an arrow. He looks to Dante like a falcon who failed to catch any prey; he might have been furious at being exposed and used. Deception rests on lies. He had been defeated by truth. I'd go so far as to say that there is something Christlike in Virgil in this canto. Jesus stood before power in the person of Pilate and remained steady and quiet, which sucked authority from the Roman ruler. Wisdom can rule by clarity of sight.

Dante is far from so sure. He doesn't weep or faint as he has done before, though he describes his fear repeatedly as they sink down. Mythical figures come to his mind. One is Phaethon, the son of Helios, who rode the sun's chariot and lost control, burning the earth in his wake. Another is Icarus, who steered too close to the sun with his wings made of wax and fell out of the sky. As both figures fell, they would have known horror, like Dante. He is far from sure this is the right path, though recalling these figures might have brought him comfort. They ascended too quickly into the sky and then fell. He is descending first. Into his mind come good omens, in fact, though he is too terrified to read them.

At the bottom of their descent are jagged cliffs. Geryon lets them off his back and darts off. They stand there, gathering themselves, listening to distressed souls screaming.

They are in the eighth circle, the place called Malebolge, as the descent deepens.

INFERNO 18
Foul

CANTO 18 BRINGS US TO THE EIGHTH CIRCLE OF
hell, and it begins with a report by Dante the poet. "There is a
place in Hell called Malebolge," he says. This is where they have
arrived.

The direct statement underlines the realism of *The Divine Comedy*. Malebolge exists quite as fully as the sun or the city of Jerusalem, for Dante.
The place occupies him more than any other in the *Inferno* by quite a
long way. It stresses the point that evil grows with subtlety, not merely
with acts.

Malebolge has a distinct shape. Looked at in cross-section, it appears
to be a funnel or giant stadium. Dante would have known the Colos-
seum of Rome, similar to a modern stadium in which people sit in tiers.
Malebolge is similarly ringed, each tier filled with a gorge or deep ditch:
a bolge. They all contain souls, lodged according to their deed. There are
far more people here than Dante could estimate or count.

The bolge are crossed by bridges, and a pathway wends its way along the upper reaches of each one. The place seems to have been designed not only to house souls but also so that the unlucky individuals might be observed. To watch the souls in Malebolge is to track the shadowy far reaches of the human mind.

The importance of Dante seeing parts of himself in the souls in this domain is stressed by Virgil. I think that's partly to extend Dante's learning, and partly because without such insight, the distinctions between each bolge might be missed. This macrocosm in hell is a microcosm in himself. He needs to chart it well so that he can be more capable of handling his destructive aspects. Malebolge is a living map, a bit like the maps of the psyche drawn up by developmental psychologists today. The Desert Fathers and Mothers of the early Christian centuries did something similar when they entered the wilderness and simultaneously entered an inner landscape, to discover their own torments, frailty, temptations, demons. Like Dante, they needed to travel not so as to escape themselves but to encounter themselves. Without the distractions of the world, the contents of their minds became clearer. It was a necessary preparation for catching sight of God.

The souls are trapped in various ways. Some manipulated others in life, others despoiled things, others again pimped themselves or profiteered or paraded false virtues, falsifying themselves and others. These are the varieties of fraudulence with which Malebolge is concerned. They are worse sins, more intractable states of mind, than Dante and Virgil have faced so far because the individual has more consciously adopted such deformed ways of life. They have used their freedom to orient their wills against what is good, beautiful, and true. Their decision, and the consequences, act as a warning and a mirror: how do we pimp ourselves, profiteer, exploit? What damage does this do and how does it take away sight of the divine image within us and the world, and so sever us from God? It's a subtle business, for all that Malebolge is full of graphic horrors.

Demons play a big part in it. They harrow, harass, attack, and tease. They are constantly watching and judging their charges, ensuring that the experience of being stuck is never forgotten. They are devilish surveillance machines, monitoring all that goes on, adding to the oppression. The sense of being watched becomes internalized by the souls of Malebolge, much as many modern people watch themselves. I think that many medieval people would look at the modern world and think we lack freedom with the way we crack the whip upon ourselves with the technology that reaches into every aspect of our lives. It might look demonic.

Dante and Virgil's exploration of the place begins as they step away from jagged cliffs where Geryon has deposited them. His guide turns left, and Dante follows him.

They are able to see into the first ditch, where souls are processing in two lines, flowing in opposite directions. One line is moving toward them, the other away from them with their backs to the travelers. The regimentation reminds Dante of the Jubilee of 1300 in Rome, when so many pilgrims came to the holy city that they had to walk across the bridges of the Tiber in a similar fashion, each side of the bridge allocated to one direction of travel.

It's an odd image to come to Dante's mind. This was the first time the Church had declared a Jubilee. It meant that if individuals made a trip to the holy sites and places, they would be freed from the consequences of sins. It seems like a generous idea. But I think it's echoed here in hell because Dante is intimating that it's too mechanical an approach to divine life. It risks turning spiritual transformation into a checkbox activity. Doing this or that because a priest or prelate has sanctioned it is not the same as becoming capable of divine sight. The implication is that the Jubilee of 1300 could take people away from heaven. It might foster an approach to religion that is about mindlessly obeying or lining up in serried ranks. It may entirely miss the difficulties of gazing into the soul, the descent that allows the light of the cosmos to be discerned within.

Looking farther into the first bolge, they see horned devils flying around the streaming souls. They freely deploy their whips. Dante sees a face he recognizes, though when the individual realizes that he has been spotted from above, he looks down. He doesn't want to be seen. Maybe he is embarrassed or ashamed. It may be a sign of regret, a precursor to transformation or change.

He is called Venedico Caccianemico who was known for having pimped his sister. He confesses to Dante that he sold her to a marquis to get on in the world. It is a hideous thing to have done. Venedico is not atypical. He is one of many who, each in their own way, sold others for personal benefit. In eternity, they face the fact that in so doing they sold their souls.

Dante and Venedico's brief exchange reminds Venedico of life on earth and he asks to be remembered above. Maybe that's why he looked down: he half remembered the light. If so, the recollection was brief. A devil swoops in from above and yells that he must keep moving. There is no pimping down here, it taunts.

Dante hurries back to Virgil's side. Does he fear he might have pimped people in life, perhaps not in such an explicit way as Venedico, but by writing about others? Did he exploit them for his own ends, his own glory? That is not mooted explicitly. But it makes you wonder if it was part of the shock of Dante's first taste of Malebolge.

They come to a stone bridge that reaches across the chasm in which the souls walk. It is relatively straightforward to climb up its near slope, and they paused at the top, where they can gain a better view of the activity beneath them. In particular, they can see the faces of the souls that, previously, had their backs to them.

This second group are seducers, experts in the opposite deeds to the pimps. They used charm and sexuality to woo. One character stands out as they look down: Jason, the mythological retriever of the golden fleece. During his travels he had seduced a woman, Hypsipyle, who became pregnant, though Jason left her with the child.

That was one side of Jason's character, though maybe only one side. I say that because, strangely, Jason's name will also be heard in paradise. He is remembered in that domain as well, in a good light. I wonder if this is suggesting that people are complex. Part of them can be in hell, part in heaven. The thought makes me sit up as a psychotherapist because a common model of the psyche describes the human mind as populated by different personalities and sub-personalities. They may cooperate or fight. They may be similar or different. The model explains how we can be various, perhaps depending on who we are with or where we are. There can be parts that are loving, parts that are greedy, parts that delight, parts that hate. Is Dante intimating he caught sight of something similar in Malebolge, as his insight into human flaws deepened?

They walk farther across the bridge, come to the other side, and are almost immediately alongside the second bolge. It's the only canto while they are in Malebolge to cover two of the bleak ditches. I suspect the crush of two is indicative of Dante's own rush to gain the wherewithal to understand what he is seeing.

A terrible stink rises from the second valley. They can't see into it, for darkness, though when they clamber onto a bridge that spans the recess, they see farther down. The stink and shadow make sense: the ditch is full of feces, as if from terrestrial latrines. Virgil and Dante cover their faces. The people in this bolge are buried in excrement to various degrees.

Their hideous condition is the result of using flattery to get through life. It reminds me of Freud's observation that gifts can be akin to shit, an association that arises from our early lives when we had to learn to go to the lavatory. Parents praise children when they perform correctly, and

Freud wondered if children experience the adulation as thanks for a gift, deposited in the correct place.

The people in the second bolge would, therefore, be the kind of individuals who exploit this half-forgotten memory by deploying praise as a form of manipulation. They are the types who use superlatives all the time: everything in life is "wonderful," "tremendous," "amazing," "fantastic" — a chain of adjectives that is a bit like the praise a parent would offer to encourage a child.

The flattery is damaging because, after a while, you can't tell whether what is being said is true or false. Everything is treated as perfect, which demeans what's good and erodes the chance of learning, discerning, improving, understanding. The habit undermines the purpose of life.

Dante recognizes the face of Alessio Interminei, from Lucca. At first, Alessio doesn't want to be looked at, but Dante calls out and Alessio laments where he has ended up because of the flatteries that, in life, rolled from his tongue.

Virgil encourages Dante to look down again and he sees the mythological figure of Thaïs. She was a prostitute who used her beauty to charm and control others. Deception was her way of life.

The canto ends with Virgil remarking that they have probably seen enough of these pimps, seducers, and flatterers. The early part of their trek across Malebolge leaves grim images in the mind.

Dante perceives the bleak bankruptcy of exchanging spiritual gifts for temporal goods.

INFERNO 19

Corruption

ANTE'S RHETORICAL OUTBURSTS FILL CANTO 19. It opens with a declaration against sin and is punctuated by others. It marks a shift of register from the personal failures of the first canto of Malebolge to focus on systemic failings across medieval society, particularly in the medieval Church. Dante the poet is sounding the trumpet. He is speaking truth to power.

"O Simon Magus, and scum that followed him," he cries. Dante recalls divine justice and wisdom, and how those who claim to follow God should stand for such things. He is outraged.

Simon Magus is a character from the Acts of the Apostles who became the type of those who seek to manipulate divine power to their advantage. He had seen Peter casting out demons in the name of the Holy Spirit, and asked Peter whether he could have the same power, and how much it would cost. He sought to buy spiritual capacities. Peter curses him, and the error leads to Simon's undoing.

It sounds like a fairly straightforward moral tale, the meaning of which is clear. But offering spiritual goods for temporal goods, and confusing the two, is a daily hazard for churches. Simony, as the sin came to be called, can become a way of life, wittingly or unwittingly. That is why it is important.

In the medieval Church it took one form in particular: the buying and selling of indulgences, which purported to save the soul punishment in purgatory. The practice became so excessive that it prompted the Reformation, though some worried about it long before Martin Luther purportedly nailed his ninety-five theses to a church door in Wittenberg. Today, simony can take other forms, particularly for established churches, as they seek to secure their position in the secular polity by offering blessings and ceremonies and moral sanction. For churches, it is a systemic problem.

Dante looks down into the third bolge and sees structures that look familiar. There are upright tubes buried in the ground, which remind him of the cylinders of the baptistry pool in Florence. Priests could stand in the cylinder, which didn't contain water, and so remain dry while they immersed those to be baptized in the holy water around them.

The image comes to mind because Dante had once rescued a child who became stuck in one such tube. He had smashed the marble to release the infant, only some said he had desecrated the baptistry. Part of Dante's purpose in canto 19 may be to tell his accusers that if they can't tell the difference between saving a life and damaging a baptistry, then they are going to struggle to tell the difference between eternal life and the obsessions of churches. It's a variant on simony, and the confusion between what's temporal and eternal. Dante may even be implying that he smashed a baptistry to save a soul, whereas the Church smashes souls to build its baptistries. That sounds extreme, only institutions routinely take on a life of their own that may divorce them from other concerns. They readily become more powerful than any of the individuals who fill posts and positions, causing those individuals to act in ways that they would elsewhere resist. The upshot is that churches damage souls in the name of blessing.

Dante sees souls in the tubes, though they are not standing. They are in headfirst, upside down. Their feet stick out. On their soles dance flames. It's a literal inversion and spiritual inversion. The baptized are said to receive the flames of the Holy Spirit that shine above their heads. Here, the lost souls must contend with burning fires that torment their feet. Dante notices that the burning is sustained by an oily substance, which is a perverse form of the oil with which the baptized are anointed. In some holes he sees only feet and ankles pointing out. In others, calves and knees protrude.

Dante notices one set of legs where the flames are bigger and the kicking more vigorous. He is drawn toward it and asks Virgil whose feet they might be. Virgil offers to carry Dante into the trench to ask the owner directly. It is a gesture he has not offered Dante before. He is able to do what the priests of Dante's time were not: assist in the discernment of what's true. The symbolism of the offer is doubly strong as Virgil is no priest, but a pagan. This is going to be an important encounter.

Virgil explains that, first, they will cross the bridge that spans the bolge and then, from the other side that is lower due to the funnel shape of Malebolge, climb back into the ditch.

They do so and draw close to the legs Dante had spotted. Dante stands alongside the cylinder, ironically enough making him feel like a priest in a confessional. He asks who the sinner might be. A voice emerges from beneath the ground, though it does not respond directly to Dante. Instead, it cries: "Boniface!"

This soul was a pope, and he thinks another pope, Boniface VIII, has just arrived. In life, the inverted pontiff was used to speaking only with senior figures. In death, he cannot imagine anyone else is worth talking to. The Boniface he thinks he addresses was one of his successors, whom he presumes has now been flung into hell as well. Power is like that. It becomes preoccupied only with the fortunes of the powerful and forgets how to hear others.

Dante feels like a friar confessing an assassin. In Florence, assassins were executed by being buried head-first in the ground, with friar or monk standing alongside to catch any last-minute confessions. The image is not one that flatters this damned pope. It must have been a discombobulating experience for Dante, when you recall the temporal power and regal charisma of the medieval papacy.

The background to the story unfolding before him is that Boniface VIII was a particularly worldly pope, among many worldly popes. He caused his predecessor, Celestine V, who had been a holy hermit, to resign in order to make space for his reign. The abdication came a few short weeks after Celestine was declared pope. But, reasoned Boniface, the papacy is not to do with sanctity.

Boniface also carries huge significance for Dante. In effect, the pope was the cause of Dante's public downfall because he held Dante in Rome when the poet-cum-politician needed to be in Florence defending himself. He was not, and so could not, and therefore was unable to do anything to prevent the events that led to his exile. Dante blamed the pope for the rest of his life. We will hear a lot more about Boniface as the journey progresses.

The pope who had assumed Dante was Boniface is Nicholas III. He was a Roman nobleman, and another worldly prelate. Even though the future of his eternal soul is now at stake, the ups and downs of Church life remain his greatest concern. Little wonder he is stuck in hell.

Nicholas has presumed Dante is Boniface because he has seen Boniface's name written in the book that records the fate of souls. Not that Nicholas is any great prophet. It wouldn't take much insight to draw that conclusion, given his own predicament. Further, his bitterness wills Boniface to appear in hell before his successor's time is up. He even has the guile to charge Boniface with his own sins: prostituting the Church for money, power, gain, and wealth. This simoniac is blind to doing the very same thing. He presumably thought his actions were justified, another way in which power corrupts. It's the failure to see the plank in your own eye, having become obsessed with the speck in your neighbor's eye, to recall Jesus's remark in the Gospels.

Dante's portrayal of Nicholas amounts to a strong indictment of the papacy as such. Nicholas is not an exception but the rule. These big institutions inevitably become preoccupied with their temporal power, with their continuity. They'll tell you it's about doing good in the world. And the complication is that, in part, it is. But at the same time, corruption creeps in. It is easy to spot it, looking back at the medieval Church, whose papacy has become a byword for depravity. But similar risks continue.

Oddly enough, for a secular age, simony is widespread in the world, as well. Think of the number of marketing campaigns that aim to shift goods by lending them a spiritual aura. Cars are associated with godlike power. Beauty products will make you glow like an angel. Candles, heavenly scenes and diaphanous curtains have become the staples of ads. Presumably the con works.

Conversely, genuinely spiritual goods are sold because of their temporal utility. Meditation is advertised as helping with the stresses of the day. The Christian gospel is said to bring prosperity in its wake. Charismatic healers and angel seers trade on spectacle.

Nicholas remains bitter throughout the exchange with Dante. At one point, Dante tries to speak back to the pope, telling him that excessive greed and preoccupation with material goods has brought great grief to the world. It crushes the good and exalts the depraved. The so-called Donation of Constantine is lamented. This was the document, now regarded as fictitious, that seemed to give temporal power to popes at the behest of the emperor, Constantine. What a terrible moment that was! If only Constantine had foreseen the cumulative effects of his gift, Dante cries!

It's an effort to break through Nicholas's delusion and highlight the sin. The pope's feet do kick more violently, though Dante is unclear whether it's out of pricked conscience or increased rage. Whatever the truth of that, a poet is speaking the truth to a pope. To Dante's early readers, this was revolutionary talk. It might still provoke a headline today.

Virgil is delighted. He witnesses his student charged with righteous anger, developing his own authority, and speaking from the good within him, resistant to the depravity that surrounds them. He carries Dante out of the bolge, as he had carried him in.

Dante describes the second embrace as close to Virgil's heart. Virgil holds Dante to his chest. They are acting, thinking, and feeling as one, at least in this moment. It brings Virgil joy. It seems that his mission is going well.

Virgil puts Dante down, and immediately they see another deep valley before them. Hell's consolations tend not to last.

Dante is perturbed when they encounter the diviners, an art he practices too.

INFERNO 20

Shock

ANTE OPENS BY REMARKING THAT THIS IS canto 20 of the first part of his *Divine Comedy*, "the one about the damned." It makes us sit up. He is drawing attention to what he calls the "strange torments" of this next ditch of Malebolge and reminding us that there are two more parts of the *Comedy* to come.

His efforts at putting what he saw into verse, thereby communicating the impact and meaning of his journey, are not aimed at putting the fear of God into us. They are to encourage us on the pathway to the transformation of purgatory and the delight of heaven. It is true that here in Malebolge, the sights are dispiriting, horrible, and vile, but they can be held and tolerated within a bigger vision. That greater context neither reduces their seriousness, nor terminates the faith in happier outcomes that may be possible.

This is the path he seeks to follow. This is the perception his poem offers. It can alter your view of reality from the bottom up.

The question is how you divine what you see, how you discern the meaning of events. Divination is the theme of canto 20. Dante knows that practices such as astrology, soothsaying, and precognition are another matter that requires careful attention. To dismiss them too fast is as bad a mistake as to fall for them too quickly.

It should come as no surprise. Dante is entirely focused on reading the signs of the times. He contemplates earthly warnings. He follows celestial lights. Doing so is his vocation. He is clear it offers truth. So, what is it that turns prophecy from divine art to hellish error?

He is, at times, interested in predicting the future. Anticipating what is to come is a feature of the poem, not least via the many souls who warn him about his own future. However, the significance of these forecasts is to do with enabling Dante to prepare for possible outcomes. They illuminate current concerns and indicate improvements of character. They work with his freedom, which is to become more godly. They are not about attempting to control or change things, which implicitly or explicitly is to seek to become a god.

Dante and Virgil arrive at the fourth valley, look in, and what they see shocks them. The pit is packed with twisted and contorted bodies. The souls are viscerally suffering. Their heads have been forced around so that eyes look back when they should be looking forward. Mouths open like blowholes. Men's beards adorn backs. Women's tears wash shoulder blades.

The figures are condemned permanently to walk forward while looking backward. They move slowly, in lines that remind Dante of a liturgical procession. They tried to look forward in life and something has gone terribly wrong. Now they will step never to see the ground beneath their feet, let alone the future into which they are moving.

They were diviners in life, and Dante lists some of the individuals they see. Some are astrologers. Some are augurs. Some are prophets. The scene is shocking because he could be one of them. Dante weeps, collapses, and leans against a jagged rock. He has not been overwhelmed by hell's revelations for some time. He is again here. He is wrestling with himself. His mood is in marked contrast to the righteousness that had so assured him before the inverted pope.

He instructs us to reflect on his tears, challenging readers of his divinatory text. We must share the disquiet and accompany him on the descent, if we are to treat his insights not as mere spectacle, as an indifferent forecaster or callous fortune-teller might do, but as troubling and transformative.

Virgil chastises the crumpled Dante. The mood of the older poet has altered dramatically. He had thought Dante was growing. Now he appears to have fallen back. He encourages Dante to look into the bolge and learn.

He names some of the souls and offers thoughts on what led them to be caught in this deep ditch. The implication is that they tried to bend the divine will to their own will. That puts you in hell because trying to bend the divine will to your own will, rather than allowing your will to conform to the divine, is to cut yourself off from God. It is the crime of so-called New Thought, the name for the practice today of willing that the universe deliver your heart's latest dream or desire. It is narcissistic: I don't have to change as the cosmos will come to me.

Virgil speaks like a diviner of the right sort, as he names souls. Raise your eyes, he tells Dante, which is to look inwardly as well as outwardly. Four soothsayers from the classical world pass by, with one standing out, Tiresias, the prophet. He saw snakes mating, became a woman, only later to see the same snakes mating again, and morphing back into a man. The strange happenstance rendered him subject to Juno's wrath, when she asked him whether men or women gain more pleasure in sex. He could tell having been both, and answered honestly — it's women — which meant that Juno's secret was out. She blinded him as punishment. Only, the curse brings a blessing, of sorts, because Jupiter, to whom Juno is married, opens his inner eye. Tiresias gains the gift of prophecy, at a price. Maybe the moral of the story is prophecy inevitably mixes the affairs of gods and mortals, which tends to go badly for mortals.

Virgil also spots the prophetess, Manto. She interests him because it was on the spot where she settled that the city of Mantua was founded, his hometown. The sight leads him into a long description of the events that led to the settlement's establishment, which can seem odd, until you notice that his manner of talking is strikingly naturalistic and this-worldly. He extols the advantages of Mantua's geographical location at great length, offering a list of benefits that would not usually have occurred to a classical writer, whose standard practice would have been to herald a city according to its establishment by the gods, divined by myth or sorcery. Think of Rome, Romulus, and Remus.

Commentators also note how Virgil speaks in a vernacular tone, rather than the lofty tragic style of The Aeneid. It is as if he is learning a different voice. He is changing. He is divining a new way of engaging with the world that abandons inherited assumptions and discovers new ones.

He ends his account with a declaration: let no false tales adulterate the truth! It is the kind of thing a prophet would say, one doing well. He turns back to Dante. But his charge is still gripped by distress. As when he met the lovers and the suicides, it will take Dante longer than Virgil to regain his mind, his voice, his equanimity. He is being challenged to change.

Virgil names a few more figures in the bolge, this time turning to near contemporaries of Dante who have recently died and find themselves here. One is the astrologer, Michael Scott, from Scotland, who was well-known for his work on Aristotle and Islamic texts. The sight cannot have calmed Dante's unease.

It's a confusing canto. The "strange torments" are bizarre and, at least partly, inexplicable. Maybe some of the diviners became too wedded to their truths. They were brilliant in their way. They lived against the grain. They found a voice that may well have helped others. But there is a risk born of such success, which is becoming identified with that voice and forgetting that ultimately, wisdom comes not from one's wit, but from kinship with God. Maybe part of the reason these souls are lost is that they believed not just in their gift but in the myths that their gift prompted about them. That would certainly be a temptation for Dante.

His anxiety continues into the next canto, though it is worth remembering his opening remarks. This is canto 20 in the first part of his *Commedia*. Purgatory and paradise are to come, or rather, it is only if the confusions and complications of life are experienced to the full, that purgatory and paradise can come. Descent is the prerequisite for ascent.

They meet the demons of Malebranche. Virgil reckons he can outplay them. Dante does not.

INFERNO 21

Games

ANTE IS DEEPLY DISTRESSED BY THE SIGHT OF the diviners. At the beginning of canto 21, he and Virgil talk as they walk, though Dante tells us he isn't going to report what was said. My sense is that his reflections arise from the impact of his experience. He knows what he must learn because he feels it. That is crucial. Being told is one thing. Understanding for yourself is something else entirely. Only then does insight become part of becoming. That is our challenge as readers, not to be interested only in Dante's growth, but in our own.

It is like learning to ride a bike. Manuals may tell you some things, but until you sit in the saddle and push off, you will be little better off for reading them. You must feel the balance in your body. Navigating a course through life is similar. Stomach and heart matter as much as head.

Love is the same. It is not until you have fallen in love, or at least fallen in love with love, that love stories speak. So, this pause at the start of canto

21 underlines that we are involved with the most important things that matter, which are only thoroughly known by being known from within ourselves. Then, Dante and Virgil arrive at the fifth bolge and walk onto the bridge that spans it.

They peer down into a different type of gloom. It holds a darkness from which, it seems, nothing escapes. It reminds me of black holes. Everything is sucked into these entities and, even to modern physics, there is something preternatural about them. Dante says it reminds him of pitch. Images of the Venetian dockyards come to him, some of the busiest in the world, to which ships would flock for a repaint of tar. It is a strangely encouraging picture because he sees the dockworkers collaborating together, some at the bow, some at the stern, some on the oars. It's a functioning society, each person playing their part.

He looks back into the bolge and notices the blackness rising and falling, as if breathing. As he stares, Virgil suddenly grabs him, yelling at him to watch out. Dante shivers. They rush farther over the bridge, and Dante casts an eye back. He sees a demon coming toward them.

The fiend is straight out of central casting. It has vast wings, and every movement it makes seems cruel. Slung over its shoulder is a soul. It is carrying the unfortunate individual like a cut of meat.

The demon calls out, beckoning his fellows, a tribe called the Malebranche. It crows that it has captured a sinner for fresh torment, before tossing the poor soul over the bridge and into the darkness. Immediately, a hundred demons with pitchforks spring into view. The condemned individual clearly knows what he has to do: stay under the pitch to avoid being poked and prodded.

It is terrible to watch, as if seeing someone deep fried. The demons jest that the human can't pilfer in the dark: this is the bolge for those who have embezzled and grafted.

The soul they have seen is an elder from the city of Lucca. He used civic office for his personal gain. However, there's more meaning to be gleaned from the sight than just punishment for another form of fraudulence.

Lucca is the city of Saint Zita, a saint who was known for her honesty and transparency, and to which the city expressed devotion. It is also famous for a relic, an image of the crucified Christ called the Holy Face, which is honored in the city to this day. The demons add to the torment because, when the elder's face appears above the pitch a second time, they sneer with a quip: it's not time to show the Holy Face. He disappears again.

The implication is that corruption can break out anywhere, especially when appearances imply it won't. Lucca is being contrasted with the functioning docks of Venice. It had concealed its bad apples, implicating the many not just the few, unlike the port that re-tarred ships.

Virgil and Dante are still hiding on the bridge, and Virgil has an idea. He tells Dante to hide while he confronts the demons. He steps forward boldly, his confidence regained. He knows about demons. He's been here before. He won't easily be fooled by this devious bunch.

Dante is not sure, which is presumably why Virgil wants him to hide. His nervousness would give the game away, scuppering their chance at safe passage.

But alarm bells should be ringing. Virgil is trying to out deceit the deceitful. If you live by the sword there is always the risk that you will die by the sword, especially if your opponents are better swordsmen. I suspect this analysis provides a clue as to how corruption can become a cancer that infects whole towns. A small compromise one day, a white lie the next, and before long, sleaze has become a way of life.

Virgil shows himself. The demons charge forward en masse. But Virgil stays cool and tells them to hear him out before resorting to their hooks and forks.

The demons agree and push their leader, Malacoda, to the front. The name means evil-tailed, which makes you think of Geryon, and its scorpion tail.

That said, Malacoda displays intelligence, though that could make him more dastardly than the rest. What does it take to become a head demon? Virgil reasons with Malacoda that to get this far through hell, he must be blessed. Surely, they can see that he is on a mission from God.

The allusion to the divine name seems to humble Malacoda. He drops his pitchfork and arrogance seemingly drains from his face. He turns to his fellows and warns them not to touch Virgil. Virgil calls to Dante, hid behind a rock, and the pilgrim rejoins his guide.

However, Malacoda is faking it. He is smarter than Virgil presumes. Virgil has stopped thinking, stopped observing. He has resorted to tactics akin to the magical, much as he did outside of Dis. They were rescued once, when the angel appeared, though now they are deeper down.

Dante looks on and detects something is wrong. He doesn't have to pretend to be in charge and that makes him more observant. He senses Malacoda is hatching a plan. Nothing can be right in this zone. He remembers where they are.

He describes his feeling as mirroring a moment in his earthly life when he had ended up on the wrong side of a battle. His compatriots were defeated, though the victors claimed to be open to a truce. They made a pact with the prisoners who could flee from the battlefield, and return to their homes, so long as they marched through the victors assembled around them. Was it a ritual humiliation, underscoring events? Was it a trap before a slaughter? There was no point in his life that Dante felt more terrified, he says. His life was in their hands.

It feels as if his and Virgil's life hang by a thread. The tension ramps up when one of the demons, growing weary of the bargaining, asks to poke Virgil, though Malacoda's authority holds, and he speaks on with Virgil. There's a bridge over the sixth bolge, he explains, farther along and to the right. He advises the travelers that they need to take that one because another that is nearer crumbled when hell felt the earthquake. It's an opportunity, Malacoda adds, as the extra walk will provide more time to observe the souls in this realm.

If he sounds like a dodgy travel agent that is because he is. It turns out that all the bridges over the sixth bolge crumbled. But Virgil, whose first trip here must have been before the Crucifixion, doesn't know that, and he is prepared to trust the demon. Dante suspects something is up but doesn't yet know the extent of the lie.

There is another indicator that all is not right, which they might have noticed. Malacoda gives a remarkably precise piece of information to them. He tells them when the earthquake occurred to the hour: five more hours and it will be one thousand two hundred sixty-six years and a day since the bridge fell, he says. He was giving himself away with that detail, as he has clearly been counting the days since the Crucifixion happened. He was terrified by the harrowing of hell, and hence is not to be trusted.

Virgil fails to be alerted by the hint, and Malacoda grows bolder. He offers a troop of his best demons to escort the pair. That is almost too much for Dante who points out that, if they have God's blessing, why do they need demons for company? But Virgil's overconfidence overrules him. He tells Dante not to worry. All is under control. And off they set.

The canto ends with a scatological fanfare. As they depart, the demons salute Malacoda by blowing raspberries. Malacoda returns the salute by doubling up to fart. The gesture is a twisted reminder of Dante blowing the metaphorical trumpet of truth at the inverted pope. How speedily in life fortunes change.

They find themselves escorted by ten demons. Something has gone very wrong.

INFERNO 22
Hunted

DANTE AND VIRGIL PACE ALONGSIDE THE FIFTH bolge of Malebolge, dark with black tar, accompanied by ten demons. How did they get themselves into this situation? Was it Virgil's pride, timidity, or Malacoda's deviousness?

Dante is uncomfortable. He opens the canto by rehearsing the bloody chaos of battle scenes, complete with trumpet calls and bugle sounds. The sounds of danger and chaos are appropriate.

He peers into the pitch. The souls within it look like dolphins breaking the surface of greasy, dingy water. There are more, collecting around the edges of the dingy fluid like frogs around a polluted pond. Above the surface push nostrils, exposing just enough to keep breathing.

Nature references abound in this canto. When one sinner is hauled out of the water, Dante thinks that his skin looks like otter's fur. It's thick and slick. It's a juxtaposition of images, as if Dante himself is struggling

90

to maintain contact with what thrives, while surrounded by what rots.

Recalling the world above helps him to stay on the right side of calm. It brings comfort. He gains strength. He searches for the wherewithal to examine the demons as they lift out a sinner, brutally to torment him. They flay the victim, their horns tearing off flesh, as they chuckle among themselves.

There's a pause. Virgil speaks to the soul who is staring at his wounds. His name is not disclosed, but he wasn't the most overt of the grafters, instead quietly pocketing money on the side. He suffers a terrible punishment now, and the question of whether he deserves the torment grows when he continues, talking about his parents. They were disastrous. His mother gave him up for service. She herself was a compulsive spendthrift, who frittered away all that her husband could bring home, so much so that the man was driven to desperation and killed himself. The story rightly raises the question of divine compassion: can their child be so fulsomely blamed? I'm not sure, but it does underline that the state of your soul directly affects what you experience after death, or to put it the other way around, your inner state of mind in life is crucial. Moment by moment, we are shaping ourselves. Little deceptions can take us a long way in the wrong direction.

The gaggle of demons are not so absorbed by their torture as to forget the lie that they are there to support Dante and Virgil's learning. They ask whether another pause would be a chance for further questions.

Virgil takes the opportunity, asking the soul with the bad parents whether there are more Italians in this mess. The poor chap barely has a chance to answer, before the demons resume their gory work on him. However, in another lull, Virgil receives a reply. There is a friar, he learns, from Sardinia, who was no mean thief but a grand barrater. He was a governor of the island and took advantage of his position continually and systematically throughout his time in office. Worse, he has paired up with a fellow corrupt governor in hell, with whom he spends time comparing notes. They are immersed in the pitch because they are immersed in their crime. It appears that they do not to want to change; it appears that they are not aware that they can change. That is the depth to which duplicity can shape a life.

Then, one of the tormented souls has an idea. He asks Virgil to get the demons to hold off for a while, on the pretense of wanting to ask further questions, at which point he will whistle. It is a sign to sinners to surface, seemingly for a breather. A demon likes the plan. Its wings are faster than human limbs, it boasts, so it will be able to get to the souls who surface at the whistle.

However, the soul who asked Virgil plans to double-cross everyone. He wants to flee for cover although, when he makes his escape, mayhem ensues. It becomes impossible to tell who is deceiving whom, who is lying to whom, who has the best of the others. The horde implodes. Fraud runs amok.

The soul who had started the whole thing off leaps back into the pitch, and the demons turn on each other in blame, tumbling into the pitch themselves. The leader of the pack manages to keep its mind, and organizes a rescue party, which pulls out the incinerated demons.

There is bedlam, but also a chance. In the confusion, Dante and Virgil seize the moment. Fooled no longer, they steal away.

Affection balances fear. Thought counters foolhardiness. They escape to fresh despair.

INFERNO 23

Knocks

VIRGIL AND DANTE MAKE THEIR ESCAPE FROM the demons fighting among themselves, humbled by the errors that led to the entanglement with the Malebranche. They walk like friars minor, lowly monks, along the top bank between the fifth and sixth bolge. They try not to draw attention to themselves.

Creeping forward, Dante recalls a tale that he believes to be by Aesop. It tells of a mouse who wants to cross a river and so approaches a seemingly friendly frog. The frog offers to tie the mouse to his back leg and tow him across. They set out until, mid-stream, the devious frog tries to plunge to the bottom of the river, to drown the mouse. He stops at a swooping sound overhead. A falcon falls on them, catches them in its talons, and consumes them both. The moral of the story is that if you mix trust and deviousness,

93

events quickly spiral out of control, and everyone ends up hurt. Or dead.

The story catches the mood and frightens Dante as he recalls it. He realizes that the demons behind them might become falcons in a swoop. They will tire of fighting each other and then turn back to them, more furious than ever.

His skin tightening, Dante turns to Virgil, who is having similar thoughts: the two are starting to work together once more. Fear returns, only this time they are better prepared. Virgil suggests that they disappear into the sixth bolge, where the demons can't go: their power in one ditch dissipates in another, like Mafiosi in a town they don't own.

They begin to climb down the slope to their right, and spot the demons approaching fast. In a touching moment, sealing the restoration of their friendship, Virgil grabs Dante, holding him to his chest, like a mother would a child. Virgil is not thinking of his own safety. He is focused on Dante's protection. He throws himself down the slope like a woman fleeing a burning house, positioned between her offspring and the flames.

They tumble down like water traversing a mill. It is a perilous fall because the bolge's banks are strewn with jagged rocks, like a watermill's blades. But they reach the bottom unscathed and look up. Sure enough, ten demons glower down, raging but powerless. They are free, for now.

It is a dramatic moment and a tender one. Dante's fear and Virgil's over-confidence has been replaced by mutual concern. They know a fresh love for each other and that creates a sense of good. They have a chance to readjust, to recalibrate and see where they've ended up.

They look around. Immediately, their eyes fall on the inhabitants of the next dark place. A slow procession of monk-like figures is moving before them. They are wearing great capes and enormous hoods. Upon first glance, the robes look gorgeous, seemingly made of cloth of gold, although looking again, Dante sees that they are gaudy: the shimmering fabrics are cheap. And he notices the faces of the wearers. They are drenched with tears. These are mourning souls, burdened by their clothes, unable to do more than continue the slow walk along this round.

Dante asks Virgil to find him a soul who he knew in life, to talk with and learn about the suffering. It happens — though, of course, nothing just happens — that there is a Tuscan nearby who overhears and offers his help. Dante turns, and sees a pair of souls walking together. They look back, amazed to see Dante speaking.

They can see his throat moving, and that he is mortal. They wonder how both Dante and Virgil can be in this bolge without wearing its cloaks.

They ask who the strangers might be, and Dante explains that he is from the city that banks the Arno, as they are.

They belonged to a group known as the jovial friars. The order ostensibly followed Saint Francis of Assisi, though they traded on the association with the great saint rather than taking the calling seriously, and led lives that included marriage and many creature comforts. They were hypocrites, and that is what holds them in hell.

Their mortal failings ran very deep indeed. The two friars were associated with opposite sides in the Florentine civil war — one the Guelphs, the other the Ghibellines — and they were brought together, as holy reconcilers, in an effort to forge a peace accord. The idea was that religious figures were to some extent independent of the antagonisms that fired the conflict, and so might bridge divides in a shared mayoralty of the city.

But indulgent lifestyles had infected their souls. Hypocrisy ruled their hearts. Secretly, the two were actually papal appointments, and the pope was supported by the Guelphs. The deception was revealed, and the opportunity for peace instead rekindled the conflagration. The civil war restarted with renewed vehemence. Their duplicity led to the suffering of many. In death, the souls suffer the duplicity of their lives.

They are so wedded to their self-importance, so unable to see that they could live truthfully and simply, that they are bowed down by their grandiosity, manifest in their clothes and infernal location. Weighty gowns conceal empty interiors. Shiny exteriors house the rotten corpses of their lives, like the whitewashed sepulchers referred to by Jesus in the Gospels.

Speaking with them, Dante stops midsentence. A grisly sight interrupts him. He spots a figure, pinned to the ground, with spikes through his hands and feet. The man is being crucified.

It is an unbearable sight. The twisted body writhes and heaves. One of the friars explains who he is: Caiaphas, the high priest who argued that it was expedient to kill one person, Jesus, in order to save many. This was the deal Caiaphas was said to have done with Pontius Pilate on the night of Jesus's arrest and trial, not because he cared for the many, but because he wanted to be rid of the so-called messiah. Hypocrisy was his way of life, and his undoing. The processing souls step on the man as they come to the place of his agony.

One of the jovial friars explains that the high priest, along with other members of the Sanhedrin, made the Jews deicides — killers of God. An uncomfortable antisemitism fills the air, focused on the poisonous belief that has slain and displaced countless Jews over the Christian millennia. It is hard to hear Dante rehearse it again. However, I think he is calling it into question. The antisemitism is put into the mouth of one of the friars who is a hypocrite. He is someone who didn't know about truth and honor in life, and clearly does not know about them in death. He can't own up to his own faults, let alone make accurate accusations against others.

Further, it is not the only moment in which Dante implicitly critiques antisemitism. The Jews that he meets en route are never portrayed via stereotypes. For instance, if he had been following conventions, rather than seeing things with fresh eyes, he would have had Jewish figures among the usurers. There were none.

For his part, Virgil is petrified by the sight of Caiaphas. He cannot understand it at all. In one way, that is a reflection of his paganism. But in another, it suggests that Virgil is stunned at the extreme punishment for seemingly sensible expediency. This is precisely what he had resorted to in his interactions with the demons. He lied to the Malebranche in a bid to outwit the liars. Seeing Caiaphas is a gut-wrenching realization, though the jolt is a blessing in disguise. He sees what is at stake in such shenanigans: the chaos that results, the spiraling down, the erosion of integrity, the loss of divine sight. I think he sees something of himself in Caiaphas.

Virgil wants to move on and asks the friars for a way out of the bolge. They tell him of a way to clamber out, though the reason why it exists, is a further shock to Virgil. They inform him of what the demons knew all along. All the bridges fell into the sixth bolge at the harrowing of hell. There is not one left intact. Virgil realizes that Malacoda was out to get him all along. He was utterly played. To add insult to injury, one of the friars throws into the discussion a truism that is so obvious it shouldn't need saying: the devil is the father of lies. Virgil missed the basics with his cleverness.

He is angry with himself, though it is a type of anger that is not bad. He harnesses it, and his fury becomes an energy for revised action. He steps off full of vigor in the direction the friars have indicated. Dante is pleased and follows closely in the footsteps of his master.

Virgil helps Dante climb from the sixth bolge. In the next is a melee of serpents and souls.

INFERNO 24
Mishmash

ANTO 24 BEGINS WITH A LOVELY EXTENDED metaphor that captures a moment of temporary peace. Virgil and Dante enjoy it after the storm of their encounter with the Malebranche.

It tells of a shepherd waking on a spring morning, momentarily forgetting that the weather is warming. He leaves his hut and sees hoarfrost on the ground, thinking it is snow. His mind races to the conclusion that the land has frozen and the fodder for his sheep will be solid as well. It happens in winter. He goes back inside, full of frustration and fear. Then, he realizes his mistake. The "snow" is a hoarfrost. Spring is on its way and, when he looks outside again, the white sheen covering the ground is lifting. The sun is shining. The seasons are changing. His heart fills with joy.

The same shift of mood flows through Virgil. His frustration at his foolishness turns into gladness that he and Dante are safe. Dante comments on the sweet tenderness of his guide's countenance. It is a moment of connection.

It is touching, and another indicator that Virgil is grappling with the meaning of the trip inwardly. He is not governed only by the outcome of his mortal life. It leaves me again wondering what this means for him, as well as for the souls around and about them. He is in hell, though psychologically and spiritually it looks as if he is becoming more capable of traveling elsewhere.

They reach the point where the hypocrites had said there would be tumbled rocks, and there are. They haven't lied. Maybe that's a flicker of hope as well. Virgil leads Dante up the slope. He carefully tests out each boulder for its ability to hold Dante's weight. It is a long trek and hard work.

The effort it takes Dante is emphasized in the poet's retelling of the climb. He remembers his lungs aching and his strength being sapped in the effort to keep going. They reach the top, and he has to stop and rest. Virgil tells him that sloth won't secure him fame and glory, which is perhaps a comment to himself as much as Dante. Fame and glory in this context refer to the lasting lights of heaven. Reaching those heights demands change in them both, and that takes patience and persistence. They are reflections for us as well, his readers.

This journey is akin to a long climb up a steep mountain. They and we must be in it for the long haul. When a horizon is reached, another one will open up. Any ascent will include wrong-turnings, false-starts, successive descents.

Mood changes also come fast on the pilgrimage of life. It is good to notice Virgil and Dante's ups and downs because, once realized in oneself, the downs can be borne more easily in the knowledge that they don't last. The snow can turn out to be hoarfrost, the seeming winter, the beginning of spring.

That said, the effects of the darkness are real. As Virgil chivvies Dante along with his talk of sloth, fame, and glory, his paganism can be felt. The hero's courage is heard in his voice. Then again, if you pay attention to Dante in this canto, you see that the primary source of energy for him is love: his love of Virgil, detected in his guide's countenance, tenderness, and care. The two aspects work together. Affection can keep us going quite as tenaciously as the manly virtues. Virgil has been likened to a mother carrying her child. Both sides are developing in him.

The description of their clamber up the side of the bolge occupies half of this canto. Dante the poet is stressing the effort in the number of verses he allots to it. Finally, they reach the top and the next bridge, spanning the seventh gorge. It is littered with rocks and hard to climb onto as well.

At the highpoint of the bridge, they stop. There is a voice. It is coming up from the depths of the ditch below them. They can't see its source. The crevasse is dark. But the voice is peculiar. It is inarticulate. Though human, it is unable to enunciate and pronounce words. Dante is intrigued. Virgil is glad. There is more to discover, and they are ready to do so.

They cross the bridge, arriving at the lower side. They see more clearly into the chasm and what comes into view is one of the most shocking sights of the entire Inferno. It is so unexpected, so dramatic.

A confused melee of souls and serpents meets their gaze. The scene reminds Dante of what happens when news breaks out that plague has reached the city. Poison and panic run through the body politic like an infection, and venom appears to flow in this bolge. Terror drives an uproar. But the animalistic activity before them is not only due to a fracas or brawl.

They focus on one soul who is being chased by a snake. The creature catches up with its prey and strikes. The damned figure is bitten between the shoulder blades and, instantly, turns into ash. A pile of cinders lies where a moment before there had been a man. Only, in the next second, the ash reforms and the soul appears again.

It is a shock. What is going on here? Dante the poet is making us think quite as hard as Dante the pilgrim must have wrestled. The soul who was bitten, collapsed, and reformed reminds him of the Phoenix rising from the ashes, only the Phoenix rises to new life, which is why it became a metaphor for the Resurrection of Christ. This soul is on a treadmill of return without a sign of any difference. It is a hellish recurrence, not a divine rebirth.

Virgil calls out to the metamorphizing individual, who reveals his identity. He is Vanni Fucci and he confesses to having stolen from the sacristy of Pisa. However, as is often the case with the souls in the lower reaches of hell, it is not the crime itself that is the cause of his current problems. The thievery is a symptom of a deeper shame. He also "stole" the innocence of a neighbor, who was blamed in his stead.

This is the inner meaning of thievery. The eternal damage done by stealing stuff is that it short circuits the effort required not to possess goods but to possess yourself. The thief is in real peril when he develops the habit of believing he can take what he wants, body and soul. He gains the knowhow of fooling others and simultaneously fools himself. The gold or garments Fucci took from the sacristy may have transformed his appearance, but they undid his insides.

It is the opposite of what Dante and Virgil have been working so hard to do, in their climb. These souls cannot enjoy the grace and love that Dante and Virgil have been sharing, which is itself transforming. Instead of being on a virtuous spiral up, they are on a vicious spiral down, suffering the strikes and bites of snakes, which repeatedly raze them to the ground like a derelict building.

The notion of stealing has a particular meaning in psychotherapy and adds to what Dante and Virgil see. It describes someone who is unable to acknowledge how they have been helped by others. A friend may have offered an insight, or a companion practical help. But these gestures are not experienced as coming from others. To such individuals, it feels as if they have helped themselves. The insight or aid is, in effect, stolen from the friend and companion. The upshot is that it shuts support out. That may explain why Fucci and his fellows are stuck in the bottom of a bolge, in which there is no grace or companionship, but a venomous, backbiting crowd.

The thief enters the same world, when he takes what he wants and assumes it's his to own. There is no recognition of others, of injustice, of hurt.

Dante recognizes Fucci and recalls that he was a man known for outbursts of rage. Fucci is momentarily ashamed. He bows his head, wishing Dante hadn't spotted him. You wonder whether there is hope for the thief. Might he be remade rather than recycled?

The short answer is "no." His seeming embarrassment turns into a cruel prophecy to do with Dante's future and the civil wars again, which Fucci spits out. He turns nasty. You will suffer, he cries!

He wants to destroy Dante for speaking truthfully about him. He strikes back as vehemently as the snake has been striking him. It is another aspect of this state of mind, and another reason he remains in the pit. Though changing continually, he is not really changing at all. The malice brings the canto to an abrupt end.

They see even more terrible metamorphoses and realize the serpents are human souls too.

INFERNO 25
Disfigured

UCCI HAS CURSED DANTE, AND HE WANTS TO
curse God as well. At the beginning of canto 25, Fucci raises a fist
upward and yells: Here God, this sign is for you! He is showing
heaven the finger, and the gesture is utterly futile.

The only thing it allows is a chance for the serpents around him to
redouble their charge. They have been enveloping, biting, and poisoning
Fucci, and now they strap themselves so tightly to him that he cannot move.
Dante thinks of the serpents as his friends because, if God can't be hurt by
the raging remarks of a haughty individual, he can.

Momentarily released, Fucci rushes off, and a galloping centaur draws
Dante and Virgil's attention. He is Cacus, Virgil says, and Dante sees that
he too is covered in snakes. There is a dragon in the tangle, around Cacus's
neck, flapping wings, breathing fire. The centaur looks completely crazy.

Cacus is the child of Vulcan, the god of fire, and became a thief in life. He stole cattle, dragging them backward to his cave to make it seem that the hooves stamping the ground were made by a stampede moving in the opposite direction. Cacus shows all the signs of a cool, calculating operator who is utterly dedicated to deception.

He was eventually caught by Hercules, who clubbed him to death. He has ended up, in the seventh bolge of Malebolge, not so much because he was violent or dishonest but because he is a fully conscious, thinking fraudster. He gallops off.

Virgil and Dante keep looking into the pit and, when a new soul calls out, they notice three shades beneath them. More ghastly metamorphoses start as one of the new souls utters a name: Cianfa. Virgil is about to speak, but Dante stops him by pressing his finger to his lips. Curious, Dante wants to watch the nauseating action. It's a striking moment because nothing like this has happened between them before. I wonder if Dante is, inadvertently, silencing Virgil much as you might before a sacred ritual, only they are about to witness a parody of a sacred performance. The gesture certainly makes us readers look that little bit harder to discern what the ensuing attacks and transformations might mean.

What unfolds is truly horrendous. It happens in two movements, involving humans and serpents morphing in various ways. The shapeshifting takes on extra resonance because it becomes clear that the snakes are actually humans too, in serpent form. In other words, this is not about demons cursing humans. There are no fiends in this bolge. Humans are mercilessly toying with each other, as thieves do. They steal from each other.

The first grotesque transformations concern a sinner named Agnel. First, a lizard-like serpent with six feet hooks Agnel with all six of them. With the middle pair, it hugs him around the stomach. With the front pair, it holds his arms. With the lower pair, it reaches around his thighs. It simultaneously bites him through each cheek on his face. The snake's tail then swings between Agnel's legs and slaps against his back, becoming rigid and stiff. Dante remarks that ivy never twisted so tightly around a tree.

It was like watching one puddle of wax melting into another, Dante says. The grim embrace of the two also reminds him of a flame consuming a page, the paper turning brown as the flame licks higher.

The other two shades look on in horror. They call out that Agnel would be horrified if he could see how he is changed. He has become neither snake nor human, nor snake-human. The amalgam of limbs and heads and bodies is too twisted and conjoined.

One of the two souls looking on, who is called Buoso, is approached by another snake. It is a black adder and fixes Buoso by staring into his eyes. He becomes entranced as smoke starts to envelop the two of them. As it thickens, the snake strikes Buoso in the navel.

Dante remarks that the bite is in the place from which an unborn child feeds. It is a perversion of the nurturing, nourishing process whereby the embryo matures and thrives, and the grim substitution continues. Buoso morphs into a snake, as the snake morphs into a human. First, the snake's tail starts to split into legs, as the legs of Buoso start to join as if a tail. Then, Buoso's arms melt into his sides, as the snake sprouts limbs from its flanks. Next, the human face flattens into a snout, as the snake's snout pushes out into a human face. Buoso has become a snake as the snake has become a man. He is called Guercio. So, what have we witnessed?

I think that the images are mockeries of the Incarnation. In the figure of Jesus, divinity and humanity are joined perfectly. The combination is the completion or perfection of humanity, to which all individuals might aspire. Here in hell, snakes and humans — the snake clearly carrying echoes of the tempter in Eden — destroy each other as they combine. The imitation is monstrous. It is as if hell, for all its drama, contains no genuine novelty. All that happens is that divine acts are spoiled, distorted, mocked. Souls are locked in raging, vain gestures against God.

It is important to consider how the divine and the human come together, not only for theological reasons, but for spiritual ones, because it is so easy to get wrong. It can be understood as if the divine must eradicate all that is human or must steal our individuality from us. But in truth, it is as the individual becomes more fully themselves that they find themselves becoming more open to the divine. The transformation is about discovery and expansion, not self-denial, as some on spiritual journeys might conclude when they read about putting others first or eradicating the ego. These strategies don't work because what is suppressed becomes more powerful. The ego turns into an inner serpent that can possess at will. It hinders or halts transformation in the act of seizing the soul.

What is lost is the harmonious relationship between God and humanity, ultimately based on the fact that all life is divine life and one. The divine nature doesn't need to force anything upon human individuals, and human individuals don't need to force anything from the divine. When the relationship is right, when souls approach God with wisdom and love, what emerges is the unity that was always there, dancing in light.

Dante says that the metamorphoses of hell are more profound than the switches and changes described by his poetic predecessors, Ovid and Lucan. It can sound as if Dante is boasting, as if he is claiming more for his art. But I think what Dante is stressing is that, whereas the classical poets described changes drawn from their imaginations, he is describing what he has seen with his eyes. He apologizes to us, his readers, if he has not managed fully to convey the horror, though that only creates a gap for us imaginatively to see whether we can make up the loss in our minds, and dare to draw nearer to this hellish reality.

The eighth bolge appears majestic until Dante understands its souls are caught in flames.

INFERNO 26
Cunning

ANTE OPENS THIS CANTO WITH A DECLARATION. It is a stately condemnation of his birthplace. Florence, which seems so grand on earth, has fed more souls into hell than any other city. Florence's enemies couldn't wish worse for the city than what Dante is seeing of its citizens in hell. He only wishes their fate were better known. It would be a mercy. A city that was founded upon the greatest virtues, and built aspiring to the most beautiful things, has lost touch with its wellspring. It has turned in on itself and is spiraling rapidly down. It has become hellish, and its children are in hell.

Dante's peroration is not only a condemnation of Florence. It is a comment on civilization as a whole, and what happens when its life and vitality grow stunted and corrupted. The nature of its charisma, the roots to its source, can no longer sustain or feed it. Civil war is one result of losing sight of a higher vision.

Ironically, the risk to civilizations ramps up as they become more powerful and enjoy the benefits of great technology and hard-won knowledge. Hubris grows with these possessions, when coupled to the conviction that the population has to rely on itself. These are bitter thoughts.

Dante and Virgil move from the edge of the seventh bolge. Again, it takes effort. Virgil helps pull Dante up. He is wrestling with the material aspect of his being, which the medieval mind perceived to be one pole of human life, with the other being the soulful or spiritual aspect. The spiritual pole is drawn up by the forces of levity, and the material pole is attracted downward by the force of gravity. Dante is feeling that heaviness. His weight and physicality are increasing in this place as they journey toward zones increasingly cut off from God.

It's an understanding of reality that draws on experience. People who are depressed will say they feel heavy. Others, who are rediscovering life's pleasures, will describe themselves lightening up. For Dante, these were not just psychological states of mind because psychological states of mind are themselves reflections of the reality. What Virgil can offer Dante in helping him climb is akin to what a therapist can offer a client. It's one of the reasons training as a therapist involves your own therapy, which is to say, your own descent.

Maybe Virgil's knowledge of the territory, gained on his previous trip through hell, allows him to stay in touch with levity and not be overwhelmed by gravity. Pulling Dante up the bolge is like helping him find a way out, with encouragement or insight or the confidence that it can be done. The sense is still carried in phrases such as "sharing burdens" or "bearing another's weight." What Dante and Virgil are experiencing together is familiar to those who have known hells on earth. Virgil's mood is marked by being full of focus, will, and desire. He seeks to share it with Dante, and so lighten his load.

It works. They reach the eighth bolge, which is to say they become capable of seeing souls caught in deeper states of despair. The sight grieves Dante more than any of the other places they have encountered, which makes you wonder whether he is seeing more of himself in this place and its torments.

His first glimpse is certainly unexpected. The souls here carry an air of eerie beauty. They look like fireflies dancing at dusk, lighting up the countryside with their brightness and choreography. They look like flames, which reminds Dante of the flames Elisha the prophet saw as he watched his predecessor, Elijah, rise into the heavens on a chariot of fire. What is interesting about the link is that Elisha could only follow the ascent so far. He couldn't see into the celestial heights and felt that Elijah was taken away from him. It was an ambivalent moment for Elisha, and Dante is reminded of it as the fireflies remind him of the possibility of knowing God.

The eerie beauty does not last. The seeming fireflies morph into mosquitoes. The prettiness of the first impression is disturbed by a truer perception that becomes clearer.

The flames are moving along this chasm and each contains a soul. It's an instructive description. The flames are not the souls themselves but are rather like the aura or charisma that might surround an individual in life. That radiance could have been a reflection of their divine spirit, but it appears to have become a prison. It cages them and holds them, rather than freeing them and enabling them to rise up.

Dante becomes engrossed. It is a risk that he faces himself. His own genius might become inverted and confining rather than creative. He leans against a boulder to gain a better look, peering so precipitously that Virgil grabs him. He is at risk of falling, in more senses than one.

He tells his guide that he must speak to one of the flames. He needs to understand their predicament better. Then, he notices that one of them has two tongues flickering from it. Virgil sees that Dante has spotted the double and explains that it is a flame of particulate note. It contains Ulysses and Diomedes.

The two are well known from the writings of Homer, in which Ulysses was called Odysseus, and Diomedes was a ruler of Argos, equally renowned for his cunning. These two ancient figures have become trapped in the same flame because, in life, their genius became destructively entangled. Dante the poet outlines several of their famous deeds, the best known of which was the plan to smuggle Greeks into Troy inside a giant wooden horse.

They are also remembered for stealing the statue of Athena called the Palladium, after the gods had told the Greeks that they would need it if they were to flatten the enemy city. Not that Ulysses and Diomedes trusted each other. They resisted working together, so much so that at one point, Ulysses raised a sword to slay Diomedes. He wanted his rival out of the way to claim the glory for himself. But Diomedes caught sight of the moonlight reflected in the metal blade and fended off the attack. He himself didn't kill Ulysses in revenge only because he knew that they needed each other if they were to secure victory and steal the Palladium. Ever since, an obligation that runs against your instinct or wishes has been known as a Diomedeian necessity or compulsion.

It is a tragedy because their shared craftiness could have been a huge asset. But it was often misused. In eternity, Dante sees them bound together, held in the flame, condemned to fight. Like tongues of fire, they lick and lap at each other.

Ulysses' presence carries significance in another way. In the Odyssey, he is remembered for escaping from the cave of Polyphemus, the cyclops. He blinds the giant by pushing an olive branch into its single eye. The story came to be widely celebrated in the ancient world which may well have reflected a growing consciousness of the age as Jeremy Naydler points out in his book, In the Shadow of the Machine: The Prehistory of the Computer and the Evolution of Consciousness. Polyphemus represents an older awareness of nature and life. It was closer to chthonic forces. The blinding of Polyphemus by Ulysses represents a break with this past. In the story, Ulysses departs and begins his years of wandering across the seas, chased by gods like Poseidon, who was Polyphemus's father. His escape was secured through cunning, but it came at a price. He found himself at war with the gods, and unsure where to settle in nature. It has been the fate of human beings since.

The stories about Ulysses clearly fascinated Dante because, in this canto, he embarks on an innovative extension of Ulysses' travels. Dante says that after, finally, reaching his hometown, Ulysses grew restless again. This time, he wanted to leave the Mediterranean altogether and travel through the pillars of Hercules, at Gibraltar. This narrow passageway was regarded as a threshold by the ancient Greeks. It was a warning not to journey farther. It was like the marking of a medieval map: "Here be dragons" would be written on more distant oceans.

But Ulysses had outgrown the constraints of old superstitions, he felt. According to Dante, he used his charisma one last time to inspire his men. He delivered a marvelous speech, talking of how human beings only live once, so it is admirable, even necessary, to use that one life well. The gods will it, he declared. Let us go and see what lies beyond the sun, he invited. I want to see all the virtues and vices of humankind, he enticed.

The men were inspired. Only, like Ulysses, they didn't understand what they were seeking. The journey was too perilous. They passed through the Straits of Gibraltar and turned left, which is to say south, though the description of their direction given by Dante is doubly meaningful in hell, left tending to be the divine way.

In this case, it was not. The sailors traveled for five months. They stuck to their southern passage and eventually come across a great mountain, the likes of which they had never seen before. In the mythical geography of *The Divine Comedy*, this is Mount Purgatory. But Ulysses had got to it by devious means. He had short-circuited the spiritual path by setting out to sea. He had not died. He did not have Beatrice's blessing. A whirlpool opened up and consumed his ship. It tossed the sailors around three times and swallowed them. Their ambition was thwarted at the last.

The story is returned to repeatedly throughout *The Divine Comedy*. Dante's invention of Ulysses' final fate is a clear expression of one he feared for himself. He is using all his skill and ability to navigate a way across the seas of human experience while inviting us to follow him. He is seeing all the vices of humankind and he will see all the virtues. He wants to travel beyond the sun. He wants to move into the divine realms out of the human realm. The question is whether he is angering the gods, losing his way, and sailing toward his own condemnation. Such doubts are part and parcel of any spiritual journey as ambition jostles with submission. Dante has a chance to become familiar with them, as do we.

When Dante insists on his strong desire to speak with the two-tongued flame, Virgil replies that he, Virgil, will do the talking. Dante needs the headspace to observe what is said, and not to become entangled in the exchange. The spirit of adventure and longing is too dangerous for him.

Virgil addresses Ulysses who tells of his final sailing through the pillars of Hercules, to the far south, and into the whirlpool.

Perhaps the mistake that Ulysses made was that he didn't understand that mortal life is the necessary preparation for the afterlife. It is a realization that was only fully fleshed out with the Christian dispensation. For Homeric Greeks, the afterlife was not a realm in which to thrive. It was the land of the shades, who faded as they were forgotten. You might say that Ulysses' ambition was commendable, but he got ahead of himself. The question for Dante is whether the time to journey to heaven in life is right for him. Has he understood Christianity correctly?

Ulysses had to fail, and descent was the whirlpool's intent. It brought him here to the eighth bolge, though perhaps to learn as much as to suffer. My guess is that this is why his flame looks beautiful as well as imprisoning, stately as well as twisting. Beauty is always a sign of hope. It is a promise of the delight that ends despair.

For now, though, Ulysses' light is in hell. What looks like a firefly in one moment becomes a mosquito in another. The canto ends with the destruction of Ulysses' ship. Dante and Virgil are left contemplating the story they have heard.

Overlooking the eighth bolge, they see a writhing flame approach. The soul says he trusted a pope.

INFERNO 27
Deals

THE FLAME IN WHICH ULYSSES IS BOUND TO DIO-
medes stands still. It stops flickering and, momentarily, conveys
an air of dignity, not frustration or fight. Does Ulysses understand himself more fully with rehearsing his story afresh? Does he sense
a moment of hope?

If so, canto 27 returns to the ugliness and bitterness that is the dominant mood in Malebolge. Dante evokes the image of the Sicilian bull. This
contraption was requested by a despotic ruler of Sicily called Phalaris. He
asked a blacksmith to make him a torture instrument cast out of bronze
in the shape of a bull. The victim was placed inside, a fire lit beneath, and
the device converted the screams of agony into the sound of a bellowing
bull. So successful was the effect that, when it was presented to the despot,
Phalaris decided that its maker should die in it by way of demonstration.

The Sicilian bull brings an abrupt switch from Ulysses' heroic tales to
the brutality of Dante's own times. They are not unlike our times. The

medieval and modern world are both littered with technologies turned to twisted ends. What cruel cunning is unleashed in cluster bombs and landmines, drones, and bots?

Dante and Virgil look down into the eighth bolge again. There are more tortured souls contained in flickering flames. Another approaches the travelers as Ulysses and Diomedes move off. It has heard Virgil speaking, though when it expresses its desire to converse with the two, Virgil turns to Dante. It is Dante's turn to address the flame. Virgil had spoken to a soul of the classical age. Dante can best engage one of his. The two are working together at this stage of the trip.

The voice within this flame reveals that it belongs to Guido da Montefeltro, an infamous military strategist. He was a successful fighter for the Ghibellines who, approaching retirement, decided to become a friar. It sounds like a pious move. Only he was enticed to rejoin the warring fray by the pope Dante loved to hate, Boniface VIII, after the pope promised him absolution for abandoning religious life, along with any other subsequent sins he might commit. Guido did a deal with a pope thinking it would carry leverage with God. That is why he is in hell.

Dante speaks to Guido at great length about the Italian civil wars. He describes how several towns and city-states have fallen in and out of freedom and tyranny, and how different parties have variously switched sides. The flame loves news of these intricacies and details: Guido wasn't changed by his time as a friar and the return to warfare, which he had blamed on the pope's empty promise, was really driven by his desire. He burns more brightly at tales of soldiery. That is where his heart is.

Dante points out that he, Dante, is a living soul and so will return to the land of the living, where he might tell of Guido's war lust. Guido mocks Dante saying, he has never heard of souls returning from this place. It shows his inability to imagine such a possibility, for Dante, for others, and for himself. He is truly stuck.

For Dante, the exchange emphasizes that the assent of the heart is what determines our place in the afterlife. Absolution from a priest won't do it, even a pope. Neither will gestures like becoming a monk. Only genuine yearning can propel people toward purgatory and paradise, because what is desired is what is enjoyed. Love cuts the pathway through life.

Blaming the pope outsources responsibility for change to someone else. Dante had seen the same attitude in the early circles of hell, when Francesca had blamed a tale of courtly romance for her falling in love with Paolo, which was really a love of romance itself. She wanted to be swept along its tides and her desire delivered for her.

It's a terrible, tangled picture of what can happen in churches when people assume that ministers and the clergy understand the ways of God. It easily happens. It happened then. It happens now. Familiar too is the repentant figure who reckons that he can sin now and repent later. When that attitude creeps in, the soul is in peril. It is not the sin. It's becoming disconnected from the heart and sidelining the genuine longing for God.

The implication is that you can make all the mistakes you like in life. But if you cut yourself off from your heart's desire, the trouble really starts. It's why Dante is accompanied by Virgil, who shares his love of poetry, and will be led by Beatrice, who fires his longing for beauty.

Just how spoiled someone's perception of reality can become is indicated by the final detail in Guido's story. He tells Dante that at the moment of his death, he thought he saw Francis coming for him. The vision is one that an erstwhile friar might expect, except that Guido expected it because he treated religious life as a transaction. He made the promise, so Francis had to keep his side of the bargain.

But on the cusp of eternity, the truths of the heart are revealed. He thought it was Francis welcoming him into heaven before the vision shifted. He looked again and realized it was a fallen cherub swooping before him. These angels are those associated with divine wisdom and, in their fallen form, they are therefore linked to fraud, deviousness, and cunning. It was entirely appropriate that a fallen cherub should appear before him, disguised as Francis. In a way, it's the only angel he could see. The angel snatched Guido and carried him to Minos, who wrapped his tail around himself eight times, before biting it for good measure, and sending Guido to the eighth circle of hell, the place called Malebolge. His brilliance has found a place to shine in hell.

Guido's light moves away from Dante. It writhes and twists, in marked contrast to the flame of Ulysses and Diomedes, which had been still. Dante and Virgil walk silently to the next bolge.

The ninth bolge entombs figures Dante regards as schismatic, themselves now rent asunder.

INFERNO 28
Fundamentalism

ANTO 28 IS ONE IN WHICH MY OWN DREAD comes to the fore. This is not because my own sins especially overlap with those in this bolge, insofar as I know. Or that the punishment is exceptionally macabre, though it is not unimaginative. It is because of a soul that Dante says he saw there. It is the Prophet Muhammad. It is difficult for me on two counts.

First, I have gained much from reading Sufi texts, particularly those of Ibn 'Arabi. To me, they are clearly inspired and contain illuminating insights. It is difficult to read a scene that denigrates Muhammad.

Second, the canto makes me ask what is Dante up to? What did he really see? Can I trust anything else he tells us? His testimony stands or falls on the veracity of his perception. He himself insists that is so. How, therefore, can a writer who fomented the distrust of others, as Edward Said explains in his book *Orientalism*, be wholeheartedly trusted?

These difficulties are a blessing in disguise, not because I agree with Dante about Muhammad, but because Dante has been insisting throughout that the truth of his journey is not found in any literal reading of his words, but in wrestling with them, to release their spirit. They are living words, ones that catalyze and channel, not program or fix. Like a religious symbol, they reflect light that originates in a source that lies beyond the horizon of our understanding. This is why The Divine Comedy, like any inspired text, can be read time and time again, each time yielding new life. It is why Dante is still read, 700 years on.

The truth is not on the page. It is in the receptive mind of the reader. We have just encountered the soul of Guido who had become lost because his mind had grown incapable of receiving anything beyond what he already knew. We must be open to more than what Dante thought he knew too. He is a genius. His work is revelatory. But he himself is still flawed. This canto can become an exercise in perceiving how even his flaws might let the light in. Such is the genius of God.

Dante introduces us to what he saw in the ninth bolge of Malebolge in the context of battles. Canto 28 opens with the description of several conflicts from history. The references are heaped on top of one another, as bodies are on battlefields, as the destruction of war devastates lives. The stories of injury and massacre form a bloody link with the previous bolge containing Guido the military strategist to this one, which contains those who stir up the discord that can spark conflagrations.

The first soul they see is Muhammad. He approaches them and is split from head to foot, disemboweled. He tears himself apart, as does the soul who accompanies him, Ali, Muhammad's son-in-law. He too is cut open. As they walk the circle of this bolge, they heal, only for devils to appear, who reinstate their wounds.

Dante is portraying Muhammad as a divisive figure because this is how he understood Islam. The condition suffered by the schismatics is of wounds that don't permanently heal, but constantly reopen. During the medieval period, the common assumption was that Islam was a Christian sect that had split from the truth. Some said Muhammad had been a cardinal who wanted to become pope. It sounds surprising today, in an age that knows about world religions. But Dante writes in the age of Christendom, when all peoples and tongues seemed to revolve like planets around the single Christian sun. The conviction became more entrenched during the crusades, which were already generations old and thoroughly incorporated into the culture of Dante's era. He had crusaders in his own family, at least one of whom he knew to have died while crusading. The logic was that Islamic warriors had seized Jerusalem, the site of Christ's death and Resurrection, so they must know Christ to be holy in some way, only in the wrong way. No one read the Qur'an.

Muhammad and Ali are not the only souls Dante detects in this chasm. In fact, Muhammad makes a prophecy that concerns a contemporary of Dante's, a Christian figure called Fra Dolcino. He led a heretical sect that was suppressed by the Church in the thirteenth century, leading to his execution at the stake. The prophecy, which Dante heard from Muhammad's lips, reveals much about how Dante viewed the Prophet. In Dante's mind, Muhammad would know about Fra Dolcino's fate because Muhammad shares it.

The schismatics see that Dante is living. Virgil explains that Dante is here not because he is dead but so that he may know the full experience of life and death before he dies. This is a potent way of putting it. Dying before you die is an ordeal that the enlightened are said to undergo, and the power of Virgil's remark is not missed by the souls. Dante reports that over one hundred turned to look at him when they heard it. For a moment, it seemed as if their suffering stopped. They found relief in the possibility of enlightenment, which is to say, an ordeal by which truth leads to unity, not division. The implication is that at least some of the souls still yearn for truth. They heard a word of truth from Virgil and recognized its authenticity. Perhaps their mistake was to have been too zealous for the truth, and so intolerant of dissent. And it raises the question again of how this round enlightens Dante, and what that might say to us?

Dante's view of Islam is complicated because it is almost certain that he had direct knowledge of Islamic learning, if not the religion itself, gathered from his teacher, Bruno Latini, who we met on the burning sands. It's known that Latini spent time in Moorish Spain and moreover had done so during the period of relatively peaceful coexistence between Christianity and Islam on the Iberian Peninsula. There are records of Latini speaking of the glories of Islamic civilization.

Interestingly for readers of The Divine Comedy, he must have been given a copy of the Kitab, or book, that describes Muhammad's Miraj, which is his ascent into the heavens. This was an eleventh-century account of the Prophet's so-called night journey. It records that Mohammad visited various levels of heaven and, underneath, various levels of hell. Modern scholars have established that Dante borrowed from this Islamic tradition to develop his own revelation of heaven and hell. He is directly indebted to the figure he sees before him. Muhammad had enabled him to perceive and articulate the truths that came to him in this intermediary space of encounter, imagination, and revelation. The Prophet expanded Dante's own powers of perception.

Dante's awareness of the Miraj is only one aspect of his indebtedness to Islam. He was informed by Islamic philosophy via his reading of Aristotle, who was received into medieval Europe via the commentaries of the Islamic philosopher, Averroes. He also finds Muslims in limbo. Other Islamic influences will be evident in other parts of The Divine Comedy.

All this needs to be born in mind when interpreting what Dante felt he saw when he encountered Muhammad in Malebolge. Further, it's only in doing so that Dante's account can carry on living, and not become an anachronism forged by medieval prejudice. The awareness of reality he seeks to convey, in form and content, requires readers to bring together the text, knowledge of the text and its times, the understandings that have emerged since, and self-knowledge. It is complicated but the promise is immense: a living engagement with life in all its fullness.

I believe that the dynamic is exemplified in the canto. When Dante talks with Muhammad, he gets things factually wrong. For example, the Prophet was not a Christian schismatic but the founder of Islam. Factual errors occur in other parts of The Divine Comedy, but they do not undermine its deeper veracity. Instead, they point to the type of truths that are more robust than historical facts — truths about human desire, human failings, and divine ways.

This illuminates my discomfort in reading about Muhammad in Malebolge. It makes me wrestle with a meaning that might come through the words, even as I feel compelled to reject the literal sense presented on the page. It is to have a moment of descent, wondering what is going on, which is the necessary precursor to any ascent. Canto 28 can become doubly valuable because it cements the pattern of Dante's journey in my mind.

They encounter further schismatics. An unnamed figure has a split face. It seems that his crime was to sow dissent within a group who were on a peace mission, thereby spoiling their chances of success.

They see historical figures, such as Gaius Scribonius Curio. He was an adviser to Julius Caesar, and encouraged him to cross the Rubicon, the proximate cause of the civil war in ancient Rome.

Another person is Mosca de' Lamberti, a contemporary of Dante. He walks around the bolge holding before him bloody stumps for hands. It's a gruesome moment in a grim canto. Lamberti had encouraged nothing less than the Florentine civil war, having stirred the original division between the Guelphs and Ghibellines. Little wonder that when Lamberti addresses Dante, Dante retorts harshly, condemning Lamberti and his clan. Dante is speaking from his heart, from his experience. Here in the deeper reaches of hell, such feelings often emerge unmoderated from the lips of the pilgrim.

A final figure that Dante sees is the victim of one of Dante's most famous images. He is Bertran de Born, a poet who excelled in verses describing the horrors of war, which suggests he must have had a deep feeling for them, perhaps a deep enjoyment of them. Dante sees him decapitated, holding his head by the hair in front of him like a lantern. The way he saw in life has become the light by which he must find his way around the bolge in death. De Born's headlight is a warning against taking our insights literally. They will forge the reality we detect around us.

The warning is reflected in a remark Dante makes to us readers. He says that we won't believe his report of the sight of the headless de Born, though that was the evidence that struck his eyes. He adds that he is as sure of it as his conscience allows. It's a fascinating confession. It implies that Dante is aware that his sight can deceive him, though he is being true in telling what he saw. His perceptions are shaped by his interpretations, as de Born's had been. That is what it is to see.

Incidentally, de Born is the occasion for the single time Dante uses the word "contrapasso," the "opposite suffering" that afflicts the souls. I've already argued that the meaning of what traps the souls here is not to be read too literally, but rather must be teased out from the nuances of their attitudes and behaviors, in part because Dante does not use the word repeatedly, but just this once. It's ironic again that the single instance is here, in the canto where what Dante reports seeing is so tricky. It informs the literalism that seems to infect this bolge. Further, it is one of the sinners, de Born, who uses the word, when he says holding his head before him is "the perfect contrapasso." It needs to be read cautiously. It is implying that the conviction that the punishment fits the crime in The Divine Comedy offers only a partial understanding of what is going on, and one that is counterproductive when it forecloses deeper insights.

Literal convictions amplify the state of mind that leads to division and schism. They are drained of the psychological and theological subtlety that better reflects reality. They are shaped by the crude and prejudiced. They cause splits and divisions because they are incapable of seeing how diversity can lead to a richer kind of unity than mere uniformity. That happens in the body politic, when citizens adopt polarized thinking, as much as in religious groups, when the only question is whether someone is for or against the cause. It's the awareness known by the fundamentalist, so there is a bitter irony that Dante sees Muhammad here. Dante is caught by the mentality of this domain and finds himself perceiving and presenting Islam through narrow Christian eyes. He knows more about Islam. Islam is integral to his project. And yet, all that awareness leaves Dante in the eighth circle of hell. He forgets it in this dark place.

We must bring all our learning, mental struggle, and imagination to this great poem. We must ask for divine inspiration and insight. Only then might we understand what we see, an issue that will present itself again directly in the next canto.

Dante and Virgil argue. The bolge is infected with the pestilence of denuded nature and humanity.

INFERNO 29
Melting

ANTE IS GRIPPED BY THE CONFUSION OF MUTI-
lated bodies found in the ninth bolge of Malebolge. Maybe it was
the sight of Bertran de Born, maybe his rage at Mosca de' Lamberti.
He is transfixed, which does not please Virgil, who issues one of his sharpest
rebukes to Dante. What are you doing staring at the mayhem, he cries? Why
are you still absorbed with it? We must push on! Time waits for no man.

The exchange between them raises a whole series of fascinating issues
that are worth teasing out. One is the question of the time they have to
spend in hell.

Virgil tells Dante that the moon is now on the other side of the earth,
compared with where it was when they set off. That means it is about 1:30
PM. They will spend twenty-four hours in hell, so they have got about five
hours left. Virgil also tells Dante that this circle of Malebolge, this particular
valley, is roughly twenty-two miles in circumference.

This piece of factual information was picked up during the Renaissance and no less a figure than Galileo gave two lectures on its significance at the end of the sixteenth century. He attempted to work out the dimensions of hell using Virgil's estimate. It seems comical, akin to calculating that the cosmos was created in 4004 BC. But the Renaissance was the time when numbers came to be valued for quantitative aspects rather than qualitative, so it reflects the concerns of the age.

When Virgil tells the time, and gives a dimension of hell, he is talking about a felt sense of things more than a measurement. Twenty-two miles implies a middle distance — at the limit of what a person might walk in a day, say. Twenty-four hours means a complete cycle of the sun, which suggests that they are going to have a short season in hell, rather than literally twenty-four hours. It's a comfort — a short season is better than eternity — although embedded in his remarks is the implication that Dante is starting to look as if he wants to take up residency in the place, to be absorbed by it, not to visit it so as to learn and move on. Dante must be careful not to become entranced by the atmosphere and infected by the spirit of this chasm. He seems to be losing his capacity to act. Virgil might have become alarmed because he sensed a divide growing between them, which is precisely what the bolge of the schismatics would be expected to foster. They shouldn't spend too long exposed to it.

Virgil is not wrong. Dante strikes back that if Virgil knew what was preoccupying him, he would moderate his alarm. It's a stinging rebuke because Virgil does tend to know what is going on in Dante's mind and, during the hours of climbing, they have felt close, and been working together.

Dante is, in fact, looking for a relative. He tells Virgil, who is able to help him. He has seen Dante's kin underneath the bridge.

The relative is a cousin of Dante's father. Commentators have identified him as a historical figure, who was murdered, although no one in Dante's family received the blood money in recompense. The vendetta comes back to Dante's mind presumably because vendettas are close to schisms and divisions, in terms of their effects on society. They cut people off from one another. Dante must be experiencing the tension within himself, inherited from his own family. He feels guilty, as if he must do something about it, if he can.

A vendetta carries a lot more meaning than just avenging a cousin. Dante feels it as the compulsion to do something about the lack of blood money, and it holds him back because he senses he ought not to leave this bolge without addressing the issue directly with his dead relative, as he has the chance. Not to do so would be to break bonds of honor and loyalty.

However, guilt is a feeling that arises more generally when an individual does something that goes against the wishes of a group. It is a sign that bonds of belonging are being challenged, perhaps deliberately. It is a separating emotion, filling the gap that is opening up. I think Dante feels it not only because of his relative but because his *Divine Comedy* might come to be viewed as schismatic. We have already seen how he is challenging the received wisdom of Christianity. He is encountering popes in hell and is reforming attitudes to supposed sins, such as homosexuality. He is likely to be declared a heretic because of his epic, which was indeed banned on occasion. Dante lingers in this bolge, in part, to develop the sense of his evolving relationship with Christianity. He is grappling with the implications of his journey being not just an amplification of how the Church understands Christianity. It is a revision, to the point of a new dispensation.

This is a good moment to feel these tensions. Given the significance of his calling, he must learn about temptations such as hubris, and contemplating Bertran de Born, carrying his head, is a good way to do so.

That said, Dante realizes he has drunk his fill. He hears Virgil's distress, and they move on, though they continue to discuss the sight of these sinners while they make their way to the tenth bolge, and last of Malebolge. He doesn't tell us what is said between them, the sign that Dante is absorbing the lessons for himself.

They reach the final ditch, and the mood changes dramatically. They are in a different psycho-spiritual space, the dimension of reality dominated by the spirit of falsification.

Souls here mistreated nature and their own life. They became cut off from the spiritual, sacramental, and divine aspects of reality through seeking to use these elements for their own ends. The case in point, highlighted in this canto, is alchemy.

In the medieval world, alchemy meant both the attempt to falsify metals, in particular presenting what is not gold as gold, and the sense of falsifying your inner state, by presenting vices as virtues. The link is that in both cases the individual deliberately confused what is worthless with what is of high value. They may have deceived others, though they ended up deceiving themselves.

It is a slippery slope. It was a risk growing in the mercantile age, when regalia formerly associated with princes, as a reflection of their birth and vocation, were becoming luxuries available to those with money. You might say that a material sparkle in this world can cause forgetfulness of the spiritual sparkle associated with heaven and the stars.

The danger is not so much in the luxuries themselves as how they can captivate the attention. In time, they can become so alluring that individuals and then societies forget that there is more to desire from life. The enchantment of material goods casts an alchemical spell over the soul, dulling the ability to sense divine glory. As a result, one is left circling in a dark chasm, which as Dante and Virgil reach the tenth bolge, is demonstrated by souls who appear to have the plague.

It is a pestilence. Bodies are heaped up on each other, inert or crawling over one another. Individuals sit picking scabs, trying to ease their suffering, though only making it worse. Dante says it was like seeing a hospital that had been overwhelmed. The smell of sickness fills the air, not the scent of returning health. It is a disturbing set of images, related to understanding nature and its divine dimensions.

Dante had a broadly Neoplatonic understanding of evil and suffering. It understood that malevolence and woe increase with distance from God, and conversely, that although terrible things can happen in any time or place, they are eased, by finding meaning, with proximity to the divine. The understanding reflects the common intuition that while suffering is, at times, inevitable, it can also prompt love, kindness, and selflessness within the human spirit.

In this bolge, however, the human spirit is corrupted. And I think the infernal pestilence they see is not a natural plague. Instead, it is a disease of the soul. After all, there can be no natural disease in eternity because these figures no longer belong to mortal life. Their symptoms are manifestations of the deeper concern, of becoming so distant from divine life that they have lost touch with its value. They wouldn't notice if spiritual light were to surround them.

Virgil and Dante look back into the bolge from the far side of the bridge that crosses it. They see people picking at themselves not because they are infected, but because they are attacking the good that is nearest to them: their very being. And attack is the right word because Dante notices that they turn their fingers into pincers, the better to pull back their skin. They don't know how to use their capacities in any way other than for destruction. They have lost the vitality to move, which is why they are in piles: gravity dominates their state, in the practical absence of levity.

Virgil calls out to the souls, asking for any Italians, so Dante can converse with someone. He explains that he is here with a mortal soul, at which heads do turn toward them. As before, there is a momentary easing of their suffering, and its hideous scratching, at mention of the word "life." They almost turn to that forgotten quality of being, though they can only half turn their heads. In a desperately tragic moment, they do no more than glance, before flopping back into their disintegrating state.

Dante and Virgil talk with two souls who are not named. One was put to death in life for claiming to be able to build a flying machine for a king, though that was only one of his obsessions. His whole life was devoted to magical arts that might assist the powerful and so also benefit him. His alchemy changed him more than it transgressed nature, and he is paying the price. Natural justice, which in the premodern world meant entities flourishing in their best place, has become a curse for him because he messed with it. He lost the ability to make good judgments and so he is, in effect, hideously judged by himself. He picks and scratches. He can't see there is more to life.

A second soul speaks who was part of a group that loved luxuries. He and his friends would throw lavish dinners and afterward trash not only the leftovers, but the furniture and venue as well. They were the godfathers of excessive consumption. When everything can be ruined, everything becomes worthless.

Dante joins in with this spirit to some degree because, in the banter with these individuals, he indulges in some stereotyping of foreigners. He declares that the Sienese are silly, more stupid than the French. It sounds like the kind of jesting that might go on at a debauched party, but it's risky because all human beings are of equal worth. Each person shares in the divine image. That is their inner value. If you become used to mocking and condemning others, you might forget that they reflect the divine light, and then forget that you do too.

The canto ends abruptly with a final pun on aping nature. We were apes in life and are subhuman here, one of the souls says. He is mocking himself, not so as to regret or repent, but simply because that is his habit. Denigration is his way of life. Nothing is not falsified.

Minds and bodies themselves begin to disintegrate in souls driven rabid by playing God in life.

INFERNO 30

Fevers

T IS NOT JUST THE MINDS OF THE INDIVIDUALS IN the tenth valley of Malebolge that are disintegrating. Their bodies are as well. The pilgrims are reaching parts of the cosmos that are so far from divinity that its hold on souls is attenuating. These souls have turned so resolutely from the source of their vitality, that they can barely hold themselves together, literally. The tendency will escalate as Dante and Virgil approach the pit of hell.

It is the effects of evil, in the Neoplatonic schema. It is experienced as the growing absence of what is good, including the quality of existence itself. Good and evil have an asymmetric relationship: evil takes hold when good becomes distant, and not because evil is a power in itself — the theory of evil known as the deprivation of good.

Dante illustrates the effects of this undoing by opening the canto with references to two accounts in the ancient world of individuals falling apart.

One concerns King Athamas, who lost his sanity to the point of not being able to recognize his wife and sons. One day, when they approached him, he thought he saw a lioness and two cubs. Depraved, he dashed one of the "cubs" against a rock, at which the lioness and other cub threw themselves into a river and drowned.

The second story is of Hecuba, the wife of King Priam and queen of Troy. With the fall of Troy and the madness of the city sacking, she saw her husband, son, and daughter die. It prompted her loss of mind for grief, after which she is said to have run around barking like a dog.

The stories create a mood of evil's reality because individuals gripped by it lose touch with reality. However, it is interesting that whereas these stories from the ancient world were understood to be the effects of abandonment or attack by gods, the individuals Dante meets in this gorge are responsible for their own derangement. That is part of the meaning of the Christian dispensation and the evolution of consciousness from the ancient world. The Incarnation implies that the human individual can become completely transparent to the divine. He can share directly in God's life. But the converse also follows, that to turn away from God's life is to fall toward the edges of non-existence.

Dante must grapple with this dire predicament because he aspires to ascend into the heavens and perceive the heart of divinity. That is his calling. That is the human calling. And it is a high calling, partly because it can go so wrong.

Virgil and Dante look again into the bolge and see three types of souls. The first have become rabid: they are rushing around biting, grabbing, and dragging other souls. The second have bodies that are leaking: they have become so distended that it is hard to see the boundaries of their being anymore, as they blur into the matter around them. The third are feverish: their bodies are steaming as their identity and integrity ooze into the environment. At several points in the canto, Dante remarks that it is becoming increasingly hard to tell where the landscape ends and human bodies begin. Everything is merging into undifferentiated, inert matter.

The soul met in the previous canto, who had devoted himself to luxury, is grabbed by a rabid passer-by. He sinks his teeth into the neck of his fellow and drags him off on his belly. The raving culprit is called Gianni Schicchi. During his mortal life, he had impersonated a wealthy man who had died, so that the deceased's son could change his father's will to his advantage. His imitation of the dead man was utterly convincing, though it raises the question of why such an act would be so severely consequential in eternity. In fact, this was only one such incident. Schicchi made a habit of impersonating others. When you put that way of life alongside the stories of gods impersonating human beings, which in classical tales they frequently do, the implication is that Schicchi had come to think he were a god. That is a dangerous delusion with which to toy, a fantasy that is underlined in Dante's report because the poet adds the detail that when Schicchi had imitated the dead man, he had asked only for a prize mare as payment. He would have gained the world, if he had understood how he is made in the image of God. Lost in the misconception that he was a god, he couldn't keep himself, or his horse.

Dante and Virgil next see Myrrha, the daughter of King Cinyras of Cyprus. She so desired to sleep with her father incestuously that she disguised herself and entered his bed. When Cinyras discovered the unnatural deception, he vowed to kill her, although the gods took pity on her and turned her into a myrrh tree. She had conceived a son by the boundary-blurring, taboo-busting union, who was born from the tree and called Adonis. Now in hell, she is unable to contain herself. Her passion has taken possession of her. Dante finds it mesmerizing, which indicates a risk for him. That happens. When the people around you can't control themselves, the madness is infectious. It can get under your skin and start to unhinge you as well.

Dante's attention switches to the second group of souls, whose bodies have become porous. They are melding with the rocks around them. One figure stands out, Master Adamo, an individual thought by commentators to be a falsifier of gold florins. His body is distended like a lute. He no longer has legs and his body is glued to the ground. He can't move, and remarks that he couldn't shift an inch in a hundred years if he tried.

His forgery messed with the nature of money. It's serious because, as Dante considered with the sin of usury, money can be thought of as creating an intermediary world of value. Coins stand for things of real worth so that they can be traded in lieu of straightforward barter. That is how coins gain their own value, indicative of which is that they are stamped with images of emperors and gods. So, creating treasures is a significant act. In the medieval world it would have been natural to think of it as magical because, as material goods should speak of spiritual blessings, so the creation of coins carries the aura of a sacrament: it is an outward sign of inner worth, which is how the whole of creation might speak to people and lead them toward God.

Master Adamo had seized this awesome power for himself. His practice had cut him off from divine life because he had ceased to perceive divine life. I imagine he is pinned to the ground because he has been overcome by gravity, having lost any of the levity that would enable him to rise. This is bitterly ironic as he would have used fire in his alchemy, fire which should have reminded him of the spirit and the heavens as its flames rose into the air. Instead, he used fire for narrow, material gain. Counterfeiters disrupt the chain of being from earth to heaven, and risk falling to the lowest domains of being as a result.

Master Adamo craves a drop of water as he lies trapped in hell. He says that his thirst reminds him of the fertile countryside of his birth and the flowing waters he used to see in the world above. It is a brilliant piece of writing by Dante because the description brings the loveliness of water to our minds, prompting a reflection on how it is a life-giving substance of both material and spiritual value, even as Master Adamo reflects on how his activities in life have turned this natural gift into a curse. His descent is momentarily our ascent, as it could have been for him too.

The attention of Virgil and Dante moves on to the feverish, steaming souls. Their lifeblood is leaking into the atmosphere. Two turn out to be infamous liars. One is Potiphar's wife, who tried to seduce Joseph in the story from the Hebrew Bible, was rejected by him, and so accused him of rape. Joseph was thrown into prison. A second is a Greek from the Trojan war called Sinon. He was imprisoned in the city of Troy, and it was he who persuaded the Trojans to open the gates and let in the Trojan horse. The deceit led to the ruin of the city.

Both acts are foul but in order to understand why these perpetrators have ended up in lower hell, it is once again necessary to reflect on their inner lives. Today, we would say that Potiphar's wife was an abuser, probably a serial abuser, with Joseph being just one of her victims. She used irresistible power to exploit individuals sexually, which ruins them either in the act of rape or in the ruination of their lives, if they refuse.

Sinon the Greek broke a different kind of body boundary, the sacred boundary of the city walls. Further, he may have done so by despoiling a sacred sign. It is likely the Trojans let in the horse because they regarded it as an offering to the gods from the Greeks. Why else would they have welcomed it into their sanctuary? The duplicity rode roughshod over the connections between mortals and deities, and Sinon is unable to maintain those links now.

A surprising thing happens next. Sinon and Master Adamo launch into a verbal joust with one another. They exchange vicious accusations, which Dante finds fascinating. Commentators note that this is because the two deploy a form of poetic combat in their fight. It is easy to imagine that a hellish version of the practice would be doubly enticing for Dante the poet. Only, it is a perverse use of the art. Used well, it was designed to encourage poets to aspire to higher and higher insights, greater and greater visions, more and more nuance, and subtlety and glory. It was poetic combat as a spiritual practice. In the tenth bolge of Malebolge, though, undertaken by Sinon and Master Adamo, it has the opposite effect. It pins them down and keeps them stuck.

Virgil notices Dante's fascination and chides his charge, which immediately fills the poet with shame. Virgil spots Dante's response and immediately forgives him. His shame has saved him, you might say, because it is a conscious response to his deadly interest in Sinon and Master Adamo, though it is painful for Dante. He tells us that he wished he were like someone who was dreaming a dream in which they find themselves in trouble, only to realize they are dreaming and so can wake, with the trouble vanishing away. It is an apt metaphor for this pit, where the boundaries between fantasies and life have led to real trouble and seemingly no escape, unlike waking from a dream. It also prompts us to reflect on the nature of reality and how dreams can carry us higher or cause us to fall. Dante is learning from his encounter with the falsifiers, as he must. He is experiencing the confusions of the place, so as to be able more accurately to discern when aspirations become curses; desire becomes lust.

The canto ends with a touching remark from Virgil. He tells Dante that if he ever finds himself caught up in futile arguments in the future, he can imagine Virgil at his side. He will be able henceforth to recall his guide's rebuke and the shame that liberated him in the tenth pit. It is a gift from the descent, which is about to become steeper.

Virgil and Dante wander into a grey zone, hear an ominous horn, and encounter giants.

INFERNO 31
Plunge

IRGIL AND DANTE ARE ON THE FAR EDGE OF
Malebolge. They are about to step into another region of reality, the floor of hell, in which the experience of being is not only
becoming more corrupted but more and more tenuous: it is a falling away
from everything.

Dante is preoccupied with Virgil's rebuke at his fascination with the
bickering souls. It pierces him like the lance of Achilles, he says, which
was famous because while its first strike injured, its second strike healed.
It's a healing image for Dante the pilgrim, though it is also an allusion
as to why they must press on into the darkness. At first, the final part of
their journey through hell will feel like it damages Dante, though it will
transform him. The lance of Achilles shows again that descent and ascent
are intimately linked.

The journey to heaven requires the reform of desire, will, and knowledge. The divine will, and desire, is that we ascend, freely and consciously.
That necessitates awakening — the second touch of the lance — and must
follow awareness of the opposite states of mind, and how ensnared human
souls can become.

The effects of the first strike are felt as Dante ceases to be sure whether
it is day or night. He is feeling disoriented as the cosmos appears to return
to a state before its creation, which included separating the light from the
darkness, the day from the night. Those life-giving distinctions are coming
undone.

The experience of becoming lost, physically and psychologically, compounds a growing terror. The lack of distinctions feeds a gnawing dread.
Uniformity is like that. It's why sameness is a tool of oppression, used by
dictators. It's why prisoners are held in windowless, grey rooms. Divine
life is precisely the opposite: a unity born of diversity, in which each can
be fully themselves and so fully open to one another.

In a hellish mush, life drains away. Nothing can reflect the divine light.
Instead, there is an unsettling absence. Dante and Virgil are moving through
it, though they are suddenly brought back to some sense of direction by
the sound of a horn blast. It is louder than a thunderclap. It wakes them
into a new state of terror.

The fanfare reminds Dante of Roland's horn. He was a leader in Charlemagne's army against the Saracens, a century or so before Dante lived.
The story came back from the Crusades that the rear guard, led by Roland,
was routed by the Muslim warriors when they fell too far behind the main
forces. Roland blowing his horn for help was the lasting memory of the
carnage. It spoke of horror. The blast of the infernal horn carries the same
sense of foreboding. Are Dante and Virgil going to be left stranded? Are
they falling beyond divine help?

The Divine Comedy has only one ending, but this does not mean there are
not real moments of dread. Even when you know there is hope, desperate
times can overwhelm you, particularly when you know that they must be
endured because they are part of the healing.

Virgil senses Dante's fear and tells him something of what they are about
to witness. Seeming towers will appear through the gloom, only they are
not towers but giants. Virgil's description of them occupies several verses in
the canto. His words sweep up and down their bodies. They stand on the
floor of hell. Their waists will appear level with the precipice that Dante
and he must descend, so what they will see initially is the giants from the

waists upward. Commentators have worked out that Dante imagines them to have been about thirty-five feet tall.

The giants' size is a reflection of their moral monstrosity. They are overgrown because they have become too proud. Dante will see three of them and discover how pride shapes their inner lives. I also sense that the giants come from an older consciousness. They are pre-Christian, from the times when humans and giants were said to have together walked the earth. Such stories are in the Bible and other ancient sources. Dante and Virgil become capable of seeing them because, much as the day and the night are blurring, so the deep past and present are too. The echoes of former times are rushing toward them and taking on tangible form once again. States of mind that to them are primitive and so nightmarish are reshaping reality, as they experience the consciousness conjured by the giants' presence.

Dorothy L. Sayers wrote that the giants of the Inferno are massive conglomerations of emotion, undifferentiated and undiscerned by reason. They exist in a raw state. This explains how they each seem to be trapped in a particular felt state of rage or incoherence. They are living matter, though matter from which soul has almost departed.

The first giant they see is Nimrod. They hear him muttering meaningless words. "Raphel may amech zabi almi!" Virgil tartly calls him a blathering idiot. Commentators have speculated about what Nimrod might have been trying to say. My guess is the words are meaningless because Nimrod has lost any grasp on meaning. He is babbling, a word that originates with the story of the Tower of Babel in the Bible, and with which Nimrod became associated. The hubris of the ziggurat is that human beings thought they could build meaning from stone, rather than discovering the meaning of the skies. The hope led to them not understanding one another or themselves. To lose touch with the language of the cosmos is to empty the soul and, in time, to cease to be able to speak in any meaningful way.

That is partly what it is to start to fall away from being. Blather echoes this desperate state. George Orwell was right to highlight its dangers. It can undo the human mind, as it can ruin a society.

They leave Nimrod to his incoherence and walk on a little farther, coming to a second, fiercer giant. He is Ephialtes. A giant from Greek myth, he was one of the sons of the earth who tried an assault on Olympus. Of course, they failed, and Jupiter defeated them. Before Dante, he looks like a violent monster, pinned down by chains. He has one arm wrapped across his chest, the other strapped to his back.

The sight prompts Dante to tell Virgil that he would like to see Briareus.

He is a giant Virgil had described in *The Aeneid* as a monster with fantastical form. Virgil had said he had one hundred limbs, fifty mouths, and fire for breath. Virgil replies to Dante that Briareus is here, though too far off, which seems a shame for Dante having travelled all this way, as it is a shame for us, though Virgil's ban is not incidental. My sense is that Dante cannot see Briareus because some states of being, some tortured minds, are too disconcerting, too dire. Dante has been wrestling with the madness of others in Malebolge. The sight took him close to the edge. Virgil realizes he must not become unhinged.

Virgil is wise because they then feel an earthquake of terrible force. It is caused by Ephialtes shaking. He had stirred with barely contained violence. Dante tells us that he had never feared more keenly that he would die. Seeing Briareus might well have been too much.

They approach another giant, Antaeus. He is also from Greek mythology, although he didn't take part in the rebellion against Jupiter, and so here in hell, he is unbound, though something else keeps him imprisoned: his vanity.

We learn this because Virgil plays on it. He knows that they need Antaeus's help to reach the floor of hell, and he is going to fool the giant into offering it by flattering him. Virgil calls to Antaeus and reminds him of the time he captured a thousand lions. For the performer of such a feat, Virgil has a modest request now: to lift Dante and him to the lower part of hell, upon which Antaeus's feet stand. Virgil adds that Dante is a mortal and so can add another tale to burnish the giant's reputation when he returns to the land of the living. Virgil continues, teasingly, that he hopes he won't have to ask Antaeus's giant rivals for the favor. They are only a little way farther along the cliff, and so it would be easy for him to turn to them.

It is a nervy moment. Virgil is using flattery against a beast trapped by flattery. It could go wrong as a form of expediency. However, Antaeus is stupefied in his eternal predicament. He can't help but respond as Virgil requires. He reaches out for Virgil, who turns to Dante and grasps him. They are carried over the lip into the final circle of hell. They descend dozens of feet and are gently put down by the giant.

It's a moment with a hidden meaning because, in mythology, Antaeus was killed by Hercules. The hero had learned that if he lifted Antaeus up from the earth, so that his feet lost contact with Gaia, the giant would be rendered vulnerable. Dante and Virgil are vulnerable, as Antaeus lifts them to the ground. It is a strange change of roles in hell, as if the action that was his undoing can do good. Hell can seem like a fixed place, though it is also one of unexpected reversals.

Dante and Virgil look up from their low vantage point. It reminds Dante of walking underneath the high towers of Bologna, when the sun passes behind a turret, casting a shadow that shoots out along the ground. It can seem as if the tower is about to topple.

Antaeus doesn't topple. He stands up again and leaves them to whatever they may encounter next.

Requesting heavenly help, Dante steps into Cocytus, revealed as a region of deadening ice.

INFERNO 32

Freeze

VIRGIL AND DANTE ARE CLOSE TO THE SPIRITUAL
nadir of the cosmos, a place where reality itself comes undone. Little
wonder Dante the poet tells us it is hard to find the words to speak
of this darkness. It is a region in which words themselves can hardly sound.
His task cannot be undertaken lightly. It takes extreme effort to write about
what they saw in the gloom.

The seriousness with which he will try contrasts with the flippancy with
which hell is often talked about today. Hell may be simply dismissed by
progressives, as a product of the overexcited religious imagination. It may
be weaponized by fundamentalists who are sure their enemies are destined
for its grim corridors. It might also be observed that we live in an age that
successfully builds hells on earth.

There are reasons that spiritual adepts like Dante have deployed all their
ability to contemplate hell's meaning so profoundly. Dante himself calls

on the heavenly ladies who are the guardians of his pilgrimage. He evokes the name of Amphion, who was said to be able to charm rocks. He will need parallel abilities to bring the deadness of this zone to imaginative life.

He does so, in part, by contrasting the music of life with the silences of this region. He compares the beauty of life with the ugliness of this half-life. He deploys the vitality of words to convey the chilly reality that confronts him. He squeezes the juice out of the experience so his readers can taste it.

That said, words and experiences recalled will not be adequate to convey what happened next. They are not crude or rough enough to capture the crude and rough states of being that they see in this hole. The most banal word carries more soul than exists here.

It is the empty region he and Virgil must navigate. He must risk falling away, as it falls from life. He must touch the lowest points, if he is to ascend to the highest.

At first, Dante is not sure where to look. He gazes upward, in the direction that the head of Antaeus has just disappeared. It is a natural response for someone who has not forgotten about levity, though he is disturbed by a voice. "Watch out!" it calls, which is a useful instruction. Watch out for the owner of the voice and watch out for what they will see.

The voice is alarmed because the mouth that called out is at Dante's feet. In this region of hell, souls are almost completely buried in the ground. They are interred up to their necks. Their bodies rot in the stinking terrain.

Then comes one of the Dante's greatest revelations in the whole *Divine Comedy*. He tells us that the floor of hell is not hot and burning. There is no fire or flame. Instead, down here, is a vast, icy lake. The infernal landscape is frozen so solidly that it looks like glass.

The fiery hell of popular imagining is wrong. Fire is heat, life, and spirit. It rises with levity to the heavens. It can burn but is never hopeless. Hell, though, is cold, deathly, and demonic. It falls with gravity to the borders of non-existence. It binds with fear and despair.

The souls of lower hell suffer it. Rigidity destroys life. You feel it in people who have become frozen from traumas or nameless dreads. The tragedy is that a thousand choices to turn from vitality and vivaciousness have brought these souls to absolute zero. Evil is not the opposite of goodness. It is its absence.

The frozen lake is called Cocytus. Dante looks across its dull surface, and sees heads bound in ice. They look like frogs poking their heads through the surface tension, or heads of wheat strewn across the field after a harvest. The warmth of these similes is in marked contrast to the emptiness they describe.

He surveys the scene for a while, and then looks down and detects, at his feet, two heads butting together like goats. Their eyes drip tears that freeze on their lips. The two are so close together that the ice glues them together, as if in a kiss.

They are brothers. They killed each other because they both desired to inherit their father's wealth. Their wicked passion locks them together, as violence and misdeeds do. Their crime resonates with the name of this first ring of the ninth circle of hell: Caïne, after Cain who killed his brother Abel.

The voice he had first heard calls out again. He is called Camicion de' Pazzi and seems to delight in telling Dante about the brothers at his feet, building the sense of treachery that infects Cocytus. De' Pazzi himself murdered a relative in life, and he seeks to ensure that the reputations of his fellow souls are slain in death: he names a few frozen souls to Dante.

One that stands out for British readers is Mordred. He was one of the legendary knights of the Round Table of King Arthur, and was said to have turned on Arthur, although Arthur pierced him with his lance, so that the sunlight shone through Mordred's body. The deadly wound is the last time Mordred knew inner warmth.

Dante glances across the lake. He sees a thousand faces looking like dogs, frozen purple with cold. To this day, he adds, when he sees an icy pond in winter, he shudders at the memory.

Virgil and Dante are already walking into a second region of Cocytus. The boundary is not clearly marked because nothing can be clearly distinguished. It is called Antenora, after a betrayer of Troy. He is another treacherous figure, although his crime was not against relatives or individuals with whom he shared a sacred bond. He was traitorous.

Dante gets caught up in the deeper perfidiousness. Whether willfully or by accident, he kicks a head. Maybe he himself can no longer tell the difference. He may be becoming half possessed. He checks with Virgil when he wants to speak to the injured soul: he is less sure of himself and so turns to his guide, who nods permission. The distressed soul is called Bocca degli Abati and was involved in the battle of Montaperti. He was said to have cut off the hand of the standard bearer and, when the flag fell, panic gripped the Guelphs, which caused their defeat.

The Guelphs were Dante's side and, in one of the nastiest moments in The Divine Comedy, Dante launches into a vicious attack on Bocca, who attacks back. Dante tells him that he deserves to be kicked, and Bocca yells back that Dante's kick is pathetic for a living man. Dante seizes Bocca's head and threatens to tear his hair out. The humdinger casts both figures in a dim light.

The ugliness is Dante confronting his own ugliness. The desire to injure Bocca, who is really without defense, exposes him to his own inner rage, murderousness, and hate. He must know them, or they will haunt him as a shadow and prevent his ascent. The scene reminds me of a comment made by the psychotherapist, Donald Winnicott, who remarked that we can't know about love until we know about hate, and so learn that love is stronger.

The horrid moment is interrupted when another soul calls out, mocking Bocca. This soul names a string of other Florentines who were involved in the civil war. The reader is reminded of Dante's earlier curse of his city, when he declared that he saw more souls in hell from it than any other city. Dante is literally surrounded by the treachery of civil war. He is looking in the faces of those who were caught in its vortex of revenge-inspired slaughter. They are bound together because taking a life binds you to that life. They are bound together because the net of collective madness drags everyone down. This is what it looks like when a civilization leans on its crumbling terracotta foot, to recall the image of the old man of Crete. These figures have no idea that there is richness to life, that there was once spiritual silver and gold.

The canto ends with a final shocking scene. They are out in the middle of the icy lake. Two more heads are locked together. One is biting at the base of the other's skull, as someone might tear hungrily at a piece of bread. It's an enactment of Saint Paul's remark in the Letter to the Galatians, that attacking another leads to being consumed by each other.

Dante wants to know their story. He promises to tell it in the world above if they speak to him, though the canto closes with a warning. He will tell it so long as his tongue doesn't dry up first. In the seeing and the telling, he risks become consumed by the foulness.

Dante and Virgil encounter Ugolino deeper in Cocytus, as well as the souls of the living dead.

INFERNO 33

Grotesque

IRGIL AND DANTE ARE DEEP INTO THE INFERNAL cold of Cocytus. Before them is a head with gore-covered lips, tearing at the brain of another.

The cannibal stops chewing and looks up. Dante does not know who he is, though he recognizes he is from Florence. Unashamedly, the figure reveals himself. He is Count Ugolino. His victim is Archbishop Ruggieri.

The story Ugolino is about to tell Dante is one of the best known from *The Divine Comedy*, and one of the most discussed because, from start to finish, it is not quite clear why his actions in life propelled him to the extremities of hell. I think Dante keeps us wondering deliberately. He has stood before these humans-cum-monsters. He wants us imaginatively to draw close as well.

The facts of what happened are fairly clear. Ugolino was thrown into a tower, along with his four sons, by his enemy, Ruggieri. The tower became a permanent prison when it was nailed shut. They were left to starve to death.

138

However, the way in which Ugolino tells the tale adds complications. For one thing, Ugolino doesn't mention that he was with his four sons until he is quite some way into his account of events. Though a father, he focuses mostly on his own suffering. He is clearly concerned that Dante pities him. He wants his side of the story to be retold by Dante in the world above.

He also emphases the archbishop's guilt by telling Dante he had a dream that presaged the violence of the churchman's deed. He saw a wolf and cubs being chased by a huntsman and hounds. The wolves are caught, and the dogs' fangs rip the flesh from their bones.

Finally, when he notices that Dante isn't weeping, he accuses Dante of callousness and reveals that his children were in the tower. He speaks of their suffering, how they turned to their father for help and sobbing, finally, offered their bodies for him to feed from. Ugolino appears to give himself away, though, because he stresses his stoicism: he remained silent at their pleas, offering no prayers or consolation. He bit his hand rather than cry. But is he heartless? And what kind of child would think that their father might eat them? Are they already accustomed to sacrificing themselves to his ambition? When they have died and he is near the end, he remarks that hunger became more powerful than grief. Is he hinting that he tried to eat them to save himself? It's not clear.

The bitter irony is that there are reasonable grounds for pity in his sorry tale. The history shows that Ugolino was an ally of Ruggieri, and that Ruggieri betrayed him in one of the twists and turns of the Italian civil wars. And yet, what matters in the afterlife is not what people have done, but the inner state of their soul. Two individuals may act in precisely the same way, and their character could be completely different.

I think Dante is realizing that this is a place from which love has departed. The two brothers, in Caïne, hated each other and killed each other. They were driven by murderous rage, though at least it was a kind of passion. Ugolino feels differently. It is as if he barely realizes that his children exist as separate entities to him. He does say that he held back his tears so as not to upset them and, when they had died, he called out their names. But he seems to be using his children's suffering to win Dante's sympathy. Did he look on their bodies as collateral damage? Is it possible to read Ugolino's story and conclude that the love that might draw him back to God is gone from him? His story is not even tragic. It speaks of a soul in an emotional void and spiritual vacuum.

Ugolino returns to biting Ruggieri's skull. His teeth grind on bone like a dog's. Dante himself responds by cursing Pisa. After all, the so-called justice of the city locked up Ugolino and his innocent sons. Dante sees to the merciless heart of the story. He is implicitly recognizing that, dire as it was, the way in which Ugolino responded to his predicament was the moment he might have been transformed by compassion and become ready for heaven. Only there was no compassion in his soul, it appears. He was only ready for hell.

Virgil and Dante move more speedily, farther into Cocytus. They enter a third region called Tolomea, named after a Ptolemy. Commentators are unclear whether it is the Ptolemy who betrayed Pompey at the end of the war between Pompey and Caesar, or a Ptolemy of the Hebrew Bible, who had various members of his family killed while he ate dinner. Whoever it is, the psycho-spiritual temperature continues to drop.

They realize they have transitioned into a still chillier zone because the heads in the ice are looking up. Previously, the souls had been looking down or forward. This new position breaks necks and freezes tears in eye sockets.

Dante also realizes that he can feel a wind, which is a surprise because a breeze is usually a sign of life and spirit. That seems unlikely, and he asks Virgil about its source. Virgil tells him he will soon discover.

First, there is more to learn about the figures before them, and it turns out that they are the souls of the possessed. These individuals are in hell, though their bodies remain alive on earth, animated by demons.

One spiritual husk speaks. He is Friar Alberigo, another jovial friar, the fake followers of Saint Francis. Alberigo's luxurious life extended to entertaining a selection of his family to dinner, during which he called for figs. It was a signal for his private militia to kill his guests. They suffered bodily death, and he died eternal death.

The depth of that loss is implied because he can't tell that Dante is still alive. Life has left Alberigo and he can't detect it when it stands in front of him. He can still be manipulative, though. He tries to strike a deal with Dante. In return for removing the blocks of ice from his eyes, providing a temporary relief, he will tell Dante the story of another soul alongside him, a Florentine called Branca D'Oria. Branca is from Genoa. He murdered family members at dinner too.

Dante could have refused to trade on another's pain. However, Tolomea is affecting him and he agrees, with the added twist that when he has learned of Branca, he fails to fulfil his side of the bargain. Three times, Alberigo asks Dante to remove the ice. Three times Dante refuses. The number reminds Christians of the three times Saint Peter refused to acknowledge his friendship with Jesus. It is the treachery of the region. It is revealing the side of

Dante that can turn betrayer. He is becoming, at least in part, no better than Ugolino or Alberigo. Being close to the center of hell is one of the greatest moments of his life, and he is failing to respond in love.

This is a part of the universe from which love and forgiveness seem to have fled. There appears to be absolutely no chance of change. These figures are condemned as if there is no God. All is becoming frozen.

Dante closes canto 33 cursing the Genovese. He calls for a genocide to wipe them from the face of the earth. He can no longer see individuals and issues a blanket condemnation. He is almost at one with the empty spirit of bleakness.

Dante and Virgil face the fallen angel of light, before an astonishing turnaround.

INFERNO 34
Lucifer

ANTO 34 OPENS WITH VIRGIL MISQUOTING THE medieval hymn *Vexilla Regis*, which usually translates, "As the banners of the king come forth." It refers to the triumph of Jesus, but Virgil twists the meaning. He adds the word "inferno" at the end, so actually declares: "As the banners of the king of hell come forth."

The words are unnerving to hear, echoing across the icy lake. It brings a blasphemous feel to the start of the last canto of *The Inferno*. A mocking tone is suitable for these regions, though it is entirely possible to be possessed by it. They are surrounded by souls to whom this has happened.

The banners to which Virgil refers are the wings of the great body of Lucifer, although Lucifer doesn't move or come forth, so the amended hymn is, in fact, mocking Satan who thought he was triumphant. In other words, Virgil is not straightforwardly blaspheming and, further, he must understand what the original words meant in order to reframe them. He is gaining a feel for the Christian worldview and dispensation. He is changing.

Virgil invites Dante to look around and see what this final ring of Cocytus contains. Dante strains to do so. His eyes must adjust, along with his mental perception and spiritual nous. Remember, he is in a bad way.

He thinks he sees a windmill, as if through a distant fog. Windmills were a relatively novel feature of the medieval landscape, and my guess is that the sight of them was unsettling. They were machines that captured the wind and converted it into mechanical power, which is to say they took a phenomenon that conveyed spirit and breath and extracted brawn from it. Might that be blasphemous?

It is not that windmills were new in themselves. They had been around for centuries, and there are records of horizontal windmills in the ancient Greek world. What was new, however, was their spread, a product of the industrializing mindset that sought control of nature for material gain. A windmill in the countryside might, therefore, have felt devilish to Dante. Perhaps that is why one comes to his mind now.

As he looks, he feels gusts of wind coming from the direction of the supposed contraption. He shrinks back and seeks shelter behind Virgil. The wind is a kind of anti-breath or anti-spirit. It sucks the life out of the atmosphere, rather than being an expression of vitality. The emptiness is intimidating.

They are in the fourth and final region of Cocytus, called Giudecca. No souls speak here. They are completely buried in ice. As Dante looks down, he glimpses them, contorted, like as many sticks and twigs embedded in the frozen waste. They are only just not falling out of existence altogether.

These souls aren't the animated dead, whom Virgil and Dante encountered in Tolomea. They are shells of a long-lost life. Dante sees the imprint of their former vitality in the frozen landscape. Little wonder he is hiding behind Virgil, though his guide tells him that now is the time to see. He must summon all his courage to understand this place and know the final sights of hell.

It is time for Dante to meet the creature who was once so beautiful, Lucifer, the being of light. Virgil presents him by saying, "Behold Dis," "Dis" being the old word for Satan. The call to "Behold" echoes the phrase, "Behold the man," the phrase Pilate had used to present Jesus to the crowd before his Crucifixion. Virgil is asking whether the significance of this creature can be perceived and understood by Dante. Can he begin to grasp what he is about to look at?

Dante the poet, in his turn, addresses us readers. We too must use all our imagination to grasp what he is grappling with. Beings here are neither alive nor dead. They are suspended in an intermediate state that is neither one thing nor the other.

They draw closer to Lucifer. Dante helps us by describing his body in detail, as he had done with the bodies of the giants. The size of Lucifer is particularly emphasized. Dante says that proportionally, as he was to the giants, so the giants are to Satan, which puts Satan at about a thousand feet tall. He towers above Dante and the surface of the ice. He is a skyscraper in this empty zone, his massiveness reflecting the enormity of his demise.

It was the result of raising a brow to his maker, as Dante puts it. In an instance of pride, his inner nature was revealed, and he cut himself off from his wellspring, from his source, from divine life. And how great was that fall. Lucifer was the most beautiful of creatures. He was, in a way, closest to God.

The tragedy takes us to the heart of the message of canto 34. The huge risk and peril in any spiritual ascent is that as the soul rises, as it shines with more divine beauty, as it comes to greater knowledge of the divine, so increases the risk that the glory switches to pride, and the overweening desire to own and possess, not reflect and enjoy. It is why ascent must be constantly accompanied by descent, in the sense of understanding and letting go of what might cause the soul to tumble. It's why Dante must visit this pit. There is no farther place to fall into. He must see it so as to grasp the nature of the pride that will accompany him as he takes the path to heaven because it is in him. The more he rises, the more useful it will be to recall Lucifer, the frozen creature of light.

Dante continues to describe Satan's appearance. He is taking in the sight. Lucifer has six wings, which means that he was one of the Seraphim who sing around the throne of God, held by love, enjoying the divine vision face to face. The fallen wings are the cause of the infernal wind. They beat like the mouth of a dead fish, head severed, abandoned on the dockside.

Lucifer has three faces — one yellow, one black, one red — that are at right angles to each other. Dante is amazed that down here, Satan hideously mirrors something of the trinitarian energy of God, the three persons in heaven who are constantly breathing life and love to each other. What was a sharing of love and vitality has become ice in Lucifer's face, a face that doesn't speak. It is immobile, only managing blindly, instinctively to chew on three souls, one in each maw.

This takes us to another level of symbolism, another aspect that this view might communicate to us, because the names of the souls Dante sees in Lucifer's mouth are Judas Iscariot, the betrayer of Jesus, and Brutus and

Cassius, the betrayers of Julius Caesar. Judas is head-first in the red face and is being raked down his back. Cassius and Brutus are in the side faces: feet-first for Cassius in the yellow face; Brutus similarly, in the black face.

Commentators have spilt much ink discussing the symbolism. I think it is good not to tie it down too fast, so that the imagery can live. Maybe Judas, Cassius, and Brutus are devilish echoes of Mary, Lucia, and Beatrice, the three heavenly ladies. If Mary said "Yes" to God, Judas said "no." If Lucia shines with divine light, Brutus in the black face shares the darkness of Satan. If Beatrice is love, then Cassius is in the yellow face of envy, malice, and hatred.

It is instructive to recall that these individuals were the friends of those they betrayed. Judas, in particular, is so fascinating because he was the great friend of Jesus. How else could he have approached him in the garden of Gethsemane and kissed him? Judas must have been a great souled person. He must have understood much of Jesus's mission to become so close. He must have shared something of Christ's consciousness. He must have anticipated the meaning of the kingdom, before he fell so far: if he had not, he could not have fallen so far. He is like Lucifer in that if Lucifer had been close to God, Judas was to Jesus; whereas Lucifer had raised a brow to God, Judas had shared the bread at the Last Supper so that Satan entered into him, as John's Gospel puts it. In that moment, there was no one closer to Jesus, no one who had farther to plummet.

Perhaps he put the cause he felt Jesus stood for above the person Jesus was? Or maybe Judas hadn't fully understood that in order to receive heavenly life, the individual must die to himself. That thwarts pride and makes space for more life than mortal life can comprehend. It is why sacrifice has a priority in spiritual life. It lets go to let in.

That is a clue as to what happens next, which is utterly astonishing.

Virgil tells Dante that they have seen it all, it is time to move from this place, and they begin an extraordinary turnaround. It happens as they reach the deepest, darkest moment. Death, even eternal death, is the gateway to life, eternal life. Hell is a realm in which occur what Carl Jung called enantiodromia, "opposite courses."

Dante is, firstly, picked up by Virgil. Dante clasps his neck and Virgil waits for the moment when the six wings move so that they can come right up to the side of Lucifer's shanks. Then, they cling to the fur and climb through a gap in the ice, right alongside Lucifer's body. It is remarkable. By following the emptiness to its nadir, they find the first steps of a pathway out.

Dante can only cling to Virgil. He must follow in faith. He cannot yet understand. It is too unexpected, too bizarre. Then again, he has built enough trust in his guide and their journey, in their descent to this point, to know that when Virgil says hold tight, he must do so, physically and spiritually.

It is a moment of metanoia akin to when winter becomes spring, darkness light, despair joy. It's a feature of the inner life of the cosmos and the psyche that, when lost in the shade, is almost impossible to imagine. Except it happens. It seems to be a feature of the universe, as it is for Dante and Virgil.

They climb down and then, suddenly, Dante realizes they are climbing up. The satanic feet that he had been expecting to see pointing down, are sticking up. They have entered an antechamber in the ice.

Dante is shocked. He thought they were descending, only they are ascending. The former has been his overt experience so far. Virgil explains that they have passed through the ontological center of the cosmos and so, having followed gravity to its null point, they can track levity to its high point.

Virgil describes the myth of Lucifer's fall to explain things further: how he had crashed from heaven, toward the earth, which was repelled by the celestial antimatter, and rushed away before the fallen angel as he fell. It forged the great hole that is hell, with the escaping matter rising up on the other side of the earth, to form a mountain. This is purgatory, which they will climb.

It is a magical moment in The Divine Comedy. The promise of light. The leap of the heart. It will never again be so bad. Further, if Dante has come to realize that evil is the absence of good, he can also detect how death is the absence of life: life makes space for death, and so still holds it, as good holds evil, as the reversal has just showed. Good contains evil, life contains death, as hell is contained in the earth. Nothing can ultimately destroy life, therefore, or what is good.

They stand in the antechamber within which everything changes. Virgil asks Dante whether he can hear the sound of a stream. It will be their guide back to the surface of the earth. It has made its way through the hard rocks and cut a path back up.

They set out along the hidden track. They do not rest during the climb. They are drawn by the promise of light and life. And sure enough, close to the surface, Dante sees a crack in the rocks through which he glimpses the sky. He spots the beautiful things of the heavens. Once more, he observes the stars.

The Inferno ends with the same word as The Purgatorio and The Paradiso: stars. It is one of the most quietly lovely moments in the entire Divine Comedy. It's a moment to pause, to feel ease, to reconnect with hope and vitality.

It is also the start of another journey, for which this one has been a mighty preparation.

II

Purgatorio

Virgil and Dante are in a world of sunlight and stars, strangeness and novelty.

PURGATORIO I

Dawn

IRGIL AND DANTE ARE IN PURGATORY, AND canto I immediately signals what a different world this is. The grey atmosphere of hell is behind them. They are in a domain of blues and greens, soft winds and soils. This is a place of life once more. Dante remarks that his little bark, which is to say the craft of his poetry, will now venture to sail across fresh waters. They are fresh because different, though also because not frozen as was the ice of Cocytus. The sails of his verse will strive to catch the winds that carry the spirit of this region of vitality.

He calls on the muse, Calliope, for assistance. She is significant as the greatest of the nine muses who help humans by converting what's going on into music and words, though Dante adds an interesting detail to his invocation. He recalls Paris, a king of Macedonia who had nine daughters, whom he named after the muses. He then challenged the muses to a competition, sure that his offspring's abilities could exceed the talents of the deities. He was wrong, of course. Dante seems to be suggesting that he doesn't want to steal what rightfully belongs to the gods, but instead to be open to their assistance in order to share in, and know, divine glories for himself.

He tells us that this section of his story will be about the purging of people's souls to make them ready for paradise. It's worth reflecting on what he meant by purging because the word carries misleading associations. It can mean the tendency to be rid of, to expel, to reject. However, Dante's purpose is to become open to life, embracing it all, not to split off aspects of life. Not doing that was a large part of the reason he had to journey through hell, so the kind of purging he is introducing is about dismantling the barriers that hinder the conscious incorporation of the whole of life into the soul.

Purging to exclude is a fool's game. It never works because it fosters a life that must become increasingly vigilant against what is not wanted. It therefore limits life and closes it down. It holds people back as they try to inhabit spaces that are deemed free of what's not wanted or liked. The upshot is to lock individuals in forms of hell. As Dante now knows, much of what sustains that state of being is the attitudes of rage, hate, deviousness, and envy that narrow preoccupations, leaving souls unable to change. They are held fast by a fear of life.

Purgatory, though, is about removing the defenses that attempt such exclusions. The past is confronted. The future is embraced. The habits and character traits that leave people unfree are challenged. The aim is release from what holds souls back, which is precisely the opposite of trying to avoid things. Purgatory is about the cultivation of virtues that expand the soul. It is about the elimination of vices that compress hearts.

It is a beautiful early morning. In fact, it is Easter Sunday morning. You will recall that Dante awoke to find himself lost in the dark woods on Good Friday. He has travelled through hell in a journey that parallels Jesus's harrowing of hell: his sight of it has freed him from it. Now, it's about an hour before dawn and what a tremendous sunrise it is going to be.

The sun is allowing her rosy fingers to reach toward the horizon. Just beginning to lighten up the night sky, Venus is shining brightly as the morning star, heralding the sun, and making the dawn smile. It's a brilliant image because if you've ever experienced that hour before dawn, you immediately know the potential and possibility it promises.

The heavens are evoked because they have returned to Dante's consciousness as the clear destination of his pilgrimage. From now on, they will always be in view, no matter how hard things become. And purgatory is difficult to navigate. It takes many souls hundreds of years, which is to say they must search into the deepest recesses of their hearts to make it through. However, they do so in a place that never ceases to speak of God's goodness.

This is not a zone haunted by the freeze of non-being. It is a place of hope. It sparkles, reflects, and knows the divine life.

The invitation to us readers, while on earth, is to develop the habit of looking up and looking out. It is there during the night, with the shining of the stars. It is there during the day, in the light of the sun. The symbols of life, which are themselves alive, surround us.

Staying in touch with that reality is about feeling into the world, not just relating to it as if it were mechanical and soulless. The imaginative quality of such a felt engagement is indicated by a detail in Dante's description. He has said that Venus is a morning star, although Venus was an evening star on Easter Sunday in the year 1300. The planet followed the sun's setting that year; it didn't lead its rising. It looks like an error, though I think Dante would have known this. He was clearly very observant of the heavens. So, by seeing Venus as the morning star, he is inviting us to see the world in the light of hope, not just empirical observation. He is nudging toward awakening spiritual perception, which is a large part of the task in purgatory. You might go so far as to say that it is truer to describe Venus as a morning star as he arrives in purgatory, because Venus the celestial presence heralds the light of the sunrise which, in his heart, he is about to encounter. Part of the purging of purgatory has to do with lifeless assumptions. They hold us to a flat-world version of reality when they exclude the liveliness that animates all things. But the journey through purgatory is going to enable Dante increasingly to transcend the perceptions of mortal life and see with the eyes of immortality.

Another detail Dante notices in the predawn sky is the four stars of the constellation known as the Southern Cross. On earth it is observable in the southern hemisphere, which is where Dante finds himself in his psycho-physical geography, having travelled through the middle of the earth, which is where hell is mythically located. It is with this mentality that he sees the Southern Cross. It is above him not because he is literally on the other side of the globe but because his journey has reconnected him with the four virtues, of which the four stars of the constellation speak. The stars of justice, wisdom, temperance, and courage shine because they are going to help guide him hereon. He must see them in his soul, so they appear to him in the sky, as a prompt.

There is a person standing nearby, Dante notices, and the figure is not someone he would remotely expect to meet. As if to stress how this part of the journey is about perceptual expansion, he recognizes Cato, a pre-Christian Roman Stoic, best known for the suicide he committed to prevent his ignoble capture by Caesar during the Roman civil wars.

He stands before Virgil and Dante as the very embodiment of purgatory. He is an ancient man with a long beard that streaks white as it divides across his shoulders. He carries a natural wisdom and authority, and Dante notices that the four stars, the four virtues, shine in his face as if he and the stars were one. There is a foretaste of the approaching sun's light in his countenance, which is symbolically a way of associating Cato's soul with the light of Christ who, like the sun, rose on this particular morning.

So, why is Cato, the pagan, welcoming them? What is Dante, the Christian, intimating by this surprising, even shocking, visitation?

A clue is found in Cato's suicide. It is a different type from that encountered so far. It is unlike Dido's, for love, and unlike those who were in the wood of the suicides, who killed themselves out of revenge, rage, and despair. Stoics deemed suicide ethical when it enabled the individual to stay aligned with the divine pulse that they detected running through the cosmos, which they called the Logos. A Stoic sage like Cato would sense that his life had reached a stage when he would be better able to resonate with this vitality by dying. He would judge that sacrificing his mortal life was required to stay in touch with divine life.

The implication is that Cato's suicide was akin to Jesus's death on the Cross, as Jesus also sacrificed his life to stay aligned with divine, rather than be led by worldly concerns. When Jesus stood before Pilate he told the Roman governor that his kingdom was not of this world. Cato, like Jesus, had realized that the life in which he could live fully and freely implied being free to leave mortal life.

Cato shines with the light of the sun because his life is illuminated by the same light as that of Jesus. Pagans can know at least something of Christ, and find themselves in purgatory, which of course is now true of Virgil as well. He had travelled through hell before, though he had not emerged on the other side. Dante is, I think, suggesting his journey not only expanded his own spiritual sight but that of his companion.

That said, it is clear that Cato doesn't fully understand the life of God. He is at the foot of Mount Purgatory, which is to say that he has yet to become fully conscious of all that it means for him and the cosmos.

Further, Cato is shocked when he sees Dante and Virgil emerge from hell. He saw them climbing out of the crevice cut by the river that flowed into the earth, and he has seen nothing like that before. He had not realized that God allows such journeys to be made. He wonders if this presages a change in divine ways.

Virgil steps forward and tells Dante that they must honor Cato. They kneel before him and, having bowed, Virgil speaks. He has the wisdom to know that they need the blessing of this venerable figure, and he tells Cato that Dante, a mortal soul, is here by divine blessing, which is to say that if the rules are changing, they are doing so with heavenly, not hellish, sanction. He, Virgil, has been released from the bondage of limbo to travel into purgatory as well.

Virgil's words sound almost like a prophecy, raising the question of whether the pilgrimage is as much to do with his salvation as Dante's.

He continues, telling the Stoic that, in limbo, he knew Cato's wife, Marcia, and he implores Cato, by the love of Marcia, to be kind to them. The invocation of love appears to help Cato because he says that he will offer them his blessing, as the visitors seem to herald a new law. It is the law of love, which he knew of in his marriage, though not in his stoicism: stoicism offered a deterministic understanding of reality, not one shaped by the freedom that comes with the forgiveness, desire, and creativity of relationships. Cato had assumed that necessity trumped affection in the cosmos, though he is reconsidering that, as he stands before Virgil and Dante.

He tells them what to do next. They must go to the lowest part of purgatory, which is by the sea. They must begin there, as an act of humility. Much as everything flows into the sea because it is in the lowest place, so they must start from the lowest place so that everything can flow into them, thereby ensuring that they are open to all of life, human and divine.

They will find a reed bed by the sea, Cato continues, and Dante must pluck a reed and make a new belt from it. Their journey through purgatory can then proceed, by following the sun, which will have risen.

The sage disappears. Dante and Virgil stand up and make their way toward the seashore. They seem relatively lonely as they walk. Purgatory has its joys but is a place of sadness and struggle as well. It embraces a range of emotions, if always within the context of change and hope.

They find the seashore and the reeds. Virgil plucks one, and immediately a new reed sprouts up in its place. This is a domain in which life cannot be suppressed.

Virgil washes Dante's face. Cato had told him that the grime of hell must be removed from the pilgrim so that his vision of purgatory is unimpeded.

The canto ends with a final allusion. Dante recalls how Ulysses had not made it to land when he had tried to sail to purgatory but had been consumed by the whirlpool and carried to hell. The implication is that Dante has reached purgatory and is ready to go farther.

For us readers, the first canto of The Purgatorio brings an air of expectation. Their first hour beneath the skies is beautiful, marked by tenderness and love. But there is also much that, as yet, remains unclear, possibly alarming. Fresh discoveries await us as well, as Dante sets his bark to traverse fresh waters.

The sun rises and an angel, with a boat of souls, speeds to them.

PURGATORIO 2

Sunrise

T IS THE BLUE HOUR BEFORE DAWN AND THE HORIzon begins to glow. Aurora, one of the sun's most enchanting names given to the orb at dawn, is casting her golden rays in flashes across the heavens.

It speaks to Dante of the cosmos as a whole. He thinks of Jerusalem that, in his mythical geography, is on the other side of the globe from where he and Virgil stand. He recalls the Ganges to the east, and the Pillars of Hercules that flank the Strait of Gibraltar to the west. The whole of earth's expanse, and human activity, comes to his mind as the sun rises. The earth turns. He sees the stars as if falling from the night sky.

It is an elaborate description of the moment. What is Dante the poet trying to convey?

My intuition is that he is evoking the felt presence of the forces with which the pilgrims must begin to contend. Unlike hell, the life of purgatory is essentially good. It is lit with the light of the sun and stars. But it can be bewildering, tough, fearsome. Dante's description of the sunrise, evoking the whole of heaven, from the north, south, east, and west, is a way of conjuring up the sense that there is no let up on the extent to which they must engage with wonderful and tremendous things.

It is part of our calling as human beings. We can become more conscious of life, though to do so, we must ourselves change. We can learn to see not only a beautiful sunrise, but spiritual light and otherworldly darkness racing across the skies. Understanding what that means for themselves and the world is Dante and Virgil's next task.

They don't know how to tackle it, yet. Their thoughts run ahead of them as they watch the indigo skies lighten. They stand stock still by the edge of the sea, confused as much as enchanted, wondering about the road that lies ahead.

Then, Dante notices a light coming from the west, the opposite side of the sky from the emerging sun. It reminds him of red Mars straining through a morning mist, though as they gaze mesmerized, they realize it is moving at great speed across the water toward them. It nears, and its light whitens. As it comes closer still, Dante makes out its shape. It is an angel.

The last time they saw an angel was outside the city of Dis. There, they felt the power and ferocity of these heavenly presences. And perhaps the memory of that shock jolts Virgil, because he comes to his senses. He tells Dante to drop to his knees. "It is the angel of the Lord!" he exclaims.

The light grows so bright that Dante can't look at the angel directly. He must protect his eyes and so he bows his head. The act is one that he will perform repeatedly in purgatory and paradise, as he becomes accustomed to the brilliance of divine light, as he learns how to see it.

He manages to spot a detail. The angel is not alone. It is perched on the stern of a boat, its intelligence and will causing the craft to move across the sea more swiftly than would be possible if it were powered by sail or oars. The boat is a ferry and is packed with more than a hundred souls, although the busy vessel makes no impression on the waves. It is as if it were without weight.

Life in purgatory often feels like life on earth. People struggle in both places. They suffer and wrestle with their faults. But, repeatedly, it is clear that purgatory is a different dimension of reality. Angels appear. People relate differently to the elements: they cast no shadows and make no impression on water. The reality of purgatory is an expansion of the reality known on earth. Learning how to see and understand that wider existence is another part of the task Dante faces.

The boat lands and they hear the souls singing. They are chanting a hymn, Psalm 114, which speaks of Israel being led out of Egypt. It also sings of vitalities that can be missed or ill-discerned. It tells of nature springing into life when Israel walked out of Egypt. The seas saw the people coming and fled from their path. The River Jordan was driven back, mountains leapt like rams, and the little hills skipped like lambs. The presence of God turned rocks into water and flints into fountains. There was a glorious, unsettling turbulence.

The psalm captures an appropriate mood. It is hard to keep a grip on what is happening. The sense of confusion deepens because, as soon as all the souls are off the boat, the angel blesses them, turns around, and speeds back in the same direction from whence it had come. Angels, it seems, never hang around. They are always on a mission.

Dante and Virgil look at the souls. They are wandering around, wondering what is happening. They see Dante and Virgil and, not unreasonably, ask for advice. What should they do? Where should they go? Virgil confesses that they arrived only a short while before them. They are pilgrims too.

As an aside, calling himself a pilgrim is a striking self-description from Virgil. Remember that he has not been to purgatory before. Consciously, he assumes that his place in eternity is fixed, in limbo. His journeys through hell have been the exception, not the rule. Only now, it slips out that he is on a pilgrimage, a journey defined by leading to a different inner, as well as outer, destination. I think he is clearly, if unwittingly, speaking prophetically. If Dante is finding his way to heaven, Virgil is beginning to find his way out of hell.

He tells the aimless souls that the journey through purgatory is going to seem like child's play compared with the journey they have undertaken, through hell. It makes us wonder how he knows that. He is beginning to discern truths of the Christian dispensation that, in his mortal life, he knew nothing of at all.

The souls turn to Dante and see he is breathing. He has a body. They turn pale in wonder, quite as confused by Dante as Dante had been by their arrival. Everyone on the seashore feels hopeful and intrepid.

Then, the sense of promise seizes the souls en masse and, all at once, they rush toward Dante. His embodied presence is some kind of miracle. He must, therefore, be a token of good news. Their movement makes me think that, unlike the souls in hell who also regularly noticed Dante's mortal form, the souls in purgatory are able to react to it with hope, even if their reaction is somewhat misplaced.

One of the souls elbows his way to the front. He approaches Dante and the two recognize each other. This individual is a great friend of Dante, called Casella. Not much is known about him apart from what Dante tells us, but it is clear from The Divine Comedy that he was a musician who had set some of Dante's words to music.

The scene is heart-warming. They share their joy at reconnecting. Neither had expected to do so this way, in the afterlife. However, the reunion carries a shadow because three times Dante reaches out and tries to hug Casella, as he would have done in Florence, and three times his arms fail to hold his friend. Casella explains that he is dead. He is a spiritual body. Things have changed.

Dante knew that his friend had died. His passing happened three months before Dante found himself in the dark woods. So, he asks, why has it taken Casella all that time to get to purgatory? Casella's reply is fascinating. He had struggled to leave mortal life. After his death he went to Ostia, which is the Roman port by the sea, and the departure point for those who have passed over. That much made sense to him because seaports are always places to embark on journeys. However, when the angel and the ferry repeatedly arrived to pick him up, he wasn't able to board. It took him three months to be able to do so.

My sense is that this is the time it took Casella fully to realize that he had died. The experience chimes with the ghosts that resist death, for one reason or another, hoping not to have to leave behind the life they knew. It might be that ties of hatred, revenge, or jealousy bind people to their earthly lives. It might be that life has been good, and too lovely to let go.

This seems to be so in Casella's case because he next volunteers to sing one of the songs he wrote to Dante's lyric, "Love that speaks to me in my mind." The friends share the joy at the prospect of the melody, though Casella wonders whether he is allowed to sing it in this place. Are there laws in operation of which they are not aware?

His nervousness is illuminating. It is as if he senses that if any song were to be sung, it should be one about love. That chimes with the atmosphere of purgatory. But, as the commentators note, the lines Casella suggests are ones Dante wrote out of love of philosophy. But what kind of philosophy can guide them here? Might invoking the wrong sort mislead them?

The song seems like a good idea, and the souls are settled by the sound. Delight fills the air. Only the mood is suddenly disrupted. Cato springs into view once more and chastises the company for becoming lost in the music. They look as if they are here only to find pleasure, he remarks, and there is much more they must seek if they are to find their way through purgatory.

Cato still has a foot in the old pre-Christian world, for all that he treads the soils of purgatory. He is not sure how purgatory operates. But he is right insofar as purgatory is not primarily about bliss. That is to come, and first they must be made ready for higher delights.

And so, the canto ends on a down beat. Casella must learn to let go. His longing for quick happiness could trap him on the shores of purgatory, as it did at the docks of Ostia. There are amazing sights and sounds to come, but the souls must learn not to seek satisfaction in lesser joys. Nostalgia will not help. Cato knows that much, and the force of his challenge returns the fear of God to the assembly. The music stops and with that, the newly arrived souls scatter like pigeons.

Dante is reminded that if he is no longer in hell, he has not returned to life on earth.

Virgil is troubled. They encounter souls moving very slowly.

PURGATORIO 3

Delay

THE SOULS ON THE SEASHORE OF PURGATORY
have scattered like startled pigeons. Cato has alarmed them and
yanked them from their reverie at Casella's song. Dante sticks
close to Virgil. He knows he needs his human god and comforter, he tells us.

The opening sets up an intriguing canto that is focused particularly on
Virgil. It is also controversial. Many of the commentators remark that in it,
Virgil's undoing begins. He starts to realize that his old philosophy cannot
find the way to paradise. It dawns on him just how different the Christian
worldview is from the one he knows. That adds up to him recognizing his
eternal destiny in the darkness. It raises the question of whether he, like
Dante, is saved? The general assumption is that he is not.

Those commentators who take this line portray Virgil as an increasingly
pathetic figure in *The Purgatorio*. But I sense the opposite. I think Virgil really
is entering purgatory, body and soul. What might be thought pathetic, I
detect is lament. He is distressed that what he thought he knew about life,

160

the universe, and the divine is wrong. That makes him anxious for his future. They are difficult feelings to embrace. But that is what purgatory is all about. It is about the kind of suffering that makes for change. He must become uncoupled from the wisdom of the pre-Christian centuries, and that is asking much.

It would make him into a new person, a different kind of poet. Cato has already intimated the type of novelty he must let in. The old sense of the divine Logos as a tendency or fate must give way to the law of love, one based on relationship, desire, fulfilment, light.

That Virgil can change, for all the worry he feels, is signaled by Dante's drawing close. If Virgil was not already becoming capable of more, the Christianity of Dante the pilgrim would already be proving more reliable in this place. Dante knows a lot about love, in particular how it can guide the mind as well as the heart. And yet, it is clear that they are bound together on this next stage of the journey quite as much as they were in hell. To my mind, it is becoming clearer that if the subterranean experience was one that challenged Virgil, this next one could transform him.

That is indicated right at the beginning of canto 3 because Dante notices that his guide is feeling ashamed of not realizing that Casella's song was a mistake. If he didn't have an intimation as to why that is so, he would not feel shame but simply bewilderment. He knows a different philosophy is required. He longs for it, with the longing that is, in fact, a key element of the philosophy of love. It is already growing within him.

He quickly recovers from his shame and steps forward with his usual unhasty stride, Dante notices, as he simultaneously becomes more aware of the height of Mount Purgatory and bemused by the prospect of the climb. Virgil comforts his charge, taking responsibility for the state they are in. He is not lost in shame or resentment, as souls in hell are. He is preparing himself for the huge effort that will be asked of them. That effort must arise from his heart, and his heart is ready for it. These are not the actions of a soul resigned to his fate, but the movements of a soul who dares to hope for more.

He tells Dante that time is of the essence, by which he means that they must stay focused, allowing every experience to seep into them, educating them. They must reflect on what is happening together.

That many commentators do not see Virgil changing like Dante stems, I think, from lacking an eye for spiritual transformation. Scholars can be very sophisticated and nuanced about Dante the poet, Dante the historical figure, Dante the Renaissance genius. But Dante's brilliance lies in his ability to show the conversion he and Virgil underwent. In this place of supernatural vitalities, some terrifying, some electrifying, the dramatis personae evolve as well. No one is a static cypher, least of all Virgil, for all that those in hell are hideously stuck. Part of the joy of reading The Divine Comedy is spotting the inner shifts. They can catalyze inner shifts in us as well, if we are open to them.

The sun has continued to ascend the sky. It doesn't stop in its divine task and has begun to cast shadows. Dante notices his and the way it reaches toward the high mountain. And then he jumps. There is no second shadow besides his. Where is Virgil, who he thought was nearby?

Dante has not noted that the other souls were surprised at his physical body, and that he is different from the dead. Virgil explains that he too has the diaphanous presence of a living soul. He speaks of his tomb on earth, and how it was moved from Brindisi where he died, to Naples, at Caesar Augustus's command. He appears to be gently grieving over his body, which is another significant detail. Grief will prove to be one of the key emotions in purgatory. It is one that precipitates change.

The spiritual body that Virgil has in the afterlife can be thought of as the body closest to felt experience. Medieval and ancient philosophers assumed that humans have several bodies, the physical one being only the most tangible and manifest. Within and through it, animating it, is the soul or subtle body. Virgil tells Dante that this spirit is made of the same substance as the light that shines from the sun. It shares in that vitality, which is why the brightness passes through his body, casting no shadow. It can transmit the light because, unlike the physical body, it is closer in nature to light. You might say that soul and light are of the same essence, when viewed with spiritual eyes, much as breath and spirit reveal themselves to be.

The sun nudges up farther. Dante's worry about bodies and shadows subsides. They arrive at the foot of the mountain, which is a cliff, and are confronted by its sheer steepness. They have no idea how they might begin to ascend.

Then, coming from afar off, another group of souls approaches. They are moving slowing. They look like a meandering flock of sheep. As one person takes half a step forward, those behind follow in the same direction. They appear leaderless, directionless, unthinking.

Dante and Virgil decide to walk toward the shuffling group, hoping for advice on climbing the mountain. The souls see the two approaching and look up, spotting that Dante casts a shadow. One of them steps forward, asking why Dante doesn't recognize him.

He is Manfred, King of Sicily, and was famous in life. This is why he expects to be recognized by Virgil and Dante, though his pride is strikingly incongruous in purgatory.

He speaks about his family, or at least he speaks about one side of his family. To Dante's first readers, it would have been obvious that Manfred was referencing his lineage through his grandmother, which was the noble and glorious heritage he claimed. He continues, asking Dante to request the prayers of his daughter when he returns to earth. She is the mother of queens. Manfred believes that her royal prayers will be efficacious. What he seems unable to do is claim responsibility for all of his life. Unlike Virgil, he is not able to lament and grieve the whole of his lot, but instead picks and choses, as if to gloss over a darker side. The shadow he doesn't want to own is that he was the illegitimate son of Frederick II, the emperor, and spent his life struggling to hold onto his crown. Manfred wants to purge his life in the wrong way, to be rid of the parts he doesn't want.

In life, his discontent produced much ugliness. He killed several members of his family in various attempts to secure power. That led to him being excommunicated, and his body being abused after his death, in marked contrast to the way Virgil's body was honored. That he is in purgatory would have been a surprise to Dante's contemporaries.

Manfred explains that he is here and not in hell because, as he was dying, he turned to God. He thereby received forgiveness and salvation, which is a seeming confirmation of the medieval conviction that what matters for the afterlife is the attitude of the soul at the moment of death. However, this is another case in which we should be wary of what souls tell us. Manfred may be saved but he is lost on the foothills of purgatory. He hardly understands anything, and so the explanation he offers should not be taken as gospel. Quite the opposite. I think Dante is using his encounter with Manfred to question the magical belief that last-minute conversions lead to everlasting life.

In her commentary on Manfred, Helen Luke recalls the line of T. S. Eliot, that the time of death is every moment. I think this is the spiritual significance of deathbed conversions. To the enlightened, every moment is an opportunity to let go and pass on into new life. Every moment is a kind of death, and so the chance to step into more life. Manfred may understand his predicament via Church formularies. But, in truth, he has everything still to learn.

Dante has everything still to learn as well, though he is in a different relationship to ignorance. Unlike the former king's pride, Dante displays humility by apologizing to Manfred for not recognizing him. Virgil continues, explaining to the souls that Dante is here in his body because he has the blessing of heaven. It puts the souls at their ease. The mention of heaven is good news to them, not bad, as it had been for the souls in hell.

In return, they display some humility and generosity by offering Dante and Virgil what little they do know. There is an entry up the mountain a little way behind them, the group indicates. They have passed it in their drifting.

The canto offers us a feel for purgatory. It contains sadness, anxiety, displays of pride and ignorance, but also an early sense that there is a way forward and things can be understood. This latter element is shown particularly by Virgil. Death can lead to new life. Maybe even those seemingly condemned to eternal death can walk the paths that lead to eternal life.

Finding a narrow path, they begin to climb.

PURGATORIO 4

Di∫tra¢tions

RIDE ADVANCES NO ONE IN PURGATORY, MAN-
fred has yet to learn, though his story engrosses Dante. Upon reflection, Dante the poet realizes that their meeting spoke to him about
the danger of distractions. They can preoccupy people throughout their lives.

It leads to a reflection on the nature of the human psyche, and Dante's
analysis that, contra Aristotle, human beings have one, not three, souls.
This might seem like an unnecessarily esoteric question to turn to right
now, though it carries practical importance.

Aristotle had argued that human beings have three souls, by which he
meant three distinctive capacities in life. The first is shared with plants and

can be thought of as the sheer desire for life. The second is shared with other animals and can be thought of as making choices about the type of life pursued. This is the inner meaning of the observation that plants tend to reach out from one place, whereas animals move around. The third soul, Aristotle said, is the capacity humans have for imagining different futures. Unlike other creatures we not only react and respond to the present but anticipate and build the future.

Along with other Christian philosophers, Dante concluded that humans have one soul. This unity points to a capacity that Aristotle overlooked, or perhaps was not available to him at the time: the ability to integrate inner life. I think that explains why polytheism dominated the ancient world. Back then, the many gods of the universe reflected the parts of human interiority that were felt similarly to be various. Polytheists looked to make sense of their lives by relating to these many gods, whereas monotheists, who became dominant around the Mediterranean with the emergence of Christianity, looked to the one God as a unified ground for an inner life that, simultaneously, became one.

Put it like this. Following the insights of Owen Barfield, I think that one of the most significant innovations that came with Christianity was the ability to say "I am" in a way that individuals in the ancient world never quite could. The new religion fostered a sense of being human that included qualities which we take for granted, like autonomy, free will, and personal responsibility. The shift is connected to the emergence of monotheism: when human beings could know themselves as individual, at least in principle, they could perceive that beneath and within all the diversity of the cosmos lay a divine reality that is singular too.

This matters in purgatory, whose main function is to redirect misdirected souls. It is the basis for redemption, namely that souls can be wholly redirected into divine life, and it also explains distractions: a whole person might become preoccupied by trivia, and therefore become divided within himself. Manfred has not begun to detect the preoccupations from which he must wean himself. He loves to marvel at part of himself. He must learn to marvel at the whole of himself if he is to enjoy the life of God.

The shallows of the self that absorb Manfred are exposed because, when Virgil and Dante find the entry onto the mountainside, they leave the king to his pride without by your leave.

The cut through the cliffs is narrow. It is a tight squeeze. Dante says that they could easily have missed it, which no doubt is another reflection on how easy it is to be trapped in what you think you know about life, oblivious of the way to more. The present moment matters and if you become preoccupied with the past or future, perhaps seeking to bask in the reflected glory of relatives as Manfred does, you might never begin the climb to greater heights.

Dante and Virgil embark on the road less travelled. And it is steep. The path is angled at forty-five degrees and, quickly, Dante finds it almost too arduous. His physical body feels the pull of gravity, meant in both senses of the word: the weight of his material presence and the burden of his heavy soul. And the suffering stirs in him a fantasy about flying: if only he could sprout wings and, born by levity, glide up the mountain. The fantasy tortures him though it is also a prophecy. In time this is what he will become able to do. He will be capable of rising to the highest place. What seems hard will become second nature. It's another way in which descent and ascent are entwined.

Virgil is attentive and, as Dante reaches the exhaustion point, Virgil is able to encourage him. They push on, reach a ledge and, stopping for a rest, they notice something else.

Noticing is always good when you seek to change, and what they spot is that the sun is on their left. It strikes Dante because normally, in the morning of the northern hemisphere when looking north, the sun would be on the right. But they are in the southern hemisphere and the observation is a prompt to explore the felt strangeness of this unfamiliar zone.

They use the skies to reorient themselves, partly because they are so familiar with how they usually appear. The position of the sun, stars, moon, and planets can offer a profound way of feeling at home or feeling abroad. Virgil pipes up about the constellations and sings of their movements, if with a touch of wariness, because he also references Phaethon, the youthful son of Helios, who rode his father's chariot recklessly across the sky and was cursed by Jupiter. Care is required in foreign climes.

They climb and the steepness of the mountainside wears on Dante again. Caught up in the effort, he complains that he might not be able to make it. The peak looks too high, which elicits another insight from Virgil. He tells Dante that as they climb higher, the climbing becomes easier.

I wonder how Virgil knows that. He has not been here before. As a pagan, he is supposed to be ignorant of how purgatory works. But he is learning to trust purgatory and that means he is starting to gain a feel for its workings. The law of love and levity is making itself known to him and that can only happen, I think, because it is beginning to change him.

Virgil is able to tolerate the suffering of the climb because he knows that there is a goal, or end, to this suffering. It is another difference between purgatory and hell. In the latter, the suffering is intolerable not only because it is great but because there is conviction that it is without end. In the former, there is hope that can help souls push on to the end.

The two are absorbing the meaning of this truth, when their thoughts are interrupted by a voice. "You'll need to sit down before then," it interjects. They have reached the location of another group of souls, a little way up the mountain. They are called the souls of the indolent or lazy, and the encounter with them brings a personal element to the canto because, once again, Dante recognizes a friend from his former life, another musician.

He is a lute player called Belacqua and the two immediately start joshing with one another. "I'm glad you're here," Dante remarks, "because if you're here, I'll not have to worry about my ultimate fate." It's striking that the minute Dante encounters this friend, as when he encounters Casella, he is drawn into their mood. With Casella, it had been the desire for pleasure. With Belacqua, it is the jesting side of life. It is touching in one way, but in another, it suggests that Dante is readily swayed by those around him and that is not a wholly helpful virtue in purgatory.

Belacqua himself suggests that he has become concerned about more serious matters. He is changing, which is why he has made some small progress up the mountain. He tells Dante that he was a late penitent. He had been careless about the state of his soul for much of his life but reformed with time to spare — just.

Much as with Manfred's confession of conversion as he was dying, there is an insight in Belacqua's admission that runs deeper than the kind of religiosity which treats conversion as a spiritual transaction: as long as you get it in sometime, you get into the better place. You can hear Belacqua beginning to sense that he might have spent his mortal life preparing for eternity. Because he didn't, he finds himself on the lower slopes of purgatory, facing a long time of preparation. His soul is still pretty wedded to life's amusing trivialities, which will take a while to work through to make space for the true delights that are to come.

In the encounter he asks Dante what he really seeks in life. What joy do your choices really bring? Belacqua shows that he is trying to ask himself these things because he next tells Dante that the prayers of those who understand grace can aid him.

It's the second time we have encountered the conviction that the prayers of faithful people can lessen the time souls must spend in purgatory. There is a formulaic interpretation of this belief, as if the quantity of efficacious intercession correlates directly with the reduction of time in reform: more prayers, less penance. But it rather misses the point and, ironically enough, probably leads to more time in purgatory.

A better understanding is beginning to emerge, indicated by Belacqua's request differing from Manfred's. The king had requested prayers from his royal offspring, his appeal reflecting his grandiosity. Belacqua has asked for prayers from those whose hearts are aligned with heaven, indicating that his perception is more acute. It's not high and mighty prayers that make a difference, but prayers that will be loved by heaven.

Belacqua knows more about what's loved in heaven. It's why he's farther up the mountain and, in a virtuous spiral, is that little bit more able to align himself with what is loved in heaven as well. It's the reason why the climb up slowly but steadily becomes easier. He is better able to receive the grace of the prayers, even as he asks for better prayers.

The more general point is that what you pray for really matters. The prayer that is right is, in a way, already answered. And the way to ask for the right prayer is to be able to look into your soul. It's unclear whether Belacqua can yet do that, but he is on the way to being able to do so.

The canto comes to an end. Virgil encourages Dante some more. He doesn't want Dante to become lost in the seductive indolence of Belacqua, having only recently escaped the grandiosity of Manfred and the merriment of Casella. The sun is at the noon's zenith. They must push on.

Meeting agitated souls, they manage to keep a focus.

PURGATORIO 5

Distress

ANTO 5 IS CONFUSING. IT IS NOT OBVIOUS WHAT it is trying to say. And yet working out how to perceive its message is no incidental part of The Divine Comedy. It is key to the poem's transformative impact on us readers.

It's worth recalling that Dante explicitly wrote about his journey on a number of levels. This was standard practice in the medieval world, a time during which many people spontaneously experienced life's vitality at a number of levels. In common with others, Dante therefore explained that he deployed understandings that are literal, allegorical, tropological, and anagogic. The first, the literal level, explains itself. The allegorical presents the moral implications of encounters and events. The tropological level is the one that fosters the transformation of the individual, often as he wrestles to understand what is being explained. The last level, the ana-gogic, can be reached by human beings as a result of this process, when an understanding of life from the divine perspective comes into view. It comes after the conversion of perception fostered by the tropological struggle.

Dante explained this in a surviving letter written to a patron, by reflecting on the psalm that sings of Israel being led by Moses out of Egypt. The literal meaning is the exodus described as if an event in history. The allegorical meaning, from the Christian point of view, is that the story of Moses is a precursor to the action of Christ, who leads all people to the promised land: the Hebrew experience is a foretaste of the Christian experience. The tropological meaning emerges from reflecting on what it might mean to move from a world of slavery to one of freedom as fundamentally an inner liberation, in principle available to all. The anagogic reading perceives that this is not just an experience for the few, or the many, but for the entire creation, in the fullness of time.

The last is the widest ranging and the simplest meaning: there are no exceptions, no qualifications, no complications of the truth that all of life came from God and returns to God. How this happens is known fully only by God, *sub specie aeternitatis*, or from the perspective of eternity. It can be known to us more and more, if we journey across the various levels of meaning. With that possibility in mind, consider canto 5.

Dante and Virgil are walking away from Belacqua, when one of the shades in Belacqua's group calls out. The soul has noticed that Dante's body blocks the sun and so casts a shadow. Dante must be alive, the individual exclaims.

Dante turns around, though not for long, because Virgil immediately warns him against looking back. "What do you care for their whispering?" he says. "Let them talk, but keep strong and push on, with me." In other words, don't be like the indolent who are swaying this way and that with every gust of wind, rumor, or incident.

Dante is embarrassed. He blushes. Virgil the pagan appears to be learning faster than him, a Christian. This might be, in part, because Dante has first to unlearn what he assumes as a Christian, something Virgil doesn't have to do, having never been a Christian. Virgil is already in the tropological state of mind, having had to discard his literal and moral perceptions.

They do push on, leaving Belacqua and the others behind, and come across another group of souls. They are chanting Psalm 51, the *Miserere mei*: "Have mercy on me, O God." Dante only gives the title within the narrative of his poem, but the psalm is worth reading. It might have been sung by someone who doesn't know what God requires, or what the spiritual journey is about. The psalmist is at wits end and pleads to learn more. It's a sign of the state of the souls at this location on the mountain. They turn to Psalm 51 to give that expression.

They display qualities of uncertainty and distraction because as soon as they see Dante approaching, they stop to marvel that his body is blocking the sun, just like the group of which Belacqua was a part. Though they are also strikingly different. Their surprise at Dante's embodied presence unleashes a rampant energy. Much of the rest of the canto is filled with images of souls rushing hither and thither, requesting this and that. Dante the poet deploys metaphors of violence, meteors, storms, cavalry, and lightening to capture the activity.

These souls have agitated psyches. They don't know what they are doing, and their lack of focus brings out their inner confusion and distress. Virgil tells Dante that he can speak with them, but the two of them must simultaneously keep moving.

It's a significant instruction. It implies that, unlike the souls bustling around them, Dante must be able to keep focused on his aims, even while engaging with them. The encounter turns into an exercise in which he practices not losing touch with his will. He can exist in a world of distraction and not, himself, be distracted. It's a useful lesson.

It's also not easy. First, two of the souls rush up to the pilgrims. They cry out to Dante, the one with the mortal body. Then, they run back to their confreres, who about turn and move as a group toward Dante and Virgil. "Be careful," Virgil implores. "They will plead to be heard by you."

Three of them speak out. The first is not named in the canto, though commentators have identified him as a magistrate called Jacopo, who fell afoul of a superior and was brutally murdered. Jacopo recalls in grim, vivid detail how his eyes dimmed as he died, a pool of his blood spreading about around him. However, he remembered to call on God at the last moment, and so finds himself in purgatory.

A second soul butts in. He is Buonconte da Montefeltro, whose father, Guido, we have already met in hell. The father was the great military leader who turned Franciscan, and thought Saint Francis was coming to meet him as he died, only it turned out to be a demon. The son, Buonconte, knew a violent life and death as well, having expired with his throat cut. However, he murmured Mary's name before he perished, and so is saved. His body was then fought over by a demon and an angel. Buonconte takes pleasure in explaining at some length how the angel won his soul, though the demon caused his bodily remains to be carried into a swamp, then swept along a river in a storm, never to be found again.

Toward the end of the canto, a third soul materializes. The appearance is striking for its difference. First, she is a woman. Second, she doesn't say much. Third, what she does say is not violent but beautiful. She doesn't give her name, which has been identified as La Pia, though she does give a brief account of her sudden death. Her husband pushed her out of a high window.

What is beautiful about her words is that she is not preoccupied by the manner of her death, as the others are. Instead, she asks Dante to pray for her when he returns to earth, after he has recovered from his journey.

So, what are we to make of the three encounters? They can be understood in the four ways of medieval hermeneutics. There is the literal meaning, of individuals who met sudden deaths but managed to call on divine aid just in time. Allegorically speaking, their stories act as a warning: sudden death might meet you too. However, this reading portrays God as a mechanical deity, which I think Dante very much wants us to move beyond. That direction of travel is fostered as the character of the three souls seems to develop from the first to the third.

What that development might be about is revealed in the wish for prayers. This is the third time such a request has been made in The Purgatorio although, as some commentators note, it now happens in a different way, at least in the words used by La Pia. She recognizes Dante's journey, as well as her own. She knows that prayers aren't spells, which might magic you from one state to another, like a frog morphing into a prince. Rather, they can be sought because they aid an individual's transformation by helping him along the pathway that the transformation requires.

La Pia is, therefore, echoing to Dante the words spoken by Virgil when the souls first appeared. Listen to them, but don't be distracted by them, he said. Listen to me, but don't be distracted by me, she says. She is showing that she has learned more about the ways of purgatory than Jacopo and Buonconte. She can be aware of others and, at the same time, take responsibility for herself.

Other details in the canto suggest parallel developments of awareness. For example, Dante finds it hard to identify the souls, hence Jacopo and La Pia are not named, and Buonconte has to volunteer who he is. The difficulty in seeing them is a reflection of their distraction: they struggle to own their wills and so be clearly themselves. In the spiritual world of purgatory, that leaves them looking hazy around the edges. Further, what is true of their wills here was true of their wills in life. It's why they managed to turn to the light of heaven only in the last moments of their lives.

This thought leads to a third level of meaning, the tropological. In attending to his own way and responding to others, Dante is learning something of self-sacrifice. For example, the canto ends with the strong sense that

Dante will indeed pray for La Pia when he returns to earth. The act of recalling the incident in his poem is such an intercession. This is to say that he is working out how his journey can be fully his own and joined with the journey of others. He can be open to the concerns of others in a way that amplifies his own insights. It is the difference between a generosity that connects individuals, and the distraction that isolates because it cuts people off from themselves.

This immediately offers a glimpse of the anagogic view because God's awareness, love, desire, and will are like that. God is completely steady, self-possessed, and focused, and simultaneously able to overflow selflessly across the whole of creation.

I think this is the meaning of a canto that, on the surface, appears to be chaotic and rather literal-minded. It can be read as an exercise in tuning into the deeper currents beneath all the turbulence of violent deaths and pleas for prayers. Dante the poet is offering us an experience of what he experienced as a pilgrim, at this stage. We can enter into the transformative spirit of purgatory itself.

Bien ondel meni queci loppicissma
ce tuoi grenoli acum loi macigne
a medza icu fioi come si am.
Viena noer la mia wima de piunge
medzua sola adi a noce chiama
cesare mo pete noma compagne.

puo nieoim enii eba meco nouenbie
no giunge quel che tu cerobe fih.
Quance nolce cel cempo che rimebie
legge monera offao acostume
hai tu murato a innonare menbie.
Et se hen nicoidi anedi lume
medzai ce simighanrea qua recma.

Dante asks about prayers and divine law, as Virgil encounters a friend.

PURGATORIO 6

Lament

DANTE IS IMAGINING THE WINNER OF A DICE game surrounded by admirers. The loser carries no interest for the crowd and is left alone, while the winner tosses coins to keep the melee at bay, as if to satiate their desire for a share in the good fortune.

Why does this picture come to Dante's mind at the start of canto 6? Does he identify with the winner, as seems right at a first pass because this is how the souls are still treating him? They bother and cajole him with requests for prayers. Or does he feel he is really the loser because, as yet, he doesn't know how to win at this game of purgatory, prayers, and passage? Their enthusiasm and trust, as if he can make a difference, leave him feeling like a fraud.

Whether he feels like a winner or loser is left open, and I think he feels both sides. He is jangled by the souls crowding around and is wrestling to stay focused on his own path as he responds to their demands. The upside is that he feels the earnestness of the sinners, and so is open-hearted toward them. The downside is that he is not sure how to react to them, and so feels he risks merely tossing metaphorical coins.

Then again, he is honest about his confusion at the start of canto 6, an honesty that, in time, goes a long way in purgatory. And he is also honoring their suffering, in part by naming some of the souls who press eagerly toward him. Benincasa da Laterina, the Aretine. Federigo Novello. Count Orso. Pierre de la Brosse. There are many. They may be confused about why they are asking for his prayers, but the asking suggests their wills are re-aligning in a better direction.

The matter continues to rumble through the canto, as Dante and Virgil have a conversation about the meaning of prayerful requests. "Oh, my Light," Dante implores. "Didn't you once say prayers have no effect in heaven? Are these souls asking in vain?" Virgil replies that he did once write that very thing, though now he has a different view. He realizes he was mistaken. He understands that there is a principle of love, which is a more powerful dynamic in the cosmos than law or justice. Virgil is coming directly to know it. He feels it as the souls crowd around. He is changing.

He tells Dante that in ancient days, before Christianity, people prayed for the wrong things. They can pray for the wrong things still, of course. Doing so keeps people stuck because it simultaneously closes them to receiving that which can change everything. Virgil admits that Dante will have to wait until he meets Beatrice — someone who, unlike Virgil, fully grasps the intricacies of grace and human transformation — to understand how it works. This will happen at the top of the mountain, he adds.

The comment electrifies Dante. He is to meet Beatrice at the top of Mount Purgatory? The promise is almost as powerful as a meeting itself. Dante becomes charged by the name of the person he has loved as a gale blowing through his life. He finds fresh energy to climb and asks Virgil whether they can make more haste.

For us readers, we note the impact of the name of Beatrice, which is a name for love. It is a partial demonstration of what they have been talking about. Love is more powerful than any impediment, confusion, or mistake.

They keep walking. The name brings hope, but they must still make the ascent. And as they climb, they spot a solitary soul in the distance. He is sitting majestically. His gaze is steady, unlike the souls they have encountered on the lower slopes so far. He is self-possessed, and it shines from him like a kind of wisdom. Virgil immediately senses that this person will be able to offer them guidance.

They draw near and, at first, the soul ignores them. This might be, in part, because the day has grown older and it is late afternoon. The sun is so

low that everywhere is in shadow and so Dante's shadow does not fall from
him. Without that particular signal, Virgil and Dante look unremarkable.
They could be just another couple of confused, passing souls.

Virgil asks which way they should go, and the soul responds with another
question. Where are they from, he asks? It is as if such questions preoccupy
this solitary figure. He sits there asking himself who he is, where he is from,
what has happened in his life, and what has gone wrong. Virgil and Dante
are encountering a different state of mind, and entering a different region
of purgatory. This soul is not manically asking for prayers. He is reflective.

Virgil replies that he is from Mantua, which jolts the soul out of his
reverie. He leaps up, declaring that he is from Mantua too.

Virgil and the soul embrace, in the way that spiritual bodies can. They
realize they are from the same place, and perhaps recognize that they are
in the same state of mind. They are both engrossed with what the right
next step might be, and how to find the way. There are no meaningless
meetings in purgatory. There will be none in paradise. Every moment offers
moments of learning.

He is Sordello, a poet, known particularly for his lamentations on war.
Some of his writing still survives today. It makes sense that they have
encountered him here because lamentation is the state of mind they need.
They must move on from the trauma of those souls preoccupied with the
violence of their deaths, and the way to move on is to see trauma for what
it is, grieve its curtailment of life, grieve its treachery, or impulsiveness, or
hate, grieve its injury, and accept the waste. That is to lament, the contemplation of which Sordello devoted his energies to, during his earthly life.

A spirit of lament fills the air and has a powerful impact upon Dante.
He launches into a bitter, even sarcastic, lament for what he has seen in his
life. The memory of the name of Beatrice, and the power of love, disappears. He vents against Italy and its slavishness to violence, before turning
against Caesars and kings who have been unable to bring peace and have
unleashed war. His cursing and acidic litany fills the rest of the canto. He
calls out to God, saying that although God was crucified for sinners, He
appears resolutely to have turned His eyes from the world He loves. Do
you not see the state we are in, Dante cries? This is the depth grief and
anger must reach.

As an aside, it is notable that Dante does not use Christian nomenclature
for God, but instead calls out to Jove, the contraction of the name, Jupiter.
I think it's a sign that he doesn't fully understand who he is calling out
to, for much the same reason that he can only wildly call out. He is a long

way from the vision of Beatrice and the altered relationship to suffering that her presence will ultimately bring.

Next, Dante rails against Florence. How hypocritical his birthplace has become! How it has utterly failed to live up to its founding ideals and best goals! How fully it has betrayed its past!

The howling verses mount up. The mourning continues. Dante does not hold back from conveying a sense of exasperation and distress. He is gripped by it, and that absorption cannot be rushed. We readers must stay with this process, much as we have stayed with the descent into hell. Beatrice's name has been invoked but there is no shortcut to the top of the mountain. The path before them is the way, and right now the way fills Dante's heart with agony, not relief.

The canto ends with a final image of discomfort, that of a person on a sick bed, tossing and turning in pain.

Virgil and Sordello embrace, and they come to a hidden valley.

PURGATORIO 7
Reflection

CANTO 7 IS FILLED WITH A SENSE OF DRAWING in and consolidating. They've moved away from the agitated souls, who had troubled lives and violent deaths. Dante has voiced the hurt and anger of his mortal life in Italy and Florence. It was a bitter, heartfelt outburst, cutting right across the flow of events. He doesn't speak in this canto. Emotion needs time to recover.

Into his silence, Dante the poet returns us to the ongoing meeting of Virgil and Sordello. They have recognized each other, and Virgil reveals who he is: a poet too.

Sordello is amazed, and he knows which poet. "You are the glory of all Latin poets!" he exclaims. "You have a deathless fame!" He had been merely greeting Virgil, but now he honors the Roman bard, much as a serf might their lord.

The adulation leaves us readers with the scene of three souls, each consumed by their own experience. Dante is exhausted. Virgil seeks guidance. Sordello is star-struck. And it is Virgil who picks up the action.

He explains to Sordello how he has been called from hell and is leading a way up Mount Purgatory on a divine mission. He was sent to limbo because he didn't know about the dynamics of love, he explains. That was his sin, of omission rather than commission. Now he seeks guidance to continue with his task of leading Dante, though it is pretty clear that he seeks inner guidance for himself as well. Is there a way permanently out of limbo for him?

Sordello lauds him with praise, but Virgil stays resolutely humble. He is reflective. He knows that his earthly life and success were not enough. He can see more in the afterlife. But how far can he go? I suspect that Dante the poet is intimating that he can go all the way. After all, if you change in purgatory, you only change in one direction, and Virgil is clearly changing. There is hope on these steep mountain slopes.

He steers Sordello away from the adulation, painfully aware of his own need for passage, and asks his admirer the way forward. "Where does purgatory truly start?" he inquires. He is asking about the gateway that all souls must pass through. It marks the moment when they move from wandering aimlessly, and being preoccupied with their pasts, and turn to the future. The threshold is a little farther up the mountain. It is as much psychological as physical. To pass through it, souls must have gathered themselves enough for earnest work on their transformation.

Sordello knows the direction in which to go and agrees to be their guide for the next stage. And he does so with a fascinating detail. It casts further light on the expanded reality through which Dante and Virgil are travelling.

It turns out that they cannot trek by night. They can only move up while the sun is in the sky, although they can move around, on the same level, during the dark hours. It's one of the details I love because it invites us to contemplate and appreciate the purgatorial dimension, which is at once part of The Divine Comedy and part of inner life as we can know it. Think of it according to the four levels of interpretation.

Literally speaking, they cannot travel by night because they don't have light. In a strange place, that is unwise. Allegorically, they need divine light to discover the life of this place and so be able to take it in and let it change them. At night, the sunlight, which in its essence is divine light, is below the horizons of their awareness. Tropologically, they can't travel by night because, in a different way, the nighttime matters quite as much as the day. It is a moment to pause so as to digest the experiences of the day and let them work a change within. At night, our minds become the present reality, in dreams and reflection. The shadowy light means we can mull over what's been seen during the day and absorb its meaning, consciously and unconsciously. Experiences become insights, which become part of who we are.

Interestingly, in *The Divine Comedy*, it is only in *The Purgatorio* that Dante dreams. He didn't in *The Inferno*. He won't in *The Paradiso*. The nights and the dreams are integral to his pilgrimage during this stage. And this is what the anagogical level knows: nothing is wasted. Ascent and descent are part and parcel of the one movement toward God, and the nighttime plays a crucial part in that.

That said, Virgil is not thinking in such expansive ways. Sordello's answer leaves him alarmed. He wants to reach the threshold and asks Sordello to take them there. Sordello comforts Virgil by adding that the gateway is only a little farther on.

They come to a hillock and, at the top of the rise, look down across a gentle fold in the mountain. It is a dry valley and exhibits preternaturally vivid colors. The grass and trees that line the incline shine like precious stones and glorious metals. The atmosphere smells heaven-sent. Maybe this valley only shows itself in this way at the end of the day, when states of mind blur as darkness falls, and an inner light can come out.

They hear chanting. There are souls in the valley singing the *Salve Regina*, one of the anthems sung during compline, the monastic office that closes the day. It calls on the Virgin Mary as Queen of Heaven to hear people's cries in the vale of tears that is our time on earth. It asks for protection through the night.

Heard here, it complements the mood of reflection in which Virgil and Dante find themselves, by bringing to mind the pattern of the liturgical day and night as practiced by monks and nuns. This charts the rise and fall of each day, like an echo of the sun's rising and setting, and in that round sings of rhythm and beauty. However, the presence of the liturgy in purgatory raises a question. Why are the souls still singing it in the afterlife? Haven't they moved on? Are they still having to call on the aids and assistance that they needed on earth? The chanting and liturgy are beautiful, but they can't go on forever. If they did, it would mean the souls were stuck in the endless round as well.

The implication is that these souls are in this valley, not having yet crossed the threshold into purgatory proper, because they are not yet ready for it. The problem is clearly not a preoccupation with violence. They are above the worries that obsessed Aretine, Federigo Novello, Count Orso, and Pierre de la Brosse. However, given the beauty of the place and the singing, it may be that they have fallen in love with the circular round of the liturgical day and are struggling to let it go.

That too can cause stuckness. It can prevent movement. Something like this is intimated because Sordello tells Virgil and Dante that they are not going to descend into the valley quite yet. They are going to stay on the lip of the incline, from where they have a vantage point, to stop, wait, and watch. Slightly above the souls below, they can attend to what happens without becoming enchanted by the loveliness that might enthrall or bewitch them.

The valley is occupied by rulers and kings, individuals who tried to lead people during their mortal lives. Many are named in the remaining part of the canto. There is Rudolf of Hapsburg and Ottokar II, king of Bohemia. They spot Philip III the Bold, of France, and Philip IV the Fair.

The naming, coupled to a few details of how they had failed their task in life, brings us closer to them. They are like specimen rulers of a certain kind. They became too entangled with the affairs of the world and lost perspective, sometimes with terrible results. Here they can contemplate the mess they left behind. They sing the liturgy as an expression of melancholy. It's a melancholy that reflects the mood of the day as the valley's glorious colors fade into nightly greys, much as the glory of their rank was tarnished by the years of their rule.

Looking over more crowned heads, they see one individual sitting on his own. He is Henry III of England. Dante says that his branches bore good fruit in the end. Perhaps that's why he is a little separated from the others. He may have been a failure but his son, Edward I, is credited with reforming English law, and at least that brought some good.

The canto draws to a close as the day does. Dante and Virgil are about to have their first night in purgatory. It feels eerie. At once beautiful and sorrowful, but increasingly uncanny.

Angels and a serpent appear, though the souls don't seem concerned.

PURGATORIO 8

Regret

DANTE AND VIRGIL ARE IN THE DAZZLING VALLEY of the rulers, inhabited by those preoccupied with their failed attempts to govern on earth. The kings and emperors are struggling to work out their salvation, as they are still diminished by the weaknesses of their mortal lives, which from the perspective occupied by Dante and Virgil, slightly above them, are in stark contrast to the lively colors of the plant life around them.

The golden hour of the evening has past, and the world is turning grey. It is the hour when sailors long to be back in port, Dante recalls. It is the moment of the day when people become nostalgic for home. Similarly, he continues, it is the time the bell tolls as night shelters for travelling pilgrims close.

The contrast in his thoughts is noteworthy. One is about return. The other is about a refuge during an ongoing journey. There is a sense, as his first night in purgatory settles in, that he is feeling the pull of wanting to return to the port of his old ways, as well as feeling the pull of a resting place from which to gather strength for a different tomorrow. No doubt, he is being affected by the spirit of the valley, as the rulers wrestle with leaving behind legacies that history will find wanting. Will they find a way into tomorrow?

Dante the poet breaks the fourth wall to address us readers. The veil that covers the truth is thinner at night, he tells us, because the darkness brings us closer to the shadows that the daylight expels. Can we see what this place means? Can we look with him into the valley? He raises the expectation of a step change in his journey, if we have the eyes to see it.

The eighth canto of The Purgatorio parallels the ninth of The Inferno, in this regard. They are actually both eighth cantos, if you treat the first canto of The Inferno as introductory, as most commentators do. They are both transitional. The first one described the moment during which Dante and Virgil stood before the walls of Dis, awaiting the assistance of an angel. Might an angel appear again? Are there fresh doors to open?

They would be inner openings, rather than the iron gates of Dis, designed to keep out the divine. The souls condemned for a time to the valley look as if they have imprisoned themselves with regrets rather than fears, with shame rather than hate. They are locked in by their preoccupations, rather than locked up, potentially for eternity.

Another liturgical anthem sounds, the Te Lucis Ante: "Before the ending of the day." It is another beautiful compline chant, praying for divine protection. Or is it, too, at risk of confining them, as the souls sing what they know, like sailors seeking a familiar port, rather than pilgrims reaching for horizons?

The implication is that they have yet to find the resources they need to work out their salvation. The consolation of church services might have comforted them as they realized their mortal life's work was coming undone. The lovely interiors of medieval cathedrals — full of the robed great and good, decorated with sparkling jewels and polished marble — encouraged them to seek glory, until it became a harsh reminder that glory was eluding them as their reigns waned. They tried prayers. They sought the counsel of priests and prelates only to realize that the clergy were as preoccupied with secular concerns as they were. The memory of worship won't lead them to divine glory. They forgot what Saint Augustine had told them, that the Church is a pilgrim on earth. Its home is another country, not the ornately adorned, richly endowed ecclesiastical haven.

Churchmen and women today risk being weighed down by what anchors them to mundane concerns as much as their medieval forebears. If they are no longer caught up in papal wars, they are in civic life and global politics, in part trying to do good, in part trying to justify their existence. The truth comes out by the amount of energy clergy will spend decrying injustice. It seems a self-evidently good thing to do — until you reach the valley of the rulers on Mount Purgatory, when it becomes clear that there is little, or no energy left for eternal life. They have only empty words, old formulas, chants. The implication is that many will have to spend long periods sitting on the emerald grass, amidst the rainbow trees and flowers, as they recall what life is really about.

Dante becomes tired of looking at the kings. Self-obsession has that effect. And he looks up.

Not one, but two angels appear. They are as green as spring leaves and have broken swords in their hands. They take up two stations, one on each side of the valley, as if guarding the miserable souls between them. Dante tries to look into their faces but is blinded by golden light.

Sordello reports that there is a serpent in the valley, and the angels bring protection, though he is seemingly unconcerned about any danger. It turns out that the appearance of the angels is a ritual that happens every night at this time and has become as familiar and uninspiring as a dusty church service.

For a novice, though, like Dante, the prospect of what appears to be a looming cosmic battle is chilling. He freezes with fear, much as he had done when he stood before Lucifer. He leans into Virgil, seeking refuge, even as Sordello tells them that they must walk down into the valley. Is that wise, Dante wonders?

They descend. He notices that none of the souls look worried. They don't seem to have noticed the arrival of the angels. Saint Bernard, whom Dante will eventually meet in the heights of heaven, would have told them that every night, devils and angels fight to enter human hearts. These human hearts seem unable to let anything in. They hardly believe it anymore. The drama has emptied of meaning. The angels might wish to offer more but they can only put on a performance for those for whom they have become a performance.

The souls are interested in Dante and Virgil as they pass. One is Nino Visconti, the grandson of a soul whom Dante saw in hell, the cannibalistic Count Ugolino. Dante greets him warmly. It looks as if they were friends in mortal life. And then Dante tells Nino, and Sordello who listens in, that he is alive. He is not a shade. The night had been concealing that from them.

They are amazed. Momentarily, Nino wakes up to what divine grace might be able to do, though old attitudes die hard, and he quickly adds that he can't believe what Dante is telling him. Nino does not turn a new leaf. He turns back to his familiar life and reports bitterly what happened. After he died, his wife quickly found a new husband, and bedmate, Nino says. "Remember me to my daughter," he adds. "Ask for her prayers," he pleads, but not for those of his wife.

Dante's original readers would have known that Nino's wife was called Beatrice. In Dante's imagination, Beatrice is a name that can only do one thing: fire him with the love that might draw him toward God. Nino's Beatrice provides a counterexample. That is how stuck Nino has become. The presence of angels can't move him.

Dante, though, is not so lost. He looks up, which is a good inclination in The Divine Comedy. If you can see the sky, you can reorient yourself.

He sees three stars. They have replaced the four stars of the Southern Cross that had blazoned the dawn. The three have an astronomical reality because in the southern hemisphere, three stars do stand out in the night sky, although much as the four stars reminded Dante of the four cardinal virtues, so the three stars here have appeared to remind him of the three theological virtues: faith, hope, and love. They are heralds. They bring the light of the qualities he will need to journey farther than Nino is capable of doing. If he can draw on the stellar light, and allow it to enlighten his soul, he will find a way through these antechambers of purgatory.

Before that happens, though, the serpent must appear. Which it does. It looks real enough, like a vicious streak in the undergrowth, though simultaneously, it seems nonchalant as well. It stops halfway down the slope and licks itself, almost as preoccupied as the souls it appears uninterested in tempting.

That said, the angels don't take any chances, or do they just do what they always do at this time? After all, they brought broken swords. They swoop down in elegant, graceful arcs, and the serpent, spotting them, instantly scuttles off.

The sight is fascinating to Dante. He is disturbed at what it might mean. But no one else has batted an eyelid, and presumably that is the meaning we readers are invited to draw from the scene. Nothing less than eternal delight awaits us, though we have to want it.

Another soul addresses Dante. Conrad Malaspina speaks out, lavishing praise on his family, and by implication himself. Further, Conrad prophesizes, his family will offer Dante refuge when he is exiled from Florence during the remainder of his earthly life.

Dante is grateful, though we are left wanting to warn him from becoming too concerned with his security, welcome though the hospitality will be. It's as if the promise of it has made Dante forget the sight of the angels already. If he were to return to this part of purgatory in his afterlife, the implication is that he would be like the wasted rulers.

The canto ends with us wondering what it is going to take for Dante to cross the threshold and begin the real work of purgatory. The answer will come in the next canto, when he has a shocking dream.

Dante sleeps and dreams. They arrive at the gate of purgatory.

PURGATORIO 9
Abduction

THIS CANTO IS ONE OF THE RICHEST IN THE PUR-
gatorio. It's packed with symbolism, information, and transformative moments. You can read it time and again and find something
new. Dante's journey takes a major step forward in it. In particular, he learns
more about how passionate love is part of his ascent. It is not an easy lesson
as he must confront the darker side of erotic love too.

It is the type of love that tends to be viewed warily in monotheistic religions, particularly in their institutional forms. They are more comfortable
when love manifests in other guises, like agape or friendship. Christianity
provides an obvious case in point. Punitive attitudes toward eros set in from
its earliest days after Saint Paul felt that sex provided a test case for how
the new freedom to be found in Christ differed from the old freedoms of
Roman citizenship. For the Roman freeman, a key demonstration of liberty
was doing what you wanted sexually, with your own and others' bodies.

But Paul preached a different liberty. It was not civic but spiritual, known through belonging to Christ. Sexual acts, of any sort, were therefore interpreted as an implicit rejection of divine grace.

"I wish that all were as I myself am," he writes to the Corinthians (1 Cor 7:7), which is to say, celibate. As Saint Augustine was later to write (in *The City of God*, Book XIV, Chs. 15–16), the one thing that erotic love reveals to us is that its surges of desire spring directly from humanity's rebellion against God. At best, it is what you might call a necessary evil.

What is striking is that these worries and prohibitions stand in marked contrast with the attitudes toward eros found in mystical and visionary traditions. These tend to take a very different view, in the West reaching back to Plato. He taught that eros is a go-between spirit or dynamic, known in the ancient world as a daimon, whose embrace widens and deepens perception. In *The Symposium*, he tells of how the priestess and prophet, Diotima, taught Socrates that the "arts of love" can lead to the highest mysteries of sight, ultimately catching glimpses of what's good, beautiful, and true.

Dante clearly felt a tension between the two attitudes toward eros in his life. His early poems describe the agony of controlling sexual impulses, particularly as they were released when he fell in love with Beatrice. Her image utterly, almost ruthlessly, seized his imagination.

He reached a pivotal moment in his spiritual and poetic struggle when he realized that exalting the beauty he saw in her could be an end in itself. He gradually found a way of harmonizing the love she inspired in him with the ascent of the soul to the divine. It required a combination of eros and logos, meaning the intelligence or insight that can discern the presence of God. This is because the divine image itself can be known as a combination of eros and logos. With that insight, Beatrice could become much more than the object of his infatuation. She could become a star that guided him through the ups and downs of eros, in his search for constant, eternal love. In short, the right use of eros is at the heart of Dante's journey, and he presents a key aspect of that realization during canto 9.

The first night on the mountain has begun. Exhausted, he falls asleep and, in the early hours of the morning, he dreams. It is the auspicious period when the individual is still transparent to God, though beginning to return to his waking consciousness.

He sees himself snatched from the mountain by an eagle. The bird descends like terrible lightning and carries him into the high heavens, much as the god Jupiter abducted the beautiful youth Ganymede. He is lifted into a burning sphere of scorching fire.

He awakes with a jolt, gripped by fear. Virgil calms him with comforting words and reveals that while Dante slept, they had a visitation.

A lady from heaven appeared. It was Saint Lucia and she carried Dante a little farther up the mountain, as the day's climb had been hard going for him. She told Virgil that she wanted to speed him on his journey.

Much ink has been spilled over the meaning of the dream, but it is pretty clear that Dante's dream and what happened while he slept are in stark contrast. The dream was a nightmare of barely disguised sexual violence, an insight that is underlined by several allusions to uncontained lust that Dante makes in other parts of canto 9.

For example, before he falls asleep, he describes the rising moon as the concubine of Tithonus. Tithonus was a mortal who was abducted by Aurora, the goddess of the dawn, and who grew old, being mortal. Their love developed a dark dynamic as he shriveled like a cicada. The moon, as Dante sees it on Mount Purgatory, is envisaged as another illicit lover of Tithonus. He also says that the concubine-moon rises in the constellation of Scorpio, who has a cold body and a sting.

Then, as Dante falls asleep, he refers to the sensation as bearing Adam's weight. This is another evocative description, referring to the mortal flesh of Adam that, following the temptation of Eve and fall, requires sleep. It's a hint at how erotic love leads astray, as much as it can lead to God.

His dream occurs toward the end of the night, at the hour when swallows begin to sing, Dante remarks. This is reference to another grim tale of love gone wrong, as the swallow is the metamorphosized Philomela. In a complicated myth, that Dante adds to in his own way, Philomela ends up killing her son, cooking him, and presenting the meat in a feast to her husband, in order to avenge his erotic betrayal.

A further violent image is referenced as Dante wakes up frightened. He says he woke up like Achilles, the Greek hero, who unbeknownst to him was carried by his mother, Thetis, to a strange island in the hope of escaping the Trojan war. It's a different image of love, one that hopes to save a son, while knowing that fate will claim the son. Thetis knows that. She is a goddess.

So, against this background that is strewn with intense, vicious, and desperate stories of love, Dante has his dream. It features a lustful abduction, though his sleep is the occasion for another love to break through. Lucia comes to his aid.

She is significant as one of three ladies who keep a benign eye on Dante from the celestial heights, alongside Beatrice and the Virgin Mary, though note: he has not one but three beautiful women loving him. This is one indicator of how eros's passion is transformed. What might be judged almost as a kind of promiscuity becomes an excessive desire, though potent power, to help.

As to the dream, I think what it implies is something like this. If inwardly, Dante had experienced the outward actions of Saint Lucia as a kidnap, almost a rape, as he awakens, he realizes how profoundly mistaken he is. Eros is actually speeding him on his journey toward divine love.

The implication is that the transformation of eros from its dark manifestations to its true character requires him to work on his perceptions. He must hold in mind both images — one of violent and lustful snatching, the other of divine embrace and carriage. In so doing, the possessive character of eros that currently dominates his mind, as revealed by the dream, might give way to the dominant character of divine love, which is of attracting and mingling participation.

The shift is key to Dante's transformational erotic spirituality, a possibility that is confirmed by Lucia lifting Dante higher up the mountain. Moreover, Virgil continues, with Dante fully awake, they are at the gateway on Mount Purgatory. It marks the start of purgatory proper, which Dante is ready to enter, having oriented himself and gained a first taste of the dramatic changes in him that the ascent will demand.

The threshold is guarded by an angel. The divine being is too bright to look at, as is the gleaming sword that it carries, though Dante can see that the gate is entered by ascending three steps. The first looks like glass, the second like cracked pumice, the third like flaming blood spurting from a vein.

The steps are usually interpreted allegorically by commentators, but I feel a more natural and penetrating way to explain them arises from the experience he has just had. He sees his image in the first step of glass, much as he has seen an aspect of himself in the dream. This is represented in the second step, which he is able to step onto because he can tolerate the cracked and troubling erotic impulses within him. And because that disturbance is born, a third step up becomes possible, when this flaming passion, in the process of being changed, can bear him to a threshold.

The angel speaks to them. It says four things, which develop the seriousness of this pivotal moment. It tells Dante to speak from where he is. It asks Dante what he wants, and where his guide is. And then it says, beware. If you enter through this gateway, you will face grief and regret. This is not a simple transition.

You might say that the dream, the carriage, and the gateway are an initiation. Dante still has a long way to go and his erotic desires will require further work. As he follows the path, he learns much more about how his ambivalence about eros has to do with human ignorance and youthful experience, as well as the painful struggle to reform his desires, his perceptions, his knowledge, and his will so he can become capable of paradise.

But canto 9 conveys a central element: that which seems monstrous, feels dark, frightening, possessive, wild — like an uncontrolled rape of life itself — is something remarkably different. If we can bear ourselves, and allow ourselves to be borne, then we will become able to enjoy a free, indulgent, and delightful awareness of what is beautiful, good, and true. Eros can be transformed, not condemned. It is a love to befriend, not reject. It can energize our steps up Mount Purgatory, and then our flight into paradise.

That said, it is in the nature of eros to go wrong. It's bound to misfire. It gets confused in its imagery and in its passion. But that's not a reason to discard it. Quite the opposite. It's a reason to stay with it, and recognize its difficulty, which I think is what Dante does. He is prepared to follow and change its energy.

Virgil tells him to ask the angel to let them through by turning the keys that open the gate. Interestingly, Dante does not do this but, instead, falls to his knees. He asks for divine mercy and beats his breast three times. He knows that what is required of him is to become more self-possessed, to take responsibility, to claim ownership for the next stage of the journey that he's about to undertake. He wants to understand himself, and change.

In response, the angel marks Dante's forehead with seven Ps. On the other side of the gate, Mount Purgatory will present them with seven terraces, and, on each, a particular kind of failure is faced. The angel tells Dante to be sure that each of these P-shaped wounds is healed. They will serve as an indicator for Dante that he is ready to move onto the next step. The wounds are a gift. That is another important insight about the way purgatory works.

A snaking path leads to a terrace of beautiful engravings.

PURGATORIO 10

Weight

ANTE AND VIRGIL PASS THROUGH THE GATE over the threshold of purgatory. It closes resoundingly behind them. There is no going back. With their eyes focused forward, Dante and Virgil don't turn around.

They have reached a point of no return and the way forward is tricky. They climb through a narrow cleft. The path that follows is zigzagged. In fact, it appears to move like a wave.

I think that Dante is experiencing the first unsteady steps of his revised relationship with love. Love has always led him but, until the dream of Ganymede's abduction, a possessive form of love has tended to dominate. He has seen how powerful that is, which has simultaneously revealed a different operation of eros: the dynamic that can carry him to heights he barely knows exist, of which Lucia has offered a taste as she helped him up the mountain to the gate.

The passageway through the gate is a tremendous moment of focus. He has a clear feel for what might be different and can gradually turn more to this new love. But it is going to take time: it is going to take the time it takes to climb Mount Purgatory. He is still fully aware of the older desires within him to seize and control. So, at the start, the path feels disorienting and dizzying. He is inclined to be pushed and pulled by the other forces in his soul, with their competing desires and fears. The road momentarily zigzags as he finds his feet.

Bright beginnings often coexist with old habits, an ambivalence that shows up in psychotherapy. Someone may be deeply troubled by jealousy, hatred, or violence. And those feelings don't easily die. However, alongside them, come feelings marked by compassion, love, or forgiveness. Part of the task of the psychotherapist is to spot these shifts and not forget them because, for the client, they may seem tiny and inconsequential, incapable of winning out over the seemingly more powerful, destructive impulses. But they are capable. They do win out. They can blossom and flourish.

A parallel transformation is reported in accounts of spiritual transformation. There comes a point at which the individual sees, tastes, and wants righteousness. It is called by various names. They enter the stream, convert, confess, undergo the rite of passage. And, at first, it may seem like not much has changed. The unrighteousness lives on. But its time is limited. Light is overcoming darkness, for all that the darkness appears sticky, tenacious, and reluctant to depart. It might even appear not to be shifting at all.

It is like travelling through the eye of a needle, Dante remarks as he tracks the trail beneath their feet. "We must keep our wits," Virgil adds.

They do. They make progress along the unsteady road and come to a ledge. It is a flat ridge looking like a shelf attached to the side of the mountain. It is the first of the seven terraces on Mount Purgatory, on which souls wrestle with the unrighteousness within them.

This first terrace looks empty. Its width measures the length of about three human persons, if they lay on the ground, head to foot. On one side is the mountain's sheer cliff. On the other, a drop.

The place is deserted and still, though it carries an air of potential rather than of emptiness. Then they notice that the cliff face is not rocky and barren. It is decorated with extraordinarily beautiful images.

They are engraved into the marble of the mountainside by an artist with a skill greater than the greatest Dante has admired in Florence, a place in which no mean sculptors have lived. The friezes convey such an intensity of depiction that what they show appears to live. They celebrate the moments of conversion of a series of well-known figures, biblical and historical. They capture the pivot point in a life when the divine definitively outdoes the devilish. They look so beautiful not only because they are wonderfully made, but because they convey the lovely moment the good shapes a life.

They see the instant that Mary said "Yes" to the angel, as the angel greeted her with, "Ave!" They see the occasion on which King David brought the Ark of the Covenant into Jerusalem and danced before it. This panel also shows one of his wives, Michal, looking on with a sneer, though the spontaneity of David's joy outshines her scorn.

They see an incident from the life of the Emperor Trajan, remembered in legend. One day, he was on his way to a great battle, dressed in full regalia, followed by his army, when a widow tried to stop him and ask for a blessing. At first, he didn't notice the seemingly inconsequential interruption to the mighty procession, but she persisted, and Trajan paused, listened, and granted her request. Though his heart was readied for the bloody passions of war, he found a different kind of care within him, and so spoke to the woman. As it turned out, that moment was more consequential than any battle. It led to Trajan, the pagan ruler, being remembered here, as one saved.

Virgil loves the scenes. He encourages Dante to explore them, to absorb them. He knows they convey a crucial spirit that Dante must take in. He must be taking it in himself, else he wouldn't stress their value. Virgil the pagan is fostering his conversion.

God loves these moments as they are part of His art, His creativity, His desire: they are instances when a heart turns back to the love that made it. The soul knows humility, which is to say that it freely, consciously agrees to the moment.

Virgil casts his eyes back across the terrace and, looking farther ahead, sees a group of souls. They are shuffling slowly toward them.

Dante raises his head to look, turning with ease from the beautiful images to the approaching shades. He is not trying to hold onto the moments the carvings so gorgeously convey. An unpossessive eros within him is freer to go with the flow. Though what he sees next is hard.

In fact, the canto comes to an end with Dante warning us readers that the sights that will assail them henceforth on the mountain will be troubling. This is the place where darkness departs, but only because the darkness has been accepted as real. There is genuine suffering, for all that it is suffering which has been freely embraced, because the individuals know that there is a greater love being born within them. Divine life stirs them up and compels them forward. It coexists and contends with foul and fiendish forces. But the effort to be wholly remade, which is required wholly to know God, is worth it.

It takes time. It requires tenacity and an ability to tolerate the unpleasant parts of yourself. When someone merely turns their back on what they
don't like of themselves, that part of themselves stays strong. It is called
denial and it is forbidden in purgatory. The road is punishing but is also
the path of hope.

The souls that approach are closer. Dante is still trying to see why they
look so odd. Virgil explains. They are bent double and their eyes can only
look at the ground. The reason is that there are great boulders on their
backs. The weights force the souls to bend over, and they beat their chests
as they hobble along. For some, the stones cause a tilt to their posture. For
others, the boulders push them almost completely to the ground.

The first terrace of purgatory is where the proud work off the effects of
their sin, though I think it is more helpful to stay with the image, rather
than to resort to the categorizations traditionally offered by the Church.
Pride can be destructive. It can grip like a limpet, but it is also a subtle
feeling. It can be good, when it enables dignity. Discerning how it is operative inside them is the task for these souls. It's why the process takes time.
They cannot simply put their burdens down. They want to carry them, in
fact, so that they can sift through the varieties of pride within them, to
absorb what is good and gradually discard what hinders their development.

Dante reflects that they are like caterpillars: worms destined to be but-
terflies, after the alchemy of the chrysalis stage. But they must undergo
the chrysalis stage.

That transformation need not have waited for Mount Purgatory. It would
have been better to attend to it before death since, left unchecked, pride
grows in life, registered as a great weight in the afterlife. Openness to the
moments when an alternative love stirs within us, when an angel, or ark,
or widow moves us, are invaluable, for all that they might appear trivial
at the time.

Canto 10, though, ends with the difficulty. The souls on this first terrace
are clearly struggling. Through their tears, falling from their downturned
faces, Dante sees that they are crying over how hard it is to go on. Though
they do.

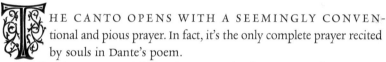

Dante speaks with souls carrying the heavy burden of pride.

PURGATORIO II

Honor

THE CANTO OPENS WITH A SEEMINGLY CONVENtional and pious prayer. In fact, it's the only complete prayer recited by souls in Dante's poem.

Virgil and Dante are with the sinners on the first terrace of Mount Purgatory. They are bowed down by enormous weights, strapped to their backs. And they hear the souls saying the Lord's Prayer.

Immediately, it strikes them as different. The souls in ante-purgatory have not prayed themselves. Instead, they've asked for the prayers of others. The individuals on this side of the threshold have a different attitude toward prayer. They are praying for themselves, which is to say they are taking responsibility for themselves on their path to paradise.

They are also praying in the vernacular, the Italian of their everyday tongue, in which Dante writes. His first readers would have felt the risky thrill of this familiarity with divine words. At the time, it would have felt provocative, possibly blasphemous. Further, they don't merely rattle off the Lord's Prayer but improvise upon it, extending and amplifying various elements within it.

Instead of only hearing "Our Father in heaven," Dante and Virgil hear added thoughts on how the highest heavens participate most fully in divine life and love, because in the highest heavens divine life and love are known and seen directly. Below the high heavens, in realms such as earth, divine life and love are known via their influence, indirectly.

To the line on God's will, "Thy will be done," the souls add an additional thought on their wills aligning with the divine. To the request, "Give us this day our daily bread," they reflect on feeding more fully on godly sustenance.

The souls sound very active in their praying. This is not mere recitation, but the development of their thoughts as they think, which is what prayer can be about: not about trying to change God's mind but to move more into God's mind.

As the souls near the end of the Lord's Prayer, they remark that they utter it not only for themselves but for people who are still alive. After all, they need not be led into temptation too. The generosity touches Dante deeply and he addresses us readers, saying that if they pray for us, we might pray for them, that together all might rise and join the wheeling stars. There is a care in purgatory that is not selfish but universal. There is an opening up to saving not only the individual but the whole world.

One prayer might lead to another, and who knows where that virtuous circle can end.

Virgil speaks as the prayer draws to a close. They are on a divine mission, he explains, and need to know the shortest pathway up purgatory. They do not want a shortcut but the short route that is the direct path, aligned with God, much as the souls have been praying. Virgil's request chimes with the moment of caring for the journey of others.

The voice of a burdened soul sounds from underneath the loads. Virgil and Dante hear that if they move along the terrace, they will find a path that they can climb.

The speaker adds that he would be glad to know who addresses them, particularly as Virgil has said Dante is still alive. He explains that when he was alive, he was Omberto Aldobrandesco. He was from an admirable family, of which one might rightly be proud.

This strikes a less comfortable tone. Omberto is not lying, but he has not worked out how to relate to his illustrious heritage. He uses the first person singular "I" with remarkable frequency, almost as if he knows he might not, and yet can't help doing so.

He is clearly in the grip of pride. He knows that he is proud of his family, and that is not a straightforwardly bad attitude. However, he is a little too proud of his family, a boast that he tries to redress while remarking that Dante and Virgil may not have heard of the name Aldobrandesco. He is aware enough not to think that they should have heard of it, as a soul in hell might have assumed, though he is keen for them to have heard it, at the same time.

This is what he is on Mount Purgatory to work through. He can feel both elements: the dignity and the vanity. By exposing himself to both, which is uncomfortable in its irresolution, he can transcend his old ways.

Dante has bent double to speak with Omberto. He is sharing in the discomfort and admits that pride will be one of the conditions he has to navigate on both sides of death. But his leaning means that his face can be seen by other souls, and one calls out. This soul is bent slightly less low to the ground and so has a bit more room for maneuver, which is to say he is a little less unfree with self-obsession.

He doesn't say his name, though he does repeatedly use the first person singular. We know who he is because Dante recognizes him and speaks his name. Oderisi da Gubbio was an illustrator of manuscripts. Dante is excited to see him, though when he calls Oderisi "the honor of Gubbio," we can imagine Oderisi wincing a little. Appropriate feelings about his gift and art are what he is facing, as he faces the ground.

He is learning because when Dante comments on his honor, Oderisi immediately informs Dante that his peer, Franco Bolognese, could color pages more radiantly than he could. Competitors in life, Oderisi benefits from his superior in purgatory. He continues, remarking that fame comes and goes like grass in a field. It only lasts so long as a greater glory doesn't eclipse it, which is to say that if someone is famous for a long time, it might only be because no greater exemplar has yet emerged, rather than because the fame itself deserves to last forever.

The discussion of fame brings to mind the insights of Boethius in The Consolation of Philosophy. While in prison, having lost everything, Boethius learns from Lady Philosophy that there is a fame that deserves to last, as there is glory, wealth, and honor too. It is the glory, wealth, and honor that belongs to God, and which the illustrator, noble, and poet must seek in life to reflect.

I add poet to the list because Bolognese suggests that the poetic glory of some might already be diminishing with the arrival of a brighter poetic light. The implication is that he is alluding to Dante.

Dante himself is being invited to contemplate his pride. He is musing on his art, its aims, and origins. He is being challenged by the spirit of purgatory to face his own mix of dignity and vanity.

He has a lot to be proud of. He is a poet of genius, epoch defining, with a stronger claim than most to be considered immortal. But might that pride become an impediment? Could it prevent him from fulfilling his goal? After all, if he can't progress beyond the terrace of the proud, he won't pen his magnum opus. Pride could still be his undoing. How is Dante to reconcile the glory of his gift with the greater glory about which his gift might speak?

He asks about another soul he sees, one called Provenzan Salvani. He was a Ghibelline chief, and sworn enemy of Dante, inasmuch as he once ordered the destruction of Florence, a plan that was only just thwarted.

It is significant that Dante sees Salvani, his opponent. It says something about Dante: that he is addressing his pride. After all, he might have used his poem to condemn Salvani to hell. There is a part of him that would have been glad to see him there. But he didn't. He saw him in purgatory, and so he reports his presence correctly. Dante is using his gift to speak of God's love, not his own loathings.

Salvani is on this terrace because of a generous act that cut through the destructive impulses that shaped him. A friend had needed to raise a ransom and Salvani responded by begging in the marketplace to gather the money that released his friend. He had swallowed his pride in the service of another.

It must have been a deeply painful decision. He would have been known for his military splendor and fearsome appearance. But in that moment, he showed that there was another impulse in his heart, one that could overwrite his pride. It rewrites his character in purgatory, as he bears the weight on his back while bending before Dante. He could humble himself like Mary, David, and Trajan, commemorated in the vivid, exemplary carvings.

A crucial lesson for us, as readers, is that the little moments in life when we can act against character, in ways that might improve our character, are crucial and transformative. They should be seized. They can move mountains, or at least might ease the weight that otherwise bears down on us and prevents us from gazing freely at the heavenly lights and stars. They are easily ignored, easily turned from as humiliating. But they are the way to fuller participation in divine life. They are a gift from purgatory.

Somewhat alleviated from pride, they encounter an angel to guide them.

PURGATORIO 12

Lighter

IRGIL TELLS DANTE TO STAND UP STRAIGHT. Dante has been talking with those burdened by pride. He was feeling it himself: the way it limits and constrains his worldview with its mistaken sense that his gift is self-given.

But it's hard to leave the souls on the first terrace of Mount Purgatory. He feels yoked to them, as oxen are to one another, though the reference to yokes smuggles in a note to hope. Jesus had said that his yoke is easy and his burden is light. The implication is that one day, these souls will know that freedom. Their yokes are simultaneously devices of release.

The comparison has wider meaning. Saint Paul had spoken of the law as preparing souls for the freedom of Christ. It is a type of teacher, Paul wrote in the letter to the Galatians, because its weight provokes a dream of liberation. Dante uses the same word for teacher in this canto as Paul does in his letter and, given the word is a *hapax legomenon* in The Commedia, it underlies the comparison Dante is deliberately making. There is hope as these souls are doubled up and bowed down.

Dante straightens himself and stands up. Immediately, he notices he feels lighter. He has lost some of the burden of his own pride. The levity surprises him. He didn't know that there was such freedom in his soul. By releasing some of his self-importance, he finds more of the easy yoke and light burden of which Jesus spoke.

That said, he realizes that pride can quickly seize on the newfound sense of the lightness, as if he had himself achieved it, as if he is not blessed but owed it. The soul can as quickly take on weight as it can lose it. Dante must learn to watch as pride comes and goes. It is a constant task on the spiritual journey. Humility is a necessary virtue, not in the sense of self-abnegation, but in the sense of self-opening, in order to be filled up with more. It's why service is perfect freedom, because service turns to the life that you don't own and can't claim, as that life is limitless.

They walk on, and Virgil invites Dante to look down again. Beneath his feet, he sees more images. Again, the carvings look as lively as real life, though they convey scenes very different from those that marked the entry to this terrace. At this end of the ledge, the images show those who weren't able to learn its lessons. They display figures who remain bowed down.

The first is of Lucifer, locked into the stone of Mount Purgatory as firmly as he had been frozen in the ice of hell. The second is of the giant whom Dante hadn't seen on the floor of the *Inferno*, Briareus. Virgil had warned Dante that Briareus was too terrifying to approach, though now that they see him realistically portrayed, Dante sees he doesn't have all the heads and arms that he had expected. He is pathetically bound in chains. You might say that Dante is able to see more clearly, which means seeing through his fearful expectations to the real condition of fallen angels and giants.

Other figures are in the marble beneath their feet, some mythological, some biblical, some historical. Dante views them with pity. He describes the experience as like entering a mausoleum. As you read names, dates, and descriptions, you ponder the lives lived, the loves lost, the mistakes made. Dante views these seemingly cursed individuals with a softer heart.

The tercets in the poem that describe these sad souls form an acrostic. If you put the first letter of each line together, you get, UUUU, OOOO, MMMM. That reads "uom," the Italian for "man." It is as if Dante is lamenting the state of many men and women. He is not revolted or angered by them, as he had been upon encountering the disfigured in hell. He grieves for them. Their walk becomes a litany of lament, which is to cultivate an attitude of humility, the first step toward freedom from pride.

Virgil remarks that it is about noon. The sun is high in the sky, which Virgil conveys by referencing the sixth handmaid of the day. Each hour was felt to be the precursor to the next, as the medieval soul felt the qualities of the day unfolding, more than the minutes of the day ticking away. It's a wonderful way to experience time because time is felt to be leading on, not running out.

Then, Virgil tells Dante to look. There's an angel approaching. He suggests that Dante will want to show due reverence and willingness to accept whatever the angel is arriving to give. It feels like an important moment: as if Dante must receive a blessing in order to continue.

Dante admires the divine creature. It is white and radiant, shining like a sparkling dawn star. He is able to look toward it, unblinded. It's another indicator of change.

The angel spreads its wings and, although Dante doesn't notice it in the moment, their brush against his forehead causes one of the Ps to be erased. What Dante does notice is feeling lighter at the breeze of its passing.

The angel speaks. Human beings are made to fly upward, it sings. How easily they are knocked off their natural course, it adds. There's a strange thing about purgation: when the weight of sin lessens, it's hard to remember what had held you down.

The angel offers guidance too. It shows them the way up, off this terrace, and toward the second. If you have ever been to Florence, the route Dante describes is like the climb to San Miniato al Monte. This church is on the far side of the Arno from the famous duomo and, from its high terrace, the panorama of Florence unfolds in all its magnificence. Dante is not only feeling lighter. He is enjoying the climb.

"Blessed are the poor in spirit!" They hear the words of the beatitude sweetly sung as they progress. The chant resounds with the insight that poverty of spirit enables the individual to see the riches of life. They are in a domain that celebrates the other side of pride, when it is relinquished.

The lovely mood of the moment continues to the end of the canto, as Virgil reveals to Dante that the angel has wiped one of the Ps from his head. He raises his hand and feels that six remain. In some ways, this is the first tangible evidence that Dante has received that he really is changing, for all the distance he has already travelled. The truth of his journey, and Virgil's guidance, is becoming manifest.

Virgil smiles. He too can feel the lightness. He too understands more of the operation of grace. He has seen the angel and sensed more of the law of love. He hasn't had a P removed from his forehead as, like the other souls on Mount Purgatory, he has none to erase. But he can feel the transformation in himself as much as in the presence around them. If he couldn't feel his own, he would not be smiling at the other.

The second terrace looks barren, but the generous sun guides them.

PURGATORIO 13

Envy

DANTE AND VIRGIL ARRIVE ON THE SECOND TER-
race of Mount Purgatory. They have been led here by an angel, to
the sound of chanting. They are in good spirits. But the moment
they step onto the next ledge, the mood changes. Spiritual progress is like that.

This zone is barren. They are not greeted by inspiring murals. Blue-gray
rock faces them. It projects emptiness and disorients them. Virgil fears that
they may wait too long for guidance. The place offers no bearings and
erodes their inner orientation as well.

However, Virgil is not entirely lost. He looks up at the sun, turning to his
right, so as to face it directly. The action looks ritualistic and, sure enough,
he next addresses the solar disk. He calls on its sweetness and warmth, in
marked contrast to their immediate environs. It constantly pours forth
warmth and light, which is to say, it never ceases to inspire illumination
and intelligence. This is the intuition Virgil seeks in his prayer, from a living
source of light, so unlike the barren rocks.

He receives it. They hear spirits flying by them. If the rocks were dead,
the air is now alive. My sense is that the spirits are a bit like sunbeams. They

didn't detect them initially, but tuned in by Virgil's turn to the sun, they hear them. One utters the words of Mary at the wedding in Cana: "They have no wine." It brings to mind the first of the miracles of Jesus which are signs of divine presence, as John's Gospel records it. There's a classical reference in a voice calling, "I am Orestes!" It belongs to the friend of Orestes, who pretended to be the son of Agamemnon in order to take the brunt of the punishment that was due the vengeful son.

Thirdly come the words of Jesus, "Love your enemies." They clarify further what this place is about: going the extra mile, caring for those who harm you, thinking of others, offering your life.

They have come to the terrace for those whose lives were shaped by envy, Virgil concludes. The results of envy are radiated by the rocks: envy drains life from those who suffer it, to the extent of seeking to destroy life in others, when the envious person feels they cannot have that life themselves. It is the kind of envy that doesn't merely want what another person has, a mood that can inspire creativity and direction. Rather, it is the emotion that grips a person when they feel that they can never have what another person has. A hatred of others grows. The envious person may first try to steal so as to possess and, failing that, will resort to destructive or murderous means, either to destroy what they lack or to ruin the person who has what they lack.

The way the nature of this terrace's flaws emerge to Dante and Virgil is fascinating. It's as if two poles of human nature are present. One is extraordinarily, wildly generous, almost to the point of madness. The other is extraordinarily, wildly possessive, to the point of destruction. It's as if, between these two dynamics, an alchemical reaction burns. The souls on this terrace feel it within them, as Dante and Virgil hear the spirit voices rushing by. It provokes a keen awareness of what has dominated their lives, and what can transform them. They must live with this tension as they are, thereby, transformed, like a transmutation in the retort.

They see the souls. They are huddled up against the bleak rocks, as if striving to feel at home. The clothes they wear are the same color as the stone, which is perhaps why Dante and Virgil didn't spot them at first.

Their appearance is beggarly. They are having to ask for what they don't have, even as the sun freely radiates its generosity upon them.

Dante notices something further. The envious have their eyes stitched shut. They look like young falcons, forcefully calmed by not being able to see, and not yet allowed to fly.

It seems cruel but there is a necessity in purgatory's ways. Envy works by projection. The envious project their own desires onto others, to the extent that they see in others what they want, and so become empty themselves. It's why envy is such a destructive state of affairs. These souls on Mount Purgatory have volunteered the deliberate closing of their eyes, so that they must look into themselves, and bear what they find. That is the only way they may recover themselves, painful though the process must be.

Dante approaches them. Virgil walks alongside him, carefully staying between Dante and the drop off Mount Purgatory. It's a generous position to adopt, as Dante enquires into the disposition that knows no generosity. It is an uncomfortable place to be, which Virgil intuits in an empathic telepathy he has with Dante.

This sharing of minds will become an increasing feature of the journey to God. It will double in intensity when Dante meets Beatrice. It arises, I think, with the realization that consciousness — meaning thoughts and feelings — is not the private feature of existence it is commonly taken to be. Awareness of what is on another's mind grows with the recognition that the consciousness of two people is, at base, one. One person's capacity to say "I" is the same as another person's capacity to say "I," for all that their character, experience, and preoccupations will differ, because underneath that stream of consciousness lies a unity that sustains everyone. This reality becomes clearer as they ascend, manifesting in part as telepathy.

It is a type of empathy, though that this is not a word Dante could have used, as it was only coined in 1904. It is a modern way of describing an older perception: when you meet another person, you don't see a body or hear a voice. You experience being with another soul. The physical presence is only the visible appearance of an invisible spirit. A living body projects that interior current, and an open mind can pick up its undercurrents, which is what Virgil does now.

Dante is staring at the souls who can't look back. He feels he might gawp at them, maybe enjoy the suffering they are undergoing, which would be damaging insofar as it distracts from fostering an awareness of how envy may or may not be operative in his own life. Virgil knows what Dante is thinking and agrees. "Yes, do speak with them, but be brief and to the point," he directs.

Dante addresses them generously, reminding them that they are here because they are destined to see once more, by the light of heaven. And he asks whether any of those present are Italian.

Sapìa of Siena calls back, agreeing with Dante that they are citizens of the heavenly city, and that he would have been more correct to ask for someone who was once a pilgrim in Italy. She was a noblewoman, though not much is known about her mortal life, beyond that she was very wealthy and gave much of it to fund a hospital in Siena, which makes you wonder why she is here. Wasn't generosity a defining feature of her life?

She confesses to Dante that contrary impulses actually shaped her soul. Her actions were smokescreens, her philanthropy a sham. In life, she reveled in others' suffering. Further, in the Italian civil wars, she came to love watching the destruction of her townspeople. She enjoyed it as they scattered across the plains of the peninsula. Sadism seized her inwardly. Or perhaps she suffered from the delusion that can grip those who give to the less fortunate: they do so because it demonstrates that they are not less fortunate and, in their fantasy, builds the belief that they don't and will never have to rely on others. The giving isolates them. It doesn't connect them with others, as the sun's warmth connects us to the earth's star.

She describes how she used to sing like a blackbird, seemingly beautifully but all the while declaring her superiority. It became so bad that she lost her fear of God. Though her name is Sapìa, she says, sapient she was not.

She was saved by a friar, Pier Pettinaio. He grieved for her, prayed for her, and she was not so far gone that she was not moved by his devotion. In the last minutes of her life, as her fragility and mortality became more evident and powerful than the delusions with which she had surrounded herself, she was able to receive the grace his prayers unleashed. Love only needs a little to overcome much. The upshot is that she is on the second terrace, becoming capable of more.

She is not so shut up with herself as to not be interested in Dante. His eyes aren't sewn shut, she presumes, and he explains that he is a still-living soul. He knows that he will return to this ledge in the falcon-like state, though interestingly he intuits he won't have to stay here for long.

This is a reflection of his self-understanding. It is not a boast. He knows he will have to spend longer with the proud — that is, closer to his core troubles — which is to say that he is not envious of others because he is aware of his great gift.

Sapìa replies that Dante's presence is wonderful. She can recognize the miracles of God, in spite of her sealed eyelids, perhaps *because* they are shut. Pray for me when you return to earth, she asks, and tell them my story, so they may learn from my flaws. The lesson may be particularly valuable in Siena, she adds. It is a landlocked city-state, prone to envy locations with ports on the coast. During her lifetime, the city's rulers had thought they might be able to dig a tunnel to the sea. The vanity almost ruined them and their fellow citizens. They would do well not to covet what life has given others, as she had, but instead accept their blessings and their lot.

In the realm of the envious, an avaricious civilization comes into view.

PURGATORIO 14
Degeneracy

ANTE OVERHEARS TWO SOULS SPEAKING ABOUT him. They have realized he is walking, and so must have his eyes open, not stitched shut like the souls on the second terrace of purgatory, working out their envy. They also know he has not yet died, as they heard his intakes of breath as he was speaking with Sapìa. They are awed by what his presence says about divine grace.

They know about grace. They are in purgatory, not hell. But their inquisitive nature did not miss the sound of Dante breathing, a detail that conveys a sense of the jealousy that shaped their earthly lives. As they talk, or is it gossip, you sense they are struggling not to wish that they were free like him.

They call out to Dante, and he tells them that he is from Florence, though he does so in a remarkably roundabout way. He alludes to being born on the banks of a river, which the souls identify as the Arno. They note that he hasn't used the name of his city or its river directly, and that launches a tirade against the people of Florence, with which Dante can only concur.

It sets the tone for the canto, which can be helpfully read against its corresponding canto in The Inferno. There the figure of the Old Man of Crete had been invoked. It is a great statue, standing under a mountain, with a splendid head of gold, chest of silver, bronze and iron legs, that are degrading into a crumbling terracotta foot, upon which its entire weight rests. It is an image of a tired, lost civilization, relying on its least valuable parts, having forgotten the gold and silver of its genius and wellspring.

In canto 14 of The Purgatorio, Dante the poet returns to the theme of cultural decline. In The Inferno, it was the source of the foul, red river that flowed to the depths of hell. What is Dante going to say about it now?

Fame is on his mind, in the richest sense of distinction and eminence, because he tells the souls that they will not know who he is: he is not famous as he has not yet written anything worthy of the name. It is a striking assessment of his work before The Divine Comedy, which was substantial and noteworthy, for all that his masterpiece would come entirely to outshine it. But perhaps he is also thinking of the fame of Florence, as a son of the city. It had been worthy of the name but had cast that renown aside.

My sense is that between the lines of this canto, Dante is asking us to think about the origins of civilizations, and how civilizations decline and fall. They are inclined to start living off their fame, their illustriousness, and their reputation. This can foster a sense of self-sufficiency and entitlement that in turn begins the process of leaning on the terracotta foot and ceasing to attend to the silver and gold. The bulk of the canto is certainly taken up with a roll call of degeneracy, corruption, and fraud, as Dante and the souls together rehearse a long series of disastrous wars, failed politics, and civic exploitation.

It raises the question of whether Dante's poem will help restore the civilization that was its wellspring. Will Dante's fame come because his journey, and brilliant account, reconnect Italy and Europe to its divine source? The canto picks up the possibility that his poetry is not only about Dante's purification or the fame of his city, but of European civilization and Christianity itself.

The lament is like reading a news review of a terrible year. It tells a tale of suffering and sorrow. It paints a picture of a time and place as rank as hell, polluted by greed, narcissism, and envy. Cities have become places in which virtue is mocked and loathed, as the inhabitants run en masse toward vice. The situation has become so bad that these places couldn't save themselves if they wanted to. The air carries demonic odors, the lifeblood is perverted. One of the souls remarks that people have become like pigs, to which we might add, with apologies to pigs: how far can things fall?

The two souls speak of their own offspring. One turns to the other and, in a moment of prophecy, describes seeing his peer's grandson running across the countryside like a wolf, needlessly murdering people. His nobility is draining away, in mindless, unmotivated violence. He springs from a cursed wood that couldn't renew itself in a thousand years.

With that thought, they pause. They have not yet revealed who they are, and Dante is keen to know their names. They speak of a world that he intimately knows, and he longs to know with whom he shares the distress.

One of the souls looks up. He says to Dante that, although he wouldn't tell them his name, they will tell him theirs. The long recollection of terrible times has made him want to act generously, to bring at least some redemption, in the spirit of purgatory.

Dante learns that he has been speaking with Guido del Duca and Rinier da Calboli. Though little is known about them as historical figures, it is likely that they came from opposite sides of the civil wars. In purgatory, they look on the calamity together. Dante was right to want to know their names. With that information, he can see former enemies united, a vision that is powerfully redemptive for Dante.

Guido admits that, like Sapìa, he is on this terrace because in life he had loved watching the suffering of others. He understands how horrible that is. He calls out to his fellow citizens, asking why they live this way. Why do they love the things that destroy others and loathe the things that can be shared? Why do civilizations forget what is sustainable, and so consume themselves?

Guido continues with a second, contrasting list of leaders. He names ancestors who were noble and virtuous, who understood how to build societies and cultures in ways that were life-giving for all. The final part of the canto is therefore in marked contrast to what came before. Light and hope make an appearance, although Guido ends his inventory by saying that it sorrows him to remember better times and, in truth, he would rather weep. It is the more appropriate emotion for his sorrowing mind. It is the right state for him to be in, as he acknowledges the part he played in Italy's decline.

Dante and Virgil leave them. They walk on, confident that they are headed in the right direction, though Dante is momentarily filled with fear at the sound of two voices, screeching through the air like monstrous gales.

Good spirits had flown by them as they entered the second terrace, and demonic ghosts pass them as they come to its end. They hear the voice of

Cain, who slew his brother, Abel. They hear the voice of Aglauros, a mythological figure who was gripped by envy when her sister found favor with the god, Mercury. As a consequence, she was turned to stone, which is to say, her feelings petrified inside her.

Virgil speaks, intoning another lament for humanity's state, remarking that even when heaven shows its light, when the stars of divine insight wheel high in the sky, people prefer to fix their eyes and keep their faces turned to the ground. If only heads could look up, he muses, instead of being face down. Virgil is right. He is learning of these things too.

Virgil outlines a way of limitless growth in life. Dante is rapt.

PURGATORIO 15

Mercy

T'S THREE HOURS BEFORE SUNSET, WHICH MEANS it's three hours before their second nightfall on Mount Purgatory. Dante and Virgil are walking on the second terrace up the mountain, facing the mid-afternoon sun. It is beginning to descend in the west, as Dante's shadow starts to lengthen.

He experiences the moment globally, reflecting that mid-afternoon in purgatory is mid-morning on another part of the globe, where it will be three hours after sunrise. It will be night in other regions. He is aware of not just the single moment that surrounds him, or of time as if governed by a clock. He knows time as a cosmic phenomenon. He can be connected to more than one moment of time, as in his mind's eye he traverses the globe. He can see more deeply into the immediacy around him and enjoy a wider perception of reality.

Canto 15 is, in part, about looking at surfaces and reflections, and recognizing that they are only the most visible dimension in multidimensional things. Through and beyond appearances are other zones with a life of their own. They touch what's immediate, though are not contained by what's immediate.

The generous mind can appreciate such scale. It is not envious of other people and places. Dante and Virgil are walking along the terrace for those gradually allowing others their lives, as they become more content with their own. Envy is a vice that limits perception, as well as damaging souls. Generosity is a virtue that expands perception and, along with its sight, enlarges the soul of the generous mind. Clinging, holding onto, possessing, coveting are qualities that constrain life. They narrow and blind.

Dante is seeing beyond these limitations as he enjoys the diaphanous nature of time, and the experience of its abundance prompts a vision. He realizes that he is becoming distracted by the appearance of a light that is brighter than the sun, and lower in the sky. At first it looks like a second sun from which he has to shield his eyes. Only it is hard to block out the new brilliance. The light bounces under his hands, which he has raised to shield his eyes, much as light will reflect off a mirror to surprise and dazzle. I think the vision comes because the generous mind sees more light as it opens onto the ways in which life shines with multiple intensities. It sees more than what is immediately manifest. It's an inner light drawing, flowing, attracting. And then Dante identifies its nature. It is an angel, rising at the end of the terrace of the envious.

Seeing it disturbs him. He has seen a few angels on the journey, most provoking a mix of fascination and fear. This angel catches him unawares. His spontaneous reaction is to screen it out, to try to block its light, though he will come to know that such brilliance can be tolerated, and then welcomed, and then loved.

Dante asks Virgil to explain what is going on, and Virgil replies that Dante should not be surprised that he is dazzled and disturbed by the angelic presence. The light is what his soul was made to enjoy, an enjoyment of which this ascent is making him capable. Such light will soon not be a burden, Virgil adds, and it is remarkable that he knows that. Wider perceptions are unfolding within him, as well as within Dante as they climb. They are both seeing more light, which is to say, they are opening up to the true nature of light. The falling sun is lovely. Lovelier is the celestial light of which the sun is a reflection.

This is the light that illuminates direct perception. It is the image that the artist sees and captures in pencil or paint. The scientific description of light is only one way of describing it, one that is self-evidently limited. The mathematician and philosopher, Alfred North Whitehead, who is said to have been one of only a handful of people who really understood the ideas of Albert Einstein when they emerged in 1905, put it like this. Entities like atoms, electrons, and photons appear in the minds of physicists because of the way that physicists look at the world. They are useful abstractions that work while you are performing experiments and using equations. But they don't work when, say, you are looking at a sunset because a photon of light doesn't explain anything about the gorgeous golds and reds. "When you understand all about the sun and all about the atmosphere and all about the rotation of the earth, you may still miss the radiance of the sunset," he wrote. It is that missing radiance that Dante is discovering in the light of the angel.

With the light comes sound. Dante and Virgil hear another beatitude, chanted in Latin: "Blessed are the merciful." Dante has heard the words countless times before. He hears them afresh in this moment, with a renewed clarity. Their truth shines out, as if beaming with the light. I think he senses that being merciful is a blessing when it is not regarded as a moral requirement. It brings bliss because those who find that they can forgive, simultaneously find that they have open hearts.

More words echo around them, this time in Italian, which is interesting because it is as if Dante is not only hearing more in and through the Latin of Church liturgy: he is hearing of divine things directly in the vernacular language of everyday life. Everyday life and divine life are closer to each other than he had heretofore realized. It's a proximity the Christianity of the Church fails to foster, with its demands to believe the creeds it sanctions, do the actions it sanctions, receive the blessings it sanctions.

The Italian phrase is unexpected: "Rejoice, you who conquer!" It is not a biblical quotation, though it sounds like it might be. It is not a Church expression. It is a riff on such things, which is to say that this place, as Dante becomes more conscious of how it shines in his mind, reveals an audacity. It's another side to purgatory's emerging generosity.

The vision of the angel fades. It has sparked a renewed yearning inside Dante and Virgil, reflected in a conversation between them. Dante is reminded of a remark he had heard earlier on the terrace, which had ventured that there is a type of sharing in life that doesn't diminish with sharing, but rather grows as it is passed around. He doesn't understand what can be shared like that. Usually, sharing means dividing up, so that there is only so much to go around. Does Virgil know about this abundance, Dante asks?

Virgil tells Dante that he must turn from perceiving with earthly eyes, which can indeed only understand scarcity and diminishment. Heavenly eyes, though, perceive love, which grows the more that it loves. As it is shared, it doesn't diminish but increases.

"I long to know more about that," Dante replies, immediately proving Virgil's point. And Virgil sketches what amounts to an entire economy built on growth of a type that doesn't consume what it desires but amplifies and broadens what it desires. Love is the example he gives, though to that could be added music, or knowledge, or art. These things do not come to an end but continually suggest wider avenues, subtler nuances, deeper reflections. They are not about accumulation, but transformation. They are not about maximizing profits, but broadening satisfaction.

The reason these things bring potentially infinite growth is that they draw on infinite life. The trick, then, is to discover the economy of abundance and, distinguishing it from the economy of scarcity, to ask whether it connects with sources of life that aren't depleted.

Virgil knows Dante is gripped by this sense of possibility. He tells him that he will come to know of it fully when he meets Beatrice once more, adding that the second of the Ps on his forehead has been removed. Dante had not yet noticed, but the angel had wiped it away.

Things are changing fast in Dante's mind and, perhaps particularly at hearing the name Beatrice once more, he falls into a trance. Virgil's explanation, that name, and the vision of the angel, with its superlative light, tips him into an ecstasy. It's an eruption within him of spiritual energy, paralleling the appearance of celestial light. It's a peak experience of the type that, from the outside, can make someone look drunk, though from the inside it is really a shift of gear that, while disorienting, is the pathway to a fuller perception of reality. It bewilders because a barely dreamed side of life is glimpsed and better grasped.

Simultaneous with the vision is their entry onto the next terrace of purgatory. Dante is swept up to the next level with three instances of life-giving generosity, that each have a twist. He sees the moment in which Mary and Joseph take the young Jesus to the Temple in Jerusalem. They lose him there and spend three days searching for him, only to finally find him talking with the Temple elders. They are distressed and ask Jesus whether he did not care that they would be worried, to which Jesus replies: "Did you not know that I must be in my Father's house?" (Lk 2:49).

It's a harsh response because Mary and Joseph have a point. The young Jesus is only twelve years old. They are his parents. But Jesus is already in touch with a source of life that exceeds parental concerns. The implication is that Dante might be too.

It's a level of awareness that can cause offense. As an adult, Jesus was to make many remarks pointing to it, and risking outrage. He told people to let the dead bury their dead, that brothers and sisters would fall out over his teaching, that he had come to bring a sword. This way cannot be understood morally. It only seems objectionable, confusing, and wrong. But Jesus is interested in divine ways and the perception of those ways by human beings. That comes by stepping into a new world, which means, at least in part, turning away from the familiar.

The second moment Dante glimpses features a Greek leader called Pisistratus. He was remembered for a story concerning his daughter. One day, she was embraced by a suitor, at which her mother, Pisistratus's wife, became incensed. She, as a parent, had not granted permission. But Pisistratus felt differently. He told his wife that when you see love, you must welcome love. It overwrites offense and possessiveness. The thought only compounded his wife's anger. But his sight was on matters other than social norms. He was looking at a higher kind of life.

Dante's third vision is of Saint Stephen, the first martyr, being killed by stoning. The story is told in the Acts of the Apostles and is striking for the loathing and hate hurled at Stephen along with the rocks and boulders. That violence, and his broken body, contrasts markedly with Stephen himself. His eyes are fixed on heaven. He is already halfway to another dimension of reality, and he asks that his tormentors and murderers be forgiven.

I think the point of these stories is that while they are clear that there is a side of life that eclipses the worst that life can apparently throw at you, it is not remotely straightforward to access. It involves all that you know being disturbed, which is why many never fully know of it. Don't parental concerns, social mores, and justice come first? Well, no, these visions say.

Dante remarks that this other life will be judged to be a string of terrible errors by many people. But the seeming errors are truths. That can be discerned.

The point is underlined because as Dante comes out of his ecstasy, Virgil remarks that Dante looks drunk, unsteady, dazed. Dante replies that he has seen tremendous things, to which Virgil replies: yes. He knows.

My guess is that Virgil underlines the point about the appearance of drunkenness because the trick with visions is not to become addicted to the peak experiences, but to work at incorporating them into life. Ecstasy can become an end in itself when, in truth, it happens on the path to another end: divine perception.

They walk a little farther along the third terrace. Together again, they move across its terrain. As if to underscore that the journey into the light involves darkness and confusion, as much as vision and sight, a cloud as black as night forms around them. One of the bleakest experiences of their time on Mount Purgatory is about to break upon them.

Blind rage becomes righteous anger. They talk about free will.

PURGATORIO 16

Will

ANTO 16 IS THE FIFTIETH CANTO IN THE DIVINE
Comedy, out of one hundred. It poses a central question at this
central stage: what is the nature of free will?

It's a crucial issue. If human beings enjoy no freedom of will, then Dante's entire journey and work will amount to nothing. His life is devoted to aligning his will with the divine will. He seeks the way of changing, or awakening, so as to participate freely in God's life, which is the pathway to paradise. He needs a proper understanding of freedom if he is to track that course. So, it is striking that the canto in which Dante addresses this matter is also one of the darkest in purgatory.

Dante and Virgil are surrounded by thick, acrid, impenetrable smoke. It had formed around them as they climbed onto the third terrace on Mount Purgatory. It enwraps them for the whole canto with a cloudiness so dense that Dante cannot see Virgil, though he clings to him throughout. "Watch out you don't lose me," Virgil warns.

This is the purgatorial state of mind. It is not without hope. Quite the opposite, it is full of hope. It is not without insight. Quite the opposite, it is the state of mind in which insights rise and grow. But it is a state of mind that can move speedily from light to darkness, from acceptance to fear, from trust to doubt.

It is about the struggle to let our desires link to divine love. It is a struggle because we are free beings. It would be automatic only if we were robots. Consciously and unconsciously, we become proud, envious, and angry — the trouble that Dante and Virgil will discover on this terrace. However, what is even more important, consciously we can set an intention to become less proud, envious, and angry, so as to become aware of the love that sustained us all along and, actually, wasn't damaged by any vices. This is what it is to participate freely in unity with the divine.

The cloud that envelops them is the rage that gripped the lives of the souls on the terrace. It didn't entirely ruin their lives, as was the case with the furious they had met in hell. But it did disconnect them from life, becoming a life of its own. Seeing through that clouded life is the work of purgatory.

It is a tricky process because anger is not bad per se. One of the surprising recurrences in *The Divine Comedy* is the frequent expressions of righteous anger. Even saints in the high heavens utter heartfelt ire. It means that the only way to sift anger is to enter into anger, to experience and understand its various manifestations and effects. This is why anger is a crucial step up Mount Purgatory.

It is frightening. Dante says that he became as terrified on the third terrace as he was in hell. He is not exaggerating. When perceived fully, anger is profoundly disturbing. He must have known that kind of rage during his life, and perhaps Virgil didn't to the same degree because he is able to guide Dante through this state of mind. I get the sense that he had never been wholly consumed by it, to the point of losing his mind.

They hear voices. The souls hidden about them are singing the *Agnus Dei*: "Oh Lamb of God, that takes away the sins of the world." It sounds as a perfect harmony, Dante reports, which is an ambivalent observation. On the one hand, the souls are producing a beautiful sound, the opposite of anger's ugliness. But on the other hand, the unity of their voices imply they are hard to differentiate as individuals, which is to say they are wrestling with the individuality that their blind rage has threatened to dissolve. They cling to the chant, as if that is all they can do to prevent themselves from becoming entirely lost in a fog of emotion. Virgil explains that they are slowly, gradually loosening the knot of wrath.

Dante hears the voice of a specific person though, unsurprisingly, he cannot tell whose voice it is. It reaches him from the darkness because it comes from an inner darkness and it is not clear with what will it speaks. Is it motivated by anger, or love, or need, or hope? Dante finds it hard to tell, though the intensity of the soul's presence strikes him forcibly. As the soul explains, he no longer experiences life as a passage of time, marked by calendars, as life on earth was known. Rather, he knows his life as a whole, with a complete immediacy and direct presence, which must be what is required to discern its light and darkness and untangle one from the other.

Dante and the soul wish each other well. They greet each other with marked charm. The soul is amazed at Dante's mortal presence, as well he might be, in part because Dante adds a specific detail to his now familiar account of travelling through these realms with divine blessing. Dante says that he is being taken to God's courts in heaven by means unknown to people of his times. It is a modern wisdom that conveys him there.

This is the first use of the word "modern" in Italian. It implies that Dante is fully conscious of the ways in which his journey, vision, and poem are remaking the received insights of medieval Christianity. The descent and ascent are not only transitional for him, but for his times. His aim is not to tell a story that illuminates Christianity but transforms Christianity. It's quite a claim, particularly at this midpoint of The Divine Comedy. Something is being underlined.

The soul says more. He is called Marco and is from Lombardy. Nothing else is known about him as a figure in history. He asks Dante for his prayers when he reaches the high places, which suggests he believes Dante's claim to be uncovering modern pathways to the divine. He wants to benefit from the new insights.

That said, Dante has a pressing question. It has been forming inside him for some time and comes to the fore at this moment because upon hearing that Dante is charting fresh waters, Marco replies that new routes are needed. The world is losing its ability to aim well at the goals of life. It needs the modern ways of which Dante speaks.

Dante agrees. Human beings are losing sight of life. They have become blind. But what, he asks, are the causes of this evil? What leads humanity so profoundly astray? Is it the stars, as many say? Are the heavens themselves causing people to fall short of their potential by raining down bad influence?

This is the astrological way of asking the question of free will: do the planets determine our lives, or are other forces at play? Today, many would ask a parallel question referencing, say, genes or upbringing. How free are we, when the significance of these environmental factors is factored in? Can we be held to account and blamed for our flaws? And if we are not responsible, how can we participate in our change?

Marco explains to Dante that there are natural forces that shape us. This is what it is to be alive in a dynamic, animated universe. We share that energy, and are molded by it, as a result of being born into it. Its life is our life. However, we bring more to our lives than the accidents of birth. While we inherit much from our time and place, our ancestry and upbringing, that is only part of who we are. With these received elements come capacities of reflection, impulses of desire, intuitions of purpose, moments when we can freely decide how to respond to our predicament.

Human freedom can, therefore, be modeled in this way, Marco continues, sharing the insights he is developing on this terrace. There are two levels within us. One is the instinctual, that can be consumed by anger and rage. It causes us to lose touch with our freedom and, instead, feel we are only led by stars or, we might add, programmed by genes. But since Marco has been in purgatory he has become aware of other aspects of life that can be drawn on. These are the yearnings he is nurturing on the mountain. It is here that our freedom is found.

He continues, saying that the application of his will to the task, connects him with a part of reality that is greater than the cosmos, the stars, and the created order. It is the divine part within him. Human beings stretch from the creaturely and instinctual, to the uncreated and infinite. The range is the cause of many of our struggles in life. It is also the hope of salvation.

One of the ramifications of this insight is a revision of Christian doctrine, at least as it is expressed in Western Christianity. Following Augustine, it teaches that human beings are born fallen into the utterly hopeless and lost state called original sin. But as Dante and Marco talk on through the gloom, they paint a different picture of a human. We are created innocent, they say, wanting what is good. It's why young children are delighted by everything they encounter. Spontaneously, unthinkingly, they reach out to touch whatever or whoever is around them, full of fascination, pleasure, and love.

This means that life's great task is not to mend what is fundamentally flawed. It is to foster, guide, and discern our desires, so that we grow beyond childish innocence into mature awareness. The initial impulse, which we inherit, can become a tremendous realization of the infinite life we participate in.

Thomas Aquinas, the medieval theologian and Christian innovator who had a deep impact upon Dante's thinking, wrote that "grace perfects nature." Grace always wills to bring nature to completion. It is the purpose and meaning of created life. It is crucial to keep sight of this vision, Dante continues, because without it, those who claim to be the shepherds of souls, fail in the task to guide and pastor. This is the bankruptcy of the Church. The implication is that the doctrine of original sin can suit the worldly purposes of ecclesiastical powers insofar as it keeps people beholden to them. It then blocks souls from the workings of freely given grace.

It is also why the Western world has lost its way. Those who should be helping humanity to remember what we are here for, don't themselves remember, so confused have they become by the clouding effects of their self-interest and concern.

What was true of Dante's time is true of ours. The Western world today has lost its way again. My sense too is that the Church has a key part to play in this confusion. It may or may not be so corrupt as the medieval papacy; that is a matter for debate. It has, though, invented all manner of new types of spiritual materialism and life confusion.

Dostoevsky captures one form of it in the exchange between the Grand Inquisitor and Jesus, in The Brothers Karamazov. The inquisitor tells Jesus that the Church no longer needs him, recalling how Jesus refused the temptation of Satan to turn stones into bread. The inquisitor argues that was wrong. "Feed men, and then ask of them virtue!" he insists. Similarly, many in the Church today argue that the essence of the gospel is social justice. That undoubtedly matters, but when it becomes the core or primary teaching, it sides with Satan and instills spiritual materialism.

Similarly, the inquisitor argues that if Jesus had cast himself from the Temple pinnacle, as Satan had invited him to do, people would have seen his divinity. After all, if he ruled the kingdoms of earth, salvation would follow. This is the desire to make the gospel more straightforward, practical, and believable, and it's mistaken. It perverts the freedom of which the gospel speaks, confusing it with the limited freedoms that a few might enjoy on earth.

The authentic realization is that people cannot live on bread alone. In the context of canto 16, this is what develops the maturing of the soul from its infantile, innocent state. Its problem is not an excess of evil, but of desire and love. They must, first, be restrained and refined to find the objects that will satisfy them without limit, and which are not found in terrestrial domains but celestial reality.

This world is not enough for us, or rather, when this world is not understood to be a realm that channels life itself, it is not enough for us. Frustration, destruction, blindness follow because the source and origin of all is implicitly dismissed. In short, this canto, at the halfway point, captures both sides of the story of humanity. On the one hand, it is lost. All has become dark. On the other hand, there is light. Purpose and freedom can be found.

Virgil, Dante, and Marco have been walking as they talked. They have traversed a substantial portion of the endarkened terrace, and Marco says he must stop. He cannot travel any farther. He knows that another angel will appear if he were to continue, and he is not able yet to stand its presence. He must leave before it sees him, he explains, turning back without offering Dante a chance to ask more.

The midpoint of The Divine Comedy is filled with a discussion of love.

PURGATORIO 17

Love

ANTO 16 WAS THE FIFTIETH OF THE HUNDRED in *The Divine Comedy*. Canto 17 contains the actual midpoint of the 14,233 lines of the epic poem. At line 7,116, halfway through, at the precise center, it is no surprise to find the one word that matters more than any other to Dante: love.

The canto itself majors on love, including what amounts to a talk by Virgil about its nature. Dante listens in and learns. It provides a pivot around which the poem's knowledge of love, new and old, can turn.

Dante and Virgil emerge from the thick clouds of the third terrace of Mount Purgatory. The experience is akin to being on a terrestrial mountain, shrouded in dense mist, as the mist starts to clear. The light level rises and the pale disc of the sun gleams through the cloud. Next, blue sky breaks through the haze, and warmth returns. Life reorients itself again, around light, not fog. They step from the purgatorial darkness formed by the rage of human anger.

224

The restoration of light raises the issue of how to adapt to it. After all, in canto 16, the soul called Marco had convinced Dante that human beings have free will. We can respond to the world around us, as it manifests physically and spiritually. How, then, is Dante to react to this particular moment of daylight returning? It is a chance for him to exercise the freedom they have just been discussing.

It is, in fact, the end of the day, the second dusk of their time in purgatory. The last light of the sun is hovering above the horizon. A few stars are beginning to twinkle. He realizes, as the sun slips from view, that it's as if another light rises, one with an inner illumination. It is intensely beautiful, as if gold, and straight from heaven. He is momentarily tuned into God, which prompts the thought that at different moments we might be tuned into all sorts of the dynamics that fill the cosmos, from Powers and Principalities, to lesser angels and spirits. They move around the universe, quite as freely as thoughts and feelings flit through our minds, if with purpose. They show up as lesser or higher lights, according to their closeness to God. They make up a spiritual ecology as rich and various as the biological ecology of nature and her creatures around us.

The twilight settles in, that transitional time of day, as if everyday reality is thinning, and amidst the porousness, poised on the moment day becomes night, Dante perceives another three visions. He is less scared of them this time, and they pass quickly. They echo what he has seen before and he is ready and able to understand them; they don't simply happen to him and leave him gawping. The three are witnesses to scenes from myth and history, conveying meaning as well as events. They are exemplars of life-destroying wrath.

The first tells of the return of Procne, who was transformed into a nightingale, having fed her son to his father, her husband, in response to his raping her sister. The second features Haman, a Persian figure from the Hebrew Bible, who wanted to kill a Jew, Mordecai, by crucifixion, and ended up crucified himself. The third is Amata, a woman whom Virgil wrote about, because she killed herself when she thought her son wasn't going to marry her bridal choice.

All three — Procne, Haman and Amata — demonstrate what can happen when rage burns uncontrolled. It kills, suicides or, at best, grossly distorts. Dante has learned the lesson, he has understood the nature of ire, and the visions pass. Incidentally, later in the canto, he will hear another beatitude which underlines the lesson. He hears "Blessed are the peacemakers," and knows the words, I think, not as a moral injunction to make peace, but as

225

a statement of what happens if you live a life of peace, rather than anger. Peace makes it more possible to participate in life. That prompts the blessedness of the beatitude, which in the Greek, as the theologian David Bentley Hart has pointed out, means bliss.

Dante is blessed, or blissed, in what happens next as well, because another angel appears. Dante is not able to see its face, so radiant is its light, though as with the visions, he is less afraid than he has been when previously confronted by them. Instead, the angel brings comfort. It assures them that they are walking in the right direction, which is what they need to know. They are headed toward the fourth staircase to the next level of purgatory.

They climb the stairs. The sun's light is gone and, as the last rays fade, it becomes hard to keep ascending. The effect is partly because of the law of purgatory, that the way up requires divine light. But it is doubly meaningful at this point because the fourth terrace they are approaching is the location of the slothful. These are souls who struggle with finding the energy to live. Dante and Virgil are beginning to experience the same state in their own minds. They are entering the next zone.

It frustrates Dante. He wants to know more, wants to push on, and yet, he can't. He hasn't the energy. It is the predicament of sloth in a nutshell. The flesh is willing, but the spirit is weak.

That said, nothing is wasted in purgatory, and this is the moment that Virgil takes the opportunity to discourse on love. It's a good moment. He describes how love, like the sunlight, can fade and temporarily vanish, though any such disappearance is the precursor to its reappearance. Love cannot wholly disappear from life, for if that were to happen, life itself would fail. Love is what pulses through, in, and around the cosmos.

He turns to Aristotle as he pursues his thoughts. This is part of Dante's development of medieval Christian teaching. As Virgil had done in The Inferno, in the equivalent canto to this one, the point about Aristotle is not that he was wholly right. The way his philosophy interpreted hell was only partially correct. However, it does lead to clearer perceptions and wider horizons. Aristotle offers a springboard from which to discern what Dante and Virgil experience.

The Greek philosophy overlays Church teaching. The juxtaposition is not a replacement, but an expansion. It precipitates a third level of engagement, through the alchemy of the old and the established mixing, fired by their direct and increasingly receptive exposure to reality on Mount Purgatory. It's what happens when free will and love mingle: everything becomes new. It's a wonderful experience to sense at the midpoint of the journey.

Virgil has three main points. First, he explains that while all human beings love, the goal of their loving can be mistaken, and the measure of their loving can be wrong. For example, pride is loving yourself rather than life. Alternatively, sloth is underpowered love.

The second point he makes is that there are two kinds of love in the cosmos. One is a natural kind, and another is a rational or mental kind. Natural love wells up within us, much as desire springs from the innocent child. Mental love is chosen, and Virgil focuses on this second type.

It is the love that can charge and guide free will. It is deliberate and consciously intentional. It can lead us if we collaborate with it. For example, it is the love an artist cultivates, as they choose a path exploring, say, paint and its capacity to represent life.

The third point is arguably the boldest. Virgil says that no one can actually hate themselves or God. It is an audacious remark, given the hate they have encountered — only here, on Mount Purgatory, human afflictions are looking different. Dante is more capable of appreciating a perception of love that reaches back to Socrates, which argues that hate, pride, jealousy, and wrath properly discerned are really forms of ignorance. The individual mistakes these moods for reality, and so feels enveloped by them. That was the experience of souls in hell, and the envelopment continues in purgatory, only now the souls know they are gripped by what might be called a real illusion. By participating more consciously and freely in their feelings — befriending them and bringing them close — they see them shift and change. They realize they were simply ignorant of how reality works. As the veil of unknowing lifts, the truth of love appears. Incidentally, this is the point Virgil is making at the midpoint of the Comedy, when the word "love" literally appears.

It is what the pilgrimage is all about: lifting veils, bearing what appears, embracing life. The soul who does not become lost in the descent will find it morphing into ascent. It's a beautiful point to make at the numerical turning point of the poem.

It is a significant moment. "I would have you discover more of these things for yourself," Virgil says to Dante. The journey will continue with the awareness that love fills all things, draws all things, illuminates all things. The question is how. Knowing more and more about that is the goal of loving, properly understood.

The nature of love is developed, before a crowd of souls rushes upon them.

PURGATORIO 18

Ignorance

IRGIL HAS FINISHED HIS TALK ON LOVE. DANTE is feeling sleepy: he is clearly affected by the mood of the new terrace, the fourth, for those wrestling with sloth.

That said, talking about love tends to fire a desire to talk more about love, and Virgil is so inspired. He knows that Dante has further questions, for all that they are suppressed by lethargy. But this is purgatory, so he encourages Dante to speak, which prompts Dante to raise a fundamental issue: what is love? Virgil eagerly picks up the thread.

It is important, he says, to recognize that the love we tend to have in our minds, human love, is not always good because it is human, not divine. That difference matters when it comes to asking what love is. Only divine love is true love, the love that fills creation, brings freedom, and draws wills.

Virgil is offering Dante a medieval corrective to the modern sentiment that "all you need is love." It's one that originated in Dante's time, when courtly love was widespread, the precursor to romantic ideas about love that so shape the modern imagination. It is inclined to believe that while love can make mistakes, it can't ultimately be wrong. Virgil isn't so sure.

His skepticism links back to what he said about ignorance. If we are ignorant of who we are, and how our life links to divine life, then our assumptions about love can easily be fundamentally mistaken. It's to be like the child who is born full of love and reaches out, willy-nilly, to anything and everything that is around it. The child's enthusiasm can be dangerous, which is why it needs a parent watching over it. So too the ignorant adult's passion can be erroneous and may have no one to offer correctives. However, all is not lost because Virgil posits a fascinating theory, one that also fits well with modern psychotherapy. From a very early age, he continues, we form living images within ourselves that are reflections of what we react to around us. It happens because the desire to reach out to this or that rests on the desire to want this or that. That desire comes from within us and is shaped by how it is met by the people and things around us.

Virgil calls it an apprehensive power. The trouble is that the child inevitably sees only part of what is there to be seen, which is also shaped by how the external world has responded to its desire. It is a child, and so apprehends only part of the world around and about, all the while assuming that is the whole of the world around and about. It knows nothing else.

The images it takes in form a model of the world inside the child, an inner microcosm that is a part-reflection, part-distortion of the external macrocosm, and so is marked by mistakes, to greater and lesser degrees.

This is where love's problems originate. The inner microcosm starts to affect what the child reaches out for, in a feedback loop. If an image is distorted, or reactive, or flawed, it will tend to compound mistakes about what is lovable and what is not. At worst, and perhaps not infrequently, the process can lead to little or no sense of divine love, because the introjected images formed by the child are too warped. Like a distorted mirror, they invariably reflect twisted versions of reality.

It is like stamping wax, Virgil continues. The wax may be pure. But if the stamp with which it is marked has faults, the image will be faulty as well.

There is good news in this metaphor in that wax is pliable, particularly when warmed, and the human psyche is the same: it can be warmed by love, and so made capable of receiving additional, more accurate impressions of reality. Further, desire knows when it is unsatisfied. When that longing is felt, a fire of love that yearns for more is stoked, creating a warming that doesn't cease until it touches the divine. This is why human beings don't find rest until they find God. It can feel like a curse, when you are caught in the confusion and turbulence, though it is really a blessing, because desire doesn't let you go until earlier errors are corrected and love reaches its goal.

Dante is delighted at these ideas. He wakes up as they resonate inside him. Virgil responds by saying that Dante will have to wait until he meets Beatrice to understand love's dynamics fully, though it can be detected, moving the world around us. It is in swelling leaves when they green, zealous bees making honey, the soulfulness radiating from all animate things.

We humans can become conscious of that energy because we can think about what tugs at our heartstrings, and so discern the direction in which we are being pulled. Unlike the plant that devotedly tracks the sun, and the animal that tenderly pursues its mate, we can reflect on and form ourselves, in response to the desires that well up within us. That is our freedom.

In fact, when Dante does meet Beatrice, she will tell him that he didn't use this freedom well. He was at risk of following corrupted, even corrosive, threads of love. It's partly why she had to send Virgil to him as he wandered in the dark woods. The thought of it might make us readers ask whether we are similarly wandering around ourselves. Can we foster better loves?

It's late in the evening. The sun has long set. The moon is high in the sky. It's approaching midnight. Dante becomes sleepy again and his mind starts to drift.

But the somnolent mood is interrupted again. Suddenly, a crowd of souls rushes toward them. They are in a frenzy, as if gripped by a bacchanalia. They are calling and crying. "Mary ran to the hills!" "Caesar rushed to Spain!" "Faster, we have no time to waste, for time is love!" "Strive to do good!"

These are the slothful, propelled by the energy that deserted them in life, even in the middle of the night. It has flooded them in purgatory, where they must learn to direct it aright. The references to Mary and Caesar are of exemplars who did so. Mary went to visit Elizabeth, when she became pregnant. Caesar didn't hang about when campaigning.

Amidst the mayhem, Virgil has the presence of mind to ask the direction of the staircase to the next terrace. One rushing by responds. He was an abbot in Verona, though not much is known about him apart from what Dante records. He is polite, apologizing for not being able to stop. His desire won't put him down. That said, he knows why he is running, unlike the runners on the hot sands of hell.

He gives a prophecy about a future abbot of the monastery, which is of interest to Dante, as Dante will find himself in Verona when he returns to earth in exile, though the abbot says that his successor will be a disaster, presumably because he will be slothful too. Interestingly, clergy were often regarded as slothful in Dante's time, not because they were lazy, but because they busied themselves with the wrong things. They were caught up in worldly tasks, political ambitions, and good works to the extent of forgetting about the spiritual journey to God.

Dante sees some of that in the rushing abbot. If he were spiritually lazy on earth, he's not in purgatory. He knows what he's about and he's cracking on with it, if somewhat chaotically.

The crowd passes by swiftly, ending with two souls who call out other exemplars of what they are fast learning. Virgil and Dante are alone once more.

They grow sleepy. Night thoughts rise. The canto ends with Dante giving in to his slumbers and tumbling into his dreams. Which piques our interest: will they be as consequential as the reveries of his first night on Mount Purgatory?

Dante has a second dream. They make their way to the fourth terrace.

PURGATORIO 19
Responsibility

IRGIL HAS TALKED ABOUT LOVE. DANTE HAS talked with the rushing, slothful souls. Now, he sleeps. And while he sleeps, he is disturbed by a dream.

The images come late in the night, almost the early morning, the auspicious time, when the human imagination touches the divine. The moon is high in the sky and has chilled the landscape, an effect doubled by the melancholic presence of Saturn, a faintly milky light. Together, they convey something of the unsettling mood that has descended.

The warning and foreboding builds as Dante refers to geomancers, individuals who look to the earth to divine the future. They don't raise their eyes to the sun or stars. They gaze down, which is a risky way of seeking fortune.

His dream is short and sharp. First, he sees a horribly deformed, stumbling female figure, with pale yellow skin. He stares at her, and as he stares, she changes. She grows more beautiful, appearing to become lovely. Seemingly restored, she starts to sing, only it's the song of the sirens. She speaks of seducing Ulysses, who would have thrown himself into the sea at the sound of her voice were he not tied to a mast. Dante knows the story, though he is still drawn to the siren song, and its lure of satisfaction.

Her lips are still open when another woman appears beside the siren. The second figure is saintly and stands erect. The siren becomes distressed, calling out to Virgil indignantly, "Who is this?" Virgil steps forward, rips the clothes off the siren, exposing her paunch. A stink comes off her, the smell waking Dante up.

He is deeply troubled by what he has seen. It's a second initiatory vision, and initiations are tricky by design. They aim to shift consciousness by discomfort.

His first dream showed him how possessive, violent love was rooted in his psyche. In this dream he is shown that he must take responsibility for it. It is his gaze that causes the woman to transform. He makes her lovely in his mind, presumably so he can have her. A facet of his desire could gaze on almost any person to satisfy its lust. And his desire, personified in the siren, encourages it, knowing that, with every seduction, its power grows.

It is devastating for Dante to acknowledge that these fantasies and compulsions live within him. It must have been doubly devastating given that the dream arose after a day spent listening to Virgil's beautiful talks on love. But dreams can be like that: they can offset delusions, correct assumptions. There is a part of him, a dark part of him, that needs to be known and exposed. It is purgatory's work. No matter how painful, he must see into his confused heart so it can approach the brilliant heart of the cosmos.

Dante wakes and Virgil offers comfort. "I called to you three times," Virgil says, echoing what Dante had heard in the dream, and also, interestingly, how Jesus had called three times to his disciples in the garden of Gethsemane. Virgil is Christlike in this moment, though Dante had thought the voice was the siren. That's how confused he can be.

Time has passed while he slept. The sun is high, and Virgil wants them to hurry to find the gateway to the next terrace. He is going to show Dante the way — again, rather like Jesus.

But it is hard for Dante to be enthusiastic. He walks alongside his guide, bent double, looking like the arch of a bridge, which reminds us of the stony bridges over the pits in Malebolge. Dante's mind is partly back in hell, I suspect because the dream, and his recognition that it was of his own making, makes him feel trapped. If that is what he is dreaming, how can he ever know God?

He hardly notices the angel who appears and greets them at the end of the terrace. Preoccupation can do that. It can miss kindly words, even the

233

brush of an ethereal wing. The angel shows them the way up, the direction that leads to the sun.

Virgil asks Dante what's wrong? He has seen what Dante has not yet detected: the angel has wiped another P from Dante's brow. His transformation is continuing unbated, for all that he feels weighed down by dread.

They talk and Virgil explains that Dante is experiencing a preparation. It is a foretaste of what he must face as they traverse the next three terraces. These are the final three, on which they will confront human manifestations of avarice, gluttony, and lust. If Dante doesn't know of these vices inside him, he will not be able to tolerate them exposed in front of him. He will reach for denial, or projection, or despair, rather than the hope of change that occurs on Mount Purgatory.

The figure he saw in the dream is an ageless sorceress, Virgil continues. She almost enchanted him and led Dante to miss the beatitude that the angel had spoken, "Blessed are those who mourn." Virgil recalls it, and it is a key to Dante's development: he must learn to mourn for those parts of him that might secretly thrill and then sadden him. He must grieve for the way he has made love into lust. Mourning is a soft emotion, wetting with tears. It can loosen the grip of fierce, distorted longings, and make way for a different future.

Virgil tells Dante to hurry. He can feel the warmth of the sun. He can feel the love of the mountain. It's almost as if Virgil is not bothered by Dante's dream, for all that he appreciates his companion's trial. I think there is a profound psychological insight in that lack of concern. It is as if Virgil is saying: "Don't worry. We all have fantasies of which we are ashamed. See them, but then let them go. There is a light ahead of us that can easily dispel the shadows. If we let the shame linger, it becomes a shadow of its own. Shadows must be seen because they are not the future!"

Dante is encouraged. He is lifted like a falcon who flies into the heavens. He turns to the sun and connects with its light.

It's a good moment to recover from his slump because they are on the fifth terrace. The sight that greets them presents fresh puzzles: the ground is covered by souls who are lying, face in the dirt. Their eyes and mouths and noses are pressed into it. They are saying a line from a psalm: "My soul clings to the dust" (Ps 119:25).

These souls are those who failed to fight avarice and profligacy in life. They had their faces fixed on worldly goods that turn to dust. Their possessions and positions seemed so appealing that these souls forgot how to look at heavenly things. Here, they face what had fixated them in its purest, transient form: their tears mingle with the muck, making it mud.

Virgil asks one of the souls the way, who tells him that if they keep the mountain's downward slope to their right, they will find a way along the terrace. Dante is otherwise distracted. He spots a face he recognizes and seeks Virgil's blessing to address the man. His guide agrees. They might both learn from conversing.

The person Dante sees was a pope, the first saved pontiff he has met since they set out. Adrian V was elected pope in 1276. He died before being enthroned, so he was never officially a holder of the chair of Saint Peter. He explains to Dante that it wasn't until he was elected pope, and reached the top of the ecclesiastical pole, that he realized how much the Church is shaped by worldly affairs, splendor, and glory.

The shock made him see that he loved heavenly things and he counts himself lucky to have died unexpectedly. It sounds noble, and in many ways it is. Adrian is here, not down below. However, he also gives himself away. He is an approachable, but loquacious figure. He is the type of person who will use three lines when one would do. Court life would have pleased him, and his very manner displays to Dante the extent to which he was seduced by worldly life. No one is elected pope by accident, which is presumably why he is working it off in the dust.

Dante bows to Adrian, perhaps seduced by the well-mannered soul, perhaps because it's the first admirable pope he has met. The reverencing pleases Adrian and tempts him. He abruptly asks the poet not to kneel before him, or his office. Such solemnities are the stuff of earthly life, and he knows in the afterlife that he is a pope no more. The former dignities are, here, indignities. Hence his face is in the dust.

It's not that all worldly things are bad in themselves. Far from it. Rather, the problem is that the human mind can be gripped by what glitters and gleams. Majesty can dominate the imagination, shaping aspirations and desires. Dante knows about that because his words can conjure similarly golden effects. He too might have to spend time face down.

Dante speaks with a soul who mourns the history that shaped his life.

PURGATORIO 20

History

ANTO 20 PRESENTS A CHALLENGE. IT TAKES time to work out what is really going on for the pilgrim. At one level, the literal, Dante seems preoccupied by the history of Italy. He laments events in his city-state and country, and there is much to bewail. However, as many commentators point out, the incidents that Dante relates are garbled. He doesn't get his facts straight, and that can be disturbing if you take *The Divine Comedy* not as a fiction but as a sophisticated rendition of a life-transforming experience. If it's a divine revelation, given to foster capability of heaven, what does it mean when the details are wrong? Does the whole edifice tumble from the bottom up?

It's a challenge we've already met, for example, when Dante portrays Mohammad in the *Inferno*. We can ask about it again because I think what it speaks to is Dante's engagement with what might be called deep history. This is not much concerned with the winners and losers, the powerful and the powerless, as is most history-telling today. It is not history as one damn thing after another. Rather, it's about Dante's liberation, and that means him confronting what he thinks he knows, sometimes to have it corrected, but mostly to see through that, and so to be free. If *The Divine Comedy* were a book overly obsessed with the facts, it might be useful in a history seminar, but it wouldn't change lives.

What matters is his, and our, emotional memory — what keeps us caught up in the past, be that the effects of the experiences in our own lives, or the legacy of events that happened before we lived. It's the causes of rage and hate, jealousy and pride, proximate and distant imperatives, mythological and historical roots, that the souls on Mount Purgatory are confronting.

This wider vision is indicated at the beginning of the canto. Virgil and Dante leave Pope Adrian to weeping and undoing the effects of the ecclesiastical power that gripped his heart, although Dante notes that he didn't want to leave. He wanted to hear more, and the departure leaves him unsatisfied. It is as if he felt he might hear something that would help him.

The state of wanting deepens as they walk on. The farther they move around the terrace of the avaricious, the harder it becomes to pick a way among the flattened shades who are grieving and sobbing in the muck. Dante feels profoundly distressed. He curses avarice itself, as a hungry she-wolf whose emptiness gnaws and who would devour anything. He calls to heaven, asking when a rescue might come? Is there a leader who can make a difference? Is there a divine power that can bring change?

No answer comes. His yearning is unabated. But he does hear one voice above the background groaning and murmuring. It calls out the names of three souls. They are examples of individuals who didn't cling to worldly goods but embraced a poverty that enabled them to be reborn.

The first is Mary, who didn't even call her body her own, but offered it to give birth to Christ. The second is a Roman consul called Fabricius, who is remembered because during the period of the Roman Republic, he refused to take bribes and died in poverty as a result. He could easily have taken them: it was the way consuls were supposed to be paid. But he saw the corruption and held out. The third name is that of Saint Nicholas, who gave from his wealth in order to provide dowries for the three daughters of a friend who didn't have access to the substantial amounts that were required. Each, in their own way, recognized that what they had — their body, their office, their possessions — could be in the service of what they longed for more.

The soul who is calling out these names speaks of spiritual insight and wisdom, and Dante wants to listen. The soul is only too happy to oblige, recognizing that Dante's presence is a sign of grace.

It's a synchronistic moment, as all moments are in this place. Nothing happens by chance. Events do not unfold by cause and effect, as the mechanical view of history suggests. Events are generated by meaning. Their importance is their gift.

The soul identifies himself, though commentators dispute who he might have been in history. He says he is Hugh, and he was a king of France, who reigned in the tenth century, three hundred years before Dante. The king relates how the intervening centuries witnessed his sons and heirs becoming increasingly corrupt. The story is a litany of individuals prepared to sacrifice family, virtue, even themselves in the pursuit of perceived glory. The end results affected Dante, as these historic decisions led to the spoiling of his life.

They created the conditions that obtained in thirteenth century Florence, and those conditions are what matter to Dante. They polluted the political air, poisoned the religious environment. It is as if Dante is coming to terms not with what he has done, but with what fortune had done to him: how it made him rich then poor, lucky then unlucky, in the ascendency and then out of favor. What life has thrown at him is what he contemplates. It's another key part of the reckoning on Mount Purgatory.

The detail that exercises commentators concerns one of the corrupt kings of France, who was said to have poisoned Thomas Aquinas. Modern scholarship has clarified that this could not have happened, and I don't suppose it did. However, the story carries an emotional truth, and so is an important story for Dante to confront. The poisoner king is said to have been Charles of Anjou, and he was in cahoots with Charles of Valois, a Charles that mattered to Dante because on All Saints Day, 1301, this Charles arrived in Florence and, as Dante describes it, burst the city's guts with a single thrust. On that day, Dante received the sentence of exile. It was possibly the most bitter day of his life. It poisoned his future.

Dante hears and relates the history in the light of the tragic truth of his earthly life. He must hear of the deep roots of his own ruin in order to change his relationship to events. He must drain the poison from his veins.

The depth of the bitterness is expressed in other ways. Dante compares the actions of another king, Philip the Fair, to Pontius Pilate putting Jesus to death. The implication is that Christ himself has been crucified repeatedly in the actions of these kings. That is how they are condemned.

It's the pain and destruction that avarice in rulers achieves. On earth, the greed may or may not be successfully resisted. In purgatory, it must be related unsparingly, with no means exempt to expose the full extent of the damage and hurt, even if that eclipses the facts.

The names of Mary, and Fabricius, and Nicholas are a counterpoint. If the darkness of night brings back the horror, the brightness of day radiates hope, which those names focus and reflect. Singing their names enables the souls to absorb their own selflessness and so reshape themselves. Healing comes through a combination of sorrow and sunlight, which is to say, via mourning and grief.

Hugh continues with his calling out, turning to names synonymous with rapaciousness. He remembers Midas, the king who wanted to be able to turn everything to gold, which meant he couldn't feed himself, though the world around him glistened. A number of other foul names are recited, Hugh explaining that he calls them to remind himself of how terrible the sins of the world can be. He adds that it was chance that enabled Dante to hear him, only it's also clear that there is no chance in the afterlife, so Hugh's calling was doubly intended. Dante needed to hear it. That is the grace of the place. Even when it appears disturbing, it is helping.

Dante and Virgil move on. Somehow, Dante feels satisfied, at least for the moment. I imagine it's the satisfaction of having faced something and faced it down. His meeting with the pope stirred up the deep history of his life. His meeting with the king gave the hurt and hate expression.

They step over prostrate bodies once more, seeking a way off the terrace, when suddenly their efforts are interrupted. A huge earthquake shakes the entire mountain. The ground itself feels at risk of crumbling. Dante goes numb with fear.

He cannot understand what it is about. Why that? Why here? Virgil tells Dante not to worry. "You do not need to fear while I am your guide," he explains, expressing faith in his task and their passage, although he simultaneously draws close to Dante's side, perhaps seeking some comfort for himself.

Then, a huge shout echoes around the hillside. "*Gloria in excelsis Deo!*" The chorus cascades up and down the mountain. It's a tremendous moment, in both senses of terrific and terrifying. Dante and Virgil will not learn what it means until the next canto, though the image of Latona giving birth to Apollo and Artemis, the sun and the moon, comes to Dante's mind, suggesting the quake might have something to do with a birth.

Around and about them, the shades return to their lengthy task. They are picking a way through prone souls once more. Never before has Dante so longed to know the truth of events, not just historical events, but the ones happening right around him.

Dante and Virgil meet Statius. The two pilgrims have become three.

PURGATORIO 21

Emmaus

ANTE IS RACKED WITH A THIRST TO UNDER-
stand. He and Virgil have been shaken by the earthquake, and
if you have ever been in an earthquake, you will know how disturbing an experience it is: the ground beneath your feet can no longer
be trusted. But they also heard God's glory being sung, as if the tremor
signified good news.

He desires to drink the living waters of divine life, like the Samaritan
woman at the well who asked it of Jesus, he says. At the same time, he
remains distressed by the souls who lie at their feet, as they pick their way
amidst the tears and grief of the fifth terrace. It is as if the experiences of
purgatory are coming to a head, which they do in this canto.

Suddenly, a shade is walking behind them. His arrival is like Jesus appearing to the disciples on the road to Emmaus. It was the last thing the two followers of Jesus expected, for all that they were engrossed in talking about the
man who they had recently seen crucified. Plus, this shade is walking, which
is a surprise. He is not cleaving to the ground. He greets them courteously

with words of peace, to which Virgil responds, adding that although he is banished from heaven, he wishes the soul the peace of the blessed.

This intrigues the shade, as well it might. The implication is that Virgil responds to his words of peace with the kiss of peace, and that is a hugely significant gesture to return. The kiss of peace is a symbolic sharing of God, as two faces draw close to each other and exchange breath, which is a physical manifestation of the Spirit: Virgil is sharing the spirit of peace, which is the spirit of God, while simultaneously telling the shade that he is banished from heaven. Little wonder the soul immediately asks how someone who is banished can be so far up Mount Purgatory?

I think what is going on here is that neither Virgil nor Dante knows what is going on here. Dante has already told us that the appearance of this new individual was like the appearance of Jesus on the road to Emmaus, which the disciples failed to comprehend. He doesn't understand the significance of the earthquake or *Gloria*, to which is added the sudden appearance of this third walking person.

Virgil doesn't understand either, though he enacts more than he knows because while he believes he is condemned, he acts as one who is saved in sharing the spirit of peace.

Add Dante's reference to the story of the woman at the well begging for everlasting waters to the confusion, and our expectations rise to a level that echoes Dante's desperate thirst. It seems that a pivotal moment is approaching for them; it's a tropological moment, one demanding that perceptions change radically for the upheavals to be resolved.

Virgil and the shade start to talk. He explains that he is on Mount Purgatory with God's blessing. It couldn't be otherwise: he is Dante's guide and Dante is a still-living mortal because, as Virgil puts it, the thread of his life has not yet been cut. It's a detail the soul had not spotted because the sun is on the other side of the mountain, and so Dante is not casting a shadow.

Incidentally, the way he describes the thread of Dante's life not yet being cut is arresting. He refers to the Fate called Clotho, who was one of three involved in spinning the thread of a life. A first, Lachesis, draws the thread out, and a third, Atropos, cuts it. It feels significant that these three are alluded to because another three have already been referenced, in the story of the two disciples being joined by Jesus on the road to Emmaus, which itself was used to describe Dante and Virgil being joined by a third who suddenly appeared behind them. Three is growing as a significant number in this canto, a thought to which we will return.

Virgil continues talking with their unexpected companion, adding that he might know Dante is living because of the marks on his forehead, though the soul does not appear familiar with the Ps inscribed by the angel of the threshold. Virgil, the apparently condemned, is telling this figure something he doesn't know.

The soul tells Virgil and Dante something they don't know, prompted by Virgil asking him whether he knows what caused the earthquake. Dante is hugely relieved that Virgil has addressed the matter that is bugging him. It was as if Virgil had threaded the eye of the needle of his desire, he explains to us readers. It's a metaphor worth pondering, as the reference to threading the eye of a needle brings to mind Jesus's remarks about how hard it is to enter the kingdom of God: it is easier for a camel to pass through the eye of a needle. That Dante's desire is linked with the eye, and so with the kingdom of God, implies that desire is crucial to the threading. Dante has mounting amounts of that.

The soul addresses their question about the earthquake. He explains that on Mount Purgatory what appear to be meteorological effects, which in the medieval mind included earthquakes, are not in fact the result of natural causes. The usual causes of wind and rain, thunder, and lightning, obtain only on the far side of the gateway through which they had passed. Once inside purgatory proper, divine causes rule, which is why the mountain trembled. It happens when a soul on Mount Purgatory feels pure enough to stand up for the rest of the climb to the summit. It is a shudder of celebration as souls know themselves to be free. That's why it was followed by a *Gloria*.

The explanation chimes with the story about the woman at the well asking for the living waters of eternal life. Jesus had explained that the source of this infinite refreshment is found within. It can be drunk internally, when found, which is to say that it takes time to locate. That sounds like another way of explaining what is happening to souls on Mount Purgatory. Their failures lie between them and the water, which the mountain celebrates when cleared. It jumps for joy.

The soul continues, explaining that in the purgatorial state, individuals feel the process of clearing and cleansing while they feel the presence of the darkest parts of themselves. The combined sense keeps them to the task, laborious and long though it is. Their lives are marked by hope as well as suffering, until the moment when they realize the path is clear, they stand, and proceed to the summit.

It sounds remarkable: the very soil can express divine grace. What is doubly astonishing for Dante and Virgil is that the mountain had leapt on this occasion because the soul right in front of them, the one who suddenly appeared, as if resurrected, was the one who had just realized he could stand. He has been on Mount Purgatory for many hundreds of years, and his time in this place has just come to an end. This is why he is walking. He is why the Gloria had sounded.

Dante is delighted. The account precipitates something of a conversion in him. He sees inwardly a little more of what salvation takes, of what his journey is about. It is as if he can take a sip from the everlasting waters. It's a wonderful moment, making the build-up of frustrated desire worthwhile.

So, who is this shade? He reveals his name as Statius. He was a first century Roman poet, a pagan, and yet he is saved. He has learned about divine grace and is on his way to paradise.

How this can be will be explored in some depth in the cantos to come. For now, Statius continues with an encomium to the poet from whom he learned everything he knows about poetry. That great teacher was Virgil, he says — not knowing that the shade of Virgil stands before him.

Virgil signals to Dante to remain silent, seeing that his charge can hardly contain himself. I think Virgil wants to remain humble. He feels himself to be changing. He has just heard that a pagan like him can find a path to paradise, the path that he is treading. The news is momentous. Like the appearance of the resurrected Christ, which Statius had unwittingly imitated, turning the walk of the two into three, it takes time to process, perceive, and understand. What does this mean for him?

Statius spots the glance of Virgil toward Dante and asks about its meaning. Why had Dante almost smiled? Why had Virgil stopped it?

It makes for a beautiful and touching disclosure. Virgil gives Dante his permission to reveal who he is. Statius had explained the mountain's tremor to them. Virgil had explained Dante's presence to Statius. And now Dante can explain something too: that the Virgil Statius loves stands before him.

It's the fulfilment of the kiss of peace. They have all shared something of the Spirit with each other. They are each on a parallel journey. The three are companions.

Statius falls forward to embrace Virgil again, though Virgil tells him to stop as they are both shades. I think he means that they are equals in this moment, each standing before the divine grace, which eclipses any inspiration that Statius might have received from Virgil. The spirit of God outshines any of that. Virgil the pagan is clear.

Statius understands. His love for Virgil is strong, but he has learned from his years on the mountain. The canto ends with the three sharing in joy. It is as if they have each drunk from the everlasting fountain.

Virgil and Statius talk through astonishing revelations on the sixth terrace.

PURGATORIO 22

Companions

IRGIL, DANTE, AND STATIUS WALK TOGETHER.
They are companions on a journey that, while carrying different
meanings for each of them, is marked by mutual care and love.
Statius has completed his time in purgatory. Dante is aware of the time
he may have to spend in purgatory. Virgil, I think, is beginning to feel he
may be able to climb Mount Purgatory again, not as guide to Dante, but
as a soul learning to stand before God.

They leave the fifth terrace and climb the staircase to the sixth, the penultimate round. Dante feels lighter now. Another angel removes a P from
his forehead as they embark on the next phase of the ascent. A beatitude
accompanies the cleansing: "Blessed are those who thirst after righteousness
for they shall be satisfied." Dante does thirst, and he has found a source
of satisfaction in the discussion on love and in meeting Statius. He hadn't
expected to do so, and he is not afraid of the angel this time, I think because
he finds he shares in its happy light. He knows the levity that wills us to

244

rise. He is full of that spirit. The three of them together are enjoying a shared grace and the promise of life.

Virgil and Statius know it as well, and much of the canto focuses on the ensuing exchange between the two of them as the three walk together. Nothing is wasted on Mount Purgatory and their conversation is replete with interest and meaning.

For one thing, they smile repeatedly at each other and smiles are no mean gestures in these domains. They indicate fresh revelations, extending insights, and shared delights, given and received in the generous air. Much that wasn't conceivable is being made visible. These are souls transforming fast.

Virgil is explicit: he tells Statius of his respect and love for the Roman poet's work. They hadn't known each other in life, though the poets Virgil met in the afterlife informed him of Statius's genius, in which Virgil had found great pleasure.

He wants to ask Statius a question which he hopes won't cause offence, particularly as they have only just met face to face. Why was he on the terrace for the avaricious? What Virgil had heard of Statius during his mortal life would not at all have suggested he was the acquisitive sort. Quite the opposite. He had gifts. How could he want more?

Statius's answer is a personal disclosure and theological revelation. He was on the fifth terrace because he had indulged the opposite tendency, to be profligate. He had been inclined to squander his talents, when he might have discovered more.

To Dante's contemporaries this confession would not have been only an interesting detail about Statius, whose work was read at the time. It would have struck them as an innovative way of understanding the human soul. Earlier medieval theologians did not link avariciousness and profligacy. Being spendthrift was not regarded as so serious a habit as being greedy, for all that Jesus had taught the value of using talents well. However, in the Aristotelian understanding that was returning to western Europe from the Islamic east, they were connected because Aristotle had understood virtues to be the mean between extremes.

Courage is a good balance between timidity, or running away, and fool-hardiness, or running unthinkingly into the thick of things. Righteous anger is neither raging wrath nor simple indifference.

It makes sense, then, that Statius learns about his profligacy alongside those learning about avarice. Comparable couplings had been encountered in hell, when Dante and Virgil had found themselves amidst hoarding and squandering souls who were trapped in a perpetual joust. They were struck because they repeatedly attacked each other. "Hoarder!" one side yelled. "Waster!" the other replied. They exchanged blind accusations. The difference is that on Mount Purgatory, when the two types come together, they are able to think about themselves, not merely project their worst onto others. That is the essence of change as Aristotle understood it, and as Dante is inviting us to perceive.

There is an art to being virtuous. Human flourishing can be learned, by making mistakes, reflecting, trying again. The process treats the soul as malleable, capable, and desiring. This is very different from a view that is widespread in Western Christianity, which is inclined to feel that the individual can do very little to see God and share in divine life without complete reliance on Christ's sacrifice on the Cross. When that obtains, it suits a hierarchical Church, of course, because in practice, reliance on the Cross means reliance on priests and preachers, rites, and approved teachings.

Dante is implying, once again, that his journey is not about the illumination of received Christian truths but the revision of them, and the meeting with Statius is shocking at a number of levels. He is a saved pagan. He knows much about God's ways. He is correcting, arguably improving, accepted knowledge. The revisioning had begun as soon as Dante and Virgil arrived on the shores of purgatory, when they were met by Cato. It is continuing and developing still.

One question answered, Virgil immediately has another. How is Statius here? How has he become a follower of the fisherman, Virgil asks, referring to Jesus — simultaneously aligning Aristotelian insights with those of the founder of Christianity?

Statius shocks Virgil once more. It was because of you, he replies. That is how he came to understand and embrace the fuller scheme of life and love.

He had read Virgil's Fourth Eclogue, which speaks of a new progeny descending from the high heavens. It came to be considered a prophecy of the birth of Christ, and Statius had appreciated that Virgil's words were full of divine radiance. They anticipated a new age, and Statius had become a figure of that transition. He was both pagan poet and expectant Christian: he explains that having read Virgil, he grew interested in the groups of early apostles in the latter decades of the first century. He admired them, particularly when they were persecuted by the emperor Domitian. Eventually, Statius was secretly baptized.

Commentators doubt that this occurred in history, but purgatory is a place for perceiving inner truths, not correcting literal facts, and in that way the story makes rich sense. The birth of Jesus was not a random intervention by God that could have taken place at any point in time. God's ways are continually unfolding. There is a meaning to each moment. Virgil's poetry, Statius's conversion, and Dante's journey are like three lamps each casting light across a common intuition. It is a joy to see the fuller picture emerging.

It is not only that the divine ways unfold across the centuries, and the advent of Christianity is a crucial chapter in that emergence. Virgil, Statius, and Dante share in the development by participating in the evolution differently from the distinctive vantage points of their lives. Virgil has the advantage of being born before Christianity, as the awareness of a new age to come was reaching ripe intensity: that yearning is what inspired his lines. Statius has the advantage of being born as the turning point occurred: he could grasp the meaning of his moment. Dante has the advantage of living in a time when the Christian dispensation had grown decadent: his dissatisfaction and alertness to truths from pagan times fosters its renewal and remaking.

It is Statius's turn to ask a question, and he has one for Virgil. He wants to know about other Roman poets. Where are they in the cosmic scheme of things? How do they fit into this story?

Virgil has encountered many during his time in limbo and he names some for Statius. They include Euripides, Antiphon, and Agathon from ancient Greek times, as well as Antigone, Ismene, and Thetis, whom Statius wrote about.

Virgil includes one particularly interesting figure on his list. "The daughter of Tiresias" is Manto the prophetess. He and Dante had met her in the fourth bolge of the *Inferno*, as one of the diviners who looked backward as they walked forward, so it is striking that he speaks of her being in limbo as well. Some commentators conclude that Dante has made a mistake but again, this is to read *The Divine Comedy* literally, and so interpret the double locations of Manto as an error. But if the poem describes a pathway that transforms the individuals who walk it, and itself transforms as more is understood, what appears to be an anomaly can be understood as indicative. If Manto has moved from limbo to the fourth bolge, perhaps as her soul shifts and alters in the afterlife, maybe Virgil can move from limbo to Mount Purgatory? I think this is part of the inner dynamics of eternity that Dante is becoming capable of discerning at this point in his transformation. The collocation is in the spirit of this canto.

They talk and climb and reach the sixth ledge. The sun is in the sky and it is mid-morning. Virgil advises proceeding along the terrace, keeping their right sides to the drop of the mountain as they have done before.

Virgil is going on the habit that he and Dante had developed, and which has worked well so far. Statius agrees, confirming the suggestion with insider knowledge.

Cliffside to the left, slope to the right, the sixth terrace stretches out before, and they see a strange tree. It is planted in the ground, but its branches appear inverted. The ones nearest the ground are short and hug closely to the trunk. Those higher up are long and spread out. The tree looks like an umbrella rather than a canopy.

So strong is the effect that some commentators and artists conclude that the tree has roots in the air, but the text implies that the reason for the widespread high branches is to catch the water that falls down from the higher reaches of Mount Purgatory. These streams are living waters. The tree does not need to draw sustenance from the ground. It uses its branches to gather spiritual nutrition.

A voice comes from the tree, though it seems as if the tree itself speaks. It tells of a ban: from eating the fruit that springs from its branches, from drinking the waters that drip from its boughs. It may sound as if they have arrived in Eden, but this is not about the knowledge of good and evil. It is about the trouble that the souls on this terrace must face.

They are the gluttonous, to use the easy label, though their difficulty is not overeating but a penchant for what does not satisfy. That's why they must see and smell what does feed the soul, falling from the tree.

The tree continues to call out. It speaks of individuals who do know what nourishes. Mary is one, because she called on Jesus to turn water into the wine of celebration at the wedding in Cana. It speaks of the women of Rome who, conversely, were said to be happy to drink water rather than wine. They knew that was good for them. Daniel, the Hebrew prophet, is also recalled. He was able to fast and, thereby, understand dreams and the future. Each of these figures knew about the relationship between food, earthly and divine.

The tree continues. There was an age, it explains, when people knew how to eat and drink well, so as to know nature's bounty, goodness, and God. John the Baptist understood as much, it persists, loving the clarity of the wilderness with its locusts and honey. And with that thought, the canto ends.

Dante meets a friend. It becomes clear how their amity didn't sustain him.

PURGATORIO 23

Appetite

ANTE PEERS INTO THE TREE THAT SPEAKS OF everlasting nourishment. He is fascinated by it. Where are the voices coming from?

It is easy to sympathize with his curiosity. A talking tree. But Virgil chastises him. He insists that in purgatory every moment counts, every attitude matters. Trying to unpick a spectacle is to become distracted. It is the meaning that counts, not the mechanism, which is a good message for a scientific age.

The canto revolves around Dante's ability to feed on divine life, to become part of its flow. Virgil, whom Dante calls "his father," can assist him with that. Right now, Virgil is not only a guide but a teacher. For his part, Dante is beginning to clarify his appetite for God, and the ways it can morph into a craving for earthly things, as well it might do on this terrace for those reforming their hungers.

Dante leaves the tree and walks with Virgil and Statius. They hear a tearful

249

chanting: "O Lord, open my lips," to which the response is, "And my mouth shall show forth your praise." It's verse 15 of Psalm 51, about becoming a co-operator with divine life, as the mouth transforms from being a means of consuming to a means of celebrating. There are souls sounding the line, and they are full of the bittersweet realization that they had become habituated in life to grasping. They had a misguided relationship with the fecundity of creation, mostly taking and not giving back.

Their bodies are shrunken. They look as if they are starving, which is to say that their inner lives on earth, which might well have been hidden, become their manifest life on Mount Purgatory. They can't ignore it anymore. They are like the hungry ghosts of Buddhist mythology, we might add, who are depicted with distended bellies and narrow necks. Their habits in life have led them to become unable to take in nourishment. They have lost touch with what truly nourishes. This is the tragedy of being greedy. It is the state in which whatever is offered is felt to be inadequate, unpalatable, not enough. It leads to frustration with life, anger at life and, eventually, hatred of life. In extremis, sufferers would prefer to spit out whatever they put in their mouths, a kind of perverse shadow of proclaiming praise. The condition does not nourish; it kills.

The starving souls approach Dante, Virgil, and Statius from behind. They look like pilgrims, focused on their way, though glancing up at Dante as they spot his shadow. He is a spectacle on purgatory's slopes. They momentarily wonder about the mechanism. But they know to refocus on the meaning of this domain for them and so, as they pass, they turn their heads back down.

Their skeletal faces remind Dante of the Latin "homo," the word for generic "man." It is as if their eye sockets are each an "o," their brows, cheek bones and noses forming an "m." They have "omo," or humanity, written on their faces. They are learning of their humanity in their bodies. They are recalling that they are made in the image of God, which is their hope as they feel the pangs. It is the truth that needs reasserting in order to make better choices about what to consume.

It's another arresting lesson for our times, in which consumption has become a mass activity, and discerning what to take is a daily struggle. A good question to ask could be: does it help realize the greatest truth about you?

The value of the question is underlined by two references made by Dante. One is to a mythological figure, Erysichthon, who cut down a grove that was sacred to Ceres. The goddess condemned him for his unthinking destruction of the trees by making him ravenously hungry. It drove him mad. First, he sold his daughter to buy food, and then he ate himself.

The second reference is to a figure called Mariam who, in the destruction of Jerusalem described by Josephus, is remembered for having been driven by hunger to kill and cannibalize her infant son. She lost sight of the good because she lived in a society that had lost sight of the good.

Again, the resonance in the twenty-first century needs little spelling out. Jesus's saying comes to mind: "Man shall not live by bread alone" (Mt 4:4). An obsession with physical needs can readily eclipse awareness of spiritual needs.

The souls are passing them, and one turns to Dante, staring out of his sunken eyes. He recognizes Dante, and it turns out that they were friends in life. He is called Forese Donati, and it is just as well he recognizes Dante because Dante would not have recognized him from his face alone, though when he speaks, Dante realizes it is his friend. It's an interesting distinction, as if Dante didn't know the soul or face of his friend in life, but only how his friend presented himself to the world, in his voice.

They speak. It is touching to read what they say. A mutual compassion is obvious. When they were in Florence, they enjoyed a jolly life together. They sparred in poetry competitions. They heaped jibes on one another. They jested artistically. They riffed on the passions of love. There is a suggestion in their banter on the terrace that Dante had affairs, though married.

However, as they meet in purgatory, it becomes clear that their communion was largely empty. It was fun but rather pointless. I imagine them enjoying an evening together but separating to return home feeling empty. Their friendship tended to reduce their lives, not feed their souls.

Forese explains the nature of the tree and tells them that they will find another on the other side of the terrace. He confirms that it bears beautiful fruits: it is heard speaking because it is rooted in eternal life and drinks from everlasting waters. It's a nice touch. Dante had been intrigued by the spectacle. He had wondered what was going on, and on these higher levels of purgatory, even inquisitive impulses can be satisfied. Divine generosity is present, teaching the souls its delights. It stresses that the way to treat gluttony and consumption is not by becoming puritanical. It is by waking up to what truly fills you up.

In their transitioning state, Forese says that the trees cause him and his fellow souls' pain as well as solace, as they repeatedly walk past the lovely foliage. Desire is a wild horse to train.

He also makes a passing, strikingly brief reference to one of the phrases Jesus cried from the Cross: "Eli, Eli, lama sabachthani," or "My God, my God, why have you forsaken me?" (Mt 27:46). Nothing happens in purgatory without meaning, but what is the meaning of this? It is such a dramatic moment in the story of Good Friday that it seems too casual a reference. Some commentators wonder if there is a contrast being alluded to, between the moment in Gethsemane when Jesus was nourished by the angels, and the moment on the Cross when he could have called on the angels and didn't. I wonder whether it is an indicator that Dante is going to put forward his own understanding of the meaning of the Cross, which I believe he does, in The Paradiso.

Within the Christian tradition, there is in fact no one settled theology of the Cross, but there are instead various theories of the atonement. A traditional way of viewing Christ's suffering is to understand it as a vicarious act: he suffered divine abandonment, so we won't. Alternatively, there is the theory of substitution which says that he offered his blood to be consumed by a deity whose holiness needed to be satisfied. I think Dante is going to opt for a third understanding, which is sometimes called the exemplar theory, and present Jesus as showing the way that we can make our way. He descended, plunging into the pit of human suffering, to show its ramifications and implications, so that an ascent can become possible, one based upon understanding and accepting. It fits with the purpose of purgatory. As Forese is learning, he can turn his descent around by realizing his mortal mistakes.

Dante and Forese continue to talk and, as friends might, Dante confesses that he is quite surprised to meet Forese so high up Mount Purgatory, so soon after his death. He had expected to see him on lower slopes.

Forese explains that his wife, Nella, is the reason for his relatively rapid climb. He turned his back on her, leaving their marriage bed cold. But she did not turn her back on him. Her love did not flag, and when Forese heard her prayers for him, his heart softened and he was able to embrace her love, becoming more capable of divine love in the process. He could take that love in. He could find nourishment in it. He wasn't as far from the path as Dante had presumed.

Forese sees a little of the future of Florence as they ponder the inner state of people's souls, theirs and others. It is not a lovely sight. He fears Dante will hear fresh reports of the gluttony of Florence in the last years of mortal life.

Then Forese asks Dante about how he casts a shadow. He explained the tree, might Dante explain his bodily presence? Dante obliges, in one of the fullest accounts of how he was rescued from the dark wood by Virgil, at Beatrice's request, was guided through hell, is now ascending Mount Purgatory, and is learning to speak praise and blessing.

The significance of his lengthy explanation, and that he delivers it, not Virgil, is that he is growing in understanding. He is absorbing what is going on, taking it in, digesting it, and so becoming more and more capable of speaking about it. He is even capable of saying the name Beatrice, without becoming overwhelmed. It can come out of his mouth with appropriate conviction, not confused stumbling. Earlier on his journey, simply hearing it had proved too much.

And he speaks the name Virgil, calling him by his name and not as a father or guide, as he had done at the beginning of the canto. I think this is Virgil being acknowledged as a soul, as a person whose name will be remembered in heaven because he, like Dante, Statius, and Forese, is also an individual on the path.

Dante and his friend talk. They encounter another tree on the sixth terrace.

PURGATORIO 24

Listening

IRGIL AND STATIUS, DANTE AND FORESE, WALK
and talk. They feel like ships whose sails are catching the wind.
They are speeding forward, though Dante notices that while Statius
could have sped straight to heaven, he hangs back with Virgil, presumably
to aid the way of his poetic muse.

Dante asks Forese about his sister Piccarda. She was celebrated for being
beautiful in body and soul, and so comes to mind as Dante contemplates
how the two aspects of human life can magnificently combine. Forese confirms that her loveliness and virtue has carried her straight into paradise.
Dante will meet her there.

The other souls on the sixth terrace are still inclined to cast Dante a glance
as they spot his shadow. He sees their sunken features, and the outline of
"omo," telling of a re-emerging humanity. They see his presence as a mortal
human being, telling of the extraordinary grace of God. The looks exchanged
speak of a play between the living and the dead, as each wonders about

the other, seeking signs for themselves. Dante asks Forese whether there are any of the passing shades that might be of particular significance to him.

Forese names several, which helps to restore their humanity. In hell, many souls had preferred not to be named, for shame. Being named in purgatory is an encouragement, and Forese lists many. It's one of the points in the poem when a happy hour can be spent tracking down the individuals mentioned, though broadly speaking, the diversity serves to bring to mind all the ways the common problem of gorging can manifest itself. There is a reference to a pope who so loved eels that he drowned them in white wine before gorging on them: hunger can become grotesque. There is another reference to a character who so loved wine that he developed the habit of reaching for a glass almost before he reached for his next breath: hunger can become addictive. Desire is not itself wrong, but the objects of desire can cause trouble. If they don't satisfy, they generate insatiable desire, and spirals of depravity result.

Another soul calls out to Dante, though Dante struggles to hear what is being said. He looks more closely at the speaker and sees that the shade's mouth is so taut that it can barely move to form the words. This is doubly painful to observe because the individual was a poet. He was a writer and speaker of words called Guittone, who lived a couple of generations before Dante.

Dante attunes himself to Guittone's voice and hears first that a woman from Lucca will be a blessing to him during his forthcoming years of exile. They then speak about beautiful styles of poetry because Guittone has realized that Dante, the inventor of the sweet new style, or *dolce stil nuovo*, stands before him. He praises Dante for developing a way of speaking about love that eluded his circle of poets, which Dante explains arose from listening more closely to love.

Commentators are very interested in this exchange because it is, in effect, a section in which Dante speaks about his work, and that his wellspring was experience and listening to experience. In terms of his spiritual transformation, it implies that Dante strove to bring together his experience of love and his intellect. That stemmed from the power of his early infatuation with Beatrice: it wouldn't let him go and so forced him to transcend the immediate experience and discern its wider meaning. He learned that the desire to possess the beautiful image of Beatrice could give way to an energy that enabled him to appreciate beauty in the world around him, including in words themselves. Hence the sweet new style. It is a type of intelligence, meant not in the sense of reason or logic, but the capacity of the mind to resonate with the divine life with which all life participates, and is radiantly intelligent and beautiful. He developed a mode of perception, an ability to see that appearances transmit an inner vitality that is ultimately one, shared, and common. The energy of this perception is love, and it can integrate knowledge, desire, insight, and illumination in the individual looking through the mind's eye. It is this awareness his poetry conveys, seven hundred years on. It is the integration that was fostered by Lucia appearing during the dream of his first night. He is learning to speak about it as he talks about poetry. It amplifies life rather than consumes it, reflects on life in words so as to reveal its radiance.

The souls start to move like migrating birds in formation. They display a correctly oriented desire, moving in patterns like flocks leaving a summer by the Nile, to head north for winter. It is a layered simile, as the Nile is the place of slavery in the Hebrew Bible, so these bird-souls are becoming free.

Forese realizes that they are signaling his direction of flight, and he must soon leave. He asks Dante when they will meet again. Dante is not sure, though he says that until his passing, his heart will always be climbing purgatory, longing for paradise, not least because his earthly city, Florence, knows nothing of divine life.

It's a moment when Dante's advancing progress is indicated because he speaks of Florence as a place to leave, rather than a place about which to feel bitter. He did feel that before. It's not his dominant experience any longer because he is in better touch with divine life. He has let that anger go.

Those who caused Florence's downfall will be punished, Forese remarks. They will know hell, he says, though Dante is slightly confused by the comment. It is as if he has left the need for vengeance and could even be wondering whether hell is a temporary state, for all that the souls there appeared permanently trapped.

They have no more time to discuss these things. Forese has lost time in the conversing. Dante watches him stepping ahead as he melds back in with his companions on Mount Purgatory.

Dante rejoins Virgil and Statius, and the three huddle together. They reach the second tree that, as Forese had promised, is laden with gorgeous fruit and dripping with sparkling waters. There are shades around it, looking lovingly and longingly at the branches, and resisting the desire to reach out and feed from it. That would be to short circuit their transformation, as a voice from the tree reminds them.

We are made to desire. We must learn to desire aright. The tree encourages them with counter exemplars. It recalls the centaurs whom Dante and

Virgil met in hell. They were known for violence, which the tree explains was often a drunken violence, fed by excess. Wine fires rage.

The voice adds a reflection on the Hebrews who joined Gideon to fight the Midianites. Gideon chose them because he noticed how they quenched their thirst from a stream by cupping water in their hands, not plunging in their faces. The implication seems to be that Gideon reckoned they could temper their desire, not be blindly led by it. They would, therefore, be better fighters.

The mood of the three settles as they pass the tree. They stop talking and become lost in thought. Their company is a silent communion.

They are interrupted by a voice. "What occupies your mind?" it calls out. Dante jumps. It is another angel, blazing with the ferocity of a furnace. It describes the next leg of their journey to the place of peace and satisfaction, onto the seventh and final terrace.

Dante feels the brush of the celestial wing as another P is erased from his forehead. It is like a fresh breeze on a May morning, moving the grass, lifting the fragrance of the flowers, stirring the leaves. It's delightful.

"Blessed are those whose love does not rouse excessive appetite," the angel intones in a remarkably Aristotelian sounding beatitude, summarizing what they have learned in their hearts among the famished. Righteous hunger is a mean between voraciousness and puritanism. Dante is weaving means between medieval theology and ancient Greek philosophy, as he approaches the stairs to the last purgatorial terrace.

Dante bursts with questions. Virgil and Statius describe our making.

PURGATORIO 25

Procreation

THEY BEGIN THE CLIMB TO THE LAST TERRACE. Dante feels the vigor of life around him. It is midday with the sun high in the sky. But there is no time for basking in the warmth and light. In these realms, life calls forth more life, which means that just as Dante feels he has gained some measure of awareness, through experiencing the sixth terrace, the awareness arises that there is yet more to learn. His desire flows unabated: he is as aware of what he does not yet know, as he becomes aware of what has been understood.

It is like being a young stork, he explains, who knows it is time to leave the nest, raises a wing, and then lets it drop again, realizing it cannot yet fly. Questions in his mind similarly rise and fall. He is not sure of the best way to ask. Everything is tremendous. Ever energetic eros seizes him. He longs to fly.

Virgil sees how tightly strung Dante has become. Release your bow! Let your arrows of desire fly, he invites.

Dante gains confidence. Maybe he senses that almost any question will do because they all reach toward new vistas. He settles on one that seems obvious, and the obvious questions are often the best because they highlight what is most basic and necessary to grasp. How can it be that the souls on the sixth terrace were starving? he asks. The conundrum is that they no longer possess physical bodies and if starving is anything, it is surely a physical condition.

It is a question with implications for understanding much on Mount Purgatory. The proud were weighed down by self-inflated burdens. The envious had eyes stitched together to focus on living with themselves. The wrathful were blinded to see the effects of the fogs of rage. The slothful were running with an excess of energy, learning to corral it. The covetous were prostrate to rediscover what they do and don't need. All were undergoing embodied tests and trials. So, what is the nature of their postmortem bodies?

Virgil replies. It is a good question because it goes to the heart of embodiment. Felt experience is a more subtle issue than the gross body might suggest. It is like the myth of Meleager, he says, who stayed alive so long as a log on his mother's hearth was not burnt up by the fire. Wisely, his mother removed the log altogether, until her son offended her, when she returned the log, which was consumed, and he expired. The implication is that he was burnt up by fiery rage.

The relationship between physical and spiritual vitality is also like an image in a mirror, Virgil continues. Movement doesn't cause the image in the mirror to move, though it does move with a perfect correlation, because the source of the image does not cause the reflection. The mirror does.

Virgil is disentangling Dante's tight identification of manifest physicality with felt vitality. It's an issue that remains alive today, having become possibly even more intense as mechanical accounts of embodied life have grown more sophisticated. Today, neurons can be watched, hormones can be tracked, biomarkers can be monitored. And yet what makes the difference between physical processes and conscious awareness eludes mechanical explanation. No one has any idea how meat might generate mind. Not an inkling.

On Mount Purgatory, where people are no longer flesh and blood, the issue becomes doubly pressing. What am I seeing? is Dante's question. What are the souls experiencing?

If it's a question for Dante, it is also one for Virgil. In the ancient Greek and Roman understanding, life's vitality was assumed to continue after the death of the physical body, gradually fading away at a rate dependent upon the intensity with which a life had been lived. It is why souls were called shades. They lived a shadowy, dwindling reflection of their earthly lives.

But having entered the afterlife, Virgil knows that souls aren't shady. They live on. In short, he has questions about this matter as well, so he turns to Statius to continue the discussion, which Statius is glad to do, saying he isn't correcting Virgil's understanding but expanding it.

Statius describes how, at conception, blood forms in the womb into an embryo. It is blood in a particular state: it carries the fullness of life's potential, not yet depleted by the life it will feed.

It is worth holding in mind that Statius is deploying insights drawn from the theory of four bodily humors. Blood here doesn't refer to the red fluid colored by hemoglobin, as it means today. It refers to the warm and moist qualities that flow around a body, manifesting as blood, and sustaining life. That hot wetness, or eager fecundity, forms into the physical body under the influence of the heart, Statius continues. Again, the heart was not seen as a pump but as a center of intelligence, a place in which feeling, spirit, and insight integrate. It is a conception of the heart that still makes sense, which is why the word "heart" can imply profundity, as in "the heart of the matter"; or sympathy, as in "my heart bleeds for you." Further, the heart doesn't just gather human capacities. It links to divine powers as well. It is a meeting place of terrestrial and celestial life. So, when Statius describes the embryo being formed by the blood and the heart, he is reflecting on the way human procreation is the tangible expression of divine creation, procreation meaning bringing forth that which is potential or nascent, which is to say already existing in the mind of God.

The creativity of God explodes at the moment of human conception, as the desire for life purifies and intensifies, Statius adds, in a wonderful allusion to the links between lovemaking, orgasm, ejaculation, conception, and pregnancy.

Gestation itself can be understood as a series of steps, he continues. First, the embryo is like a plant, which is to say it has the type of soul, or vitality, that responds to stimuli around it. Then it develops a sensitive soul, or the capacity to have feelings and emotions, as animals do. Finally, it forms the human soul, which adds elements of reflection and self-awareness, as well as the ability to appreciate that life draws on the life of God, from whence it originates.

God delights in this combination of natural and supernatural processes, Statius explains. God breathes divine life into the embryo as it passes through these stages. It is a vision of life that combines a natural reaching up for the divine with a divine reaching down into natural life. The plant, animal, and mineral, as well as human manifestations of life, can be imagined as extending across a chain of being, each enjoying its aliveness, each expressing the fount of life in its own way, like as many springs. The sun turns the moisture of the ground into wine, via the vine, Statius continues, thoroughly warming to his theme with another metaphor.

Physical life does not last, clearly, which Statius explains as the body leaving the soul. It is the mortal aspect of life, subject to decay, though as life itself exceeds its physical form, so life continues in the ongoing life of the soul. It makes its way to the threshold of hell, the shores of purgatory, or the heavens of paradise, full of what has been learned in life, be that for good or ill. The soul is the subtle location of memory, understanding, and will, and those qualities continue to determine what the soul is capable of knowing in the afterlife, as they had shaped what the soul is capable of experiencing during mortal life.

In particular, and to come back to Dante's original question, the post-mortem soul shapes a spiritual body around it. It is an airy body compared with the physical body, hence not casting shadows. It might be likened to a rainbow, which from the visual point of view is made of an elusive mix of the substantial and insubstantial. So, it is with the bodies of the dead that Dante has seen, and it is with these bodies that the dead experience their ongoing transformation. They can speak, feel, suffer, desire, hope, think. They can be happy, weep, and laugh. They can starve as they learn to absorb the food that lasts for eternity.

It is a wonderful myth, meant in the old sense of an account or story that makes sense of experience. It "saves the appearances" to use Aristotle's phrase, gathering together all that human beings detect of life. In this way, it is a myth superior to scientific accounts, as the latter must discard substantial parts of experience, not least that we experience, in order to make its mechanical explanations work, for all that the machine understanding has clear advantages as well, particularly in the domain of medical science. Incidentally, I don't think that the emergence of modern science would have troubled Dante. He was aware of other accounts contemporary to him, not least those from the Islamic world, and recalls Statius referring to the insights of Averroes in this canto. What is important is not the theory itself, but the extent to which it illuminates actual experience. If it fails to do that, it not only offers a limited explanation of life, but it also risks reducing the sense of life in those who believe it.

They have climbed as Statius talked. It was a long explanation and, in the time it took, they have reached the seventh terrace. Another purgatorial zone is before them.

The first thing they notice are bizarre flames. They appear to be shooting out from the side of Mount Purgatory across the ledge on which they must walk. The horizontal fire would leave no space to do so but for a wind that rises up the side of the mountain, pushing the flames up at their ends. The pilgrims will need to proceed carefully, neither being burnt on the one side or falling from the other.

Something important is being expressed in this setup. A narrow path must be trod, with the metaphors of burning and falling bringing to mind the feature with which this terrace is concerned: love.

Dante is terrified. His fear rockets when he next sees that there are souls in the flames. Two are seemingly burning, while singing a hymn: God of Mercy. His fear lessens enough for curiosity to grow. He looks more closely at them in the blaze, and suddenly they shout, "*Virum non cognosco!*" "I know no man!" This is what Mary said to the archangel Gabriel. She bore divine life without the physical excitements of erotic love, implying that this is what the conflagrating souls are contemplating. How might such a way be possible?

The question is left unanswered as the canto draws to a close. Dante leaves us with two more images of love and lust. First, the chastity of the goddess Diana is celebrated. Then the faith of married couples is proclaimed. Dante realizes that the souls in the conflagration are healing the final wound in a cure of flames and diet of affirmations.

The mention of wounds echoes back to the start of the canto. Virgil had described Dante's desire to know about physical bodies as an open wound. Statius had healed it with insight and understanding. That is the heart of the healing the final terrace offers, though it will be terrifying as well as tremendous.

Dante is before the flames that can purify his love. He pauses.

PURGATORIO 26
Flames

ANTE, VIRGIL, AND STATIUS ARE WALKING IN single file, keeping to the narrow strip between the hot flames and the edge of the ledge of the seventh terrace. If there is heat to his left, the sun is pleasantly warming Dante's shoulder on the right, as it begins to sink in the sky. His shadow falls across the fire, deepening its red. The change is noticed by the burning souls who turn, approach as close as they can without leaving the furnace, to see who is passing.

You can imagine it swiftly dawning on Dante that their predicament is his future. Love has been his passion, for good and ill, throughout his mortal life. Before long, he must join them as he joins battle with this powerful dynamic in his life. Fire is spirited: it rises, it lights up, it kisses heaven. But it also burns, it purifies, it licks, it transforms. It is a meeting place of heaven and earth, which is why candles convey what's holy and sacred fires are not left to go out. This correlates with the account of conception and birth that Statius has just explained, as another point at which natural forces are energized by divine delight.

The flames come at the top of Mount Purgatory, after so much else has been faced, which suggests something about how erotic love is purified. It is not burnt away, as if a basic impediment. If that were the purpose of the fire, it would have greeted them on the foothills of Mount Purgatory. Rather, the flames strengthen love, like a blacksmith tempers a sword, so that desire can widen, deepen, reach further, yearn for more. That happens as hindrances like pride and envy are overcome. Love can then refocus. It can put aside quick attempts at satisfaction, that the slothful and greedy might try. It can carry the soul to the goal of all desiring.

One of the burning souls calls out. He comments on Dante walking reverently behind Virgil and Statius, which we can imagine is no comfort to Dante. His position in the line reveals his nervousness.

Dante is on the cusp of explaining why he is here and alive, perhaps to distract from his fear, when he stops abruptly. He sees another group of souls approaching through the flames. They are walking in an orderly file toward the group that Dante had first seen and, as they approach, the static group separates to let those approaching move through their midst. They pass each other and greet one another with a kiss of peace. They look like ants, nuzzling their fellows, asking directions, and affirming friendliness. They share a love that meets, greets, and wishes the other well. The love is deliberate and focused, wholly unlike the love of Francesca and Paolo in hell, that swept them about like stormy winds buffet autumn leaves.

The ones who approach call out, "Sodom, Gomorrah!" The ones who are approached call out, "Pasiphaë was mounted in her lust!" They each rehearse the excessive version of the love to which they incline. Sodom and Gomorrah's crime was not the homosexual act per se, which in the medieval period did not only cover same-sex desire but non-procreative sexual acts as well. It was the desire to rape. Pasiphaë's indulgence was not sexual love per se. It was the desire to steal from the gods. The souls, who in life loved too lustily, are reforming themselves. Their problem is not the form of their love, but the spirit in which it takes place. In a moment, Dante the poet challenges and overturns centuries of Christian teaching about sexual love, same-sex love in particular. He does so by understanding and seeing more deeply into it.

He watches the lovers divide, graciously passing each other, and is reminded of migrating cranes and how one group will fly north, the other south. He is saying the object of your love doesn't matter, any more than the destination of the cranes, be that for a person of the opposite or same gender. It is the manner of your flight north or south that counts. Both can lead to heaven.

The soul who first called out is still keen to speak. His face glows as Dante turns toward him to explain how he is here, chest breathing, heart pumping, flesh living. He presents himself as a sexual being, which is appropriate, though indicates he understands the nature of erotic love, by explaining he has received grace from heaven by a lady, Beatrice.

He can see how love for her woke a desire in him that was not primarily for another person, though it had powerfully seemed like that at first, but was for divine life. She was heaven-sent so that he might be sent to heaven. Following that beauty, as opposed to trying to seize a reflection of it, will transport him higher. This love stirs intelligence in him because he can perceive more of what it wants, and participate body, mind, and spirit with what it enjoys.

The souls listen avidly, and Dante wishes them heaven's spaciousness, as he explains his story. It is a lovely touch. Another way in which erotic love is purified is by becoming more capacious, the opposite of infatuation, which is narrow. It does not obsess, it embraces.

There are poets in the flames, and they are particularly struck by Dante's presence. He has managed to reach these heights without dying, which is to say that he has managed to understand a dimension of love that drew them, but ultimately overwhelmed and defeated them before they died. They are only just learning to appreciate what he is speaking of and will write about.

"Blessed are you who can take these insights back to earth," the soul who first called out chants! It's an inventive beatitude, from an individual who is grasping how love sees novelty, becomes creative, and adds to received wisdom. Love achieves these insights when it kisses life, rather than grabbing life. Letting go is as much a part of loving as meeting, greeting, and wishing well.

This figure, who has still to reveal himself, adds that the group which had approached them shared the fault of Caesar when he had been called a queen, which is to say, when the young, statuesque Julius had prostituted himself to manipulate a king. He confirms that his trouble was uncontrolled lust.

Dante is interested in who are afflicted by these difficulties and asks for some souls to be named. Whose company will he be keeping? There are many. There's not much time to list them. But the one who has been speaking identifies himself. He is Guido Guinizelli.

This completely stuns Dante. He falls silent. Words fail him. Guido is a poet whom Dante acknowledges as one of his poetic fathers. He wants to rescue him, as the sons of Hypsipyle rescued their mother from the rage of her owner, the king, Lycurgus. He recognizes that Guido had written sweet and graceful poetry, and inspired poets better than he. If they understood love so as to be able to write about it with genius, and yet need to burn, what does that mean for him?

For a moment, he is lost in thought. Then, recovering his wits and in the spirit of the place, he offers his service to Guido. Perhaps he is thinking of a prayer, a poem, or a record of their encounter in his book.

Guido is deeply moved, seeing that his poetry and Dante's are similar in reaching a level of nuance that hopes to raise desire to its richest, fullest heights. He calls Dante brother, not son. Dante is acknowledged as belonging to the poets who spoke of love not to titillate, not to seduce, not to coarsen, not to impress, not to show off, but to enlighten. There are others in the flames who sought its greatest truth as well.

Guido requests a Paternoster from Dante when Dante enters paradise, and then disappears into the flames, like a fish diving back into deep water.

Another soul takes his place. He is Arnaut Daniel, and some of his lines, written as if by him though composed by Dante, conclude the canto. He speaks Provençal, not Italian, and had written in a complicated, hermetic style, so that wrestling with his words might shift the consciousness of readers. Here, on Mount Purgatory, Dante has him speak more simply, perhaps because his transformation is nearly complete.

Arnaut's poem from the flames welcomes Dante, explains how he is recalling follies and anticipating joys, and asks that Dante remember him in the elevated regions to which they both aspire.

The poets understand love. They can look at life and let life flow through them. They can run with delight and follow beauty so as to let their desire and will align to it — to discover spacious zones previously unimagined.

And yet, Dante has still to step into the flames.

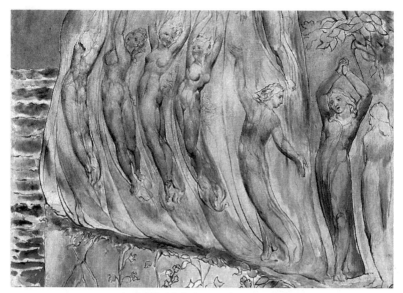

Dante is afraid but finds the strength to enter the flames.

PURGATORIO 27

Courage

THE SUN IS SETTING ON MOUNT PURGATORY. Dante notes that means it is midday in the east where the sun will be boiling the water of the Ganges, midnight in the west at the pillars of Hercules, and dawn in Jerusalem, the center of the Christian world as the historic location of God's Passion. His experience of time has grown expansive, as his awareness of the significance of events deepens. He is present to this moment and simultaneously to others.

His way of telling us the time at the opening of the canto signals that he is fully alert to the importance of the moment. An angel appears singing "Blessed are the pure in heart": happy are those whose desire is intense, willed, and focused. He appreciates its beauty and truth. Then, the angel adds a sting: they can walk no farther along this terrace without entering the fire. They have heard all they can on Mount Purgatory. To hear more, and there is much more to hear, they must undergo the purifying effects of the flames.

Dante feels like someone told they will shortly be buried alive. The thought terrifies him. Maybe this fire is the kind that tempers metal, and cleanses dross from souls, but he has seen the flesh of humans burn, and he still carries his mortal body. He has heard the screams. His exile was on pain of such a death.

He also knows about the complicated desires of the soul, and how much courage and concentration it takes to undo their tight knots. Dante is no longer fearful because of what he doesn't know, as he had been when walking through hell and climbing the lower slopes of the mountain. He understands much more at this point, and the prospect carries fresh dread. Matters of love are the heart of his life. Will the flames discover his possessive, violent fantasies? Does his youthful infatuation remain alive inside? Can he let the heat carry him higher? Will he spontaneously, uncontrollably fight the testing of that most intimate, delicious longing? Might he become stuck in the conflagration, caught by a perpetual inner struggle?

My guess is that he knows he is free to turn away. He could walk back down the mountain, ride the boat back to Ostia, and return to the dark wood of his life. It would be miserable, but it would be easier. Of all the moments on the journey so far, this one is marked by awareness and choice. One of the paradoxes of The Divine Comedy is that its joyful ending is not a foregone conclusion, for all that love cannot but win in the end.

The angel said that there is life on the other side of the flames. Virgil continues the encouragement. There is pain in the heat, but not death, he insists. There is not even singeing. He reminds Dante of how he had protected him on the back of Geryon, adding that they are nearer to God here, and so are beyond being deluded or tricked. Test the flames with your robe, he suggests. It's time to put fear aside.

Dante stands still. Ashamed, he can't step forward. What secrets of his heart will be proclaimed from the rooftops? What burning humiliation awaits him? His entire life has been shaped by love, with lust as well as longing in the mix.

Virgil grows frustrated and pulls out his trump card. He mentions a name: Beatrice. "Only this wall stands between you and her," he declares.

The thought brings to Dante's mind a myth of two earthly lovers, Pyramus and Thisbe. They couldn't meet in life and, through the ups and downs of the story, finally meet in death. It is as if Dante is wrestling with what must die in him to embrace the love of heaven. What might he be clinging to as if it were life, when it is in fact a poor shadow and faint reflection of the light on the other side?

And so, his heart purifies. His commitment grows. He discovers the childlike simplicity that is not naivety, but clarity.

Virgil steps into the flames first. It is another occasion on which he leads, Christlike. He asks Statius to enter last, as if in support. And Dante enters the heat.

He tells us that he would rather have jumped into boiling glass. That viscous fluid would have offered comparative relief. Virgil comforts him, saying he can almost see Beatrice's eyes. That's encouragement for Dante. It's a promise of salvation for Virgil. To see her eyes is to see heaven.

The intensity doesn't diminish, though they hear another angel singing on the far side. "Come, blessed of my Father," it calls.

They make it through and step out. The angel stands before them, its radiance too much for their eyes. However, there is no time to pause. The angel instructs them to make haste as there is not much daylight left. They make their way through a passageway cut into the rock and ascend a little farther. The sun is indeed so low that they walk in shade. They must make a bed for the night.

Nightfall comes, and the mood changes dramatically. Dante describes a peaceful, pastoral scene. The vast expanse of the sky is above them. The vivid color of the day has morphed into the quiet shades of the night. They are like a goat and two herdsmen, Dante being escorted by Virgil and Statius, the two shepherds of his soul.

They each take a step along the walkway and lie down. It makes for one of the most gentle pauses during the whole journey. The stars cast light down, looking larger and brighter, more vivid or alive, than on earth. They are in a different dimension of reality, with eyes that can see more keenly. The fire has intensified Dante's capacity to participate in spiritual light.

The rest is profound, the sleep deep. As if in an instant, it is the hour before the sunrise, and Venus is rising as the morning star, heralding the sun. It is the time at which Dante has his third dream.

He sees a woman walking through a meadow, picking flowers. She will make them into a garland. She sings of her name, Leah, the first wife of Jacob, and how she spends her day gathering blooms to decorate and please herself when she looks in the mirror. She adds that her sister, the second wife of Jacob, Rachel, lives differently. Rachel attends to another mirror, that of her soul, and contemplates who she is inwardly.

Dante wakes up with the blaze of the dawn. His dream is unlike those that troubled him before. It tells of what is to come, rather than how he has been. It confirms what has changed within him, Leah and Rachel possibly representing two now activated dynamics: love that makes beautiful things, and love that knows beautiful things. The next canto will illuminate the dream further. For the moment, it is inviting, exciting.

He rises to his feet and Virgil explains what the day holds. He will receive the apple that brings peace to the soul. He has spent the last night of The Divine Comedy. From now on, there is only day. This is the dawn of the everlasting day. They are at the threshold of eternity.

Levity and lightness fill Dante. As he walks, it is as if wings lift his feet. They climb the remaining steps without effort.

Then, Virgil turns again to address Dante. Though Dante doesn't know it, these are the last words his guide, companion, father, and friend will say to him. They are Virgil's last words in the service of Dante's future, spoken by a soul who knows of love.

Virgil fixes his eyes on his charge. He tells Dante that they have seen the fires of time and eternity, during the days and nights on Mount Purgatory and in hell, where there is no day or night. Skill and intellect have guided them and, from this moment, pleasure and beauty will be his guide. In the words of Saint Augustine, Dante can love and do what he wills. There is more to learn, much more. But love will no longer lead him astray.

They have arrived at the border of Eden. The grass and flowers before them radiate a supernatural vitality. They grow not naturally but preternaturally, drawing directly on divine life. Dante is free to wander and enjoy, until the eyes that he has been longing to see, find him, and come to greet him. He no longer needs Virgil. He shouldn't expect signs from him. And Virgil crowns him the lord of himself. His heart is pure. His will is correct. His heart is free.

They are in an enchanting forest. A solitary lady approaches at Dante's request.

PURGATORIO 28

Enchantment

THEY ARE IN EDEN, ON THE PLATEAU SUMMIT of Mount Purgatory. A verdant forest pulsates before them. Birds sing. Leaves hum. The morning light softly zings. A gentle wind brushes their heads, moving constantly in the same direction. It is not a disturbance of the air but a flow of life.

Dante steps eagerly into the welcoming canopy. He is soon enveloped by its lush undergrowth. He pushes forward and then stops. A stream of clear water appears at his feet. It is extraordinarily transparent and strangely dark. No light breaks its surface.

He looks across the water. Its low swell sweeps in the same direction. Then, on the far bank, to his surprise, he spots a woman. She is gathering flowers. She is singing with enchantment. He is reminded of his dream.

Canto 28 is full of mystery. Commentators have tilled its soil repeatedly in the search for its meaning and message. In particular, debate revolves around the identity of this woman. Is she historical, allegorical, mythological,

271

seasonal? In this canto, little indication is given, which is presumably the point. Dante wanders in this extraordinary place of wonder. We are invited to be fascinated too. How could an initial arrival in the earthly Eden be otherwise?

It is a forest at a different pole of reality from the forest in which Dante woke up, midway through the course of our life, to realize he had strayed from the path. The mystery of this place does not arise from fearful drifting, but expectant purpose. The trees undulate with devotion. The air moves with aim. All that lives reaches toward the east, where the sun rises, where radiance originates. The mix of luminosity and impenetrability, caught in the surface of the stream, will characterize whatever happens next.

Not unsurprisingly, the shining woman draws his attention. There are echoes in Dante's description of his gaze to a well-known medieval theme: a lonely man walks into a forest and meets a solitary woman who promises to satisfy his desire. Only Dante is reminded of other myths as well. He requests that she comes nearer to the stream so he can hear the words she intones, and maybe understand better. "You remind me of Proserpine," he says, who was kidnapped by Pluto, carried to the underworld, rescued by Mercury, but not before she had eaten pomegranate seeds, which condemned her to return to Hades for one quarter of the year, each year. Does she make him think of the fall that took place in the biblical Eden, following consumption of forbidden fruit? Does she make him long for the eternal spring that, on earth, is interrupted by winter?

She turns elegantly, eyes inclined modestly, and approaches him from the other bank. At the edge of the water, she looks up. Her eyes blaze with love, holding him as insistently as Venus sought Adonis after she accidentally scratched herself with one of Cupid's arrows.

Dante is reminded of Leander, who fell in love with Hero from across the Hellespont. They could not meet by day, because social norms forbade it, so they met by night. Leander would swim the channel, guided by a light from Hero's tower. Until one evening, the light failed, he drowned, and Hero threw herself in the water too.

Proserpine and Pluto. Venus and Adonis. Hero and Leander. The references conjure the mood of young love, beautiful, compelling, untainted but not a little dangerous.

He wants to cross the stream and wishes it would part like the Red Sea before the people of Israel. It is as if he sees the promised land in the ground on which she stands. He can feel its presence. He wants it. He is not able, yet, to enter it.

I think Dante is beginning to appreciate that while his love is purified, and his will is a true guide, there is still much to transform within himself if he is to participate in divine love unalloyed. He is preparing for the next phase of his journey. We are being offered intimations of the excitement and intrigue, the interest and challenge.

She sees that Dante is not alone. Virgil and Statius have arrived beside him. She knows from the amazement on their faces that they have not been to Eden before either. She offers to explain with a hint from verse 4 of Psalm 92. It speaks of delighting in the works of the Lord, which might have made Dante recall his dream, in which Leah and Rachel delight in creation, in modes of activity and contemplation. As two aspects of himself, the imagery can encourage him to weave together the gentle action of the moment with an appreciation for it. Somehow, the meaning of the encounter is within its strangeness. He must speak and he must listen to discern its resonances.

He has been told by Statius that the higher reaches of Mount Purgatory are not natural. The earthquake was caused by celestial joy, not terrestrial • tension. He tells the woman that he has noticed how the water and wood reach toward spiritual, as opposed to solar, light.

She confirms his observation. What they see is life before the fall. The wind moves because it is spirit, a link remembered in the ancient Greek and Hebrew words, "pneuma" and "ruach" respectively. They mean "wind," "breath," and "spirit" simultaneously, recalling how life participated in God with a love that was at one time uninterrupted, unimpeded, unmediated. The trees and flowers spring with this aboriginal vigor. They do not sprout from seeds. Nothing needs to die for their life to rejuvenate. This is the nature of eternal springtime. There are no seasons, autumns, or snows.

Owen Barfield called it original participation, the period of human history that he detected in the ancient meaning of words like "pneuma" and "ruach." The myth of Eden might well recall it, reaching back to a time when people experienced meaning all around them in the breezes, winds, and gales. The difficulty was not detecting that they had significance; the difficulty was understanding their significance. The aim of divination and ritual was to learn how to move with the gods, not to attempt to bridge the gap between humanity and God, as opened up after the fall of Eden.

At the end of the canto, the woman affirms that she is living in the Golden Age that the ancient poets had tried to recall. She still has the ancient consciousness in which inner and outer, work and worship, being and doing are seamlessly joined. Further, the distance between then and now is not absolute, she continues. She tells of how some of the flowers from Eden still drift down to earth, which is to say that we can still catch sight of the dimensions within which life is experienced as synchronous and sacramental. It's in moments of wonder and ecstasy. Many know it, when they contemplate a flower, look into a tree, spot an unfamiliar bird or bug engaged in its mundane habits. The experiences make us ask where life came from and what it is, in ways that complement the scientific explanations of evolutionary theory. She is speaking of the fire that is in the equations, to recall Einstein's phrase.

The stream before them is called the Lethe, she continues. They will also see another brook, called Eunoë. The Lethe is a river of oblivion, known in ancient mythology as offering a baptism that erases pain and distress. The Eunoë is Dante's discovery. The name means good mind, and he will have to drink from them both: first to be freed of past troubles, then to be reconnected to all that he is in order to be complete. How that will come about is unclear. The woman knows that it will.

It reminds me of Barfield's insights again, that the period of original participation is broken by a period of alienation, before being recovered anew by a revived type of participation. This final participation, as he called it, is like the first, in that it enjoys the felt consciousness of divine connection; it is unlike the first in that individuals know themselves more fully in that participation. They come to realize that the alienation was not a mistake, but fostered an intensification of their sense of themselves, born through pain and distress, but leading to a reunion with God that can be welcomed deliberately. The rituals that will involve Lethe and Eunoë enact the pattern of Dante's journey, as well as Barfield's evolutionary history.

Virgil and Statius are delighted by the reference to the Golden Age. They had intuited that they were in touch with more perfect times in their poetry, when the gods lived among men and women. Meeting this alluring woman is meaningful for them, as well as for Dante.

The canto ends with Dante turning back to absorb her loveliness. Virgil was right. Although thoughts about the fall, the risks of love, and the origins of winter and spring, had flashed across the surface of his mind, and although he is far from clear what will happen next, he has not lost touch with the sweetness of her words. He senses their truth. He can turn toward her and ask her to turn toward him. There is a sense that whatever he encounters from this moment forward, he will be able to draw on wellsprings of love, which will expand and unpack with meaning and carry him farther, as the rivulets on the water and the leaves on the trees of Eden ripple in the direction of the divine.

He follows the enchanting lady. A flash of light initiates an extraordinary vision.

PURGATORIO 29
Pageant

THINK OF THE MOST SPLENDID CEREMONY YOU have ever seen and then add more majesty. Think of the most moving ritual you have ever shared and then add more meaning. Think of the most overwhelming encounter you have ever had and then add more feeling. Add further noise, color, dance, and lights. Don't forget the buzz, the expectation, the numinosity. You are ready to read what happens to Dante next.

The canto opens with Dante held by the enchanting presence of the lady. Love wafts on every breeze and she sings a beatitude: blessed are those whose sins are covered. It's a prophecy of what happens in Eden, with its two streams and divine presence.

She walks along the far bank, treading deliberately through the dappled light, in and out of the shadows. Dante mirrors her steps, mesmerized. Every moment is weighted with significance and meaning.

The streams bend to become parallel. He faces east and the sunrise. With less than one hundred paces done, she stops, turns to him, and says: "My brother, look and listen." She has readied him for something tremendous.

The atmosphere splits with light. The incandescence persists, unlike lightning, and grows. A gentle melody drifts toward him. He curses Eve, and all that has stopped him appreciating this view before. It's a harsh moment, though he is feeling the weight of all that has frustrated him and veiled God from him. He is also about to learn that Eve is not to blame: he must take responsibility for his life.

The music intensifies, the light strengthens, and he calls on the ancient muses for help with expressing what he sees. He asks the mountains of Helicon to bless him with their waters. He seeks the assistance of Urania, the spirit of the heavens. He is gathering everything available, past and present, to bring to memory the fullness of the moment.

There are seven golden trees a little way off, though with drawing closer, he sees that they are candlesticks reaching to the sky, processing toward him. "Hosanna!" resounds from them. Bewildered, he turns to Virgil, who is struck silent in amazement. He is with Statius too, stunned by the riverside.

All that is unfolding is now close, just over the waters. Figures dressed in supernatural white appear in the light, their own luminosity bouncing from the surface of the streams, dazzling the pilgrims further. Twenty-four elders advance, singing blessings to a woman whose beauty exceeds all of Adam's daughters, which is to say, is above all women. The commentators explain that the twenty-four allegorically represent figures in the Hebrew Bible, though their impact on Dante does not come with deciphering their meaning but with hearing their chant. Can Beatrice be about to appear? Is the one who has shone love to him more than any other nearby? The entrance to transcendence is marked by the most intense longing of our lives.

Four figures in green come into view with wings covered in eyes like peacock tails. Read the prophet Ezekiel, Dante tells us, to gain a sense of it, though don't forget the vision of Saint John the Divine in the Book of Revelation as well, he adds. The vision is building, mirroring the apocalyptic texts in the Bible, apocalyptic meaning unveiling of truth. There are people, streamers, rainbows. The sight is a ceremony that transmits nothing less than divine life.

A two-wheeled chariot materializes. It is more splendid than any Roman emperor knew, more dazzling than a sun god's. It is pulled by a griffin, with an eagle's head and lion's body. The eagle speaks of looking to heaven. The lion is firmly, magnificently rooted to the earth. The two-fold beast has wings that stretch directly upward, to a height Dante cannot see, dwarfing the participants in the pageant.

Beside one wheel of the chariot are three ladies, in red, white, and green respectively. They dance, with the lady in red leading the other two. It speaks to Dante of faith, hope, and love — white, green, red — the symbolism conveying life's inner dynamics, the virtues that enable and form life's flow. Beside the other wheel, four ladies are in purple, dancing with the souls of the cardinal virtues: the wisdom to know how to act, the justice to know how to be in harmony, the courage to know how to be fearless, the temperance to respond well.

A further series of twenty-four figures process next, variously described. One carries a sword. One has the bearing of a doctor. They are the writers of the parts of the New Testament, ending with Saint John the Divine, whose eyes peer into hidden parts of reality. The enchanted forest, the golden tree-candlesticks, the dancing figures, the tremendous carriage, the griffin reaching from heaven to earth. This is the deep history of life, historical, mythological, spiritual. Everything Dante might draw on has appeared.

Suddenly, there's a monumental clap of thunder. The ceremony halts right in front of Dante. It's there for him. And the canto ends on a huge cliffhanger. What does this all portend?

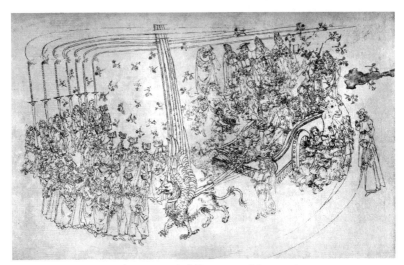

Beatrice appears, Virgil disappears, and Dante weeps.

PURGATORIO 30

Weeping

THE FINAL CANTOS OF THE INFERNO, THE PAR-
adiso and *The Purgatorio* are each concerned with revelation. In
hell, Virgil and Dante encountered the frozen Lucifer. In paradise,
what is to be revealed awaits. At the summit of Mount Purgatory, Dante
is rocked by a confrontation with divine ways that, at least initially, leaves
him completely wrung out. We human beings are free to know God, but to
do so means knowing ourselves because it is in ourselves that God becomes
known. The agony that leads to ecstasy is no more keenly felt, and expressed,
than by Dante in canto 30.

It opens with a meditation on Ursa Minor, the constellation of the Little Bear, which includes the Pole Star at the end of its saucepan-like shape.
Also called the North Star, it is the point around which the heavens turn. It
doesn't set, and so speaks of the spiritual axis around which reality unfail-
ingly turns. The great procession is stationary before Dante. The elders who
were leading the array turn toward the two-wheeled chariot pulled by the
griffin, as if looking at the turning point of the heavens.

A chant begins. "Come, Bride of Lebanon!" It is a line from the great love poem of the Hebrew Bible, the Song of Songs (4:8). A female figure is being called upon as the spiritual center. A great call breaks out. "Hallelujah!" It is akin to the Last Day of the apocalypse with its volume and effect: a hundred angels, the ministers of God and eternal heralds, rise above the chariot, singing "Blessed is the one who comes." The biblical origin of the phrase reads, "Blessed is he who comes." There, it is a great accolade for Christ. Here, Dante's modification makes room for the lady anticipated by the cry from the Song of Songs.

Flowers fall from the air like summer rain and Dante recalls hearing lines from Virgil as they tumble. "May our hands be full of lilies!" It is a festive shout from *The Aeneid*. The Hebrew Bible, the Christian hope, and Virgil's exclamations are all singing of the glory about to appear. I think the implication is that all of human life in some way anticipates this moment, and that all of human life can become capable of this moment. This is because true revelation is free and limitless, able to shine and rejoice in any situation. It is not possessive. It does not insist on sanctioned ways, governed jealously by the Church or any other body. It is abundant. It longs to be known. It is a treasure at the secret heart of being, which is in all beings.

Dante invites us readers to call to mind the sun rising after a completely clear night. The sky has become sapphire blue. A mist has formed above the horizon. Through it, we can watch the disc of gold appear — first its bright edge, then its glowing shape, then its vivid circle, heralding in blazing light the beauty of the day.

So rose a lady in the chariot. She is dressed in white, green, and red, the colors of faith, hope and love. She is wearing an olive crown upon her head, the sign of Minerva, goddess of wisdom. It is Beatrice.

Dante is instantly a youth again, on the streets of Florence, astounded by the sight of a woman walking by. Maybe because her appearance rejoices in ancient signs as well as Christian, maybe because he is rocking inside between his young and adult self, Dante turns spontaneously to Virgil. He assumes his guide is behind him. He is like a child wanting its mother to share a moment of delight, surprise, and confusion.

But he is absent. Virgil, who is mother and also sweet father to him, the parent to his new life, is not there. It is a body blow.

He was going to quote Virgil another line of poetry, one Virgil had written for Dido to capture the moment when she felt her blood throbbing with love, which is both new and ancient. There is a hint of prophecy in the reference too. Dido's love for Aeneas had led to her death, when love proved too much. Dante's love for Beatrice will lead to life, if he can tolerate its richness. But there is no Virgil. There is an empty space.

Instantly, it is as if the extraordinary unfolding on the other side of the streams collapses. Dante weeps. The joy around him cannot hold back the tears. Virgil has disappeared. We never learn why, though I think it is because Virgil's service to Dante is done, and he must henceforth attend to the redemption of his own soul, as Dante must take responsibility for his.

Dante is called back to the vision by the sound of his name, the first word Beatrice speaks. Dante.

It is the only time he will use it in *The Divine Comedy*, and Dante apologies for recording it as he heard it, because medieval writers felt that using your own name in your own work was arrogant or gauche. He must do so because the call is to him, the calling to the individual being absolutely crucial in the path to God, whose I AM can only be known in the mirror of your and my "I am." It is the central meaning of the Incarnation. It is why she reflects the divine presence as Jesus had done and can appear as Christ to him.

Do not weep for Virgil, Beatrice says, because you will have to weep for another wound, which is the losses of your life. It is a warning, and Beatrice begins to reproach Dante in relentless, bitter, aching words.

She chastises him. She speaks piercingly to the core of his life. It is pitiless, seemingly without mercy. It is so harsh that Dante casts his eyes down, by chance seeing himself in a reflection from the stream, and he can't bear the sight. He shifts his gaze. He can only manage to stare at the grass. He is like a child before its mother again, only now, wracked by guilt, exposed.

The angels dancing at Beatrice's side take pity. They start singing a song which includes lines about not feeling shame before God, because of the spacious openness that surrounds the divine. Dante is moved. He feels their compassion and his petrified heart begins to ease and soften. It is like winter mountains catching the first rays of spring and filling with the sound of tumbling water as the melt flows through valleys.

Beatrice fiercely interjects. She rebukes the angels for competing with her. It's a fascinating moment. It is as if the angels who are free to see God's face, because they never fell from grace, cannot understand Dante's predicament as a human being who must return to God's presence, by fully acknowledging all that he has become and is. That way, he can stay free. He must grieve and lament. There is no part of him that can hide in the shadows because, before God, anything hidden will burst like a long-forgotten, buried trauma, unexpectedly causing collapse.

Human beings, unlike angels, have been given not only the blessings of the divine spirit, that are breathed into them at birth, but also the blessings of the cosmos, with which they participate in mortal life. At first, it looked as if the seeds of stellar influence upon Dante, which today we might attribute to his nature and nurture, were going to germinate and sprout, Beatrice continues. He sought the sun. His potential appeared to be manifesting in his life. His poetry was on the way to developing into nothing less than an expression of divinity, conveying joy, channeling grace.

The secret of his seeming success was the sight he caught of her. That stirred the fullness of love within him. He woke up. But then she died and left him for heaven, and he failed to realize that this was her transition to divine realms, of which her earthly beauty was a radiant reflection. He became despairing and then distracted. His erotic longings sought simulacra of the good. He strayed, and so his work fell away from its early promise.

Her love endured from the other side of the grave. Unlike his, it did not waver. What was a human encounter, an everyday tale of young love, was also an opportunity. To recall the four levels at which *The Divine Comedy* can be read: this is Beatrice telling Dante that romantic love carries more meaning than a promise of happiness for the lovers. Their love shares in the love of creation which can be reached if the experience of disappointment and loss becomes a turning point, transforming first love into everlasting love, which was always its essence.

She tried to communicate this to him after she died, Beatrice explains, through dreams at night and inspirations by day. All sorts of beautiful sights on earth might couple to the beauty of their meeting to help him see that they all share the same beauty, of God. This is the perception of love first written about by Plato: that when the nature of love is pursued, it leads the inquirer to the ever-present origin and source of love, that which is not only beautiful, but which beautifies.

Eventually, Beatrice concluded that nothing could reach him, short of descending to limbo, pleading with Virgil, and securing the divine sanction for his journey. Dante would listen to Virgil speaking to him at the midpoint of his life, if he would no longer listen to her. It worked. Dante awoke to being lost.

They made their way through the infernal woods and lands, climbed Mount Purgatory to Eden, and are on the verge of paradise. But Dante cannot simply drink the waters of the Lethe and forget all that has led to this moment. He is not like an angel, fixed in divine life. He must know the full weight of human life, to become responsible for it, and complete. Then, all he is will be able to rise to God, though that moment is not yet. The canto concludes with Dante's necessary tears.

Beatrice continues to berate Dante. He collapses and is carried through the Lethe.

Washing

BEATRICE IS IN FULL ATTACK MODE. SHE IS mocking Dante, and not holding back. What stopped you from following the line of beauty in life? He looks down from the other side of the streams. She commands him to look up. Her sword plunges and twists as well.

It is profoundly uncomfortable to read. It is not what you would expect when a saint and sinner, let alone two lovers, meet on the verge of paradise. It makes you think very hard about what is going on. Why is Dante spending dozens of lines of his poem, over two cantos, forcing us to wrestle with her scolding criticism?

There is a clue in William Blake. In order to enter the state of mind Blake called Eternity, the individual must engage in what he called "wars of love." These are not primarily fought with others but are a battle with ourselves. The conflict embraces "Self-Annihilating," which for Blake, living before Freud, does not refer to routing the ego, but rather eroding the desire to control others, limit ourselves, or possess life. Wars of love are a mental fight from which he will not cease, to cite his well-known phrase.

The experience can feel unwanted, ruthless, ferocious. In his epic poem, Jerusalem: The Emanation of the Giant Albion, Blake describes Albion embarking on wars of love by throwing himself voluntarily into Los's fiery furnaces. But the heat is the judgment born of love, not condemnation. The aim is not subjugation but liberation, so that the self no longer blocks life but can become the receptacle of more and more of it.

Dante says he snapped like a bow. But there's just enough of him that remains intact to know that this is love's work. In hell, he saw how the individual self-annihilates so as to self-destruct. On the slopes of Mount Purgatory, he witnessed voluntary suffering sustained by hope. He knows that Beatrice came to limbo to call on Virgil. He can tolerate what is happening now in Eden because there is a place secured for him and he is being invited to occupy it fully, without remainder.

Beatrice asks him for his confession, for his freely given, open assent to all she has been declaring. Does he see it for himself? He admits yes, weeping. It all makes sense. She replies that with true confession, the hone that sharpens the blade of rebuke becomes the stone to blunt it.

There is a pause and sense of relief, as if the comfortable way of love will return. Only, she immediately fires up again. She wants him to be secure in the knowledge that when he hears the siren's call in the future, echoing from within him, he will resist.

Didn't you know that when I died, my body would turn to dust, she asks? Did you not think that the image you took as the epitome of beauty would decay? Why didn't you learn that lasting beauty is not found on earth? Why did you not grow wings and fly to the heavenly realms, first with your imagination and then with your virtue, which can carry you in the afterlife following death? What drew you to the simulacra? Why did you believe what promises happiness and delivers suffering?

He has to take it on his bearded chin. He is no longer a youth, as he had been when he first cast eyes on her. The humiliation heaps higher. He looks to the angels, who previously offered succor. But he must look at her. He must agree to his suffering, his mistakes, because that, rather than avoidance, expands the soul.

He looks up, mustering his dignity, to see, in a final blow, that she has turned from him. The griffin has stolen the full attention of her loving gaze. The creature who reaches between earth and heaven, who bridges worlds, is beautiful to her. In that moment, observing her regard, he keenly feels how close he came to losing everything. He could have scuppered, smashed, and scattered his life, and become trapped by the infernal realms. And here in Eden, he collapses in a dead faint.

I think it is Dante's symbolic death. It is a crucifixion, the experience of knowing, like Jesus on the Cross, of being seemingly forsaken by the divine because he has all but killed hope himself. It is a point of intense crisis, and it becomes the point from which recovery begins.

He comes around and finds that he is being carried through the first stream, the Lethe, by the mysterious, singing lady. He is in her kind embrace being led through the waters. She tips back his head just enough for him to drink from the stream. Then she continues to draw him to the farther bank. Cleansed, he hears music. "Wash me and I shall be clean," intones through the air.

He is changed instantly. All is different. The stream has lifted the burden of his past life. He joins the four ladies dressed in purple, dancing the cardinal virtues. They assemble around him like a living cloister. He can dance with the qualities of heaven, which is to say with an undefended perception of courage, wisdom, temperance, and justice. His history no longer presents any barriers to virtue.

It is a foretaste of the harmony of the sun and stars. The virtues are not just personal qualities that we manage, more or less, to embody. They are characteristics of reality, which become known as they flow and move within us. The pulse of life is their beat, their shaping its direction.

Look into Beatrice's emerald eyes, they suggest. Which he does. The memory of his original infatuation is rekindled alongside a thousand fresh flames. He can see in them what she was gazing at. The twofold nature of the griffin, flipping between earth and heaven.

Dante turns to us readers and invites us to contemplate it. He can't bring the two realms together into one. But he enjoys the pirouettes. One love leads to the other.

An echo of what he sees might be felt in a moment of reconciliation, or beauty, or poignant breakdown. His struggle to hold both sides of her contemplation together is like being moved though not overwhelmed or overwrought, neither sentimentalizing nor sneering. It is the instant that music carries you beyond itself, as the sound discloses a deeper silence. It is the mood in a dream that ceases to be a hope, aspiration, or fantasy, but is known as a way of life, offered, and shared. It is the inner meaning of the word "exquisite," which mixes pleasure and pain.

Dante is drinking in the experience, developing a taste for it, in this period after his immersion in the Lethe and before the Eunoë. The three virtues of faith, hope, and love join the cloister. They dance, speaking to Beatrice of what they call a second blessing. Unveil your mouth, not just your eyes, they suggest to her.

It is a further initiation, for her smile will be a beacon. It will reflect heaven's light to him, in measured doses, as he rises through the planetary spheres.

And she smiles. He looks. The canto ends with Dante lost for words. Even the poets who climbed Mount Parnassus, and had mastered all their ability and art, would have been silenced, he says.

Dante receives a vision of spiritual corruption.

PURGATORIO 32
Fall

DANTE IS GAZING INTO BEATRICE'S SMILE. HE IS
quenching the thirst of years. Entranced, there is no other reality
than the beauty of her face. He has drunk from the Lethe and
been freed from the burden of himself. No longer held by the concerns of
his finite mind, he can absorb her presence.

But it is dangerous. The goddesses of faith, hope, and love, who stand to
his left, notice that he is beginning to descend into divine madness. He is at
risk of losing his mind in her divinity, as can happen when people become
gripped by love, psychedelic, or paranormal experiences. Overwhelmed, they
are unable to hold onto themselves as they are flooded.

They call out that he should not look so hard. The virtues would know
because they are the form that individuals, and the cosmos, must have in
order to be containers of divine life.

Dante hears them and knows that he has indeed been blinded, much as
someone who has stared too long at the sun. He couldn't really see what he

286

was seeing. He was caught by the dazzle, though also caught from falling. Their warning sets a theme for the canto. He is temporarily in an innocent state, which will remain until he drinks from the Eunoë. It means that he is not completely himself. He is like the child without discrimination, who reaches out at whatever sparkles and shines, and so is as likely to be hurt as made happy.

He recovers from the immediate dangers of Beatrice's effulgence and notices that the procession is moving off. The elders, the virtues, the griffin, and the chariot have wheeled about and are retracing their steps toward the golden candlesticks and the glorious sun. The maneuver looks military. Troops and colors appear to be marching. As the chariot swings about, Statius and Dante fall in, alongside the inside wheel that described the tighter arc.

The martial allusions are, partly, to the Church militant on earth, as the liturgies put it, which is to say the hierarchical assembly of prelates and people who are the heralds of God's presence. That is the allegorical reading of the literal about turn, though there is a tropological sense as well. The procession is moving off with a different intent from the one that had brought it to stand before Dante. Beatrice later explains that it has raised its sights higher and will show him things that are for the whole of humanity, not just him. He must record and report them as fully as the personal encounter he underwent.

The assembly travels a short distance through the lovely forest, roughly the ground that would be covered by three firings of an arrow, Dante recalls. Beatrice steps out of the chariot, leaving it vacant, which I think means that it is ready to carry other vessels of divine life, though as Dante will see, none of them manifest beauty comparable to hers. Quite the opposite because, as a pageant of history unfolds, with various creatures and figures swooping into and crashing about it, it is as if they are more or less failed attempts at bringing God to earth. They are in marked contrast to Beatrice who, for Dante, embodies incarnate perfection.

Before that begins, they come to a standstill by a tree without fruit or leaf. It is another purgatorial tree with boughs that expand with height, capturing heaven rather than shading earth. This one is even larger than the trees Dante has heard can be found in India. The reference to the east, beyond the lands of Christendom, stretches our imaginations, reminding us that what is about to be seen does indeed relate to the whole earth.

The griffin is called blessed because it does not eat of the bark of the tree. It would be deadly for its belly and cause it to writhe in pain, the elders remark. The two-natured beast replies that, in this way, the seeds of righteousness are preserved. It is preserving a right balance between earth and heaven.

The remark is a reference to the story of Eden, with Adam and Eve falling because they ate what they could not digest; they sought to understand things that were, at that moment, beyond them. So, the griffin who doesn't eat from the tree is reaching back to prelapsarian times. Using the terms of Owen Barfield, this is the period before the alienation remembered in the story of the fall, when human beings and the whole of creation enjoyed an original participation. It was a time in tune with divine life, shining with that presence unconditionally.

Dante is taken back to that time with what happens next. The griffin touches the tree with the pole of the chariot, this container for God's presence on earth, and sure enough, the tree bursts into life. It blossoms as if it were springtime. The leaves and fruits are colored in hues somewhere between a red rose and deep violet, Dante remarks, displaying an aboriginal freshness.

A hymn is sung, which Dante doesn't comprehend. I think that is because it is the music of an old dispensation of which he has no understanding. It is from a time before the consciousness that he, you, and I know. It is a consciousness effortlessly transparent to spiritual realities. Interestingly, he falls out of consciousness as this ancient awareness envelops him. He is lulled into a mystical sleep, perhaps akin to the deep sleep that Vedantic texts say is a state of pure consciousness, unclouded by the limitations of time and place. Dante describes the experience by recalling a story. Syrinx was a chaste nymph who hid from Pan by becoming a reed bed in the river. The reeds made a hypnotic sound when Pan's breath moved across them, so he turned them into the pan pipes, which can put people to sleep. The experience is akin to Dante's lapse at this ancient vision. He feels like Peter, James, and John who fell from consciousness, overwhelmed, by the vision of the transfiguration of Jesus. He told them not to be afraid, but rise, which is an invitation to extend consciousness: to attempt to catch sight of eternity.

He is roused by the singing lady, and awakes gripped momentarily by terror, another indicator of his innocent state of mind, crying out for Beatrice. The lady assures him. Beatrice is sitting amidst the roots of the tree with the newborn leaves.

The procession and griffin have left her and returned to heaven, the singing lady says. Beatrice is alongside the chariot, accompanied by the seven virtues. Events have entered a different state of consciousness from the one that put Dante to sleep because the bridge between earth and heaven has withdrawn. The vision is moving into a different phase in which the shared participation of earth with heaven has been disrupted or broken. It is one familiar to Dante, after the fall, in alienated consciousness, with the upshot that he can stay awake.

He sees an account of the nature of human awareness. It moves through seven stages. These may map actual events in history, as commentators try to decipher, but I think they also characterize seven qualities of our times. The vulnerability bestowed upon him by bathing in the Lethe exposes him to the undercurrents of the centuries, which he sees now.

First, an eagle, the bird of Jove, swoops down from the skies. It crashes through the foliage of the tree, ripping off leaves, damaging blooms, before hitting the chariot, which rocks like a ship in a storm. The bird could stand for the spirit of the heavens descending in unsteady, unready times.

Next, a lean and hungry fox runs into the chariot. Beatrice scolds the bony beast, and it slinks away. Maybe this is a time in which there is a yearning for divine life, and it is sought with cunning and skill but little understanding, so it cannot be absorbed. There is too much reliance on the rational mind that does not perceive the need for the soul to resonate with beauty, which is why beautiful Beatrice turns the fox away.

The eagle appears again and momentarily settles in the chariot, shedding some of its golden feathers. This could be the periods in which people try to live by God and the Spirit, though they make the mistake of fabricating artifices of glory from their own plumage. They do not know how to reflect divine light. It is the period when the veneer of ecclesiastical pomp occludes divine life, as the Church confuses its importance with God's, becoming uncoupled from the ground of being.

Little wonder, a dragon bursts through the bottom of the chariot next. It has a poisonous tail, reminding us of Geryon, and this fourth state is one in which corruption, hypocrisy, and deceit shape events and rule hearts. These vices rush into the vacuum left by the desire for God being forgotten.

That gives way in time to the fifth stage that Dante sees. The chariot becomes covered in foliage, which is described as an undergrowth of good intentions. It looks verdant but is actually thin and weedy. It is a covering of seeming vitality that conceals an inner deadness. I wonder if this moment reflects something of our times, when advances bring tremendous material goods that distract from spiritual emptiness, but leave people struggling truly to connect with life, because they don't know how to sink their roots into it.

The sense of meaninglessness spirals out of control and generates growth for growth's sake in increasingly desperate attempts to find sustenance. The chariot reflects this next, in a sixth stage, by growing monstrous heads. It becomes unrecognizable to Dante, as if it could never be a receptacle for divine life at all.

That brings about the seventh stage. In the chariot are a woman and a man. The woman looks like a harlot, the man like a giant thug. He is unintelligent power, she unintelligent desire. Every so often, they kiss, with the lust of possessiveness and envy. Then, the woman casts her eyes toward Dante and, sure enough, the man becomes jealous and rages. He rallies his strength, tears the monstrous multi-headed chariot from the tree, and rides it into the darkness of the forest. Dante watches it go until he can see them no more.

Held by ignorance and vice, humankind can only chart a way blindly. It becomes lost in the shadows. The canto closes with the devastation brought to the natural world and the human soul. It is a tragedy, one that Dante has known well, when he wandered lost in the forest. The seven visions are moments of history, moments in the collapse of the human spirit, and moments he himself now fully understands.

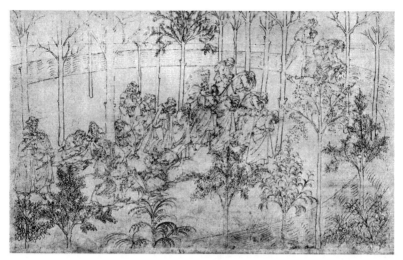

Beatrice prophesizes on Christianity's future. Dante is ready for the stars.

PURGATORIO 33

Ready

THE SEVEN GODDESSES OF THE VIRTUES INTONE
a lament. Faith, hope, and love chant; then wisdom, justice, temperance, and courage. "O God, the nations have laid Jerusalem in
ruins." They have watched the rehearsal of humanity's downfall. Beatrice
reflects the sorrow in her face with them, her grief reminding Dante of
Mary weeping at the foot of the Cross.

It's a downbeat mood to start the final canto of The Purgatorio. The feeling is going to revive, though that can happen only with conviction by
not holding back in this first moment. Descent and ascent are linked. The
profundity of the problem Dante has seen enacted leads to the brilliance
of the remedy. This is not just about a reset, renewed push, or revival, but
a remaking of human-divine relations.

Beatrice is central and she stands up like an erect flame. She is resolute and
quotes words of Jesus from John's Gospel. Jesus had said to the disciples that
they would not see him and then, after a little while, they would see him. He
was prophesying his death and Resurrection, and Beatrice uses the words to

291

indicate a similar pattern. The eagle, the fox, the dragon, the monstrous heads, the giant, and the harlot successively occupying the chariot demonstrate that Christ has been lost to the Church and the world. So, what will happen now?

Beatrice organizes the seven virtues in front of her. She nods to Dante, Statius, and the lady to move behind, and she steps out toward the wood. Dante is not ready for the advance and almost immediately Beatrice turns back and fixes his eyes. "More haste, keep pace!" she says. "You will need to hear my words." You are with me, she continues, calling him brother, which is remarkable given her recent reproaches. But the chastisement was not an end in itself. It was a catalyst, a readying. He is accepted, without condition.

Dante is flabbergasted. She is a god to him, an object of longing and terror, and she calls him brother? He reels, gobsmacked. "You know my wants and how to meet them," he replies, to which she retorts words that say, in effect, grow up! This is no longer a dream. This is about reality.

The reckoning with Dante's time, which I think still applies to now, returns as Beatrice continues to speak in apocalyptic language. She refers back to the chariot, the receptacle that is supposed to be able to incarnate divine life, and observes that it is broken. The brokenness may refer to the Church, to the world, to individual souls. But know it is ruined, she insists. And know as well that God won't linger. He will remake things.

Just how God will do that has provoked lots of discussion because Beatrice talks in prophetic words. An advent is near, she says. Stars are in her sights. God's emissary will be born. Commentators wonder if she is referring to a secular leader to govern an empire after settling the Italian civil wars, or a Church revival much as occurred with the birth of the Franciscan and Dominican orders. Whatever the truth of that, she must be referring to change from the bottom up, not merely a tweaking of the current order. The vision with the chariot has made that clear. A shift of consciousness, an influx of spirit, change from the inside out must be on her mind.

She implies this is so by saying her riddling will be understood like the riddle of Themis and that of the Sphinx. These are classical allusions. The prophetess Themis had spoken of putting the bones of the dead behind you, which sounds like Jesus's remark about letting the dead bury their dead. Burying the dead is, of course, a sacred task, so the reference to Themis suggests that what Beatrice has in mind will be a wrench into the future, causing as much offence as hope.

The allusion to the Sphinx is to the riddle that asks about the identity of the creature that walks on four legs in the morning, two at noon, and three in the afternoon, with the answer: man. The type of person the Sphinx had in mind is an everyman, not a great figure of history, which is interesting. I think it means that Beatrice is not thinking of an individual who might turn things around as a leader, ecclesiastical or military, the kind of savior Dante's contemporaries might expect. She also says that the renewal will come about without loss of life, as political, religious, or military change would inevitably entail. So, who might she mean?

I think she answers her riddle straightaway, as riddlers tend to do. The person she has in mind only seems obscure because her thought is audacious. But immediately she addresses Dante. Mark my words, she tells him directly. Write them down. Tell people on earth what you have seen and what I am saying. This, I sense, is the answer to the riddle. The apostle of remaking is Dante. A poet is going to communicate it. He will bring a vision. She instructs him to write about how life is a "race to the death," in one of the phrases from *The Divine Comedy* that has become famous. This life is a preparation for the after-life. It is the opportunity to become capable of more life, here and hereafter.

He must speak of the prelapsarian state, the aboriginal fall, the alienation and distress that has entered the world. He must speak of the fullness of life, its darkness and its light. He will address the wait, the pain, the agony, which for Adam lasted five thousand years, which is to say, a very long time.

Dante is confused. His mind clouds over. What she speaks of seems fright-ening, awesome, lofty, as it would if he senses she is speaking of him. But he is going to bring something new. *The Divine Comedy* demonstrates that.

She offers another hint. If he can understand the meaning of the inverted tree, he will perceive what she sees. It grows wider the closer it comes to the divine. Its height is great because heaven is deep and high. It can't be climbed in the usual way, because it offers no branches low down. It is not just a question of grabbling a bough of knowledge and a stump of good. Innovative means are required to rise into its canopy, which Dante is going to acquire as he rises through the heavenly spheres.

He hears her words, if not completely understanding their meaning. They imprint him like a stamp on wax. Dante tells us readers that this is what he heard. He must wrestle to understand, so he can convey its fullness in poetry, though he doesn't doubt that what he seeks to speak about is true. It will exceed the new learning of Aristotle and the knowledge coming in from the Islamic world, she continues. It will draw on genius theologians of Dante's time, like Thomas Aquinas, and spiritual adepts, like Bernard and Peter Damian, whom he will meet in paradise. And it will discover, disclose, and delight in more. He must struggle, in order to come to appreciate how profound the revelation will be. It is as far from how things currently are, as the earth is from the highest of the spinning spheres, she insists, which is to say, about as far as can be.

Dante becomes confused again, thinking she is talking about the distance between him and her, which he feels was never that far. She chuckles and remarks that this is the effect of the Lethe speaking, the waters of forgetfulness that have rendered him innocent of his inconstant past. But henceforth, she will speak clearly to him, and he will stay close to her meaning. The promise is made as the sun offers its clearest light, having reached the zenith of the day.

The seven virtues come to an abrupt halt. A lightness descends on the group, after the heavier, apocalyptic mood. The place they have arrived at is cool and shady, perfect for midday. It offers refreshment and relaxation in the form of a spring. Dante sees that the spring is the source for the two streams, the Lethe and Eunoë. He is surprised. One source becomes two flows. My sense is that his surprise is not that he finds this unusual, but that he recognizes how the dividing spring mirrors the spiritual dynamics of Eden, which links two worlds in one place, uniting heaven and earth.

He becomes solemn, addressing Beatrice as Holy Wisdom. What light will he bring to earth? What spirit will illuminate minds? And what is the meaning of the source and streams?

It is the end of The Purgatorio. In part these questions are for paradise, and for that, his preparation must now be completed, though Beatrice asks the singing lady to answer the last question at least, and names her in so doing. She is Matilda. It's a touching moment. Matilda says she already told Dante what must happen. He must bathe in the Eunoë so that, to the relief of the Lethe, can be added the conscious knowledge of who he is. He can then be free to rise. Beatrice quips that Dante probably forgot what Matilda had said because, since the Lethe, he has had a lot on his mind, namely her.

Beatrice asks the singing lady to lead him into the Eunoë as she had done the Lethe. Matilda graciously obliges and invites Statius to come too.

The canticle ends with Dante addressing us readers. He hasn't the words to describe the sweetness of the waters, he says. He hasn't the space either, because this section of his poem is ending. It is a lovely moment. Even at this culmination of the second journey, he thinks of us. Why wouldn't he, given what Beatrice has prophesied? He is there for us. He will continue for us.

Dante is ready to rise. He is remade like a tree that bursts back into life. It is a powerful metaphor with the inverted tree still in our minds. His branches will embrace the heavens. He will move among the stars.

The word is the last of The Purgatorio. It was the last of The Inferno. The stars are his destiny, though it will take the journey through paradise to discover how.

III
Paradiso

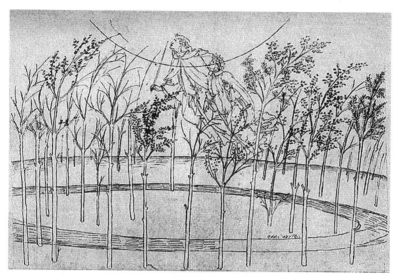

Dante's intellect and desire, guided by Beatrice, draw him into the heavens.

PARADISO I

Rising

ANTO 1 OF THE PARADISO IS AN INTRODUCTION to this third, last, and most extraordinary part of Dante's journey. Dante calls on the gods for their gifts of poetry, in order that he might communicate and be worthy of discussing all that he's seen. Simultaneously, the canto stirs up in us the desire to follow him, if we possibly can, into the highest heavens.

All our love and desire are going to be needed, our curiosity and intellect, he insists. The journey is going to be daunting and difficult, but ultimately, it's going to take us into paradise, which we are destined to discover anyway. It is an invitation to become more conscious of that destiny, and to know more about the preparation possible in mortal life.

The opening terzet contrasts markedly from the opening of The Inferno where he began, frightened in a dark wood, midway through the course of our life. Now he speaks confidently of the glory of God that is the source of all movement in the cosmos, which itself seeks to reflect God. This vision of reality is a perception of cascading light and glory, enabling the whole of creation to participate in the life of the Creator. His awareness will draw us as readers, with the aim of enabling us to share it. It demands our intellect, which is not just our understanding, but the openness consciously to resonate with the divine. It demands our desire: the yearning impulses that can drive us through life blindly or, conversely, more intentionally toward the light.

Dante assures us that he speaks of what he knows. He has seen the highest heaven that reflects the divine light unalloyed. This is not a journey fabricated by a tremendous imagination. It's a journey that is possible to describe because Dante's imaginative genius can convey what was revealed to him. He penned words that bridge to heaven by unveiling it to us.

The words will fall short of the full experience, but they can enable us to catch glimpses and reflections of the celestial heights, and so feel the divine orientation within us. And that is the important part. The point about knowing God is that it is an awareness from which words spring. It is a direct sense of reality, and so outside memory or inference, and within which reflections and insights are rooted. We can develop the eyes to see and the ears to hear such things. It's a question of tuning in.

He calls on other gods to assist him, particularly Apollo: Dante's vision leaves nothing out, classical and Christian, old and new. Everything is gathered together, because everything that ever was or will be is present in the divine mind and knowing that is crucial to sharing in the divine mind. It is about bringing all things together and seeing how they integrate and mix into the glorious whole.

Apollo is the god of light, and I wonder if Dante calls on him also because the word "Apollo" means "not many" in Greek: Apollo brings the many into the one. He is a god associated with Mount Parnassus as well, so it is appropriate, here at the top of Mount Purgatory, to think of Apollo on the top of Mount Parnassus, calling us toward the light. Dante references the laurel leaves of Apollo's crown in another detail. This is calling on Apollo as the one who crowns poets, when they are recognized by the gods, which is to say when their work has become divine. He is signaling that the third part of The Divine Comedy is the most tremendous part and the most difficult, and potentially the most glorious for Dante, pilgrim and poet, insofar as it channels the most glorious.

Life's shadows are not forgotten amidst these hopes because recalling Apollo also brings Marsyas to Dante's mind. He was the satyr who challenged Apollo, for which Apollo flayed him alive. It's a viscerally appropriate image, indicating that the purged memory of everything that Dante has seen, including the violence of hell and the suffering of Mount Purgatory, will be integrated in this last part of his journey. Even the things that might destroy us, that can be excruciatingly painful, are somehow part of the ascent.

For this reason, it takes all the virtues to develop the eyes that can see and the ears that can hear. There are the four classical virtues of courage, the balance between foolhardiness and timidity; temperance, the appropriate response from moment to moment; justice, meant in the older sense of being able to see the harmony between things; and of wisdom, the ability to see with insight. The four are combined with the three Christian or theological virtues of faith, which is being able to see more than what lies visibly ahead; hope, which is turning to what's good, even when things feel tricky; and of love, which is the cultivation of the desire to be with God.

They are evoked by an astronomical allusion. Dante says that the four classical virtues are like the four circles that encompass the earth: the circle of the horizon; the circle of the ecliptic, which is the plane that the planets move through; the circle that joins the north and south poles running vertically, if you imagine the globe of the earth standing on its end; and the circle of the equator. These four circle the earth and meet at three points, pointing to the three theological virtues of faith, hope and love.

Dante describes them in this circuitous way because this is about tapping into qualities that are part of the cosmos. We can see the virtues outside of ourselves, as much as cultivate them within ourselves. That awareness is important because The Paradiso is about seeing with the inner eye into that which is outside of us, as much as within us. It gives us a clue as to what the journey is about: cultivating the qualities that we feel in ourselves and can detect in the world. It is to come to know "the inside of the whole world," as Owen Barfield put it.

Another crucial dynamic is signaled because throughout this first paradisal canto, Beatrice is said several times to be staring at the sun. Dante marvels because mortal humans can't do that, but Beatrice is in her blessed state. She is seeing more than just the guinea sun, to use William Blake's phrase, when he looked at the sunrise and saw more than a round golden disc shining brightly in the sky, as if a guinea hanging in the air. Blake famously declared, "No, No, I see the heavenly hosts crying, Holy, Holy, Holy." Being able to see more than just physical light, but what physical light heralds, is a key part of being able to journey into paradise. We need the eyes that can see more. We need to know how to look at light aright. Learning to do that is going to be crucial throughout The Paradiso.

Dante will be helped repeatedly by recognizing that Beatrice already sees more. Time and again, when he sees Beatrice enjoying the sight of the highest heavens, it fosters in him the desire which becomes for him an increased capacity to see. This gives us another hint as to how we might rise into paradise. When, in life, we see individuals radiating with joy because they see life's spiritual light, we should contemplate them, because their enjoyment will advance the capacity for us to see more. Notice what feels alluring in life. Sometimes it will lead you astray, but sometimes it will lead you to more. It's falling in love with that which is good and learning to discern where your erotic desire leads you. It's following that which is beautiful, and letting it lead you rather than wanting to possess it.

As Dante describes looking at Beatrice in this way, he realizes he has already begun to rise. He sees sparks and fire and detects that they are flying up. There's a message in that departure: perhaps we have already embarked on the journey into paradise without quite knowing it. We can become conscious of what is already going on in our lives, as well as hoping for more.

The word Dante uses for this take off is the most famous neologism in *The Divine Comedy*: the verb "transhumanize." Dante says he was transhumanized. Just what he means by this he can't quite tell at this point. It will take the journey to discover. But as a first guess, it seems akin to when the fisherman, Glaucus, ate a magic herb and became a sea god. The herb seemingly unleashed his humanity, intensifying his ability to love, to prophecy, to live.

Transhumanizing also echoes Saint Paul, who in his Second Letter to the Corinthians, wrote that he was carried up into a third, ecstatic heaven, much as Dante is being carried. Paul says that he does not know whether he was carried in his body or not, an uncertainty that Dante shares. That said, Dante's eagerness to understand what's happening to him has already been picked up by Beatrice. They're mutually sharing as they individually participate in this experience, because at heart it is a communion in the oneness of God's life, and so she knows what's going on for him. He asks her to explain things, which is to say, to bring what is happening more consciously to his mind. This is part of the ascent. It's only misperceptions that stop him from seeing more clearly already, and she explains that he is rising because humans are destined to rise: it's our misfiring desires and lack of perception that stop us. It would be strange if he hadn't started to rise, she adds, like a waterfall that tumbled upward.

The canto ends with Beatrice gazing once more toward the heavens. If paradise is beginning to manifest itself to Dante in Beatrice's sight, it may be beginning to manifest to us in Dante's poetry. He leaves us wanting to know more about the journey. Desire at the beginning of this third stage is alight.

Beatrice warns Dante that the journey is risky. They arrive in the heaven of the moon.

PARADISO 2

Warning

ANTE ISSUES A WARNING. HE DOES SO DIRECTLY, straight to us readers. Stop reading, he advises, unless you are ready to follow him all the way. It would be better to dock in the seas of hell, or stay on Mount Purgatory, than become lost on the vast oceans of paradise.

The caution makes sense. You can read The Paradiso for the poetry, and it will delight, though in delighting leave you lost in waves of pleasure. It can hypnotize and entrance, but fail in its true task of illuminating reality. That happens when the mind becomes caught in the mystery, unreceptive to the full vision. It is to love the peak experience, not the whole of life. It is to trip, not be transformed.

Follow my little ship, Dante insists. Keep close in its wake. If I pull too far ahead, catch up, because you risk being diverted by the currents. Don't just enjoy the imagery, but sharpen desire, broaden understanding, and participate in what I see.

Dante needs guides as well. He calls on Minerva, the goddess of wisdom, and again on Apollo, the god of light, to fill his sails. He calls on all the muses to fire his poetic powers with the right words and song. He invites anyone to eat the bread of angels if they long for knowledge of God and the fullest truths of which the human mind is capable. He will track a way, one that can be made your own, though you should be prepared to see what you don't expect.

Jason's Argonauts had to be ready for the unexpected when they retrieved the Golden Fleece, he notes. They saw fields ploughed with fire-breathing bulls, and dragon's teeth planted in the soil morphing into an army. Events may appear random, encounters alarming, but they each play a part.

The unknowing he is inviting us to embrace is different from the fear that filled hell and the dazed uncertainty of the lower slopes of Mount Purgatory. This is expectancy, receptive thirst. It wants more. It is the imaginative love that delights in the extraordinary. It is drawn by subtle beauties. It is akin to Wordsworth's feeling intellect, to William Blake's golden thread, to Barfield's sensitivity for the energy transmitted by words. It is like the meditator who has stilled the mind enough to detect a subtler perturbation of compassion, kindness, and happiness, and who can then attend to it, to foster, and amplify it. They then watch it become the world.

As Dante discusses this third mode of travelling, he realizes that he has already entered the first planetary sphere that characterizes the lower reaches of paradise, that of the moon. To see is to arrive. To fly is to ride on inner movements. To perceive is to share in the qualities of the realm perceived and so, knowing directly, to be in its state of mind.

The light of this lunar domain is diamond-like, though it simultaneously has the creaminess of a pearl. It has viscosity as well as brilliance, which is doubly hard to describe because Dante is also conscious of his body being penetrated by the heavenly atmosphere. There is no clear distinction between his vitality and its life. To be here is to become part of it.

It is a crucial insight. Spiritual passageway is found in stages of union. The direction of travel is indicated by a flow of life not over, under or around him, but within him.

Dante thanks God. He speaks of his gratitude at the expansion, an act that itself amplifies the experience of life within the zone shared by the moon. His thanks represent a receptive humility that the moon knows as well, because it receives and gives thanks for the light of the sun. That said, Dante wants to understand. He seeks to grow his knowledge to meet this level of consciousness, not simply be swept along by it. He has a question, of which Beatrice is aware. She suggests he give it voice, his voice. He will begin to learn to sing the song of eternity.

His question arises because, when seen from earth, the moon appears to be marked by shade and darkness, as well as light. But now that he has moved into the life of the moon directly, he sees that there are only diamonds and pearls in a uniform light, and he wonders if some received wisdom of his times explains the difference.

According to a medieval tale, the moon visibly bore the curse of Cain. Its mucky greys were a permanent stain and reminder of the ugly shadows that fall across human life. Something of that sense is remembered in the states of mind with which the moon is still associated. Wandering lunacy. Waxing and waning. Tides and surges.

Beatrice explains that this is wrong. The error is to draw celestial conclusions from empirical senses, which is to say, to use the methods of terrestrial science to understand the heavens. Observation and measurement work well on earth. In other spheres of consciousness, alternative methods are required. They may well be illuminated by terrestrial analogues, but not discovered as if they were straightforwardly terrestrial phenomena. In particular, there is a need to cultivate feeling and sympathy coupled to discernment, rather than neutrality and distance driven by abstractions, because this is a zone in which subjective knowledge is absolute, not disconnected conclusions.

Beatrice is referring to the original meaning of the word "subjective." Before the seventeenth century, it referred to what is unchanging and reliable. It is the ability to steady the mind, and peer through the ups and downs of life to detect the constant awareness and steady presence that is at the heart of all things and is the essence of existence. The meaning flipped with the emergence of modern science, which developed Aristotle's method of gathering information and making deductions. Called objectivity, it became an idol, a god that it was assumed could defeat the subtleties of subjectivity with the weight of tangible evidence.

What gets overlooked is that such objective conclusions are the ones that keep changing. The history of science is the story of their continual modification. It's what makes science interesting though inconclusive, which may explain why a number of contemporary physicists are rediscovering the absolute nature of subjectivity once more. Every so often, one will announce it, declaring that reality is mental, the universe is a thought, or existence is an observation. As the potter and philosopher Rupert Spira puts it: "Any honest model of reality must start with awareness. To start anywhere else is to build a model on the shifting sands of belief."

Beatrice trusts the subjective, and she explains that the domain of the moon is where such awareness strengthens and forms. To be in the diamond-pearl light of the moon is to be in the state of mind where the immortal begins to shine through the mortal, the necessary emerges from the contingent, the incorruptible radiates through the mutable. It is a place in which false imaginings are corrected, much as happens when it is realized that the moon's light is a reflected light, not one generated by itself.

With a childlike enthusiasm, Dante posits another idea about the seeming variance of the moon, which to modern ears sounds more scientific. Is it the case that the darker regions of lunar domains are denser, and the lighter less dense? Beatrice replies that this is not the case either. If that were so, the cosmos would be a smudge of greys, incapable of reflecting white divine light. It could convey no intimations of perfection and would be an endless repetition of flaws.

I think they are talking at cross-purposes here. Dante still has one foot on earth — he is transhumanizing — and so is treating the moon as an object in the sky, whereas Beatrice is trying to show him that he can absorb the celestial consciousness with which the moon is associated. She is driving at an alternative way of perceiving the being of things, not one that reduces paradisal to earthly experiences, and so invites him to imagine standing in front of two mirrors that are the same distance from him, with a third that is twice the distance of the first two. Next, she continues, he is to imagine a candle behind his head that is reflected in the mirrors. He would notice that the candle would look larger in the nearer mirrors, but also that the quality of the light would be the same in all three, which is to say, unaffected by distance. The intensity of all three would be the same.

She is offering him an indicator of the difference between heavenly and terrestrial awareness. The latter is preoccupied with quantities, as is modern science, whereas the former focuses on qualities, which is to say, on the felt nature of phenomena. She is nudging him toward an appreciation of subjective truths over objective conclusions.

Dante is confused, though Beatrice explains that intellectual bemusement is a stage in his developing perceptions. It is the gift of the lunar state, which moves through phases and modifications, so his confusion is a sign that he has taken the first step to perceiving divine light, pure and unmediated. The lunar heaven is the first heaven for a reason. Its virtues foster the capacity to be bewildered, an important stage in the transformation of perception.

The journey through paradise is like the life of the blacksmith, she adds, who must work and mold the metal to refine its qualities and polish its surfaces. Dante's perceptions will gradually become like a body, she continues, which while composed of various parts, each with their own genius, has to work as one. Dante begins to see that the universe is not full of matter, but of intelligences, souls, lights. They shine with one vision, much as the night sky can dazzle with complexity and simultaneously convey an impression of a single, glorious eternity.

Dante wrestles with reflection and reality, as Piccarda appears.

PARADISO 3
Qualities

BEATRICE WAS THE SUN OF HIS YOUNG LIFE, Dante declares at the start of canto 3. He is tuning into the inner life of the heavenly light, seeing that they are akin to the warmth of her presence, which is to say that planetary light and love's energy share in the same spiritual sources.

We still say as much: "his face lit up like the sun," "she shone," "the thought is illuminating," and so on — turns of phrase that are not empty but living metaphors. Outer light and inner light have much in common.

The sun and the planets are not the source of these influences but are associated with various qualities of spiritual vitality that their manifest appearances celebrate and reflect. The ways in which this is so will be a key part of his celestial discovery.

He is learning to experience the moon's light properly: it participates in an inner illumination that he has felt in Beatrice's introduction to the qualities of its light. Her proofs and arguments, as he calls them, referring back to the discussion about mirrors and candles, are an elucidation: they are not a fixed deduction but a helpful inference, and the shift of focus, onto qualities, is clarifying and brings lucidity. Beatrice has not demonstrated a truth, as if in a physics class. She has conveyed something of the radiance of truth, a beam of light that he can follow. She was a sun in his youth. She is proving to be so in his adulthood. He looks into her eyes and enjoys the gaze.

Then, he is distracted. Pale faces appear around her head. Having gained a little more depth of vision, he spots what had been invisible before. More details within the lunar sphere emerge, revealing other aspects of its life.

At first, he is confused. He thinks he is being tricked by reflections. He still has candles and mirrors on his mind as if he were in a laboratory, and so he turns around, presuming that the new faces are behind him. But he is like Narcissus, confusing image with reality. He turns back again and keeps looking ahead.

Beatrice smiles at his naivety. He can trust the sights of heaven, she avers, and talk with the materializing faces, as they are souls.

They look like pearls adorning a brow, which is to say they seem at first to be silky white upon creamy white, and so barely distinguishable. Referring to pearls again is an arresting way of describing them, given that he has already described the moon's light as pearl-like: he is discerning that pearl signifies a quality or characteristic, which the faces share. It is a quality or virtue that he is becoming able to discern with more subtlety.

They are the souls who share the life of this domain. He sees one in particular, Piccarda, the sister of his friend, Forese Donati, whom he met on Mount Purgatory. He had confirmed that her beauty carried her straight to heaven, and he greets her.

That said, he is confused as well, as he had expected her to be in a higher heaven, though she reveals that this is the right place for her. She is happy to be in this apparently lower domain. And there is a reason for it, she explains. During her mortal life she broke her religious vows, having been a sister of the Poor Clares, the second order of Franciscans.

Dante knows her biography though the detail troubles him. Doesn't she yearn to be in a higher heaven, he wonders? Doesn't she long to be more loved by God?

She smiles, as do more souls who have become visible around her, and Dante sees that her face comes alive not only with the pearly moonlight but with the "first fire" of God's light. It turns out that she is in two states at once: one in the moon, the other in the perfect domain of divine light, though in truth her lunar manifestation is a dim reflection of the fuller delight.

He begins to see that while not everywhere in heaven seems to shine with an equal light — which is just as well for him because he must become accustomed to more — at the same time, everywhere in heaven simultaneously shares the supreme grace and sweetest light. It is a case of both/and, not either/or. She can be here, in the sphere that moves the slowest because it is closest to earth, and there, in the realm of undiminished dynamism. Moreover, she has appeared here to help him understand the way this reality works.

Momentarily satisfied by her explanation, he absorbs its meaning, though quickly hits upon a further apparent problem. She is glad he has more questions as she seeks to aid him, and further, because she shares in the divine consciousness, she also knows telepathically what he wants to ask: why did she break her vows, and how does the episode relate to the moon's light?

Piccarda had a second brother, alongside Forese, and he was a warlord. When he needed to secure an alliance by wedlock, he had her removed from the convent and married her off. She broke her vows, for all that she was forced. Her religious life that was once full, like the moon, emptied of its light, like the waning lunar cycle.

Dante is confused. Isn't that an injustice? If she had not wanted to leave her sanctified life, why has God seemingly punished her by linking her to the light of the moon? How can she be completely happy and claim to know divine bliss?

She explains that she has freely and fully accepted what happened in her mortal life. Moreover, it was precisely by embracing its waxing and waning that she became aware that her true life is bigger than a particular episode, shattering though it was at the time. Suffering opened her to a wider life, which is the eternal life of God. So, paradoxically, her association with the moon is the reason she knows the highest heavens as well. It's why she can appear in both.

Moreover, looking back on her mortal life now, she no longer feels that she was forced to do anything, but rather realizes that her fate enabled her joy. She has come to welcome what happened: saying "yes" to life whatever it brings, not "no," has made her capable of all of life. You might say that the family connections that oppressed her were the occasion to find her dignity, and that expanded her soul. She rose above her personal tragedies by understanding why her losses were losses. Similarly, she can rise from the sphere of the moon to God.

Dante listens. He seems to be learning something about how to face his own bad luck and downfall, as we might too. His situation may look disastrous and may be unjust, but the obstacles can become the way. Descent and ascent are linked.

"His will is our peace," Piccarda remarks, in a phrase that has become famous. It can sound platitudinous and pious, or as if God demands submission, but it is another reflection of the higher understanding to which Piccarda is pointing. Taken literally, it might imply that the individual has no freedom and must blindly accept the will of God: if fate is embraced, peace is found. But Piccarda has already shown Dante there is more to it than that. Allegorically, the phrase can mean that morally, you should be obedient to God's will, perhaps because God is envisaged as Lord or Father, who not only must be obeyed but should be, as He knows best. But that doesn't make sense either because Piccarda clearly delights in freedom and joy.

The third level, the tropological, nudges toward the shift of perspective she is inviting Dante to comprehend. It is aided by the light of the ambiguous moon because it is a shift that is enabled by wrestling with the apparent injustice of the dictum: if God's will is our peace then what about unfairness and suffering? Does God will such things? And if so, how can that ever produce peace?

This discomfort, even rage, is what can precipitate a fourth level of understanding, the anagogic. It is what Piccarda has achieved: her love of her life, and not wanting it to be any other, mirror God's love. His will is her peace. She gained the wider perspective when she saw that the seeming hindrances and setbacks of her life were the chance to raise her sights beyond her mortal life, and with that came the consciousness of divine life. "His will is our peace" is an expansive invitation, not a brutal diktat or chilly injunction.

Piccarda tells Dante about another soul. Beside her, in the milky brightness, stands Empress Constance. Commentators believe that she was a nun too, so they have religious life in common. Further, Constance was also removed from her convent because of political machinations, which is what made her an empress. She is another example for Dante to ponder, another soul to see in the radiance of acceptance. Not that it is cheap or passive acceptance. It is hard won. Dante feels the difficulty. He didn't understand it in Piccarda, at first, and was confused. But he gave voice to his questions and learned by owning his distress at her story.

Constance and Piccarda disappear. They dissolve into the moon as if sinking in deep waters. As they go, Piccarda sings, an *Ave Maria*. As we will learn, Mary, is in the Empyrean, and Piccarda is hailing the Virgin because she is returning to the Empyrean, having helped Dante. She is sinking back onto the unimpeded fullness of life. Piccarda knows where her heart and home are, within the first fire of love.

For his part, Dante has experienced the generosity of paradise. Souls will descend from the heights, like saints and bodhisattvas returning to aid those suffering.

Dante turns back to Beatrice. Another light flashes from her and he is dazzled. He has absorbed one level of understanding and Beatrice offers another, maintaining Dante's direction of travel. He is transitioning, trans-humanizing, and will have more to learn and ask.

ff fe di quel che fir no ft conuenne.
E'omal menina che dico pregaro
tal padre fuo la propria madre fpefe
p non poter pietà fe fe fpietato.
N quefto punto uollio che di penfe
che la forza al uoler fi mifchia e famo
fi che fcufar non fi poffon loffenfe.

et non manebi ti con altri tem:
challa uoftra ftatura nò ften parta.
B iarmco mi guardo con ltcechi pieni
et fumile di moi cofi diutni.
che uincci mia uertute die leretti.
E quafi mi parto cò licechi chim.
Comian uo. Cap: Doue abfolue laqftione
celnoto facto uel poterere Capitolo:

Dante is dazzled by the paradoxes of paradise. Beatrice comes to his aid.

PARADISO 4

Confusion

T HE PATH INTO PARADISE IS POWERED BY LOVE
and light, and by questions. Canto 4 opens with Dante caught
between two matters that he longs to resolve, though in this place
of clarification, he suffers an embarrassment of riches. Which concern might
he relieve first?

"I am like someone starving offered two delicious dishes, unable to choose,"
he cries. "I am like a lamb stranded between two wolves and so failing to
run, or a mad dog confronted by two does that lets both escape."

It is a confusing set of similes because one has the figure in the middle
as a victim, and two have the one in the middle ideally going for the kill.
As we try to keep focused, a comparable tension transfers to us. Which one
does he mean?

There is also an echo back to the early stages of The Inferno, in which
Dante had encountered those who didn't make anything of their lives
because they couldn't decide anything for themselves. Dante saw them
mindlessly running with the crowd. A comparable sense of being rudderless

confronted him and Virgil on the lower slopes of Mount Purgatory. The souls knew they had left mortal life but wandered listlessly, unsure what to make of their new state. In this third realm, paradise, Dante is enveloped by wonders and unsure which way to turn because everywhere looks inviting.

It is an ambivalent, hesitant predicament that can ruin a life. There is an agony about not being able to decide in a world that offers many choices, as does the modern world. The person who has no inner compass as guide can spend decades spinning in all directions. Free from impediments they fail to discern what all the freedom is for.

Maybe Dante is nervous about his questions as well, because of the answers he might hear. Heaven is a place of novelty, which means letting old assumptions go, which are likely to be familiar and comforting.

The lunar sphere is a good place to confront the issue and settle it. The moon is the great undecided light in the night sky, moving from being full to invisible and then back to being full again every four weeks, coupled to which each day it rises later. It manifests hesitance.

Beatrice spots the confusion and comes to his aid. She is Daniel to his Nebuchadnezzar, recalling the Babylonian king whose mounting frustration with the indecision of his dream interpreters was relieved by the Hebrew prophet.

She speaks for him. He can't find the words, which is striking as he had only recently been encouraged to voice questions for himself. He is in a state of flux with his learning. She can see that he is caught between two matters that, between them, generate a conundrum. He has become confused again by what happened to Piccarda and Constance. They had been forced to abandon their vows and had accepted that. But hadn't their wills been constant, he is thinking? And isn't that what matters?

The second question has to do with predestination. Piccarda and Constance's acceptance has prompted the thought in his mind that they might always have been destined for the moon. Was that written in the stars and in the mind of God? If that is so, then how can they feel free? The same question arises in the modern world in relation to the apparently determining forces of genes and upbringing, time and place. Might there even be an arbitrariness to paradise, as if souls are outrageously allotted random heavenly positions?

Both questions raise doubts about the desirability of heaven. If paradise were a slavish place, fixed by God and forced upon humans, Dante might come to the conclusion of Satan that John Milton was subsequently to describe in the seventeenth century: "Better to reign in Hell than serve in

Heaven," the fallen angel famously asserts in *Paradise Lost*. Is Dante wondering whether paradise might slip from his fingers if he can't help but consider it unjust? His issues are similar to those of modern skeptics who reject heaven because they conceive of it either as "pie in the sky when you die," or a patronizing reward for doing good, which is more admirably sought for its own sake.

The answers Beatrice supplies do not directly address the questions. Instead, they respond by leading Dante toward wider perspectives within which his issues dissolve. That is often how paradise works. There is a third position, beyond the options that alone put people off or would catch them out, were they to choose. Moreover, the frustration within the conundrum provides the energy to rise to the higher take on things. This is what Piccarda was displaying when she described her desire to embrace her life, so as to gain the perspective *sub specie aeternitatis*. Carl Jung called it the transcendent function, the struggle through which horizons expand.

Beatrice first confirms what Dante has already seen, that all souls share in divine bliss, from the apparently lowliest to the highest, because in heaven the lowly are lifted up, as the high up willingly bow down. There is a circulation of vitality, as Dante saw when Piccarda shone with the first fire as well as the moon's pearly light, and when she disappeared into the depths to return to the Empyrean. However, souls also remain themselves, which is a manifestation of freedom: no one is mechanically conformed to divine life, and so the manner in which souls share in the divine bliss does differ.

This is a provisional answer to his question, she adds, somewhat conditioned by what he can understand at the moment — which is another vital point: there is always more to grasp in paradise, but the subtleties often elude immediate understanding. Dante must be patient, though he can rest assured that the transcendent function of paradise will never stop opening up further vistas that settle questions. He can also rest assured because, if on earth, questions tend to threaten received wisdom, in paradise, questions amplify and deepen insights.

There is a further detail. Nothing should be taken literally in heaven because the literal binds. To do so would be rather like someone who has read in the Bible that God has hands and feet, demanding to see God's hands and feet upon arriving in paradise. The request would keep them stuck at paradise's door. A fluidity of mind is required to step in and travel.

Beatrice refers to a dialogue of Plato, *The Timaeus*, because in his allusion to predeterminism, Dante had drawn on what he took to be Plato's argument, that souls return to their stars upon death, as if destined. This was the received wisdom of the time that Beatrice corrects, with what I take to be the real meaning of The Timaeus too. The important detail to note is that the dialogue is called, by Plato himself, a "likely story," by which he means one that, while offering much insight and illumination, should not be taken as the final word. It is an account of the creation of the cosmos. In fact, it offers various such accounts, with the aim of expanding the reader's appreciation of cosmogony, and the wonders of the universe, across a variety of perspectives. The upshot is that Dante would be wrong to read Plato as a determinist. The ancient Greek was an explorer. He had insights, but they were provisional, and simultaneously invaluable because they enabled more to be pursued. We should like "likely stories."

How could it be otherwise, Beatrice continues. The cosmos is not a machine. It is an organism of intelligences, principles, and souls. It contains living spheres of awareness like Jupiter, Mercury, and Mars. They are animated and interact. They are consciousnesses, though they can appear as objects, and much changes in the infinite dance, while everything is simultaneously a glorious set of variations on eternal themes.

Dante's ambivalence is morphing into a springboard, his conundrums are becoming propulsive forces. They generate intuitions, rather than settle matters. That is the way of paradise. This is the nature of its life.

There is a further nuance that Dante might appreciate, Beatrice suggests. Insofar as it is true that Piccarda and Constance were forced, they tacitly agreed to their marriages as well: they did not call on their ultimate freedom, which would be to die rather than comply.

It is a tough, harsh remark, one that seems brutal without the surety of the life beyond mortal life, and cruel even with it, and I think Beatrice makes it to push Dante a step farther. She wants him to consider the perspective of martyrs, who embrace the ultimate freedom while still on earth. They live with knowledge of eternity, she explains, when most of us, including Piccarda and Constance, have mixed allegiances. Dante appreciates that this has been true of him as well.

The agony is particularly keenly felt when caught between two evils. Piccarda and Constance had faced that situation. Should they have left the convent or risked being put to death? Both would have ruined their lives, though it can be better to die, as the example of Cato in purgatory had demonstrated: there can be a seemingly suicidal choice that is closer to remaining in life. Beatrice cites an extreme case, that of Alcmaeon, who felt obligated to kill his mother to avenge his father. Perhaps he should have sacrificed himself?

The main insight is that there is always another option when everlasting life is held in mind. That is the point of considering these difficult cases.

Beatrice expands on this by explaining that human beings possess an absolute will, which is the divine part of ourselves. It is constant, never not fixed on what is best, and always aware of the good, beautiful, and true. It is the presence of happiness within us. However, it can be eclipsed by the conditional will, which is inclined to focus on what is tricky, dire and, sometimes, seemingly impossible.

Eternal life is known during earthly life when the absolute will is not lost to the conditional. Unveiled, it brings a steadiness and quiet joy to life regardless of what happens, because its knowledge of divine life is sure. It is God within us and is the ground of the life we lead. The martyrs, the saints, the awakened, the bodhisattvas, the enlightened know it.

Dante thanks Beatrice. He feels truth flowing through him, as the light of the moon mingles with the light of his soul. Then she grows dazzling before him once more. He can no longer look into her eyes. He feels he might faint.

Beatrice shows Dante something of the freedom to align with divine life.

PARADISO 5

Conflicts

ANTE'S QUESTIONS ABOUT VOWS AND COMMIT-
ments are not exhausted. He is dizzy with them, though at the start
of canto 5, I think that wobbliness is compounded by the growing
awareness that he needs to abandon a legalistic approach to life, if he is to
continue in paradise. It is the spirit that gives life, even when it appears to
go against natural justice. He must abandon the attitude that is inclined
to bargain with God, as if God were a tyrant. Rather, God wills that Dante
know more, which, because Dante is free, might involve times of trouble.

Beatrice sees the tension in him, and she explains that the light in her
eyes dazzles him once more partly because it conflicts with his inclinations.

316

The meeting of two worlds, secular and divine, is temporarily unbearable, though Beatrice assures him that the seeming conflict is to be expected. He is entering new spheres, not merely exploring the farther reaches of the sphere with which he is already familiar. In time, that exploration will show him that there was never truly any conflict, but rather the conflict arose from his constrained perceptions.

His particular issue now is whether a broken vow can be remedied by moral works. Part of him knows that he is suggesting a way that bargains with God, as if someone could buy a place in heaven or offset bad with good, though Beatrice implies that it is best that he air his confusions and clarify his mind. That way lies the grace that will be kindled within him.

And it is not just about him. This is for us as well. Dante makes it plain by remarking that Beatrice's invitation was the way in which she opened this canto. He has addressed us directly many times before, but this breaking of the fourth wall is so that Beatrice can address us. It is a dizzying moment. Beatrice in the heaven of the moon, talks with Dante in the heaven of the moon, dictates to Dante the poet writing this canto, which reaches us reading it. There is a direct line of transmission.

Beatrice meets his concern by taking a step back from it, as is becoming her habit. Freedom of will is the greatest gift God bestows, she avers, referring to more than just the capacity to make choices, but highlighting the ability consciously, gradually, and resolutely to become aware of divine life. It happens in the big moments of life, though more commonly and, in a way, more significantly, in everyday moments. The will is operative, at some level or another, all the time. It is the attention and intention brought to each situation, coupled to the desire to know more. Free will brings purpose, meaning, and clarity to life, and so can be cultivated continually.

She expands on the gift. As it is given by God, it will be honored by God, in both senses. When used to align with God, God is already aligned with us. When used to move from God, God will not interfere.

It also works in a sacrificial way, which is to say, that the will is supported and grows when what is received is offered back. For example, if someone shows kindness, it is good intentionally to offer kindness back. If something beautiful is seen, it is good purposefully to offer a beautiful gesture in response. This dynamic of to and fro is opening, and it can be freely chosen, moment by moment.

Her account of free will explains why trying to compensate for broken vows doesn't work. Attempting to buy your way into heaven is transactional, whereas free will is transformational, and it is transformation that transports. Free will is about the whole of us, whereas bargaining with God splits us, into the part that desires the divine and the part that desires to have it our way. And yet, Dante thinks, there are individuals who are released from their vows, seemingly with God's blessing. So, how does that work?

Beatrice explains that a happy release from vows happens when the individual breaks them so as to reach for a higher intention. The early promise ends because a greater desire dissolves it. This kind of change extends the goal of free will, which is to know God, as opposed to trying to manipulate events in an attempt to secure lesser goods. In practice, it might mean that one set of vows is replaced by another, she explains, though it is the inner movement that is crucial. That must honor the importance of making vows, even if a specific vow is ended.

It takes Dante time to absorb, assimilate, and digest these nuances. She reflects further that when a vow is made, two things are happening at once. At one level, there is a promise to do something. It is a decision. But at another level, there is the act of making a vow. It is an exercise of freedom. I think Beatrice is alluding to the different types of will, discussed in the previous canto. The conditional will makes the decision, as it must to be in the world. The absolute will loves the freedom to do so. When the conditional and absolute will are aligned, the whole person is engaged.

Beatrice illustrates the point by referring to a Levitical injunction in the Hebrew Bible in which the Jews are told that they can make a substitute sacrifice as long as it represents more of themselves in the giving. It is a change of vow, which develops the initial intention. Alternatively, it is like moving from the number four to the number six, she says, which is to say that the number six contains the number four. If a new vow contains the spirit of the old, by being greater than it, the change is good.

She also refers to the silver and gold keys, the silver key representing the ability to act, the gold key representing the authority to act. Both have to be turned. At a personal level, I think this refers to the capacity to make a change coupled to the capacity to understand what change is being made. Both are needed for an advantageous exercise of freedom of will.

Another set of examples illustrates the point negatively. There is the story of Jephthah, who bargained with God. He said that if God were to give him a victory, he would sacrifice the next thing he set his eyes on. That turned out to be his daughter. Neither must we be like Agamemnon, who sacrificed his daughter, Iphigenia, to secure winds that would carry his ships to Troy. That was to make a deal with the elements.

The examples convey the importance of practicing freedom of will in the little moments of life. If we wait for the crises, it is likely that the panic of the moment will shape our promises involuntarily. We are likely to vow anything to take the unpleasantness away, which doesn't work because vows, will, and freedom should not extract us from life. They should take us deeper into life, not least when it is painful.

Dante turns to us as readers again and underlines that life can become full of such rushed vows. It is a moment when he is checking with us that we are following closely in his wake, and not getting lost. The nuances matter. I think he is asking whether we can feel the risk they have been discussing, and how we might move beyond it. After all, not infrequently, religious life can become a series of bargains with God. Can you get me a parking place? Can you make me not late? Can you make him like me? Can you make her better?

He has further questions, only Beatrice has raised her eyes. She is gazing into the heart of the divine light. It brings a stillness and silence to his mind, though it is simultaneously a transition and, suddenly, they are in a second sphere. It happens quicker than a bow would stop quivering when the arrow is released, Dante notes.

The next heaven is not named yet, emphasizing that fresh dimensions of reality emerge almost before we have noticed. However, Dante knows something has happened because his experience changes, which suggests that monitoring our states of mind is a good gauge of our plane of existence.

They are in the sphere of Mercury, and the radiance grows as they arrive. It is like balls of quicksilver joining together to form a bright dome of liquid metal, the larger surface reflecting more light. Souls rush to greet them, increasing the light, love, and dance. They are glad to welcome the arrivals and enjoy the growing brilliance of Beatrice's presence.

Imagine what it was like, Dante invites us. Suddenly, I was in a sunnier state and place. This is, itself, a mercurial way of putting it, almost teasing us. Can we imagine it? Can we follow him? He adds to the joshing by teasing us with the proposal that he stop here and now. He might say no more! Imagine the yearning that would rise in you, my readers! It is a way of passing to us a sense of his desire to learn more, which has now become markedly playful. The confusions of the moon are changing into another mode of realizing.

One of the souls speaks. It addresses Dante as one particularly blessed by God and offers him the chance to ask questions and understand more. Beatrice encourages Dante to do so. Treat these souls as gods, she says.

He sees that the soul is nestled as if in its own light. He spots its eyes, which is significant because it will be the last time he sees the human features of the souls he meets for some time, and there is something to understand in that detail. Dante's journey through paradise is, in part, an awakening to the divine light within him that is also within the souls of eternity. To see it is to perceive the glory of creation, which is no more intensely focused than in the faces of the beings whose will and love, intelligence and pleasure, consciously harmonize with it. They not only reflect God, as all creatures do to some degree, but actively participate in the image of God. That is going to be too much for Dante to tolerate through the rest of the planetary spheres. It's too dazzling for the while, so he only sees the light of the individuals he meets, though he will be ready for the full vision in the higher heavens.

This soul has its own distinctiveness, which shines within the shining that is the consciousness associated with Mercury. It is as if there is a slight competition between the lights, the personal and the celestial, which is to say that it is akin to the light of the planet Mercury, that is in a perpetual though unwinnable competition with the light of the sun, as it frequently disappears in the greater glow. Deploying another metaphor, Dante explains that the soul before him appeared to shine as the sun might through a mist at sunrise, with a light that cannot last when the blaze of the daylight grows.

Maybe competition is not quite the right word because in one of his earlier works, The Convivio, Dante explains how the mercurial state of mind is one of dialectic. Dialectic is an advance from the lunar puzzles and conundrums that he has been grappling with. Mercurial dialectic invites the participant to put his best case forward and recognize the limits of what he says, so that further insights can emerge in the space created by the impasses. It generates greater insights not by voicing confusions but by saying, "I know this much and know there is more to know." It's playful in the sense of being willing to let go, as well as being teasing.

The soul before him is shining with this type of light. It is exploring how it resonates with the greater light, when it harmonizes with the greater, when it doesn't, and the opportunities such recognition brings for expansion into the greater light. The next canto will tell us more, Dante concludes. It's another mercurial tease. Keep reading.

Dante presents a big-history view of his times and invites us to consider events.

PARADISO 6
Rule

ANTO 6 OFFERS READERS A GREAT SWEEP OF history, from the Roman period to Dante's age. It includes details of thirty-eight or more kings and rulers. One way to read the narrative is to sit down with the text, and a commentary, and go through the names and the sagas, reflecting on Dante's record of them.

Here, I'm going to focus on the big-history itself and ask what currents across time Dante is sensing and portraying. It is a complement to the encounter with the Old Man of Crete in The Inferno, and the ways in which civilizations can lose sight of their gold and silver, to lean and tumble on weaker terracotta legs. It is a next step from the contemplation of history in The Purgatorio where, in the valley of the rulers, Dante had observed a bunch of kings who were unclear, drifting, and purposeless.

His aim is to peer through the surface of history, the chronicle that tells of one thing after another, and see it from the perspective of eternity. What he sees can be summarized: the irony of history is that when very good things happen, truly terrible things are usually unfolding beneath the surface, and vice versa. To use Tolkien's word, history is a series of eucatastrophes, so far as God is concerned. Tragedies devastate, though don't have the last word. If we can see that, without denying the suffering, we can see heaven.

Dante cared deeply about what was going on in his times, as he lived with the generations-long bloody civil wars between the Guelphs and the Ghibellines. He was involved with them. However, at the same time, an actively pursued detachment from events is possible, and it can detect deeper purposes unfolding. It's a crucial capacity, not only because it offers consolation in the face of tragedies, but because it builds an awareness that history is not the only field upon which destiny plays out.

It is significant that Dante contemplates the incidents of the centuries in the sphere of Mercury. The mercurial view accepts that things are not all that they seem. It knows that there are bridges to other worlds within the immediacy of this one, which is why Mercury is a go-between, messenger god. All that glistens is not gold, and light shines in unexpected places.

The soul whom Dante had met in the previous canto speaks for the entirety of this one. He is the Emperor Justinian, which explains why his individual light is competing with — or is it complementing — the divine light. He is a great exemplar of history because his reign as the sixth ruler of the Byzantine age was a real mix. Sometimes, he seems to have been a weak figure, especially alongside his extraordinary wife, Theodora. Sometimes, he is judged a great legal reformer, almost a saint. And it was also Justinian who built Hagia Sophia in Constantinople. He was clearly a pious man, though he simultaneously sought fame and glory: he could champion admirable actions, horrific atrocities, and mindless deeds. For example, he closed Plato's Academy in AD 529, after it had existed, in one form or another, for 900 years.

The point in paradise is not to sort the good from the bad, as if the aim of eternity is to rectify history. It is to see everything equally, and to judge so as to accept. This is Dante's task, as he sees the back story of the events that ruined his earthly life. It is an achievement, and an undertaking, to move on from lambasting and lamenting the crimes of dukes and popes.

Justinian speaks uninterrupted, which is perhaps what he grew accustomed to in life, though the habit is put to good use in paradise, enabling us to contemplate the history unimpeded, and let the wider perspective emerge. It creates a sense of seeing the woods as well as the trees. The former emperor indicates that he understands that this is his role in eternity because his long story ends with an account of a chap called Romeo. This individual was a wandering and humble soul who became employed in matters of court and proved himself very useful. He married off the four daughters of a nobleman to the nobleman's substantial political advantage. Then, life at court betrayed him, because his success prompted jealousy in other courtiers, though the spirit of the pilgrim had not died within him; he had not lost it to worldly success. He retook to the road and rediscovered the path to God. He knew the relative significance of the historical events in which he willingly played a part.

He played his hand as best he could when he was drawn into society and politics, which is how it should be. The eagle of time sweeps across the years, Dante muses, blessing some, cursing others, and individuals must attempt to harness warmer winds when they can, as well as fend off gales.

Justinian's own life can be interpreted similarly. For example, he tells Dante the story of his conversion to Christianity. At first, he thought Jesus was a god on earth, though he was corrected and accepted the truth of the Incarnation: that mortal and immortal realms are one in human souls. His sight became divine sight in that instant. Then, there were his legal reforms, which produced the Code of Justinian. It was an attempt to sift the best of Roman law from the bad and preserve the former. The aim was to bring order to a frequently disordered empire, which is a good aim, although order inevitably brings injustices in its wake, when the few are sacrificed for the greater good. That is the tragedy of rule and history.

Justinian also straightforwardly perpetrated crimes, though as he speaks to Dante, he is inclined to modify the facts. He tells of handing over the business of war to his great general, Belisarius, so as to devote himself to religious matters. In truth he did devolve the waging of war to Belisarius, though he didn't leave bloody matters only to his general. He blinded other military leaders when they failed him.

There are three levels of history intertwined in Justinian's story: the good, the bad, and the complicated. Incidentally, there are factual errors and distortions in it as well, though Dante's aim is not to offer a history class, but to reflect upon history. This is the sphere of Mercury. We are required not to take everything at face value, but to make Mercury's message from the gods our own.

Another detail offers further illustration. Justinian talks about Tiberius, the third Caesar after Julius Caesar, as Dante records it. He is well-known as one of the debauched of the Julio-Claudian emperors. Further, within his reign, Jesus was crucified. The central figure in Christianity was the victim of one of the most torturous deaths humanity has devised, and Tiberius deployed it liberally.

And yet, at the time, crucifixion brought the death of a man whose life proved a pivot point in history. Secretly, *sub specie aeternitatis*, it was saturated with God's way. It was terrible, monstrous. And a tremendous good.

The Crucifixion highlights the great difficulty of living through history, engaging with it, and simultaneously remaining detached. It requires an acceptance of suffering, to the point of feeling utterly abandoned, as Jesus seems to have done. I sense this is another reason why Dante remains silent in this canto. He has good reason to feel sorry for himself, and worthy of pity, as well as angry with worldly affairs, meriting revenge. But as Justinian speaks, he can tease out the differences between the truth and lies in Justinian's story, why Justinian presents things in various ways, and so consider how he loves and hates the historical events in his life, so as to rise above those reactions. Cries for morality and justice have their place. But there is more to grasp, and that is the path of liberty.

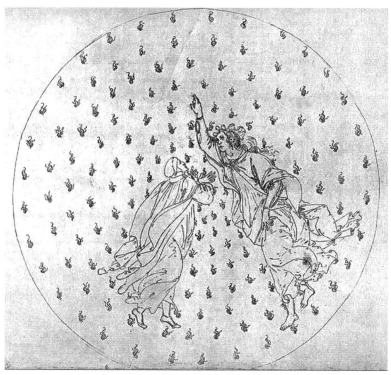

Dante is dissatisfied with the account of the Crucifixion. Beatrice offers a new vision.

PARADISO 7

Heresy

USTINIAN SINGS A HYMN. HE MIXES GREEK AND Hebrew to praise the Lord of Hosts who illuminates the realms of heaven with fire. He starts to whirl, becoming "entwoed" into one light, Dante remarks, presumably seeing the light of Justinian's earthly glory enveloped by the light of God: it was only ever a refraction of the divine radiance, after all. Other souls are stirred into similar whirligigs of delight, before they all, suddenly, disappear into infinity.

Two qualities, seemingly disparate, sometimes at odds, can combine by the operation of Mercury. The result is not just harmony, but revelation.

Dante senses the Empyrean as the sparks shoot off. Justinian shows that he brought the mixed light of his reign into alignment with the light of heaven as his glory submitted to a greater fame. At the last, his life leapt into eternity unimpeded.

Dante is not able to follow them immediately, and he is left with a burning question. He wrestles with himself, as Justinian must have wrestled. Speak, speak, he says to himself, though he is still partly intimidated by Beatrice, partly in awe of paradise, and it is she who breaks his silence.

I think he fears that his inquiry might present him in a heretical light. Is he allowed to ask? It might be the presence of Mercury that brings such difficulties to mind. The god is a trickster who likes a little chaos and loves to break boundaries.

Dante looks at Beatrice. She has love in her eyes. He remarks that the sight of it would gladden the heart of someone who was condemned to burn, which is to say, who was guilty of heresy. Is he?

She speaks in a way that seems heretical as well, saying that her wisdom is infallible and can't be touched by error. Her response means Dante can risk asking anything. An incarnation of Sophia stands before him. The opening tercets of this canto raise our expectations: what revision, revelation, or novelty is to appear?

Dante's latest question is a big one, though he can hardly foresee the conclusion to which Beatrice will lead him in asking it. The question springs from his reflecting on Justinian's remark, which the emperor had made almost in passing, that the Crucifixion of Jesus was a redress for human sin, which was itself then avenged by God in the destruction of the Jerusalem Temple in AD 70. This is a reference to the antisemitic thread that runs across Christian history, which brands the Jews as God-killers. Dante isn't immediately concerned with that. Instead, he says that he is confused by the issue of God's need for vengeance, first for sin, then for the act that avenged human failure. Why would God need to punish anything, being God? And if the Crucifixion were part of God's plan, why would God need to castigate those who were involved in it? It is a very good question, for all that it questions God — or perhaps, because it questions God.

Beatrice replies from a wider point of view, so as to enable the question to become an opportunity to see way more. She first lays out the Christian version of history's mythology, beginning with the creation of Adam. He originally knew God's life, though he became uncoupled from it, which set a pattern for humanity of falling into the abyss of alienation from God. Jesus descended from heaven to reunite estranged humanity with its Creator.

It sounds like the standard story of salvation history: Soteriology 101.

However, Beatrice also undercuts the account. This is the heaven of Mercury. Let us pay it more attention, she suggests, although to do so, she ramps up the tension, seemingly complicating things further for Dante.

The Crucifixion pleases God, she says, because it satisfies God's just need for punishment. However, it also pleased those Jews who wanted to see Jesus dead, not perceiving God's ways. This is doubly uncomfortable to read, antisemitism on stilts, and Dante feels it. Internally, he is asking whether there wasn't another way. He is tying himself in knots trying to discern an alternative.

It is worth remembering that Beatrice is rehearsing an account of Jesus's life first proposed by Anselm of Canterbury, in the eleventh century. He wrote a meditation, entitled *Why God Became Man*, which proposed what is now called substitutionary theory. In short, instead of humanity dying, a god-in-man was substituted, who died on the Cross.

In the two centuries before Dante, Anselm's work became part of a surge in devotion to Jesus the man, recorded in the art that survives. The figure of Jesus on the cross was increasingly depicted so as to emphasize how he offered himself freely out of love, suffering greatly so that others would not have to suffer. However, the devotion simultaneously prompted a reaction that celebrated the vengeance of God, who appeared to need a pure offering to preserve divine holiness. Christians who felt themselves to be redeemed by God also felt free to condemn others whom they deemed were not, not least the Jews.

Such are the perversities of humanity and history. I think tricksterish Beatrice's aim in ramping up the tension, and making Christianity's shadow self-evident, is to uncouple the vengeance from the love. People rarely manage to do so, she explains, much as arrows unleashed from a bow rarely hit the mark. The difficulty is seeing things from God's point of view, which she tries to explain to Dante next.

After Adam, God had one of two choices, she continues. God could have simply offered humanity forgiveness. After all, what does it matter to God if human beings fall short? Clemency is well within divine possibility. The drawback is that while such leniency looks compassionate in the first instance, in the longer term it is demeaning of human beings because it does not take their freely chosen actions seriously. It overwrites their will with an automatic correction from above, and so diminishes them. It makes human beings children to God's indulgent parent, meaning they might never grow up.

The second possibility was to let human beings reform and atone for themselves. God has bestowed free will on people, and a desire for divine life, so perhaps that could have been allowed time to play itself out and redeem humankind? However, a moment's reflection leads to the conclusion that this is unlikely to happen. Human beings are not, on the whole, very good at self-improvement. Moreover, allowing a single flaw into the diamond of divine life would render it a flawed diamond, a reduction from perfection. So, what was God to do?

This is the trick. Mercury's wit is God's wit. Dante is being presented with a seemingly impossible binary choice, when the joy of paradise is the realization that heaven is not patterned by dualisms. Conundrums and paradoxes are what the dialectic of Mercury transcends.

To precipitate that expansion, Beatrice invites Dante to look into another abyss, that of God's beauty, love, wisdom, sight, capacities. If he does, she says, he will see that the way God responded to the predicament of humankind is to do what God always does: continually to unfold more life into creation, more beauty into life, more goodness into souls. And this is how God redeems.

Properly understood, the birth of Jesus is a repeat of the original creation. As Adam was made a human being with unmediated access to God, so was Jesus born likewise. Beatrice is explaining that the crux moment of salvation was not the Crucifixion but the Incarnation.

It is no less a response to human failure than the response sought by the vengeance-mongers, only it is without shadow. The Incarnation is not a divine pardon but a divine reassertion: the created and natural order comingles with the divine and uncreated order, and absolutely nothing can shift that. Nothing can separate humanity from God, for all that humanity goes wildly astray. What God had done in mythological time, with the creation of Adam, was also done in historical time, with the birth of Christ. There is no either/or when it comes to participating in God's life, for life is participating in it always, already. The question is how clearly that is appreciated. I think Dante is saying that Jesus lived to restore a pure awareness, not to avenge a raging, puritanical deity. It is what souls on Mount Purgatory are learning, and souls in paradise are developing — and, I would add, what souls in the *Inferno* will one day discover.

It is a tremendous vision. But how could it be otherwise, given God is eternal goodness, brightness, and glory? To avenge would tarnish God, to introduce impurity into the light. As Beatrice puts it: good loves to do good, and divine good can only do good, so bringing more goodness into the world delights God. The birth of Jesus is better than simple mercy, even, because it is a positive act. It doesn't just wipe away; it further magnifies the timeless truth of divine abundance.

The Resurrection was a repeat of divine creativity too, Beatrice explains toward the end of the canto. She concludes it with a shortened version of the story of transient nature reaching for God, and tells Dante that in the same way that divine life was breathed into his soul when he was formed, so divine life will be breathed into him again when he dies. This is what the Spirit does: it fills all things with life, continually.

Human beings are always called to know freedom, to know life, to bridge the mortal and immortal, the finite and the infinite. Beatrice has presented Dante with a reformation of what had become the standard account of Christianity since Anselm. It is an extraordinarily harmonious and beautiful portrayal of divine action. It is also unflinching in its awareness of the human predicament. It redeems not by fixing but by attracting, not by fighting darkness with violence, but by bringing shadow to light. Discord dissolves in a higher melody. Why did God become man? Because that is what God does.

pui comincato in lialm fenafim.
fenne aquei che pui nang apanm
fonaua ofanna fiche un que pm
din udir non fu fenci dalino.
Ind fi fee lun pui premb anoi
efolo comincio tuen fien prefu.
almo piacer p che di noi aguoi.

monte tront euerce in mare fgoign.
fulgem gu infonte la corona
di quella terru chel cu nubio nga
pm che lempe reccfche abandona.
Labella rmmachia che caliga
tra puchmo epoloro fopra ilgolfo
che uccue ca enlo magior brigu.

They are in the sphere of Venus and encounter souls to discuss diversity and unity.

PARADISO 8

Friendship

ANTE HAS ARRIVED IN VENUS. HE AND BEATRICE
left Mercury without Dante noticing, though he might have wondered if they were transitioning to a deeper perception of reality
given the revision of Christianity Beatrice had shown him in Mercury. It
takes nuance to appreciate it, and he knows they have ascended farther
because Beatrice radiates more beauty. The power of love disclosed with
his understanding of God's work can be explored more keenly.

Venus is the goddess of love, though she shines with qualities that might
seem strange at first. She is associated with complex, diverse qualities of love
from generativity to contemplation, fortune to exuberance. It makes sense
that Beatrice and Dante can contemplate these aspects of life, to deepen
his focus on God's primary activity: pouring life, like the sun pours light.

The canto opens with a description of Venus as the goddess was commonly understood by the polytheistic imagination. She throws out frenzied
beams of love in collusion with her son, Cupid, causing confusion and

mesmerizing people. Dante references Dido once more, by way of illustration, she for whom love proved too much. But Venus is also the morning star, wooing the sun back from the night, and she is the evening star, celebrating the brightness of the day. She dances around the sun as she switches roles, delighting in the beauty of the one light.

Dante is incorporating the heavenly dynamics celebrated in polytheistic myths into the monotheistic worldview, drawing them together without loss of difference. It's a useful step because, without a sense of center, love does cause chaos, turn in on itself, and overwhelm. Monotheism is, therefore, a development of polytheism, not a replacement, born of the insight that can perceive how diverse qualities relate and are held together.

Dante is reminded of the embers within a fire, as he sees the souls in Venus. They are not changing lights, as they had encountered in the moon, or competing lights, as they had seen in Mercury, but harmonious lights, sustaining the flames. The souls shoot down from the high heavens of the Seraphim, the angels closest to God, and greet them. Dante sees them taking on divine light much as a silkworm spins its cocoon: deliberately, as a great task. These souls show him more clearly how to participate in divine life. Mercurial playfulness has been subsumed into Venusian delight.

He is ready for it. He enjoys Beatrice's beauty. He basks in the emerging glory, welcoming the new souls' generous appearance, which he knows will lift him. There is a distinctly erotic mood in the gathering, as one soul interpenetrates another, not to possess or capture, but to delight and elevate. They are like musical notes sounding together, and they want Dante to know their ecstasy. They have come to offer pleasure. They are flirty even, reciting a line from one of Dante's poems back to him: "O you whose intellect spins Heaven's third sphere." He had written about them and they return the compliment. There is a mood of joy as hosannas are sung in marvelous tones. Recalling the moment moves Dante the poet, as he writes.

As if seeking her blessing, he turns to his beloved, Beatrice, and she rays bliss back, assuring him that he can return the pleasure without disloyalty to her. There is a type of promiscuity that is divine because there is only more to give. So, he asks the flame who has approached nearest: who are you?

The soul doesn't offer his name. Dante doesn't see who he is. He does reveal that, on earth, he was a potentate because here, in heaven, he shares in the angelic dynamic of the Powers and Principalities. He describes his rule, as extending across parts of southern Europe.

Dante recognizes him, and a sense of warmth spreads between them. Commentators have worked out that he is Charles Martel, the King of

Hungary. In life, he stayed for a short while in Florence, and it seems Dante became acquainted with him there. They saw kindred spirits in each other, fostered by a shared love of love. It transcended their different ranks and brings them together in heaven. Dante rejoices to meet him again in the sphere of Venus. He feels how their joy echoes the divine joy. Their friendship is triangulated: it flows between them as it flows from above to them. They know the center from which their rapport emanates and around which it circulates.

Charles mentions his brother, Robert. His sibling was also a ruler, though Robert was not so fortunate. The reason, Charles explains, is that Robert was ungenerous with his power, as a result of being corrupted by mingling with souls as heartless as his own. If Charles and Dante's friendship had been a virtuous spiral up, Robert's circle had dragged them all down. Worldly love can do that when it turns in on itself.

Dante finds mention of Robert a jolt, a disruption to the Venusian meeting, but Charles explains that divine love can embrace everything and there is something to learn from his brother. That which is behind us on earth can be placed in front of us in paradise because love here is free, not anxious or constrained, he explains. Dante is glad because he has a blunt question: how can the same family produce such disparate characters? Why is it that the two brothers were so unalike?

The issue is related to the matter of freedom and determinism, will and disposition. By asking about the brothers, Dante is relating the question directly to inheritability of nobility, which we would think of in terms of nature and nurture. Dante is concerned about the transmission of aristocratic qualities, like graciousness and decency, which makes sense given the erosion of nobility during his lifetime. He lives in the period where the meaning of the word "noble" itself divided into honorable, on the one hand and on the other, titled. The uncoupling of dignity and status would, today, be perceived as declining standards in public life. Can the rot be reversed?

Dante knows that what shapes a life doesn't automatically limit a life because, as he has learned from Piccarda, the shaping can become a pathway that leads to greater life. Similarly, inheritance provides building blocks, though a life must still be constructed from them, and everyone must live a particular life: their life. In other words, there is no such thing as inevitable nobility, any more than every painting, sculpture, or poem is certain to be regarded as a great work of art. What matters is what a life receives, channels, amplifies, manifests. A good life is akin to the planet Venus, which shines with glory as it reflects and revolves around the sun, and that radiance can take on many forms. Qualities can be incarnated in many ways and still be unified in their intent, much as the heaped embers in a fire are distinctive and contribute to the uniform heat.

Charles understood this nobility during his rule. His brother did not. Charles tried to order his kingdom around the principles of complex harmony, rather than singular rule: it is hard to live well under an autocracy, terrible to live amidst civil strife, frustrating to live in a world where everyone is allotted a place simply by birth. He tried to embody the ancient notion of justice in which each person is fulfilled and contributes to the fulfilment of others. It is difficult to achieve on earth, though arises in heaven with the development of desire and understanding; individuals then become able to be themselves and to be one.

The vision illuminates divine love. It is not like romantic love that seeks to merge with another, losing the sense of self. It is not like family love, in which each person has a prescribed role. It is not like agapeic love, as if differences don't matter because love is shared equally by everyone. It is close to the love called friendship, in which each person is fully themselves, in love with others who are fully themselves, and attuned to the love that exists between them. That, in turn, is a manifestation of the love that made them.

As the lights of Venus dance around Dante, he feels their warmth. The array radiates the one love and life.

Dante meets lovers and discovers more about heavenly ascent.

PARADISO 9

Lovers

DANTE THE POET TURNS TO CLEMENCE, THE widow of Charles Martel, at the start of canto 9. He tells her that Charles informed him of forthcoming plots against their children, though insisted that she should let foul acts pass. The plotters' deeds will catch up with them. They will pay with tears.

Charles turns to face the divine brilliance, the source and delight of his life. It is sufficient, it is good, it is the backdrop against which mishaps and abuses on earth will be judged.

There is question for us in this moment too. What is my soul directed

334

toward? What is my heart's true love? They are key matters for the sphere of Venus.

Another light moves toward Dante, flaming in its eagerness. Dante checks with Beatrice, to be sure of her consent to another playful exchange, and then flirtatiously speaks to it. "Prove to me that you know my thoughts!" he says. He means it as a celebration rather than a test: souls in paradise are aware of each other's feelings because they know of the life of God, within which all is known.

The soul is Cunizza. Beautifully and extensively, she describes her birthplace and state in heaven. Her speech reflects her extravagant character. During her mortal life, she had four husbands and two lovers. She was a celebrated paramour who suffered in love, as well as causing others suffering. Finally, after an about turn, she spent the last part of her life in charitable works.

That is when Dante knew her, and it is fascinating for him to understand why she shines, as a notorious lover, with the light of Venus. I accepted all that love brought me, she explains, the rough with the smooth, the heartache with the delight, the infamy, and the consolation. She hadn't tried to pretend that her loving was other than it was, and that she wasn't responsible for the moves she made. A pretense is what Francesca had adopted in the *Inferno*, when she blamed her affair with Paolo on a book. Everything will be seen, Cunizza realized, much as Charles had wanted communicated to Clemence, and so Cunizza had made no attempt at covering up her deeds.

Her undefended honesty — the opposite of seeking to blame others — means that she is in harmony with divine love. Its light can shine in her because she doesn't harbor shadows. Its radiance can fill her because she holds nothing back. The mirror of her soul seeks out the "white radiance of eternity," to quote Percy Bysshe Shelley, because for all the ups and downs of her love life, ultimately it was a questing love that ruled her, not one turned inward, possessively or manipulatively. She could smile at herself, which meant that she could welcome the smile of God bestowed on her. What matters is not her wrongdoings, but what she did that was right, for all that the two were mixed up during her mortal life.

It is another way of putting Dante's growing sense of redemption. In the afterlife, the quality of love that a person embodies counts, because that dictates what they can enjoy. Her life had been chaotic, but it had a center. She was not swept about entirely meaninglessly in her romantic exploits and she is, in paradise, only thankful for her life. She can affirm it.

This soul beside me was famous, she teases next, without naming who it is. Its fame on earth, which was substantial and lasting, is not the most important thing in heaven, where divine fame outshines it, Cunizza contin-ues. The abiding element is that the figure cultivated passion, which is an asset insofar as it desires not only recognition, but, at least in part, divine splendor and brilliance. The fame could transmit eternal qualities. The triumph could mirror divine praise.

Still without a name, the conversation about the famous soul grows dark. Cunizza outlines the bitter times the individual also knew, telling of another person — a bishop of Feltre — whose religiosity and passion backfired. This prelate clung zealously to the letter of the law and, as a result, caused great bloodshed. He lost touch with the spirit of love. He acted out of moral rectitude rather than compassion.

The contrast with Cunizza is striking. The bishop obsessively sanctified his life to God, and it led to his perdition. She ardently gave her life to lovers, and it led her to God. The truth of the soul will out, regardless of appearances.

Cunizza turns her gaze back to the higher life that fills her and rejoins the Venusian whirring throng. The famous soul steps forward, appearing like a ruby reflecting solar rays. It's a significant appearance because there was a belief that the light of a ruby could burn away vanity.

Dante reflects that the joy of heaven makes souls glow more brightly, a truth intimated on earth because a smile will precipitate a smile. Conversely, in infernal realms of existence, a smile has the opposite effect: as he has wit-nessed in hell, joy elicits bitterness, shame, regret. He speaks to the famous soul, flirting again that the soul knows what he is thinking, because "I inyou as much as you inme," as he puts it, forging neologisms to convey the sense of commingling. So why, oh spirit, do you not speak?, Dante adds.

The soul reveals himself. He is Folquet de Marseilles, a troubadour and poet, though as Cunizza had done, he uncovers his identity slowly, via colorful circumlocutions. He had clearly enjoyed his life, for all its difficul-ties. He also references, in quick succession, a number of myths that tell of lovers who were consumed by passion and so died for love. They include Dido, who was abandoned by Aeneas; Phyllis, who was turned into an almond tree by the gods; and Iole, beloved of Hercules, who was envied by the hero's wife. She made Hercules the coat soaked in the blood of the centaur Nessus, believing it would act as a love potion, without realizing that Nessus had tricked her. The blood killed her husband.

The rehearsal of these stories makes us think about where love can lead. Folquet echoes Cunizza's advice to learn to smile at yourself, because smiles on earth echo the mood of heaven. When you do that, you do not distance yourself from your passion, with its mistakes, but draw it close, to foster and perhaps reform it. At the end of the day, it is not the sin that matters but the underlying desire, he explains. That is God's way. It's a lesson Dante can appreciate in paradise because he has seen the effects of perverse desire in hell.

Folquet sees that Dante seeks to know another flame, sparkling nearby like water struck by light, and he satisfies Dante's desire by revealing her identity. She is Rahab, the so-called whore of Jericho, who, in the biblical story, hid Joshua's spies and saved them. The implication is that while, as a prostitute, she gave her body to men, as a human being, she was able to offer her life for others. She never lost touch with her heart.

Rahab is praised fulsomely by Folquet. She is said to have been the first of the pre-Christian souls to have entered heaven, almost as if Christ rushed to find her. His priority underlines the primacy and potency of erotic love: when it does not seek to possess, it is able to carry.

The Church does not understand this truth, Dante laments. Priests follow the letter of the law and miss the spirit. They seek to pin down, in ever lengthier discussions about the dictates of canon law, and in so doing direct their passion away from God, and toward the margins of life. It is a tremendous warning about how the religious spirit readily pivots from God, in legalism, obsessions, and fundamentalism. It is a curse upon life, and risks condemning individuals, if they forget what life can bring.

It can be easier to become a prude than to accept the wild excesses of passion. Puritanism can be preferable to overcoming shame. But we need the energy of eros. We must remember to smile. If love wells up in life, it means the spheres of heaven are welling up in us.

They arrive in the heaven of the sun, the light most manifest to mortals.

PARADISO 10
Threefold

LOVE IS THREEFOLD. ITS TRINITARIAN NATURE may not be immediately apparent, though Dante celebrates it in the opening lines of canto 10. He notes how God the Father looks on God the Son with a love that is itself a breath of love, God the Holy Spirit. Similarly, for us, the lover and the beloved generate loving, which fosters more love. Love begets love. The Trinity is a synonym for the dynamics of abundance.

Dante invites us to look at the heavens and contemplate a comparable generation: the skies inspire awe, delight, wonder. They move us as they move, that joint movement awakening a third: a sense of nature's working, cosmic intelligence, God's presence. The contemplation is simultaneously an enjoyment of space and of mind, of outer space and inner space, the two domains shining together and speaking of the divine third.

Dante develops the experience further by reflecting on the great circles of earth and heaven, the equator and the ecliptic, which cross at the equinoxes and are oblique to the turning sphere. That obliqueness contains its own beauty because it makes for the seasons, as the sun rises and falls in the sky across summer and winter. The entire system breathes, pulses, swings. The rhythms of the celestial organism reflect a divine art, a majesty that modern science celebrates in its own way when it notices the so-called fine tunings of physics and the emergent story of the universe reaching back to the Big Bang, or before.

Stay at this feast, Dante invites us. Eat some more. They have arrived in the heaven of the sun.

They reached it instantaneously: Dante is ready for solar revelations. The significance of this state of mind is that it recognizes the fullest, brightest, and most glorious manifestations of eternity, much as the sun is the fullest, brightest, and most glorious light in the sky. And it simultaneously seeks more, knowing that the glare of daylight conceals as well as reveals.

The sun is an inflection point in the heavens, the fourth sphere out of seven that Dante and Beatrice are traversing. The moon, Mercury, and Venus — characterized by phases, games, and smiles respectively — reflect experiences well known on earth. The sun is the culmination of this familiarity, given it is known by all, and leads on to Mars, Jupiter, and Saturn that shine with less well-known insights. The sun is, therefore, a midpoint on a series of outer and inner illuminations.

Plato called the sun the "child of the good." It is the living power in the heavens that is self-evidently, undeniably good for us. Life depends on it, physically and spiritually, for it brings energy and intelligence. You know it when you don't see the sun for a while. Electric light is useful but dulls with its empty glare. Sunlight is alive and invigorates with its incandescent gift. That is why it brings life.

Beatrice invites Dante to thank the angels of the sun and rest in the moment. He feels God in it, and yields to the divine, momentarily forgetting Beatrice is at his side. That is significant. It is the first time he has wholly trusted himself to paradise.

The experience is at once ecstatic and shocking. When he comes to himself, he checks, though she is not displeased, but delighted. She knows that her light, the sun's light, and God's light are one light. She smiles.

He takes the next step, explaining that the sun shines with glories that, strictly speaking, are beyond speech. Here are gems too precious to bring back to earth. He is partly tantalizing us, to foster our desire to imagine them. He does not seek to report and tell, but to stir up and show. Imagine the sun and then imagine more, which is what he sees as souls start to appear before him.

These souls enjoy a brightness that outshines the brightness of the sun. After all, the sun's most astonishing brightness is not its physical light but its spiritual aliveness, and the souls enjoy that consciously, which is to say even more radiantly. It's like the happiness brought by the return of the day, or happiness at the return of a friend or an ideal or a lover. We say they light up our lives, and it's true.

The souls of the sun spin around Dante and Beatrice, as the stars spin around the celestial pole. They make of themselves a crown for the visitors' heads. The heavens are turning about them, then stop. It is like the pause in a dance, and one soul speaks. The light acknowledges the specialness of Dante's presence in the sun, given his mortality. It would no more be possible not to respond to your tremendous presence, this sign of God's grace, than it would be for a river not to flow into the sea, the soul declares, continuing with an announcement that it will unveil a crown of spirits that exemplify the genius of the sun.

A number of great philosophical, mystical, and theological spirits emerge. They shone brightly on earth in their words, reflections, communications, and insight, and they are associated with the realm of the sun in paradise. They knew about divine life not with the complications of worldly demands, as the souls in the spheres of the moon, Mercury, and Venus had. They knew about it directly, with their living intelligence. They could see it with the mind's eye, listen to it with the ears that can hear, discuss it with words that echoed the Word. They rose with God's light, as does the sun. They celebrate that now.

The soul that speaks is Thomas Aquinas, the Dominican genius who, along with Dante and a handful of others, was remaking Christianity in medieval Europe. He has much to say to Dante. They have much to discuss. Both were fascinated by Aristotelian and Islamic knowledge. It revitalized Christian knowledge, though only after official resistance and rejection.

The other lights that appear in the crown had a similar relationship to ecclesiastical powers. There is Albertus Magnus, the teacher of Thomas and a great Aristotelian scholar in his own right. There is Siger of Brabant who was known for communicating the insights of Averroes, the Islamic scholar. There is the Venerable Bede, the historian; Peter Lombard, whose sentences prompted dialectical reflection; Richard of St Victor, the great contemplative; Dionysius the Areopagite, who described the hierarchy of the heavens; Boethius, whose *Consolation of Philosophy* witnessed to true wealth, glory, and fame; and others. There are twelve in all.

Perhaps the most controversial figure, for Dante's contemporaries, is Solomon. The Bible says that no one exemplified wisdom more fully in his life, so why wouldn't he be here, except that Solomon was not a Christian. He is in the growing group of figures stretching the membership of heaven. Dante has just met Rahab. He will meet other Hebrews and pagans. There was a great debate in the medieval world about Solomon's destiny. Dante asserts: the question is settled.

This is not Dante being a controversialist or provocateur. This is Dante speaking of the life he has seen. He is not only naming presences but describing a presence he knows in names. Their voices are an echo of the voice of God. This is what he saw in the light of the sun. He rejoices in the truth of it.

Another extended metaphor engaging astronomical awareness follows the appearance of the wise lights, which runs through time, rather than space. There is a clock tower, Dante says, that chimes with the sweet music of the morning as the bride wakes with the bridegroom at her side. The allusion might be thought to be about the Church, as the bride, and Christ, as the bridegroom, though that interpretation risks reducing the erotic charge of the couple's awakening, side by side, early in the day.

Dante refuses to let us forget it. He describes the pulling, thrusting, pulsing mechanism of the clock tower. Its movement swells with anticipation, he says. It chimes with a readiness for love.

The metaphor of the clock tower links back to the canto's opening, that celebrated the heavenly organism, noted for its rhythms and movement. The trinitarian awareness of love is in it too, with the bride and groom waking to a love that blooms between them. And there is the erotic manifestation of love which, like the sun, is undeniably present in earthly life, bringing life, lighting lives, prompting people to wake up. Such amatory joy is one with eternity, Dante says.

Thomas Aquinas on the life of Francis and the light of the sun.

PARADISO II

Poverty

HERE ARE MANY WAYS IN WHICH PEOPLE WASTE
their mortal lives with misguided, useless strivings, Dante insists
at the opening of canto 11: obsessions with canon law, medical
anxieties, priesthood, fraud and force, theft, ambition, pleasures of the flesh,
indolence. These vanities launch souls in downward flights toward emptiness.
It seems like a harsh thought for the sphere of the sun, in which he and
Beatrice have been wonderfully welcomed.

Dante's point seems to be that while some activities are good in principle,
like becoming a doctor or lawyer, civil servant or priest, the risk is that they
become ends in themselves, enveloping souls in associated petty preoccupations and narrow affairs that block out the sun. When it comes to participating
in the entirety of reality, the prostitute might be better off than the priest,
because at least the prostitute is under no self-congratulatory delusions.

The twelve wise luminaries dance around them, like as many rays flashing
from a radiate crown. They settle, becoming as glorious flames in a candelabra. Thomas Aquinas, effulgent, speaks. He has more to share with Dante,
greater insights that will deepen his understanding and delight. His acumen
is the source of his shining, which the sun mirrors. It can be known on
earth in moments of discovery when a "eureka" prompts an ecstatic leap,
or in moments of perception that are like a blast of light.

342

Thomas has seen two questions in Dante's mind. The pilgrim is confused by remarks made by the saint, one referencing a path that leads the lambs to fatten, another claiming that Solomon's wisdom is unequalled. The specifics will be answered, as all desires are satisfied in this place, though first by way of inviting Dante to contemplate a wider vision that makes sense of them.

That vision features a light who was so bright it changed the course of events in history. An individual was born within whom the glory of God shone at such intensity that he could not be ignored. Indeed, the power of the beam this person shot across the lands of Europe reached around the world and reaches us still, across the centuries. Francis of Assisi is on Thomas's mind. His life was like a break in the clouds, reminding Christianity of the blue skies of divine reality.

In secular and moral terms, his witness could be easily confused with madness. His embrace of poverty, his carefree devotion, and his feeling for creation have all been tamed by familiarity, though at the time, he disturbed as much as inspired. The aftershocks of his life were still reverberating during Dante's time, as Francis died only decades before Dante started work on The Divine Comedy. The impact of his sanctity was still unsettling. It was not only that he held a mirror up to a corrupt Church and found it wanting. He unleashed a spirit that, in time, scholars argue, would spark the Renaissance, the modern concern for the individual, and an empirical appreciation of nature that led to the scientific revolution.

Thomas tells the story of Francis's life in an arresting way. He focuses on the poverty, stressing that Lady Poverty found a worthy spouse in Francis for the first time since she had married Jesus. This way of putting it stresses the feminine manifestations of divine life. They focus on bringing new life into the world as a way of remedying what has gone wrong. Francis shone with the light of the Seraphim, Thomas continues, which is to say the angelic vitality that exists closest to the divine, and lives on love. He contrasts it with the light of the Cherubim, with which his monastic founder, Dominic, shone. This is the light of wisdom. So, love and wisdom are paired in a dance as Thomas, the follower of wisdom, speaks about the bearer of love.

Francis was born in Assisi, which carries an inner meaning because the name of the town means rising. The Umbrian town is set on eastern slopes appearing to hang above a wide valley, much like a sunrise across the world. His father was a successful merchant, like Dante's, gaining from the thriving mercantile culture of the late medieval period. Workshops manufacturing cloth were precursors of the factory and fostered tremendous economies of scale, from which owners and traders benefited. Francis rejected this way of life in a famous public performance. He removed his clothes in the marketplace of Assisi, donning spiritual simplicity instead of material finery. This glory is what his followers detected beneath what his critics saw as a foolhardy, offensive gesture.

Thousands joined him before he died. Many more have done so since. He approached two popes to validate his order, Thomas continues, and preached to the Sultan. He didn't win converts among Muslims, Thomas remarks, but returned to Italy to receive the final seal of his authority, the stigmata. He was canonized within a couple of years of his death. His light was like that of the sun: undeniable, bright, obvious. Little wonder, people wanted to center their lives around him like as many orbiting planets.

Having celebrated the story, Thomas returns to Dante's first concern, about the path along which the lambs can fatten. It was a reference to his own monastic order, the Dominicans. It has lost much of its original charisma in its first one hundred years, he says. The Blackfriars have become like sheep gone astray, feeding on pastures that don't nourish.

It will turn out that the Franciscans have also taken a wrong turning. They have been seduced by the flatland anxieties with which Dante opened the canto — those of too many doctors and lawyers, civil servants and priests — the obsessions that prompt much flapping about, only to drag souls down.

Dante contemplates the circles of light in the sun, and the life of Dominic.

PARADISO 12

Authenticity

HE TWELVE LIGHTS IN THE CROWN THAT CIRCLE Dante and Beatrice are revolving again. They are like a golden millstone whirling. And then another ring appears: a second round encircles the first. Motion is matched by motion, song by song. This is the virtuous spiral upward, the opposite dynamic to the narrow concerns that can dominate interests on earth. Can we feel the rising vibrancy within us, Dante implicitly asks.

The two crowns are dual manifestations of the same reflection, like the double arcs of a rainbow, Dante explains. The white light of their common origin is powerful enough to refract and refract and refract. His description invites us to see this dynamic with the eye of the mind, to feel it in our souls. Francis and Dominic are sung by the saints of the sun, the bearers of love and wisdom. When these two elements resonate, increase follows.

Within the outer circle rise twelve more luminaries. The twenty-four together are like garlands of evergreen flowers, arranged so as to offset and

345

enhance each other. Or they are like trained dancers, whose coordinated movement and synchronous grace delight the soul. Dante sees the sweet source of earthly harmony. He detects the music of the spheres. Tunes are supernatural, in fact. In terms of the physics, they are merely vibrations in the air. In terms of harmonics, they are notes arranged across scales and intervals. But in terms of experience, they are songs and melodies, feelings and invocations. Music transmits qualities that exceed the analysis of the acoustician or musicologist.

The musical analogies are relevant in another way. As more theologians, philosophers, and mystics appear it becomes clear to Dante that, even though they often disagreed on earth, they chime together in heaven. Their voices could sound discordant in disputatious argument, even jarring, though the spirit of the sun converts the dissonance by revealing a deeper harmony. The double circling is a sign of higher resolution.

They are like two eyes moving as one, or friends rejoicing together. In this cosmic dance, the shifting shadows of the moon and the dialectical tensions of Mercury have been changed by the loving alchemy of Venus into the radiance of the sun. Tracking that metamorphosis is tracking a path into heaven. It is the tropological shift rendered in astrological terms, as the literal is freed by allegorical insights to precipitate anagogic perceptions. The marriage of Francis to Lady Poverty is a case in point. Literally, it seemed mad. Allegorically, it felt disturbing. Tropologically, it moved followers. Anagogically, it brought light to earth.

One of the lights shines brightly. It attracts Dante like a compass needle seeks north, which in the medieval understanding was a response to celestial rather than terrestrial magnetism. The flame is Bonaventure, one of the great visionaries of the Franciscan movement, and so a counterpoint to Thomas Aquinas. He described the heavenly ascent as the pathway minds can follow to God, and is a fascinating figure for Dante to encounter because, while they shared the same conviction about the possibility of divine illumination, they disagreed in the details, contradictions that in the sun will prove advantageous.

Bonaventure sings the praises of Dominic, balancing Thomas's praise of Francis. He celebrates the founder of the Dominicans for wedding faith and zeal for Christ. Dominic was a powerful communicator of Christian insights, his order becoming known as the preachers. They responded to the mendicant uprisings of the late medieval world, of which Franciscanism was a part. The rejection of riches represented a groundswell of enthusiasm for figures who seemed to be returning to the origins of Christianity over and against the corruption of the Church, and Dominic was instrumental in welcoming this evangelical poverty without rejecting the intellectual riches of the Christian past. He could speak authentically, having donned the rags of the wandering sage, and helped people track the path to God.

His order was quickly recognized by the Church, as were the Franciscans, no doubt in an effort to contain the outpouring, and the Dominicans became key advocates of the Inquisition. But while his abilities were undoubtedly courted by ecclesiastical powers, Dominic himself tackled heresies not so as to secure power but ensure holiness. For example, the Dominicans did become embroiled in crusades, not least the Albigensian, which committed atrocities against the Cathars in southern France. The word "genocide" was coined to describe what happened. The world had not seen religious violence like it. It was horrendous. But Dominic's approach was to convert people, not with threats but insight, not with fear but out of a desire for God. He lived a life that exemplified truth's beauty and hoped it would draw people back.

Like Franciscanism, it spawned cumulative effects. An ability to understand the gospel meant educating people, which became a priority. The Cathars, though persecuted, could be persecutors as well. For example, they were fond of asceticism and rejected the material world, which in practice often morphed into denigrating women. Dominic founded religious houses that supported women who fled: safe houses, if you will.

Bonaventure includes the myths of Dominic's youth in his biography. The founder of the preachers supposedly had a felicitously named father, Felix, and appropriately named mother, Giovanna, which means grace. From his early days, he demonstrated his wisdom and devotion. A nurse was said to have asked him why he slept on the ground? Dominic replied that he sought to be wedded to poverty. Dominic was sensitive to God's ways from childhood.

That said, Bonaventure continues, Dominicans in Dante's time, one hundred years on, are becoming less attuned. They are walking backward, away from Dominic's storehouse of treasures. They are growing like tares not wheat, he remarks, in a reference to Jesus's parable about the weeds that threaten to choke the crop. Criticism is not withheld in paradise. It is spoken with deliberate clarity. But it is not persecutory, like the crusades. The aim is conversion of heart, not the subjugation of populations.

The new lights are named as the canto draws to a close. Bonaventure confirms his identity and then calls the eleven others. They include well known figures like Anselm of Canterbury, who had written *Why God Became*

Man, Saint Chrysostom, and Hugh of St Victor. There are lesser-known flames as well, like a Franciscan called Augustine, a rhetorician called Donatus, and a biblical commentator called Rabanus. Finally, he names Joachim of Flora who was influential among the Franciscan Spirituals, a group who felt that a new age was arriving, in which the Holy Spirit would rule. On earth, Bonaventure had attacked these Joachimites. He stood for a rational approach to ascent, the clear light of the intellect that listens to God, whereas Joachim preached passion, apocalypticism, and enlightenment through prophetic power.

However, together in the light of the sun, Bonaventure and Joachim are joined. On earth, and despite their disagreements, both sought to point above and beyond themselves. That core aim links them in this glorious, solar fellowship. The light was never their own, and they knew it, and Dante sees how it lit them both magnificently.

Imagining the movement of the stars prepares us for further solar perceptions.

PARADISO 13
Judgment

ONSIDER THIS SCENE, DANTE INVITES US. FIX this picture in your mind's eye.

Imagine the fifteen brightest stars in the sky. From the great canopy of the night sky, and gleaming blanket of the Milky Way, hold in sight the most stunning. They dazzle like jewels mounted on a background of glittering diamonds. Add to those fifteen, the seven stars of the Great Bear, the constellation that circles the night sky of the northern hemisphere, without setting, summer and winter. And add to those twenty-two, the two brightest stars of the Little Bear, and remember the third at its tip. This is the North Star, which stays stationary. The three together appear as a horn or trumpet, blasting silent music from the fixed point.

The picture is composed of twenty-four revolving gemstones, forming great arcs across the wide dome of the heavens. The circles can be compared with a single constellation, the Corona Borealis, which is almost like a double constellation of two mini-arcs, appearing to turn like wheels inside one another. Think of the magnificent twenty-four doing likewise, splendidly. The outer twelve rotate more speedily than the inner twelve, closest to the North Star.

If you can perceive this glory, Dante says, you might gain a faint glimpse of the glory he saw around him in the heaven of the sun. Nowadays it is, in fact, not so hard to do. A long exposure photograph of the night sky records the trails of the revolving stars, as circles of light emitted as if along the grooves of a disc or wheel. But Dante's aim is not so much to find an analogy for celestial sights visible from earth. It is to exercise our imaginations, because this is what enables appreciation of the deeper glory of paradise. If you can create the image in your mind, as opposed to relying on technology, the inner patterning of the cosmos becomes visible. It is not just the stars you will know to turn. All manner of lively intelligences will come to light.

Further, you will know of the deity that the twenty-four saints praise. Three persons are One, they sing before Dante and Beatrice. One person is human and divine.

The idea that one can be three echoes Aristotle's perfect number, which is the unity that holds the beginning, the middle, and the end. The three in one echo the trinitarian nature of awareness, felt as the knower, the known, and the knowing. Or there is the light, the mind that perceives it, and the loveliness of the light it sees. These unities of experience are diversities of interdependent elements. If you can sense part of what I am inferring, Dante continues, you are on the way to sharing the sights of the heights, though it is also true that the arrays of heaven make the wonders of earth seem like the sluggish Chiana river, which ceases to flow in the Italian marshland.

Spiritual exercise over, Thomas Aquinas steps forward again. He has remembered Dante's second question about the unequalled wisdom of Solomon, which had puzzled the traveler on the presumption that at least two figures had surpassed the Hebrew king. One, of course, is Christ. A second is the human being who was born aboriginally with unalloyed divine awareness, namely Adam. These two were created directly with

God's touch, whereas most human beings, including Solomon, are made when natural generation meets divine breath, forging a mix of earthly and heavenly qualities. They carry the imprint of heaven, Thomas says, which is tremendous. Nature is like the hand of a great artist, who knows his craft, though suffers a trembling hand, such is the awesomeness of the task. Imperfections inevitably slip in. Nonetheless, divine life cascades down the heavenly hierarchies, through the nine levels from the Seraphim and the Cherubim, to the archangels and angels, which the natural world reflects in myriad lights. The downward movement itself is perfect, for all that the upward striving is not — except in the exceptional cases of Adam and Christ who lived wholly or, for the period before fall, without impediment. So, where does Solomon fit in?

Thomas describes the birth of Adam and Christ in a fascinating way. First, he refers to the rib that came out of Adam's side to form Eve, implying that Eve must have shared in the primordial wisdom as well. And second, he refers to the lance that pierced the side of Christ, which is to say that it came out of Christ like Adam's rib. There's a parallel. The rib and the lance were both creative, one giving birth to Eve, the other giving birth to grace that perfects nature. The implication is that the Cross is not sacrificial. When seen correctly, it is inspired: it is another manifestation of the continual outpouring of divine fecundity. The linking of the rib and the lance by Thomas are part of Dante's reassessment of the significance of God becoming human. Adam and Christ are alike, as different movements in the one action.

It is a doubly significant observation to make in the context of a discussion about Solomon, the ancient Hebrew who some Christians felt might not make it to heaven. If you see God's action aright, Dante is saying, you'll see that Solomon is fully able to share the divine life.

The insight explains what Thomas had meant when he said Solomon's wisdom was unequalled on earth, because he was referring to those born by natural means, as opposed to the supernaturally originated Adam and Christ. "I was referring to his wisdom as a king," he tells Dante. He asked for wisdom in that task, not bothering with what did not concern him, which is why he brilliantly succeeded. Solomon knew focus. Therein lay his judgment.

The clarification leads to a series of reflections on caution being wise, avoiding speedy conclusions, and staying with seeming contradictions. Have slower feet, Thomas advises. Don't force paradoxes or insist on a swift "yes" or "no." Steadiness fosters contemplation, transformation, and depth of vision. Many philosophers do not take time, preferring logic to patience, settled decisions to gradual emergence. Haste breeds heresy, he continues, as in the case of those who fail to understand the trinitarian nature of God, or the twofold nature of divinity in Christ. Is it three or one, they demand, one or the other? And they miss the point. So, rest in tension. The transcendent function will work its alchemy.

Perseverance is close to prudence for another reason. "Mr. and Mrs. Know-It-All," as Thomas concludes, insist that they judge with God's eyes. The one who steals is clearly at fault, they will say; the one who gives alms is clearly saved. But they do not know what will happen. They do not understand the future. The first may rise, the second fall. Those who rush to condemn, a tendency particularly appealing to the religious mentality, not only get it wrong, but they also cloud their sight of the light.

God's ways dawn in people's minds like the vision of the wheeling heavens. Seeing it correctly requires subtlety, imagination, love.

Contemplating the divinization of humanity, Dante arrives in Mars.

PARADISO 14
Resurrection

ANTE IS ON A ROLL. THERE IS A JOY IN EXPE-riencing the unveiling of truths that once seemed impossible to comprehend. It happens when love and longing link to insight and intelligence. One builds the other, as articulation colors the space created by desire. Part of the dynamic of paradise is that one delight precipitates another. It is enthusiasm in the truest sense: inspiration coupled to interest, perception enhanced by passion.

It is like watching the ripples in a tub of water race from the edge to

353

the center, and from the center to the edge, seemingly delighting in their freedom to bounce and race, Dante explains. The switch of direction, with no loss of energy, continues as Beatrice speaks. She has discerned another question that has arisen in Dante's mind.

His inquiry has to do with the meeting of the human and divine, prompted by the discussion with Thomas that has enlarged his appreciation of the meaning of creation. Life comes from God and will return to God, much as the breath of the Spirit fills the soul and lifts the individual higher. But this raises the issue of how the natural, mortal, and transient will be brought to the heavenly, immortal, and infinite. Will the physical body that dies permanently pass away? Will it be transformed? Will it be resuscitated?

Within Christianity, this is to raise the question of the general resurrection, as it is called. The common understanding is that while people clearly die, there will come a day when everyone is raised. On that day, the whole of creation will rejoin God. That is a theoretical way of putting it, though Beatrice asks very directly: how will you, Thomas, be able to tolerate the intense radiance that you do now when, presumably, your mortal eyes are restored? How can it be that your old mode of sight, which couldn't stand bright lights without blinking, is not blinded in the celestial glare?

The circle of saints is delighted by her directness. I imagine that the issue of the general resurrection fascinated them during their mortal lives. Explaining it is a central challenge for any Christian theologian. They have an awareness now from the vantage of heaven, so are glad to speak of it, and spontaneously sing of the triune life that encompasses all without being encompassed. Imitating the bouncing ripples, they praise the oneness of God, which flows into the twoness of the knower and the known, which without gap prompts the threeness sprung from the joy of knowing. That in turn delights the knower and the known, who know of their unity in the knowing.

The reaction gladdens Dante. He feels like dry soil bathed in fresh rain. He knows that the pleasures of life on earth are anticipations of life in heaven.

He hears a gentle voice from among the twenty-four lights. It reminds him of the archangel Gabriel addressing Mary at the annunciation. It is not immediately obvious which of the luminaries speak but the implication is that it is Solomon. Like Gabriel, he lived before the birth of Christ and so witnessed the Incarnation. He speaks modestly like the archangel because he senses the enormity of which he speaks, though he also knows the answer to Dante's question. The good news of life in the afterlife is no Christian possession.

God desires that we know about life in all its fullness, and the greater our vision, the greater our love for that life, which fosters a greater shining with it. There is a virtuous circle that enables us to embrace more and more of life. It can be felt on earth. It is the essence of life in heaven. Death, Solomon continues, is therefore a moment of emergence into greater life. It is as if the white heat of the coals, that sustain the cooler orange flames of the fire, migrates into the flames as well, which grow white as they unite with the source. Similarly, our physical bodies will be strengthened to bear more life. Their potential, which is partly manifested during mortal life, will reach its perfection in the actualization of the afterlife. These brighter bodies are our bodies, and they will express, and be capable of reflecting, more than our bodies on earth could have.

Solomon's explanation is akin to the remarks made by Paul in the First Letter to the Corinthians. We are born with physical bodies and resurrected with spiritual bodies, he says, which are partly a continuity of life, partly a discontinuous completed creation. The description also chimes with the Resurrection appearances of Jesus in the Gospels. Sometimes he appears to have a physical body that can do things like eat, sometimes one that can move through walls; sometimes his body is recognizably him, sometimes it is not, so changed has he become. What it takes for the disciples to detect the resurrected Jesus is an expansion of their vision. Not that this is anything new. Throughout his life with them, Jesus had asked them whether they had the eyes to see and the ears to hear. Dante is being invited to contemplate the same.

A terrestrial example, not in Dante, suggests how much more can emerge, given time. Take the fact that the ancient Greeks didn't have a word for "blue." It seems odd because they lived in a very blue world, that of the azure-skied, turquoise-watered Mediterranean. If there were one word they might need it would be "blue." The difference was that they described the sea and sky in terms of its qualities. The sea was experienced as rich and luscious, and so likened to red wine. The sky was experienced as expansive and luminous, akin to the heavens. So, in a way, they didn't need the word "blue," which is more of a category of color: blue is not red or yellow. That way of seeing the world developed subsequently, which raises the prospect of how differently things may come to be seen again, not least in heaven.

The souls around Solomon love his response. It prompts a third ring of lights to appear: in this very moment Dante's sight is expanding. What the third circle reveals is widely discussed by commentators, though the emergence of a third is never far from the threeness of the Trinity, which is to say the perfection of awareness in the life of the Spirit.

In that way, the appearance of the third ring may be a reflection of the teaching of Joachim of Fiore, one of the twelve in the ring of Bonaventure. He argued that there had been an age of the Father, an age of the Son, and that a third age was dawning, that of the Spirit. It would be one that renewed and developed the understandings of the first two, revolving around the themes of creation and incarnation, to introduce greater truths. And this is what is appearing to Dante now.

It seems to me that this has been his dawning sense through paradise. "Oh, sparks of light that are the Holy Spirit!" he calls. It is as if he sees what Joachim had foretold, as had the words of Jesus, which promised that a paraclete would come that led people into further truths that could not be yet understood. Eyes that see farther, and ears that can hear more, are being fashioned. Like the resurrection body, they are strengthening for fuller perception.

The third ring is not the only novelty. Beatrice appears more beautiful and fairer, which Dante finds hard to express in words. He is in the process of absorbing the intensification, though staying with it, when he looks up, and notices the light around him changing. They are already in the fifth heaven, that of Mars. The light has ruby reddened. He offers a sacrifice of praise.

The reference to sacrifice is to say that he is in the Martian state of mind. He has become conscious of it, and it bursts forth in a tremendous vision as he sees the Cross. The experience is not easy to describe, he says. It forms in the lights around him and Beatrice, and has equal arms, tracing a circle, unlike the usual shape seen in churches. Crimson lights move across the arms: souls are manifesting the Cross for him. It is their sacrifice of praise, in response to Dante's sacrifice of gratitude.

The wonderful reaction to his offering speaks to the nature of the sacrificial spirit reflected by the light of Mars. It is not the kind of sacrifice that requires loss of life, like a war, or the type that attempts to quell a raging god or bloody tyrant. Nor is it the sacrifice that seeks to purify, by loading impurities onto an offering that is handed over and killed. It is the kind of sacrifice that harmonizes with the flow of life, which is a constant process of receiving and passing on. It is about a relationship that grows because shared. It is the true nature of gratitude, which is not about gratifying a giver, or making the receiver feel more comfortable, but offering back the delight experienced in the receiving. It may also have to do with the age of the Spirit and becoming more porous to God. It seems certainly not about the theory of the atonement that Jesus died on the Cross to die in our stead.

Heavenly Mars is similarly unlike the mundane martial attitude of valor on the battlefield. Its passion is to participate in the cascading outpouring of God. It is linked to the give and take that is the virtuous spiral of paradise. It is like the image with which the canto began: the ripples of water dancing across the tub, joyous in their expanding reflections.

It is hard for Dante to grasp. He realizes as much when the darting souls of the circular cross start to sing. He doesn't understand their words, though the music is entrancing. Just a fragment of its meaning enters his mind, as he understands the words "arise" and "conquer." They speak of the spirit of this realm, though that simultaneously makes him confess how little he grasps of it.

But it is beautiful and desirable. Nothing he has heard before is comparable, though as he thinks that, he recalls that he has not yet looked at the eyes of Beatrice in this sphere, and they will undoubtedly have become more beautiful. She will be more ravishing.

Dante meets Cacciaguida, who offers a vision of previous times.

PARADISO 15

Ancestry

XQUISITE MUSIC, RUBY LIGHT, AND ACTS OF
praise have been Dante's arrival in the heaven of Mars. They sup-
plement the firework display of a buzzing circular cross. Sacrifice
is on display—sacrifice in the sense of offering what you have as a step
toward receiving more. It's an attitude that can be practiced moment by
moment by inwardly returning each breath, movement, or action, in thanks.
Consciousness of the whole becomes possible as the divine entirety from
which partial perceptions, expressions, and views are derived. Surrendering
your best take on what's good, beautiful, and true to the good, beautiful,
and true allows the full vision to be enjoyed.

The theologians and philosophers of the sun who disagreed on earth had
made such a sacrifice and so, in Mars, Dante appreciates the dynamic to the
full. It is the magnanimity found by true lovers who forego themselves in
the service of what they love, Dante remarks. It is the opposite of the envy
and self-inflation that traps the narcissistic.

Then, there is silence. The souls surrender their pleasure to a pause. Expectation fills the stilled ethereal air.

One of the fiery lights darts along the horizontal arm of the cross to
the center. Separating from the red blaze of its fellows, it shoots toward
Dante like a meteorite dashing across the sky. The image comes to his mind

358

presumably because meteorites are sacrificial in their appearance: they throw themselves into the atmosphere of earth to die in a blaze of glory. The approaching soul reminds Dante of Anchises, the father of Aeneas, who rushed forward to greet his son in the Greek afterlife of Elysium: a meeting of relatives, and that will turn out to be prophetic.

The light speaks to Dante in Latin. Its formal voice intones: "Oh blood of mine. Oh, grace of God. To whom else, as to thee, was heaven's gate opened twice?" The words carry the feel of an initiation, the twice-opened gates echoing the aim of the ancient mystery religions, which was to die before you died, in the rites. The blessed initiate thereby became conscious of the process of death and so able to embrace it, and the life beyond it, when his actual death arrived.

Dante is spellbound. He looks for Beatrice, who is glowing with such a light that Dante feels he might be glimpsing the highest heaven, not only Mars. I think this is a reference to the observation in medieval astronomy that Mars is the first of the planets to fall outside of the shadow of the earth. It is unaffected by mortal concerns, which is why it is the natural heaven of the martyrs, those individuals who realized while they still lived that immortal life is more valuable than mortal life, and so happily offered themselves in death. Mars is a step on from the sun, where the souls celebrated their previous disagreement; the next step is Venus, in which the souls celebrated the essence of their loves on earth; then Mercury, where the light of terrestrial glory gave way to divine glory; and the moon, in which the ups and downs of secular affairs were put aside.

The identity of the soul before him is not yet clear. His perplexity grows when the individual starts to speak in a language Dante cannot understand. It is only when the words express the mystery of the Trinity, the lofty paradox human intuition can just about grasp, that they fall within his comprehension. Dante hears the soul expressing delight at how God has blessed its offspring.

He stands before Cacciaguida, his great-great-grandfather, though Dante doesn't fully know that yet. Cacciaguida learned of Dante's journey in the book of the future, he explains. It surprised him, as mortals tend not to arrive in Mars, and he is delighted to be present at the fulfilment of its prophecy. He knows Dante has a question. His mind is connected, like all the souls in heaven, via awareness of the divine mind within them. It enables the sharing of thoughts, though he invites Dante to voice his concern, so that Dante's mind can be explicitly heard in this sphere and Dante can feel at home in it. The sound would delight a great-great-grandfather too.

Beatrice beams her blessing and Dante speaks. He celebrates the perfection of love and intellect expressed in the lights around him, as they delight in God's fullness. He thanks them for entertaining the imperfect love and intellect of a mortal in his own voice. He feels like a bird with feathers that enable it to swoop up, though only spiral around. That said, he will offer his voiced flight in the sacrificial spirit of Mars, knowing it will return more.

Cacciaguida responds and reveals who he is. He then spends much of the second half of the canto describing the Florence into which he was born, generations before Dante, when the city-state was in its heyday. It knew its purpose and mission. It understood its divine calling. It was the time before Florence fell.

Dante is being invited to touch a richer part of his ancestry. The encounter clarifies his bloodline. Cacciaguida represents his true nobility. The time in Mars is a moment when he can become more aware of who he is by reaching beyond his own life to another life with which he is connected. That extension mirrors awakening to the fuller life which is so clearly present here in the higher heavens. It is also healing. The generations closer to Dante had messed things up. They had polluted the waters from which Dante drank, with dire consequences for his mortal life. Meeting Cacciaguida is, therefore, a chance to establish a renewed connection with his life spring. It is part of his recreation. You feel him drinking it in as he listens.

Cacciaguida explains that his life ended during the second crusade. He died a martyr's death on the mission that aimed to reconnect Christian Europe with its terrestrial wellspring, Jerusalem. In history, the campaign-cum-pilgrimage was a bloody mess. Cacciaguida acknowledges this in his account. But in eternity, his purity of heart is honored. In spite of the ugly complications of mortal life, you might say, exacerbated by the vanity of rulers and the Church, Cacciaguida did not lose touch with the divine. His mind remained clear in its focus on heaven. He embraced immortality while living, and knew it in death.

The tragedy of Florence is rehearsed, though a deeper love and life is seen.

PARADISO 16
Flow

W E ARE HALFWAY THROUGH THE CANTOS OF THE
Paradiso and, as with the midpoint of The Inferno and The Purgatorio,
it marks Dante's widening perception.

Dante has been listening to Cacciaguida, his great-great-grandfather. He
now cries out against the corruption of the nobility, and much of the canto
is a rehearsal of the collapse of Florentine values. However, it is heard in
paradise, in the sphere of Mars, and I think what it means for Dante is the
recognition that everything on earth is subject to death and is cut by time's
scissors, as he puts it. This includes the loss of possessions, culture, and life
itself, though in the light of this heaven, loss can be seen to precipitate
depths of life that were formerly inconceivable. If we can learn from the
cost of demise and passing, the value of life and longing can be sustained.

The transformation is underway in Dante's imagination. The canto is
an extended reflection on that inward assurance which settles not because
it denies what happens, but because it faces events and sees more. This is
Mars who strengthens warriors and brings resolve amidst harm and injury.

Dante begins to feel how that works because Cacciaguida's nobility is not
based upon social standing or rank. It arises from his awareness of integrity
and honor. Dante reveres his ancestor by addressing him formally, using the

361

medieval Italian equivalent of "thou" and "thee," adding that these respectful pronouns were falling out of use in his times, as principles declined. Hearing it makes Beatrice smile because, previously, he had used "thou" of her. Dante remarks that her smile reminded him of the lady-in-waiting who coughed when she saw that Guinevere loved Lancelot. The cough was a warning that the illicit desire was a threat to the reputations of the legendary knight and lady. Beatrice's contrasting smile is, conversely, her blessing upon Dante. His heavenly promiscuity makes for noble not ignoble ends.

It is the type of desire that carries souls higher. He has let go of the possessive types of love that became so evident on Mount Purgatory. He is connected to sources of everlasting delight that can be freely enjoyed because they are abundant. Nothing can alter their flow. He feels his soul filled with streams that endure, and testifies to this more within him, saying: "I am more than I am."

The expression is crucial. The life of which he has been aware is but a reflection of a greater life; his spirit need not flag, because it is a refraction of the Spirit that never wanes. He is like a wave on the ocean that rejoices in the unfathomable tide feeding its modest swell. It is reconciled to its own rise and fall because it knows that movement is a facet of the ocean's being.

The awareness of plenty prompts him to ask Cacciaguida about the Florentine decline. It is as if he knows he can accept what happened across the generations to his time because he is in contact with these wellsprings. In hell, he had cursed his fellow citizens for their failures. On Mount Purgatory, he had revisited the story as a tale of woe and lament: sorrow had shifted his relationship to the past. In paradise, a third phase in this process unfolds. It is a type of apocalypse, not in the sense of a terrible judgment day that pours fire and brimstone to scorch and destroy. A heavenly apocalypse is one that discloses truth, pushing through the terrible elements without flinching to expose the unshakable ground. It assesses not to condemn but to re-establish contact with the bedrock of life. It accepts denial and rage, and tends sorrow and collapse, with a recognition that any particular story is a chapter in the great story of unceasing divine creation.

The civilization of Florence is eroded. It happens to every city, country, culture, even religion. There is the moment of birth at the meeting of earth and heaven. It produces an original charism that inspires and ignites the human spirit to experiment, build, explore. The historian, Arnold Toynbee, called it the phase of etherealization, during which the tangible manifestations of a civilization are direct expressions of its inner spirit. But inevitably that connection weakens, as interests such as power, gain, and the need simply to keep going come to dominate. Leaders seek other means to sustain a nation or culture, from violent wars to the manic replication of growth for growth's sake. They stop trusting the wellsprings and start trusting their own power, technology, capacity to control, or sense of self-sufficiency. So, it is only a question of time before that grows unwieldy and topples. It may happen because of overt corruption or because people forget what they are fighting for, and so just fight.

Utopia literally means "no place." Heaven is not found on earth. Plato had shown in *The Republic* that humans will attempt to build ideal cities and states, because that is what humans do. However, it is the virtues cultivated by such efforts that matter, not the buildings, institutions, and ways of life themselves. The virtues last when everything else crumbles. To try to prevent the crumbling breeds only strife, suffering, and vice.

Our destination is elsewhere, not mortal realms. Virtues can guide us to this other country, which is why it can also be sensed on earth in imagination and longing. Dante sees how death and decline do not compromise creation but are part of the return to God.

Throughout Cacciaguida's baleful litany of internecine murder, bribery and sleaze, papal scheming and regal depravity, the light of Mars does not fail. It shines steadily. Dante accepts what has happened and so transcends the tears and resentment. It would be called the art of engaged detachment in Indian wisdom traditions. Within Christianity, it is called taking up your cross: the ability to embrace life, whatever falls, because the falling reveals the life that lies behind what is immediately happening. Vicissitudes are passing. What awakens is the perception that travesties do not have the last word and existence is not a tragedy. It is a comedy because it sprang from love, intelligence, joy, and glory. And these things abide.

It is confirmed that Dante will be expelled from Florence upon his return to earth.

PARADISO 17

Exile

NCIENT MYTH TELLS OF HOW PHAETHON
wanted to know whether his father really was the sun god, Helios.
He asked his mother, Clymene, who said Helios was his father
and that he should ask Helios for himself. Helios confirmed his paternity;
Phaethon persuaded Helios to let him drive the sun chariot across the sky.
Unable to control the horses, Phaethon fell to earth and died.

Apart from anything else, the story conveys the wisdom of the old saying "Be careful what you wish for." Dante has it on his mind. He wants
to ask his great-great-grandfather, Cacciaguida, about his future. He has
repeatedly heard ominous predictions of exile and suffering coming his
way from the souls he has met while travelling through hell and up Mount
Purgatory. Are they true?

The question comes because Dante must be able to tolerate the truth if
he is to continue to rise. The truths that are often the hardest to bear are
the ones about ourselves. He will need the courage of Mars not to live in
fear of the vicissitudes of his mortal existence. He needs to be able to see
beyond them to know divine life.

He is troubled. Trusting in God sounds easy. It is hard to do when there are
misfortunes ahead, doubly so when you know torments are coming and will
last for a long time. Dante sets *The Divine Comedy* in 1300. He will live until

1321, meaning he faces two decades of uncertainty and dislocation. He will lose companionship, home, Florence, and face a continual threat of painful execution. Even Jesus asked for the cup of suffering to be taken from him.

There is not only the risk of fearing the future, but of trying to control or change it. This was the fault of the diviners he and Virgil met in hell. They saw the future and it tempted them to think they were God.

The initiatory experience of Mars requires him to see the future, including suffering and death, and so learn that there is more life. Then he might know that the contingencies of life and blows of chance are not lasting features, because life is underpinned by eternal verities. Dante is at that turning point. It can only be a true turning point if he truly confronts his plight. It is another way in which descent and ascent are linked.

Beatrice sees that he is agonizing and knows what the difficulty is. She encourages him to speak. That way he can not only have the truth confirmed but drink from the consolation found in these high places.

Dante asks, and Cacciaguida confirms what he dreads. He will have to flee Florence, he will have to keep unsavory company, he will feel all the blessings of his earlier life have gone. He will feel naked, abandoned, abused. There will be periods of grace amidst the distress, moments of welcome and hospitality while he wanders. But he must learn to accept them not as an escape, or as a route out of difficulty, but as a sign that love is not altered by what happens. Eternity is unchanged by suffering. The light does not darken even when everything else falls under shadows.

It is about the relationship between contingencies and eternity. From the divine perspective, there are no random acts. It all carries meaning, though not because everything is preordained, Cacciaguida insists. There is genuine change and novelty. However, God sees things as if watching a boat navigating a river from a high cliff. The person in the boat experiences the journey as a mix of turbulence and calm, not knowing which will come next or where it will end. From the clifftop, though, the destination is clear, and happenstance is the story of how that end is reached.

To put it another way, God sustains all things but not like a puppet master pulling the strings. It is the flow of life, the energy of being, that never ceases. How we ride those waves of animation is, in part, up to us. The decisions we make, the way we cultivate our freedom, truly matters. We can turn from virtue to vice, and vice versa.

Cacciaguida explains the attitude Dante must adopt as "becoming your own party." His exile will separate him from his seeming allies, in particular the Guelphs, and that is an opportunity. The aloneness can become a space within which to develop his own mind, pull back from groupthink, and cultivate an independent sense of what is good and true, away from the collective mentality of the crowd. The masses become particularly powerful in times of crisis and tragedy. They will try to draw him in, so staying on the road less travelled and seeing the way ahead is hard. But it is the pathway to eternal life.

It is another reflection on Dante's remark in the previous canto, "I am more than I am." The immortal aspect of the soul cannot be undone by life, though it can be lost sight of. He might be swept along by events and pushed about by others but there is another part of him that can see things from the high cliff, that can keep focused on the destination. To do so, he must become his own party. His path and particularity matter, but because it is within our centers that we find the divine center. It is then that we can know our eye and God's eye is one eye, to recall Meister Eckhart's phrase.

And there will be people to lean on, Cacciaguida affirms. In particular, he refers to the great Lombard, Bartolommeo della Scala, who was one of the individuals who took Dante in and gave him a home in Verona. He and his younger brother, Can Grande, were to become very important to Dante. He can be grateful for them — and, in fact, Dante dedicated The Paradiso to Can Grande. And yet their acts of kindness can be received with precisely the same engaged detachment as the doings of the cruel. They can be embraced for the time they last, and then released, when there is no loss of the wider perspective.

Cacciaguida mentions another risk, that of envying his neighbors because they don't suffer in the same way. It is a temptation, particularly for Dante who has enjoyed fame, renown, and some riches. Envy is dangerous because it invites you to want another's life, not your own. When it really festers, it invites you to want the ruination of another's life because it cannot be your own. Don't go down that path, his great-great-grandfather tells him. In heaven, there is an eternal flame, in eternal glory, with an eternal welcome that is ready for him. He can feel it, if he looks, because it is within him, amidst mortal life.

Dante is grateful to have these eventualities spelt out clearly to him. I am a timid friend of truth, he admits in a touching self-reflection. He shows his vulnerability, which is crucial for building courage. He is also not unconcerned about how his poem will be received. Might it even be ignored? It contains harsh truths, tricky verities, as well as hope and inspiration. Accessing the good means fostering the sight and motivation to ride with the bad. It means becoming your own party and knowing that you are more than you are.

Dante must write what he has seen, Cacciaguida encourages. He must not tell lies and not worry about how people might read his words. That is up to them. The bitter herb may be a nutrient, Cacciaguida explains. The soul grows when it seeks not happiness but meaning, often found on the other side of suffering.

A final comment from Cacciaguida is worth noting. Dante has encountered so many famous people on his journey, as opposed to regular folk, his ancestor tells him, for a reason: so that more people might learn from the experience. It will add longevity to his poem.

He is referring to us. Endurance is possible. Life can be embraced. Jealousy can be resisted. We can become more than who we are, because that more is who we are already.

A deeper symmetry appears as they ascend to the heaven of Jupiter.

PARADISO 18
Justice

DANTE IS CONSIDERING THE PROPHECIES AND
advice offered by Cacciaguida. The experience is a mix of bitter
and sweet. His mind twists and turns. In one moment, I sense, he
sees the truth of himself of which his ancestor speaks, but then, in another
moment, he tries to offset the unpleasantness of the future predicted for
him with sustaining thoughts of the help he will receive along the way. That
is to treat life as a balancing act, or a battle between the bad and the good.

It prompts an interjection from Beatrice. "Remember that I dwell with
the one who carries the weight of all suffering," she suggests. "Don't get
lost in other thoughts." Dante has momentarily forgotten the view from
the high cliff. The way forward is the contemplation of unchanging light,
not attempts to ward off darkness.

They are kind words and Dante turns to look at her. Her eyes are full
of divine love beyond description, and he detects in them the joy that is
everlasting. Her radiance reflects the divine brilliance, the fullness with
which longing ceases. It's what he needs. Pain is real, as is death. But by
leaning into them, not turning away from them, dimensions of existence
are discovered that remain steady and reliable throughout.

There are other souls in this heaven in whom the same light can be seen, Beatrice continues. Have a look.

He does and notices that Cacciaguida is beaming with a deeper light. It is not that Cacciaguida has changed, but that Dante can see more of what his great-great-grandfather has been driving at all along. When Dante can see his life in the round, he can see around his life, and so catch sight of the source behind, beneath, and within it. That origin emanates from Cacciaguida's eyes, which he can appreciate because he sees it with his own eyes, from within.

His great-great-grandfather has something further to add. He invites Dante to look again at the circular cross. In it, Dante sees souls whose lives have been celebrated from the higher perspective. They appear in a flash of light as Cacciaguida names them. Joshua, Judas Maccabeus, Roland and Charlemagne, Guillaume d'Orange the crusader, and others — nine in total. Their lives had the quality of epic, which is to say their exploits and deeds were akin to the tales told by Virgil in *The Aeneid* and Homer in *The Iliad*. The particular figures who come forth from the cross are ancient Hebrews from the Bible and medieval nobles whose lives became legendary.

They are meaningful for Dante because Joshua's life, for example, was one of conquest in Canaan, including terrible bloodshed and the destruction of Jericho. This to say that, in earthly terms, it was marked by suffering and riddled with moral complexity, but in heavenly terms, the deeper pulse of events is clear. This is not to overwrite all that happened, for good or ill, but it is to see more than the surface allows.

Homer and Virgil still reveal these archetypes to us. They communicate the interior dynamics of history and foster the capacity to feel that pattern for oneself when facing tragedy and change. It is why they are consoling to read.

Cacciaguida rejoins the ruby throng from which he had descended. It is an act that places Dante's own life alongside the terrible and tremendous tales spoken of by his ancestor and the other souls in the sphere of Mars. Dante will, in time, become a teller of legend himself, for which the sense he has gained from Cacciaguida is crucial.

He turns back to Beatrice, asking what he should do. And nothing remains still in paradise. The light within and around her is already changing. There is a new purity and luster beaming in her eyes, which Dante feels transmitted to him. He detects that they are moving in a greater arc, the transition to the next sphere happening as quickly as a blush flickers across a face. They are in the clear, white light of the heaven of Jupiter.

This is how revelation works. We are at a threshold and, if we can remain alert, our perception has already shifted, as light dawns and insight welcomes us. We must be alert to catch the moment, as grace invites us to step farther.

Dante's awareness of moving in a greater arc is a particularly fine detail. At one level, it is a reference to celestial astronomy, and Jupiter's larger orbit compared with that of Mars. But at another level, it is a psychological observation. He has more space. He is in a wider world. He can see more broadly across the heavens. He has gained a vantage point that is higher up the cliff. It is the opposite experience to the mounting claustrophobia of the descent into the narrowing, confining circles of hell.

The spirit of Jupiter immediately feels different from that of Mars. It is not just jovial, as is remembered by the modern use of the word "Jove," which might be misleading if it is taken to mean mere jollity. The state of mind that Jupiter reflects understands balance and symmetry, integrity and justice. This is not the justice of rules and regulations but humanity and friendship. It does not punish or rectify but incorporates everything into the whole. It brings a profound sense of harmonious completion. It is the awareness that a season of suffering or an untimely death can be as beautiful as a clear insight or noble act. It is unlike justice on earth, which is often an exercise in compromise or a manipulation of the law. It calls forth an inner justice, or natural justice as it is sometimes called, and Dante sees it.

He calls on the divine muse to help him find the words to convey the emerging sight, and sees what look like birds in the sky, full of vitality, as if a dazzling murmuration. They are individual spirits moving as one, not as if regimented, but as if dancing. They are in full possession of themselves and, because of that, fall into perfect synchronicity.

Letters form in the jovial air before him. Gradually, the meaning of the sign becomes clear. *Diligite Justitiam Qui Judicatis Terram*. The souls are writing the phrase, "Love justice you who judge the earth," the first sentence from the Book of the Wisdom of Solomon. It is a clarion call from the heavens to those who administer justice on earth.

The sign shifts again. The final letter of the last word, the "m" of "Terram," morphs. The middle stroke extends vertically upward and, is it rises, the two outer strokes extend outward and downward. From the shifting "m" an eagle appears, the rising stroke forming its head, the outer strokes its wings. The splendid bird of high heaven, the creature who can see into the sun, is joined by a shower of cascading lights. Like sparks deliberately leaping from a fire, they assembled on the eagle, marking its crest, neck, and brow. The activity reminds Dante of birds building their nests, driven by an inner intention and imperative.

It is a tremendous sight: heavenly justice as individual lives fully expressed and chiming with one another. It prompts Dante to contemplate the efforts to bring justice to earth. He detects it fails because people's vision becomes clouded by hypocrisy and constraint. It is like the money changers who turned the Temple into a marketplace, when it might be a house within which souls receive the bread of heaven. It is like the popes who practice simony because they do not know the value of blessing, peddling pardons and indulgences, excommunications and annulments, as Dante puts it. It is like those in authority who wield their power blindly, not knowing that true power empowers others by passing on insight and light.

The canto ends on a low point, though only so as to highlight the great aims to which the human soul can aspire.

The heaven of Jupiter reveals divine plenitude, readying Dante for more.

PARADISO 19

Plenitude

HE TREMENDOUS EAGLE, FORMED FROM LIVING lights, sparkling like rubies catching the sun, speaks. It is unimaginable, Dante tells us. If he had not seen it, he would not have thought to dream it. Moreover, the assembly speaks in the singular as if one, at the same time as Dante hears it speak in the plural, as if many. "I" and "mine" merge with "we" and "ours," he recalls.

It is a fractal vision. Seeing a part is seeing the whole. Each soul is wholly itself and wholly in sympathy with the souls around it, because it is wholly in sympathy with the divine. It is like the jewels in a crown, each stone set as a perfect specimen of glory, within the crown that conveys an entire world of glory. It seems to Dante that the eagle is there just for him as he enjoys its brilliance, or rather the bird is like the sun: it pours its light onto everyone fully and equally, without reserve, with each individual picking up the munificence of the whole.

This is an eagle speaking with conscious intelligence, not a parrot cutely imitating words, Helen Luke remarks in her commentary. Each soul speaks from its direct experience and knowledge of ruling justly on earth, sustained by maintaining a clear image of justice in heaven. They tell Dante that they are manifest in the heaven of Jupiter because they strove to bring Jove's justice to the towns and cities of earth.

There is a message in the image for the still earthbound, the eagle adds. Seek the reflection of divine justice even in the actions of poor rulers and leaders. There will be some likeness of it there, however faint. Even the wicked know as much and might be encouraged to find it admirable. Conversely, if disillusionment really set in and everyone stopped yearning for justice, justice really would depart from the face of the earth.

The souls are like the coals of a fire, each burning in their own way, each contributing to the glow. Or they are like flowers in a field, each delighting in its own bloom, while offering that to the loveliness of the meadow.

The sight is amazing, though it stirs an old question in Dante's heart. He has asked it a few times and he seeks another take on it again. Here in Jupiter's glow, there is no better place to ask how those who have not heard of Christianity can be condemned by God?

It just seems so unjust. If you were born before Christ. If you lived in a place in which Christianity wasn't known. If you heard about Jesus but found the message incomprehensible, unappealing, or implausible. After all, like many who claim to rule, many who claim to follow God, fail to do so, which raises a deeper take on the issue: how can any human individual or tradition, which is inevitably tarnished and limited, hope to reflect the divine light which would invite all of humanity home. How can the finite convey the infinite, the compromised reveal the good? Further, can the divine majesty really be known at all?

Dante does not quite put it in these ways, but I think his repeatedly returning to the question suggests he has these many layers in mind.

The eagle replies from its plenitude. It does not seek to excuse God but observes how God creates from an inexhaustible resource and an impulse of excess. There is always more to see, to love, to know, to desire. It is making a subtle point, as well as an extravagant one. Limited creatures can know of that which is unlimited by becoming aware that what they understand and see is but an element of what can be understood and seen. It is like Isaac Newton's perception that he is a boy, standing on the seashore, diverting himself with a smooth stone or a pretty pebble, when before him stretches a great ocean of truth. Divine plenitude meets human finitude in what remains to be discovered. It is sensed by loving, longing, and yearning to see more. It is a bit like the fractal eagle: to see one living light is, in a sense, to see the whole.

Lucifer couldn't tolerate this fact, the eagle continues. The creature who was the most beautiful and nearest to God couldn't endure that, with accepting its part in creation, it could participate in the whole of creation. No creature possesses life, but every creature can enjoy the life that freely flows within it. The mystics call it the cloud of unknowing, the dazzling darkness, or the emptiness that is full because it is able to receive without impediment. It is a bit like treading water and being aware of the depths of the ocean. In the shallows, the eagle explains, the seabed can be seen, but divine life is not shallow.

I understand your question, the I-we voice continues, but how can you pass judgment on God? Humans barely know themselves, and rarely rule their societies well, so with what ignorance do they declare that they have divine authority to judge others? Their arrogance cuts them off from seams of gold.

The bird flies around Dante like a stork tending its young. Though it speaks with force, it does not seek to condemn, but to enlighten. Its remarks can feed the hungry mind if that person has accepted his need and so yearns for more. The fact that divine justice is incomprehensible is not to bamboozle but to invite. And the incomprehension cuts both ways, the eagle goes on. Maybe a time will come when the non-Christian condemns the Christian because the unbeliever is able to see the truth more clearly. Following God is not, ultimately, about belonging to the right church or following the right tradition. It is about knowing God.

It is quite a thing to hear in the high heavens, and a list of individuals who claimed to rule in God's name, and did nothing of the sort, underlines the point. The eagle specifically cites about a dozen kings from places right across Europe. It is as if the creature is underlining that the failure infects all Christendom.

The eagle is talking of Christianity beyond Christianity. It will do so explicitly in the next canto, answering Dante's question about justice conclusively, in my view. For the moment, the message is to know there are good and bad rulers, much as there are good and bad aspects within ourselves. If we live judging and condemning, we are like the farmer who, in pulling out the tares, uproots the wheat, to recall Jesus's parable. Further, the wheat may be confused with the tares, risking the destruction of the plant that will bear fruit.

We human beings are not good judges because in condemning others, we are often secretly wishing not to find ourselves condemned. Instead, in mortal life, we must wait for the immortal. What matters is preparing the heart, embracing the limitations to be ready for more, because even when we are walking away from God, we are discovering how far God's life and love reaches. Nothing can separate us from it.

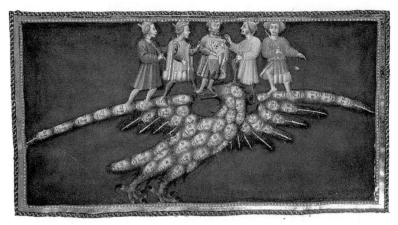

Dante never expected to see the souls who are encountered in Jupiter.

PARADISO 20

Universalism

HE EAGLE FALLS SILENT. DANTE IS REMINDED
of the moment when the sun sets and the brilliance of the day
gives way to the enchantment of the night. It is not really a transition from light to darkness, any more than the eagle going quiet lessens
the praise echoing through Jupiter's sphere. It is a shift from one kind of
light to another, the latter emerging as the sun sets. The stars were always
there, only concealed. Something of a comparable unveiling is stirring in
Dante as the question of who knows God is pressed, and the apparently
clear light of Christian orthodoxy sets to reveal a subtler reality.

The constellations wing across the night sky, and so the eagle readies
itself to speak again. As sound forms within its bejeweled body, Dante is
reminded of the murmur of a stream tumbling between rocks. Or it is like
the air vibrating within the ribs of a lute, stimulated by the strings, amplified
by the soundboard, and singing from the rose opening carved into its body.

Music is nothing without its flow, as the cycle of light from day to night
would cease without the celestial turning. That revolution speaks to Dante
because, like the eagle composed of multiple souls, the sound he hears from
the great bird is a moving harmony.

The eagle has not yet fully answered Dante's question about the salvation of those who don't know of Christianity. It has spoken of not judging God, and the importance of seeking to reflect divine justice on earth. But it senses just how profoundly the issue troubles the pilgrim. Indeed, in passing, the eagle has restated the formula that distresses him: salvation is found only in Christ. It is a gentle ratcheting up of the tension which, in heaven, tends to precipitate a revelation. Dante has returned to this quandary repeatedly and his persistence, like the widow banging on the door of the judge in Jesus's parable, is to reap a reward. By staying with it, not seeking quickly to resolve the issue one way or another, Dante will see more — much more than he could have imagined.

The eagle invites Dante to gaze at the souls within it, focusing particularly on the lights in its eye. This is a crucial part of its body, as the eagle was said to be able to look directly at the sun, which is to say, look directly at the divine brilliance without being dazzled. Attending to the eagle's eye is to attend to the capacity to see God.

In the center of the bird's pupil, he sees the soul of King David, the writer of the psalms. David is there, Dante hears, not only for his songs that understand and express every mood of the human soul. He is there because he realized that all the genius of his compositions was only a steppingstone toward life in all its fullness. But it was a crucial steppingstone. It left him open to the divine, so that the divine could be discovered in him. That is why he is in the pupil of the eye. It is the portal that connects Creator and creature.

Look at my eyebrow, the eagle invites Dante next, at which Dante raises his eyes and sees five souls. They share King David's awareness that what they knew on earth was bounded by a horizon over which there is so much more to be perceived. The recognition has carried them to this high point. Their limitations, worked out to the full, became a threshold over which was found the satisfaction of their yearning. They, thereby, fulfilled their inherent affinity with God.

The first of the five is Trajan, the Roman emperor. It is something of a surprise to see him so exalted, he not being a Christian, though Dante and Virgil had passed the celebration of his life in the vivid murals on the first terrace of Mount Purgatory. Additionally, there is a legend that Trajan had come back to life after he died because of the prayers of Pope Gregory. Coming around, the emperor converted. The story, I think, circulated as a literal way of expressing an inner truth: the act of noticing the request of the widow, which the murals commemorated, was not only morally commendable but had shown he was open to people and concerns that might be assumed closed to a supreme ruler and military leader. He was, therefore, receptive to a heaven his paganism did not fully disclose, and he finds himself in it now.

The second soul in the sparkling raptor's brow is Hezekiah, the king whose life is remembered in the Hebrew Bible. His presence would, again, have struck Dante and his contemporaries as significant, given the question of whether Jews were saved. Dante has seen Solomon in heaven, which makes sense given the great king's wisdom. But Hezekiah might be less expected. He was a successful leader of Israel, not least because he was a reformer. The implication is that capacity for change fostered the elevation of his soul in the afterlife.

The third light is Constantine, the Roman emperor who became a Christian on his deathbed, it was said. The eagle explains that Constantine's awareness prompted him to move the capital of the empire from Rome to Byzantium, where upon he renamed it, Constantinople. He left Rome to the papacy and ecclesiastical corruption.

It might be described as a capacity to invest in the future, as opposed to trying to preserve the ill-gotten gains of the past, and this is the quality that shines from the light of the fourth soul. He is William, King of Sicily, renowned for his efforts to redeem the exploitation inflicted on his subjects by his predecessor. William was not a perfect ruler, though he seems to have acknowledged that as well. A consciousness of failure, with a corresponding desire to learn, led him to heaven. It is another manifestation of the dynamic shared by David, Trajan, Hezekiah, and Constantine. They had an eye for divine justice, and how it must judge the mundane exercise of power on earth, and so they find themselves above the eye of the eagle.

If this mix of Jews, pagans, and one late-convert Christian is partly explicable, the fifth soul throws out any easy interpretation of the conviction that only Christ saves. Dante sees a soul who is otherwise almost invisible in history. He is Ripheus of Troy, a hero whom only Virgil recalls. In The Aeneid, Ripheus is described as "foremost in justice and zealous for the right." It was this attitude that carried him to divine life.

Dante is shocked. Who on earth would think that Ripheus knows more of God's depths than many Christians? The eagle is delighted at Dante's surprise. It knew it had surprises to unveil and appears to sing and swoop like a lark.

Dante cannot contain his perplexity. How can it be, he exclaims — which is ironic given he is receiving an answer to his question: whether or not you are born before Christianity or without Christianity has no bearing upon your salvation. He is struggling to accept it. Incidentally, it is also worth noting that Virgil's judgment of Ripheus was right, implying that Virgil understands enough of these things to save him, too.

The truth is that what matters is not whether an individual has accepted Christ explicitly. What matters is whether the individual has the capacity to cultivate the openness, desire, and assent required to embrace the reality for which Christ stands. I think the implication with the appearance of Ripheus is clear: everyone is bound for heaven, when they are willing. Everyone is able on account of having been breathed into life by the spirit of God. In principle, everyone can say, I am more than I am, as everyone is a child of God.

The eagle describes it as being baptized before baptism, which makes sense because the rite of baptism is only the sign of dying to self to welcome much more than oneself. He has seen that being filled with the virtues of faith, hope, and love means that an individual can share in the widest reality, which is similarly shaped by faith, hope, and love. So, too, receptivity and delight are qualities that bring individuals into divine life.

Dante hears words that could not make this point more clearly. The kingdom of heaven will suffer violence, the eagle explains, meaning God is prepared to let everything that people assume about the kingdom of heaven be rocked and shaken to the core. What matters is the desire to know God. It meets God's desire to be known. Birth, creed, and rank do not count. Love does. If your soul can harmonize with reality, like the many souls in the sphere of Jupiter beaming with as many iridescent reflections of divine light, you will participate in reality, at depth.

Predestination is also on the eagle's collective mind. The jovial bird explains that the point of this doctrine is not to disturb, confound, or belittle human beings, as if God were writing off lives before they had begun. It is, rather, to show how divine wisdom exceeds human attempts to grasp it. Affirming what is not known matters as much as asserting what is felt to be established. The seemingly proven is likely to be undermined in heaven. That is good because it feeds the fires of love, which opens the mind to greater insights.

It is the spirit of Jupiter and the essence of divine, as opposed to Church, justice. The souls glow more brightly, rejoicing in the extensiveness of God's love, which Dante appreciates. It reaches across all creation. How could it be otherwise, when all creation is already sustained by the Creator?

Dante is in Saturn, though its glory must be disclosed gradually.

PARADISO 21
Receptivity

ANTE IS GAZING ONCE MORE AT BEATRICE. HE
has turned back to her, having received the eagle's revelation. It is
a natural response. He has seen more and knows that this is likely
to precipitate further cascades of glory.

She is not smiling, not out of displeasure, but for his safety. If I smiled,
she tells Dante, you would become dust like Semele, who had asked to see
Jupiter's splendor with her own eyes and had not been able to bear the sight.

It is possible to see God too soon. It can be a terrible thing to fall into
the hands of the living God. The risks are manifold: ego inflation, flooding

and psychosis, the severance of head from heart, spiritual bypassing that is addicted to love or, conversely, a fear of the awesome fearlessness of love.

Dante is not yet ready for additional wonders although they are already in the next heaven. Their arrival in Saturn is seamless. Knowing that all can be saved, and why, has opened his eyes wider, and he must adjust. After all, it is quite a leap. Christians, then as now, do not expect heaven's gates to be open to those whose hearts are open. They would prefer a name check at the door.

Saturn's light is appropriate for the next stage of Dante's ascent. Saturn is the father of Jupiter, which spiritually speaking implies a closer proximity to the origin and source of things. The saturnine period was, therefore, associated with peace and harmony, though it was the age that witnessed the birth of time, as creation sprang from the divine and so fell away from the divine. It is for this reason that, in common speech, the saturnine refers to a melancholic consciousness, the mood that arises with an awareness of decline and death.

The heaven is quiet. It withholds its brilliance for Dante's benefit. He is grateful. He does not want to be a tree blasted by a thunderbolt, he reflects. He must evolve, as he has been doing through the planetary spheres. There is no reason to rush the seventh and last. The moon taught him that qualities shape reality. Mercury taught him that qualities are revealed through paradox. Venus added the love that can see beyond the manifest. The sun's brilliance revealed the subtler lights of glory. In Mars, he learned about the inner sacrifice that participates in the unceasing flow of life. In Jupiter, he saw that divine generosity is open to all. In Saturn, he will learn how the individual responds to that generosity by becoming a willing receptacle of divinity. It's a process. He wouldn't want to be shattered.

Dante looks at Beatrice, still beautiful, if not smiling. His trust in her is paramount in this heaven. He needs his guide.

Look around, she suggests. Turn from my face. He must adjust to the unfamiliar, which means turning toward it while monitoring how he responds to it. He must watch for the moments that feel overwhelming, pause, and then seek out the qualities within him that can rise to meet the qualities he feels around him. He will discover how he can match Saturn's virtues, and know how the glory around him is within him.

A ladder materializes in the air. It gleams, reaching beyond the limits of his sight. It is akin to Jacob's ladder that, in the patriarch's dream, stretched between earth and heaven. It is the ladder that will lead Dante out of the planetary spheres and into the region of the fixed stars.

Myriad golden lights descend the ladder, as if the stars in the sky were pouring down. Dante is reminded of crows that, in the morning light, variously stand to catch the early rays, wheel about to find the best spot, or fly off to try another perch entirely. There is a sense of having to find your own way to feel the divine warmth. The process is dynamic and personal. Some will sit still like a hermit. Others will try different modes of life. Others again may turn to alternative traditions altogether. It doesn't matter, so long as the individual loses nothing of themselves, nothing of their love, nothing of their focus.

A soul from the throng moves toward him, seemingly sent, and delighted by the opportunity to welcome Dante. Dante is quiet. He doesn't want to get ahead of himself, though Beatrice tells him to release his deepest desire and speak, which he does. What have you to tell me, he humbly asks? You have come from extraordinary heights! He adds, Why is this heaven quiet? I have heard music below.

There is no singing because the sound is closer to the music of the spheres, which is beyond the range of mortal ears, the soul replies. Similarly, Beatrice's smile is concealed because her love is one with the love that burns above.

The reply raises a thought in Dante's mind. How is it that this soul, whoever he is, was capable of absorbing such an intensity of light, when most souls are not capable of it while alive on earth? Remember that the souls in paradise appear to Dante at levels which reflect what they learned while alive, for all that they share in the highest glory too. He might also have predestination on his mind, a subject that had only recently been raised by the eagle. Does God ordain what we learn on earth?

The light starts to spin. It luminesces from within, revealing an internal energy that strikes Dante as like the momentum gained by a millstone revolving at speed. The vitality is distinctly alarming.

The soul was a contemplative in life. He became able to know divine light on earth without impediment because he recognized that his being was, at base, divine light. His way of life revealed this perfect receptacle. God's light focused on me, he explains. It pierced the light of life that otherwise already held me. That power combined with my own powers of perception and sight, so that I became more than myself, capable of actively participating in the brilliance of the source of all light. You see my joy in the bright clarity of my presence.

Then again, he continues, do not seek to understand what I describe. A seraph close to God could not explain it either. But it can be known, it can be experienced: that awareness is the goal of life because it is the condition of life. So beware, he adds. If mortals on earth seek this light, they will find their vision clouded by the smoke of confusion. If angels in heaven cannot explain it, no human mind can grasp it, and no human mind should presume to do so, though this is only because it cannot be achieved, only realized.

It is the lesson the mystics learn. A point is reached at which their efforts, their discipline, their learning, stops. The giving way is a letting go. If they don't realize this truth, their efforts turn against them, as the ascetic life becomes merely harsh, ramping up to extremities that grow masochistic. The path is joy and freedom, not punishment and repression.

Dante is fascinated. He asks the soul its name, which the light reveals as Peter Damian. He was a well-known contemplative in the medieval period, and it is doubly interesting to hear what he says because he was famous for his discipline, to the point of being a disciplinarian. Ecclesiastical authorities sought to capitalize on his charisma and enthusiasm, and he wore the cardinal's hat for a while, becoming a prince of the Church. Only, he took it off. My sense is that Peter Damian is telling Dante that he learned that severity does not lead to spiritual illumination. If anything, it dulls and, potentially, destroys it.

Instead, he entered a hermitage, lived simply, and discovered true receptivity, which he can demonstrate to Dante in Saturn, at least to some degree.

He offers Dante a glimpse of bliss but does not hold back from lambasting the Church on earth. His hermitage has grown degenerate, he continues. The life of cardinals has become decadent, with prelates needing servants to support their bloated bodies. When they ride on horses, he adds, it is hard to tell where the equine behind ends and the priestly posterior begins.

His critique is fierce. I am not exaggerating it. Its strength reflects the magnitude of the blessing that these priests have discarded and obscured. Spiritual materialism is quite as destructive as being burnt to a cinder by the sight of God.

More souls descend the ladder. Their radiant whirls envelop the rungs, in a crescendo of lovely light. They assemble around Peter Damian and, while coming to rest, let out a tremendous, terrible cry. Thunder could not drown it. It is so loud that Dante is at a loss to find a terrestrial comparison. He cannot hear what the souls might be saying. And with the roar, the canto abruptly stops.

Dante becomes capable of the light of Saturn as Benedict descends the ladder.

PARADISO 22

Awe

DANTE IS OVERCOME BY THE THUNDEROUS CRY
that resounds through the sphere of Saturn. Like an alarmed boy
darting to his mother, he turns to Beatrice, seeking her steadying
presence as the boy seeks safety to recover.

You are in heaven, Beatrice explains. Nothing here happens that is not
motivated by a zeal for righteousness, as everything is holy. You are shaken
by a shout. Imagine if the souls had sung, or I had smiled!

I think of the moment as like hearing the crashing chords of a great
symphony, or seeing a vast horizon suddenly appear over a mountain ridge.
It is terrific: terrifying and tremendous. It is the jolt of glory. Dante has been
on his long pilgrimage to prepare for these moments, so that when he sees
the ray of divine light lighting up his soul, and realizes that this brilliance
is the radiance of all creation too, he is not turned to ash by the shock. It
must also be that when the presence of divine intelligence illuminates the
shadows of his life, he is not mortified.

The exclamation is a prayer, Beatrice continues. It is for God's judgment,
which you will understand before you die. It comes at the right moment,
neither too speedily nor too slowly, except for those who fear it.

The remark is hard to understand. Commentators tend to wonder if it is a reference to events Dante will witness before he dies, as if God will right wrongs in the Italian civil wars, though I am inclined to conclude that she is referring to the timelessness of judgment. It is always acting to expose error and failure, which can feel like vengeance and a sword, though is aimed at remedying and redeeming.

Don't be concerned immediately with that, Beatrice says. Instead, look at the souls who are flowing down the ladder into this heaven.

Dante is anxious. He is being asked to reach deeply within himself to join the hundreds of eminent, blazing spirits. They are flaming balls reflecting light as if an array of perfectly aligned mirrors. It is beautiful and dazzling. He is alarmed but longs to know who they are. The most magnificent globe of light moves forward, reading Dante's silent desire to understand. It knows that Dante is burning, as he seeks to comprehend the contemplative wisdom that had been described to him by Peter Damian. He is in the right place. The love that illuminates the approaching soul perceives his desire and will not hold back from responding to it.

The soul reveals who he is and, in doing so, tells Dante much more than he thought he sought. It is the generosity of heaven: desire is offered knowledge that brings a satisfaction which exceeds what desire can imagine. The light is Benedict, the founder of Western monasticism. He describes establishing his monastery on Mount Cassino and does so in an interesting way.

Benedict reminds Dante that before he arrived at the place, it was inhabited by pagans who worshipped the divine in older ways. They lived in a time before the one who came down from heaven, he explains — the one who had revealed to humanity how to see God in a new way. The pagans were not mistaken. Rather, Benedict had good news: the Christian dispensation was inviting them to receive the riches of reality in a way that had not been possible before. It was extending their consciousness, not threatening condemnation.

I think Benedict can be understood as referring to the development of the individual so as to become capable of perceiving the divine I AM. This is only possible when, unlike Semele, souls can look on God and not feel themselves crumbling. As Owen Barfield argued, the first step is self-knowledge. It is a quest that had begun to emerge in the centuries before Jesus, with the birth of Greek philosophy and the cries of the Hebrew prophets. The time was right for the man from Nazareth to instantiate the type of personhood that could know itself completely, and so completely know the life of God. That had not been possible before, which is why Yahweh had told his followers to turn their backs as the presence passed by.

Canto 22 seems to invite such an interpretation of the unfolding, not only because Peter Damian has already stressed the individuality of the contemplative way, but because everyone who appears in the canto is described in terms of their parentage. Dante has already been referred to as a son before Beatrice, his mother. Toward the end of the canto, the planetary deities are identified by the names of their parent. The effect is to stress the significance of the next generation, as if Christianity is part of a long process of evolution.

Western monasticism is the way of life necessary to incarnate this promise. It readies the individual, by demanding that they search themselves in a shared life, so as to become a receptacle fit for the conscious awakening of God. Benedict is not just an illustrious soul, though he is that. He is a key figure in the shift from the ancient perception of reality to the medieval, which finds its fulfilment in the mystical capacity to participate directly in the heavenly light.

The prospect continues to attract and unnerve Dante in equal measure, as well it might. Can he tolerate the experience,? Does he have grace? As a sort of test, he asks to see the details of Benedict's face, here and now. If he can bear that, it would be a comfort: Benedict shines as a soul who actively participates in the image of God, so if Dante can bear the sight of the saint's face, as opposed to just the saint's light, it might imply that God's unmediated presence would not crush him.

Dante has not seen the faces of any souls since the sphere of Mercury. He has been acclimatizing to their luminous vitality. And Benedict replies that this is not the moment, Dante cannot see his face, though the time will come, in the highest levels of heaven. That is a place with no pole-guiding north star, Benedict adds, which is to say it is in a domain of reality beyond the celestial heavens marked by the planets and stars. If Benedict had brought a change of consciousness to the pagans of Mount Cassino, Dante will discover that shift of awareness before his journey is done.

He is being invited to maintain his course, to stay the path, and it is a good call. He feels himself opening up like a rose in the sun. Part of what must happen, I sense, is that Dante must see his own face in a true light. Then, he can see the faces of others, and God.

The task is not aided by the decadence that has overwhelmed the foundation on Mount Cassino, Benedict continues. People may hope to climb the ladder to heaven, but the basis of monasticism, his rule, is no longer worth the parchment it is written on, he explains. As he looks back to earth, he sees lives dominated by worldly obsessions. He sees souls trapped in a mundane flatland. He offers yet another condemnation of the contemporary Church, though it serves to highlight the path ahead for Dante, by way of contrast. It also invites us to consider whether secular anxieties have overrun our lives, with the implication that they probably have.

Reform is always possible, Benedict insists. The people of Israel thought the end had come when they approached the Red Sea; they were saved by an extraordinary occurrence. Strange things happen. The lost are found. What is dire rediscovers wonder. Hope does not die. Benedict rejoins the souls on the ladder and, with a gesture from Beatrice, Dante is swept up to follow behind them. Swifter than the speed of thought he ascends the ladder to find himself in the constellation that follows Taurus, which is to say his own: Gemini.

He tells us readers that he looks back on this transition by weeping for how far he falls short of the great revelation he knew. It is as if, during the rest of his life on earth, he forced himself to see himself, which must be a result of the experience of communing with his birth sign. Gemini represents many things but, in part, it carries the memory of the instant the divine spirit reached down and breathed life into him as he was born. It is where his mortality meets immortality; his humanity is enwombed in the divine. It is the place of his aboriginal blessing and he sings Gemini's praises.

He visits Gemini because, within its particular aura, he can reflect on his individuality. It is where he first became capable of uttering "I am," the crucial step to consciously embracing the I AM. He wasn't only made human, he was made Durante di Alighiero degli Alighieri, as his baptismal name is thought to have been.

Dante feels how he is loved by the time of his birth. He feels the life that became his life. It is the distinctive way in which the universe shaped him.

You are very close to blessedness, Beatrice avers. This felt understanding of your incarnation presages a felt awareness of God. And so, look down and see where you have come from. Take it all in.

From the vantage of the fixed stars, Dante peers back. He sees the earth. It looks paltry, and human preoccupations seem trifling. He is having an experience that many have felt, whether in dreams or as out of body experiences, when they look at themselves from above, perhaps way above, and see the twists and turns of their lives like a winding river in a deep valley: markedly modest compared with their destiny, the great ocean of being.

He sees through the spheres of Latona's daughter, the moon; Maia's offspring, Mercury; Dione's child, Venus; Hyperion's descendant, the sun; Jupiter's son, Mars; Saturn's son, Jupiter; and Jupiter's sire, Saturn — each living power and intelligence described in parental terms, each speaking to Dante of what his life was and what lies ahead. He sees how much has changed for him, and how change is the way of the cosmos. The change is a return to God, a return that he perceives consciously and self-consciously, as he is held by the constellation that was present at his birth.

He is ready to move on. His turns from the planet that he thought was his home, earth, and gazes once more into Beatrice's eyes. He knows that his true home is elsewhere.

In a series of shattering visions, Beatrice helps Dante steady himself.

PARADISO 23

Blaze

BIRD TENDING CHICKS PERCHES IN SILENCE
through the quiet hours of the night. She looks at her offspring.
She looks for the first sign of the sun. She longs to restart her work,
to forage and bring food to her young. Beatrice looks similarly vigilant to
Dante, at the start of canto 23. The image recalls the pelican in her piety
who nourishes her brood with blood from her breast, imitating the love
of God for humanity.

Dante waits, as well. He longs to feed. He yearns to mature. And he lets
himself absorb the richness of his anticipation, which is spiritual food in itself.

He doesn't have to wait long. Beatrice is watching the zenith, the high point
of the sky which, when the sun reaches it, means the daylight is at its greatest
intensity. Like the bird watching the horizon, she expects a bright dawn.

This is a canto of visions. The first is, briefly, of Christ. A second, of Mary,
lingers. And the first one breaks in the heaven above Dante, blazing with

389

stars. They share the same spiritual light as the sun, and the poet describes them as being lit by the sun. Beatrice is reveling in the sight and she declares them, the Host of Christ. Her holy happiness and flaming face pass beyond description, Dante tells us, as the source that she anticipates shines.

Christ is like the full moon, outshining the sparkling glory of the night. He is the living light that is the luminescence of all other lights. He is sun of the sun. Instantaneously, if momentarily, Dante sees it, though Christ is so bright that Dante's eyes cannot endure the sight. For the blink of an eye, he perceives the mystery of humanity's embrace in divinity.

He is stunned, and calls to Beatrice: Guide, sweet one! She explains that he has seen the wisdom and power that bridges earth and heaven, which is the cause of all fervor. It has overwhelmed him, though it is a foretaste of what he will see — perhaps in part a consolation, having not been able to see the face of Benedict. He has experienced a strength that can never be overcome, and he will know it once more, at the end of his journey, which is the goal of all life.

Her explanation causes his mind, momentarily, to burst again. It is like a cloud which builds up so much charge that it ruptures in lightning and thunder. He cannot yet consciously contain Christ, though he is about to see the women who could, and he will learn how.

Beatrice springs to his rescue. Look at me, she commands! He comes back to himself, as if waking from a dream. She infuses the exact amount of delight he can embrace, which is no mean amount. Dante says that all the muses could not have provided one thousandth of the verbal power he would need to convey the loveliness of her face, glowing with truth.

Dante addresses us. Be kind, he implores, if the vessel of my poetry struggles to navigate a clean path through these glorious waters. I am mortal. I seek to speak of immortal things. The weight is bound to make me stagger. Then again, he continues, if he were not prepared to risk everything, he would have no chance of transmitting even a fraction of what he sees.

We must make a leap too, over his words, as he leaps to the ineffable heavens. Love can do that, powered by desire, for all that descriptions fail. He will give his all, as he has learned from the wisdom of Mars and Jupiter. He will be filled with the origin of all that is, as were the whirling flames of the ladder in Saturn. For now, the failure fires further fervor.

Restored, Beatrice asks why Dante looks at her. The second vision has appeared. Look there!

It is Mary. She is described as a garden flowering with Christ. She is a rose that bore the Word of God, and is surrounded by lilies that are the apostles, the souls who first perceived the new way. A beam of sunshine will break through the clouds and bathe the land in golden light: the effect is an echo of Mary's presence. She is the morning and evening star, the forerunner of the sunshine and the remembrance of sunlight. She is the one who ensapphires the sky, Dante continues, with a neologism: the azure blue mirrors her gorgeousness. The light we see with mortal eyes is a manifestation of the light that can be known by the mind's eye.

I think Mary appears at this point because Dante has reached another crucial juncture. He has seen more of himself than he had known. He has seen, for an instant, the incarnate Christ. So, he sees Mary in order to initiate learning from the one who agreed to become the birthplace of God. And he can see her. He is ready to begin to learn.

There is music, which makes earthly song sound cacophonous. An angel descends with a crown of stars. Commentators suggest this is Gabriel, who appeared at the annunciation and appears again to encircle Mary once more and lift her back to God.

Dante cannot track her return, as yet, though he lifts his arms in the same direction, like a child reaching out to its mother, grateful for food. His gesture reflects the love he perceives in the celestial entities that blaze in Mary's wake. They sing the *Regina Caeli*: "Joy to thee, O Queen of Heaven!" Dante praises the abundance of the cosmos, and the wonders of life. He will follow her. The fascinating question is how.

Dante must delight Peter with his insights about faith.

PARADISO 24
Faith

EATRICE PRAYS TO THE FELLOWSHIP BEFORE
them, which enjoys the feast of heaven. She asks that they might
bless Dante, who by the grace of God travels to these heavens
before his death. She asks, Can they bedew him with a few drops from the
source of all insight to quench his thirst?

The happy souls begin spinning in circles, like comets swirling around
poles. They remind Dante of the wheels and cogs in a clock, each moving
at their own speed as determined by their construction, informing the
movement of the whole.

The brightest light in the dazzling array spins away from the joyful
ensemble and, amidst music so exquisite that it lifts Dante's mind out of
time, and so also out of memory that is a function of time, circles Beatrice
three time.

It is Saint Peter. He has been released to them from the high sphere by
the love in Beatrice's request. He is driven by munificence. Beatrice asks

that he test Dante on matters of faith, which raises a question: how can a test be a kindness?

"Faith" is a word easily misunderstood, as is the suggestion that Dante is to be tested. To my mind, this is not an examination in the usual sense. It is not as if the continuation of his journey rests on achieving a pass mark. Rather, Dante's task is to celebrate faith in a manner that reflects the richness of this eighth heaven of the fixed stars. He will show that he is fully in harmony with it, and can willingly enrich its song, and so participate without resistance in its life. Dante's "test" is a chance to express the way his intellect, love, and sight are ready. Peter comes as his partner in joy.

It is the right moment because he has learned, with the vision of Mary, that rising to the greatest experience of God is about being infused with the extraordinary light of God. Her womb became a meeting place for heaven and earth. Like the contemplatives, she was simultaneously enwombed by the divine. Dante will manifest his own readiness for God consciously to reside in him, as he resides in God.

This type of faith is not about a forceful assertion of convictions, or a nervous fealty to God. It is about knowledge: a living awareness that life is rooted in divine life, with that being the basis from which awareness can grow. It is the faith that seeks understanding, to cite Anselm's phrase, which means that it is already to some substantial degree understood. If Dante's faith were really ignorant affirmations, it would not have carried him this far. There is no place for either fundamentalism or fideism in paradise. The soul must embrace the light, through and through.

Dante's intelligence, in the sense of mindedness not cleverness, increasingly resonates with divine intelligence. His speech can carry a ring of truth, which will show up in the way his words cause the souls to whirl and dance. Like the presence radiated by a great work of art, this is the sense communicated in his words. This is what Peter wants to hear and delight in.

The saint is asking in a manner akin to the medieval mode of inquiry called *disputatio*. A student would stand before an examiner and be asked a question. The task of the pupil was to respond in a way that expanded the perceptions of the listeners. The aim was to show that the inner meaning of the matter at hand is known as a direct experience, not as a report, confession, or proof. It is the opposite of learning by rote. Neither is it modern artificial intelligence that increases with processing rates. In a *disputatio*, a response would explore this and that aspect of a question, playing and riffing, keeping the subject open and alive, before building to a climax of silence, as the one speaking and those listening touched the majesty of realization.

The doors of perception would be cleansed by the exchange, revealing the infinite, to use William Blake's phrase.

Dante's desire can bring down such insight. All that he has undergone has readied him for it. The erotic can join the intellect, as Dante feels in the brilliant presence of Beatrice who stands beside him. As Peter asks him to talk about faith, he feels the living waters from the eternal fountain welling up inside him.

He begins with a familiar expression, reaching for the words of Paul: "Now faith is the assurance of things hoped for, the conviction of things not seen" (Heb 11:1). Faith is sure understanding, known as an energy inside the soul. It generates confirmations of the reality hoped for, in the form of experience, argument, and action, and it fosters the emergence of greater insights to come. It is a framework within which desire, personal development, and rational discernment can blossom.

Peter asks Dante to raise his game. What comes first, he continues: the sure understanding or the confirmations of the reality to which the understanding attests? The understanding, Dante replies, otherwise any confirmations would be built on sand. Faith is not the same as sophistry or persuasion. Its purpose is to illuminate not fabricate. It might speak of things that seem impossible though, with the eyes of faith, the seemingly fanciful or implausible can be seen taking shape.

"Do you have this faith?" Peter addresses Dante directly, and he answers with an uncompromising declaration: "Yes I do!" It is the coinage with which he lives his life, he continues. It is polished with use in his pocket. It is shining with heaven's brightness. Dante's affirmation mirrors Mary's affirmation. He is ready to bear the divine.

Peter pushes on: How did you gain this coin? It is a gift and possession, Dante replies, received from the living Spirit of God, channeled through the pages of the Old and New Testaments. He has read the Bible with insight. He knows how its words reach to a meaning beyond the words. This is partly shown in the miracles of life, he continues, as Peter asks for more. By miracles he does not mean exceptional events that demonstrate God's existence, as if God mostly sat around doing nothing, bar the odd intervention. One of Dante's great interlocutors, Thomas Aquinas, has corrected him on that. The theologian had explained that miracles can't be divine interventions because the whole of existence, all of the time, depends upon God's activity for its sustenance and maintenance. The moment God stopped "intervening" would be the moment the cosmos ceased to be. What people consider to be miracles are, therefore, moments when they wake up to the ongoing, uninterrupted divine endeavor. They reveal the truth of reality. They create an experience of growing awareness into the expansiveness that is always, already here.

Peter takes a dig at Dante, using an old debating trick: isn't your argument here circular, he jests? Aren't you assuming it's all miraculous in order to confirm the miraculous? Dante replies in the same spirit. Don't tell me you can't simply look at the cosmos and not see the miracle of creation, he retorts! It is what you, Peter, experienced as an apostle: you are associated with so-called miracles, but the real miracle is that Christianity took root and grew. It did so because people responded to its truths in their hearts.

The joyful assembly around them is delighted. Like the *disputatio* that comes alive, the souls break into singing. "*Te Deum laudamus!* We praise thee, Oh God," fills the sky. Dante's answers are answered with elation. Or rather, the elation was there all along and Dante's discussion of faith has made it manifest.

As if to precipitate more gladness, Peter asks Dante to capture his creed in a phrase: can he offer a summary? He can, with a combination of Christian and Aristotelian insights. God is the unmoved mover, he begins. This is Aristotle's intuition that God's eternal existence prompts all else that exists to incline toward it. Dante adds to it with a Christian inflection: the movement is love; the inclination is desire. All things that exist want God. This truth has come to him through study of the natural world, study of the spiritual world, and study of the Bible, he stresses. Each speaks with one voice.

The eternal three in one and one in three emerges from this perception, he continues, because like the diversity of creation, which forms a unified pattern in the manifold instances of the longing for God, so God can be known as a unity in diversity, and diversity in unity. "Is" and "are" are equally applicable, Dante asserts. His summary kindles a flame in his mind. It is like a star in the heavens.

Peter welcomes his words like a master embracing a servant bringing happy news, though with their Aristotelian inflections and coming from the mouth of a poet not priest, they might have been regarded more warily by Dante's theological contemporaries on earth. But here in heaven, they prompt benedictions. Peter circles Dante three times, as he had Beatrice. That is quite an accolade. But the joy is not over yet. There are two more tests to come.

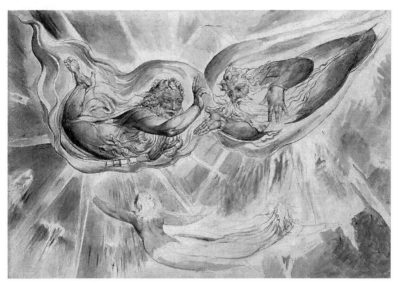

James, the light of hope, joins them, as Dante celebrates this virtue.

PARADISO 25
Hope

MAYBE THIS POEM, COMPOSED TO BRING DANTE'S visions to people on earth, will convert the minds of those who exiled him from Florence, he muses at the opening of canto 25. He was a lamb to their wolves, though with a mature voice and a golden fleece to show them, he might become their poet, to be crowned with a laurel wreath at the font where he was baptized. After all, no less a saint than Peter has just made himself into Dante's crown, spinning around him three times.

It is at once an expression of hope against hope, when it comes to secular matters and, when it comes to the celestial, a confession of the knowledge that his words have been blessed in heaven. He believes his poem is a receptacle in which heaven and earth meet. He has labored to forge it. He has changed and donned a garment of authority like the one retrieved by Jason and the Argonauts. Dante almost asks, If his warring compatriots don't see it, will you, dear reader?

396

His hope of release from the punishment of exile is undiminished, though that thwarted longing — which will cause him devastating heartache — does not lessen his awareness of a future in the heavenly city. The latter hope is called forth by the approach of another saintly light. It is James, the name that is associated with hope in the New Testament. I put it like that because there are several figures called James in the Gospels and epistles. James the Great was one of the three inner disciples who witnessed the transfiguration of Jesus, the raising of Jairus's daughter, and the suffering of Jesus in the Garden of Gethsemane. They are three intimate moments which speak of hope. James the Less was the author of the epistle that bears his name, and which discusses hope. There are two other people called James as well, also associated with the virtue. So, the James approaching Dante from among the fixed stars bears the archetype of hope and personifies its presence.

He descends alongside Peter and the two apostles greet each other like doves. They coo and nuzzle as love birds, joined as if married by the love that they know and share. Dante is astonished. He resorts to a Latin phrase to express his delight: *"coram me!"* he says, "before me!" There is an intimation of the marriage of Francis to Lady Poverty in its use, because the word "coram" appeared in Thomas Aquinas's biography of the saint. You might say that Francis placed his hope in poverty, trusting it would bring riches, and his hope is implicitly remembered here again.

Beatrice speaks to James. Illustrious life! You have written of the abundance of heavenly life. Make hope resound through it now! In short: ask Dante to celebrate the second theological virtue.

James cannot help himself. The very thought advances a summary of hope from him: all that rises from the mortal world will find its fulfilment in divine love, he says.

Dante looks and listens. He can tolerate James's light. He can take it in. He has faith and is ready to celebrate hope.

There is a link between the two virtues, which is implied in another feature of the canto. James is repeatedly referred to as the second flame. It is as if Dante is intimating that the two flames, James and Peter, become one when faith and hope are combined in love. To put it another way, it is as if the presence of faith and hope automatically precipitates love, as will happen when the third apostle, John appears. The three virtues are linked in a manner that mirrors the three of the Trinity. One quality leads to another, much as the godhead emanates three persons — the faith of understanding being akin to God the Father, the hope of return being akin to God the Son, the love of that return being akin to God the Holy Spirit.

James then obliges Beatrice's request. What is hope, he asks Dante? How does it prosper in your mind and where does it come from?

It is highly significant that not only is the second question answered first, but that Beatrice answers it. Her intervention is, I think, a beautiful development of the moment Dante had encountered his beloved in Eden. At the top of Mount Purgatory, she had chastised him relentlessly for hoping in the wrong things. She had instilled wonderful love in him, and he had turned to distractions. He had hoped in other loves, other beauties. She even silenced the angels who took pity on Dante and tried to sing a psalm about hoping and trusting in God.

She is recognizing that, in the ascent through paradise, he has learned to trust in the right hope. His hope is now secure, and so she tells James that as she sees into the mind of God, and so also into the mind of Dante, she finds a heart overflowing with hope. She explains that this is why he is making this journey ahead of his death. The implication is that even in the darkness of the wood, when he had strayed from the path, he remained receptive to hope, and could respond to Virgil, whose appearance brought hope to him.

Her answer is a lovely touch. Nothing is left unresolved in paradise. Her gesture also saves Dante the tricky task of having to boast of the hope within him.

They are working together, and Dante speaks next, singing answers to the first and third questions. First, he cites a sentence from the theologian Peter Lombard. "Hope is the expectation of future bliss, given by God's grace and received by human merit" (*Sentences*, III, xxvi, 1), he says. The two elements must work together. After all, divine blessing is all around, wherever there is light, a smile, a pattern, a desire. But it must be accepted, which requires an inner adjustment, or merit. Without such excellence, hope can misfire, as Dante's did, for a season — though the wonder of divine hope is that it uses such errors to reveal the ignorance, thereby fostering longing, which brings the knowledge, that kindles right hope. This is Dante's experience, and it's an instance of the way in which human beings are invited to cooperate with the divine. Without that invitation, they are left seemingly at the whim of a deity who chooses some and excludes others, perhaps most. Far better is Dante's vision, that God pours hope on all, indefinitely. Like the sunlight, it remains steady, and so waits to be felt and received.

This vision of hope was instilled in Dante, he continues, responding to the third question, via the light of many stars. David, the composer of the psalms. James's own letters. Dante adds his own name to the list as well. He knows that his own poem will instill hope in the world. He sees that he is a co-worker with James: the dew that James brought to humankind precipitates further showers, of which Dante's art is one. It may seem like a boast, on Dante's part, but it is not. Like his clear affirmation to Peter's question about whether he has faith, he is affirming that he knows of hope and spreads it. At this stage in his journey, he can state truth unashamedly, joyfully. He can share the light.

James is delighted. He flashes like lightning, which reminds Dante that James the Great is called one of the sons of thunder in the Gospels. He has savored Dante's replies and so asks for more. He continues, What was the promise which this hope imparted to you?

Hope is found wherever you look, if you look aright. This is effectively how Dante replies. It is in the Old Testament. It is in the New. It can be detected from the beginning of time to the end, and throughout the whole of creation. The hope of joining the marriage feast of heaven is in the prophet Isaiah. The wedding garments are celebrated in the Revelation of Saint John the Divine.

The whole heaven breaks out in a psalm: "Let them have hope!" Beatrice isn't silencing the angels anymore. She can answer for him. He can answer for himself. Their now harmonious, joint response is itself a celebration of hope. Like the love birds, Peter and James, they too seem married in their joy. Don't hope for too little, the image seems to say.

This reading carries us to the final set of images in the canto because the theme of the wedding feast comes to the fore, as a third flame emerges from the same source as Peter and James. It shines so brightly that if it were a star in the Crab constellation, which is high in the sky in the dark winter months, it would turn winter into a continual day. It would dispel darkness, which is an indicator that the third flame is that of John, and the light is that of love.

The blaze rushes toward Peter and James like a bride happy on her wedding day. Beatrice stands alongside, sharing the glow. She confirms that the third flame is John, saying this is the one who lay on Jesus's breast at the Last Supper, as well as the one who looked after Jesus's mother following the request of her Son from the Cross.

That said, Dante becomes confused. He looks at John, presuming he would be able to enjoy the brilliance as he had done James. But he can't. Worse, he is not just momentarily dazzled but blinded. After the triumphant delight following his articulations of faith and hope, he finds he cannot see. Here I am in the high heavens, he says, not able to see paradise, not able to see Beatrice.

My sense is that Dante is able to see faith and hope but is still learning about the linking element of love. It is the bridge between heaven and earth: it is the quality embodied in the Incarnation, it holds the human and divine together. And he needs to understand more, and can't quite as yet, which is why he is blinded when he looks at John. It also seems that superstitious stories about John have flooded his mind, and they obscure his vision.

One in particular is a legend that John bodily ascended into heaven when he died. John detects it in Dante's thoughts, and explains to Dante that he did not. During his mortal life, he did not become fully transparent to the divine, the combination that led Jesus and Mary to ascend. John adds that Dante should explain that to his contemporaries by including the explanation in his poem, as he has.

To put it another way, Dante has tried to detect a miracle in John's bodily assumption, having only just decried yearning after such exceptions. Or it may be that he is not yet ready to see the faces of saints, as Benedict had explained, and in trying to see whether John is manifest before him in an embodied form, as opposed to as light, he has reached out too quickly, too soon.

We are left unsure as well, and the canto ends surprisingly. The music ceases. The air stills. In his imagination, Dante sees rowers pausing as the whistle goes and blades are raised from the water. There is silence from the river, as there is silence in heaven. We too are held in suspense like the oars, waiting for the next move.

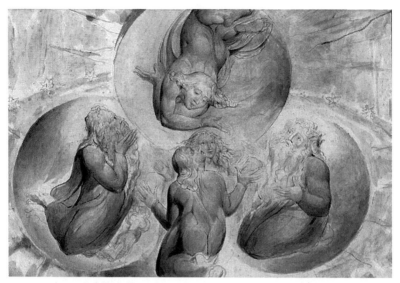

Dante is blinded and must reignite his capacity to see in heaven.

PARADISO 26

Love

ANTE IS BLIND. HE HAS NOT ONLY BEEN DAZ-
zled by the appearance of John, the apostle of love. His sight has
disappeared entirely. He cannot even see Beatrice.

This extraordinary moment is in the heaven of the fixed stars. Since he
entered paradise, Dante's sight, understanding, and pleasure had seemed
to be building uninterrupted. My sense is that he has tried to look at John
in the wrong way. He is backtracking. A further development in his ability
to see his own face is necessary first.

One point is clear. While the high heavens are replete with rapturous
feelings and marvels, as the bounty and accord of reality becomes clearer
and more evident, the difficulty of discerning more does not lessen. Each
nudge toward greater intimacy is precise. Each inflection grows more consequential. Remember: Lucifer fell from the greatest height.

Dante is temporarily knocked off course, though the souls around him,
including Beatrice, do not seem alarmed. They know another feature of

paradise: nothing goes eternally wrong. Seeming misturnings, including catastrophes and condemnations, are reincorporated into the path. I think this will ultimately prove to be the case even for the most beautiful of God's creatures, locked in the wasteland of hell.

John assures Dante. Beatrice can restore his sight as quickly as it disappeared, much as Ananias cured Paul after his vision on the road to Damascus. There is a clue in that reference. Paul thought he was on the right path. He was full of zeal for cleansing Judaism from the error of Jesus. He was on a mission of love. But his love was misguided. Being struck blind stopped him in his tracks. He was forced to reconsider, reflect, and reset.

Many spiritual traditions speak of moments of disorientation close to enlightenment. The Sufi's call it bewilderment. There is also the risky absorption of passion so as to understand its every nuance, as is practiced in Tantric traditions. Apparent setbacks must come close to the summit because they would simply dislodge a quester if they struck any earlier. They are particularly associated with paths that follow erotic love. It is a powerful way of aligning with the divine. It is tremendous but tricky. If the possessive element of eros has left Dante, he is still learning to let love carry him forward, prior to the juncture when it can be born within him, as it was in Mary at the hour of the Incarnation.

Dante has not had a Damascene experience. His is a correction or adjustment, which John works by telling Dante to focus on his soul's desire. Look inward, the apostle says. It is the most reliable of spiritual instructions: if in doubt, seek to know yourself further, because there you will find God and that which blocks your awareness of God.

Dante retreats within himself. He returns to his center. Love addresses him in various ways he remarks. As he reflects on his experience again, he sees how love can strike boldly, as it did when he first saw Beatrice, or with nuance, as it does more commonly, drawing the individual toward what is beautiful and good. Love is always calling in the soul, Dante continues, referring to love as the Alpha and Omega. But however it calls, the calling must be understood to be followed.

John's encouragement continues. Dante must find a sieve, he says, to sift through love, which is to say that Dante must speak of love, as he has of faith and hope. He must say what love is, and how he has established himself on its way, and the very act of speaking will bring further clarification. And he does so, with clarity and focus, and notably, without using extended similes or extravagant turns of speech. It is a tender moment of consolation. Inner intelligence regains its shine again.

Love comes from God, Dante avers. Its stamp can be detected throughout life. It is known in the good, and the more the good becomes known, the more love becomes evident, in a virtuous spiral of longing. In this way, it orients the soul increasingly firmly.

As that happens, a concurrent dynamic becomes clearer. This is the realization that the things, creatures, people, thoughts, and perceptions that can be called good are themselves reflections of that which is good and lovely in itself. The path of love does not just open onto the good in the cosmos. It directs toward God.

This truth is attested in the story of Moses being shown God's magnificence, Dante continues. It is embedded in the opening lines of John's own Gospel: "In the beginning was the Word" (Jn 1:1). Only a mind that sees love could write that.

You are speaking truly of love, Dante hears John reply, so say more. What other ties draw you toward God, how does love bite into your life? It is a striking metaphor. I think John wants Dante to say more practically how he knows love works. He has described that the arc of life tends toward love, so how does it actually achieve that telos?

Dante provides examples. Awareness of existence itself comes first, the sense of being alive. The bliss of being, with its quiet astonishment and shine. Inner reflection reveals the presence of sustaining love.

It is why people give their lives in love, he says next. Jesus is the exemplar. Others do it in big and small ways every day. They know that life holds them in love and that they can let go into life. Ultimately, there is nothing to lose because everything always was given by love. The giftedness of life speaks of it.

Life shows love in its beauty too. It bites into him quite tangibly when he sees a leaf and becomes aware that every facet of the natural world is the garden of the eternal gardener.

With this final remark, he hears sweet music break out around him. "Holy, holy, holy!" the host of souls cries. The music is back. The silence is broken. Moreover, his sight begins to return. It is like waking from sleep to the daylight, he explains. First, an undifferentiated glow penetrates the eyelids. Then, the individual blinks and strives to focus. He feels Beatrice driving out everything that had clouded his vision and, further, realizes that he is seeing better than he had before.

The improvement is proven because, before him, as he sees again, are not only the three flames and Beatrice, but a fourth light. Another soul has joined Peter, James, and John. Heaven always has fresh delights to reveal.

But this one doubly surprises him. He feels like a treetop pushed back by a gust of wind.

It is Adam, the first human being that the Creator made. I think Dante sees him as the next step to seeing his own face, which is to say, his humanity. The process had begun in the constellation of Gemini, when he had experienced being loved by his time of birth. He is now seeing the love at the birth of humanity, which is to say the love that sustains all human beings. It is coalesced in the extraordinary sight of the aboriginal human figure — Adam not as a historical individual but as an archetypal, embodied presence, though I also don't think the medieval mind insisted on such distinctions in the way that modern perceptions require. Adam was created aligned with God and enjoyed communion with the divine, before the fall. Seeing Adam, Dante is seeing himself, in the lost innocence of original participation, to recall Owen Barfield's phrase.

Immediately, Dante has questions. He knows Adam is aware of them, given paradisal telepathy, and says he won't speak so that Adam can speak sooner. His desire is back to full strength, with his extended sight.

Adam trembles like an excited animal. A pulse of delight ripples through him. He is only too happy to oblige. He knows Dante wants to ask four questions. How long ago was Adam created? How long was he in Eden? What is the truth of the fall? And what language was spoken before that happened?

The questions have an inner logic, which Adam unpacks by answering the third question first. It is the most important for Dante who is on his return to communion with God, and Adam's remark is very interesting.

Adam explains to Dante that the problem in Eden wasn't eating from the tree of the knowledge of good and evil. It was the way the first humans rushed to eat it. They bit into its fruit too early. They were like Lucifer, and not wholly unlike Dante had just been, when he rushed to detect the truth of the legend about the apostle of love. He was thrown, for a moment. They were thrown for an age. They could no longer see the narrow gateway through which participation with God, coupled to consciousness of themselves, might be found. They followed the possessiveness of love before they understood how it could carry them from Eden back to paradise. This fall is why Dante has had to make his journey: to learn what had not been learned before. And yet, there is wonder in that. Dante has the benefit of learning it for himself, not simply being born into it. The fall is a blessing to him and humanity. It makes possible a new creation and incarnation, within which even estrangement and death has no power in separating people from God. Instead, it leads to an expanded awareness of the extent of love.

Adam turns to Dante's questions concerning timings. He explains that he and Eve were in Eden for six hours, and that they were created many thousands of years ago, which means that their return to paradise took many thousands of years as well, in the wait for the birth of Jesus. It is the quality of these periods of time that matters, not their precise durations. Adam is saying they fell quickly, overwhelmed by the richness of Eden, and that their recovery of the path to God was long, arduous, and costly. The human story is a comedy, but the sense of alienation is profound.

And yet, however entrenched, nothing is ever completely lost. This insight is embedded in Adam's answer to Dante's last question, about the language of Eden. They spoke a divine language, Adam explains, that emerged by osmosis from creation itself. I imagine it seeping into Adam's being as he enjoyed the being of the creatures around him and felt the being of God. It means that language is not random, as modern theories of its origins tend to imply. They assume that language is basically functional: it evolved as a way of sharing information about sources of food, the proximity of predators, or the moods of companions. But Adam is saying that language was firstly a way of sharing joy about the wonder of creation, the intricacies of its operation, and the love of God.

I find this theory more persuasive. As Barfield demonstrated, language has always been metaphorical. Words have always carried soul. The inner meaning of communication is always active and alive in speech. No doubt, language brings, and has brought, copious instrumental benefits as well. But its utility was the byproduct of a delight in life that language identifies, amplifies, and renders conscious. Coupled to desire and perception, words reveal paths back to God. Dante, the pilgrim and poet, needs no persuading of that.

That said, and maybe because language has such powerful practical side effects, people quickly forgot, and forget, about its magic. The power it brings can eclipse the delight it imparts. Adam appears to reflect on this element by noting that language changes, as leaves on a tree fall and fresh growth springs up in their place. This is why so many languages are spoken, and that they can drift a long way from the aboriginal music of words.

A second, parallel rupture occurred in Adam's relationship with God. He explains that originally, he knew God as "I." He related to the divine as one person to another, one subject to another, commingling. God wasn't "it" or even "thou." But the early intimacy and fusion was quickly lost, in those brief six hours. God received other names, like "El," meaning "might" or "strength." Humans grew more interested in power, fostered by the power inherent in language, and projected that onto God.

From being blind to seeing back to the first day: the canto draws to a close. Dante has received another remarkable indication as to the goal of his return. It will be a recovery, with differences, of that initial experience. When he can truly say "I am," he will spin with the divine I AM as Adam had once done and does so again.

Dante is full of heaven's abundance, as Peter condemns the Church.

PARADISO 27

Reversal

EAVEN SINGS. THE UNIVERSE SMILES. "GLORY to the Father, Son, and Holy Spirit" fills the celestial air. The sound is exquisite. Dante drinks, breathes, and takes it in. He delights in an inexhaustible wealth, perfected love and peace, a manifest rapture. Seamlessly, it flows through him. He is inebriated.

The creation of Adam, and humanity, was from abundance. God's desire is to share divinity. Dante sees what we are made for.

Peter starts to glow more brightly. The apostle stands out amidst the general brilliance as his radiance alters, which he explains to Dante should be no reason to wonder. His luminosity shifts as if he were the eagle of Jupiter donning the plumage of Mars. The white light of the heaven of harmony is merging with the red blaze of the sphere of self-sacrifice. Peter is preparing to demonstrate what the Church on earth has failed to do.

He launches into a long, extended, and wholehearted invective against the institution that has become so preoccupied with its own concerns that it has forgotten divine life. Its own glory, fame, and wealth matters more than God's. What Dante has just enjoyed in ecstasy is utterly unknown to priests and prelates.

His tirade could hardly be put more strongly. The early popes, including him, shed their blood to realize the joy of heaven on earth. The medieval

Church is drinking that blood. It is cannibalizing itself in order to indulge its corrupt, petty, degenerate impulses.

Peter has one pope particularly in mind, the one on the throne in 1300, Boniface VIII. However, his diatribe clearly has wider reach. He cries to heaven, asking God, why do You hold back? Why do you allow this state of affairs to continue? It is remarkable. Peter knows the mind of God. He sees the divine wisdom. And still he cries.

The fourfold interpretation of events in these domains unpacks the meaning. Literally, Peter is a human being who gave his life for the cause and sees it dishonored. He expresses his distress and rage. Allegorically, Peter is a saint who yearns for change, for right to be restored, and delight to be spread once more. He expresses his heartfelt desire. But tropologically, Peter understands divine ways. He sees God's intelligence. His cries prompt the need to think through what it might actually take to bring about change on earth. God is not doing nothing, of course. God is doing what God always does: radiating divine abundance. Which leads to the anagogic question: how can he, we, and Dante identify that, align with it, and participate with this life? I think this is ultimately the reason that Dante hears Peter's condemnation here. There is no need for another rehearsal of ecclesiastical failures, literally or allegorically speaking. The repeat now points to the anagogic challenge. This is why it is heard in the high heavens.

Peter comes to two possibilities as his oration continues. There may be a secular solution. He talks about a great leader who might appear to bring order. He recalls Rome's defeat of Hannibal, which established the Roman Empire, though my sense is Peter refers to it in order to condemn the Church again. He is implying that the pagan Romans have done better than the Christian Romans. The earlier empire brought the Pax Romana with the rule of Augustus, which Peter knew in his mortal life.

Then, secondly, Peter turns to Dante. He addresses the pilgrim directly. You who will return to earth must not hold back in telling what you have seen, experienced, and heard. You must repeat the words you have heard spoken. Put aside their unacceptability. Be a prophet. Be a herald of a new spirit. Be the container for a new incarnation.

My take is that this is Dante's calling. His poem will be part of a new dispensation. It was spoken about by Beatrice in Eden and is repeated by Peter in paradise.

His work will resonate with other movements of the time, initiated by Francis and Dominic, as well as the injection of intellectual life, from Islamic and Aristotelian wellsprings. It will see through the nostrums of the age and toward a Christianity beyond Christianity, as I have put it. That can recover and remake the heart of it. That can expand the vision, which is to step closer to its fulfilment in a universal scope. I think this is implied by Peter's reference to Jupiter because it was there that Dante met David, Trajan, and Ripheus sparkling in the brow of the eagle.

Dante is about to move to the ninth sphere of heaven, the Primum Mobile, on his way to the source. He is returning to the origin to bring again the origin to earth.

As if in confirmation, the lights, flames, and souls of the eighth sphere leave the fixed stars and move back to the Empyrean. They are reconnecting with the truth, and they do so in a fascinating way. They fall upward. They are snowflakes tumbling to the clouds rather than the ground.

The center of gravity has switched. There is no longer any question of being dragged down. Levity rules. The heart of all things always did belong with God, and the high heaven knows it. The souls are falling back to their natural place, in the divine.

Dante watches them disappear. He can't yet follow them. There is farther to go. Lower your sights, Beatrice says. Look back one more time from where you have come.

He did so before, to take in his journey and transformation. He could see how his mind and perception have expanded enormously. I think this second gaze has a different purpose. Dante describes it: he is not worried about earth as he looks. He sees beyond Cadiz, which is to say where Ulysses sailed and dashed his hopes, and realizes that the earthly threshing ground, as he puts it, can be left to its flailing, at least for now. He looks down this second time to confirm that he is about to fall up to his true home, as the other souls have done.

Quickly, he turns back to Beatrice, the focus of his love and hope. She embodies wisdom. She knows the center and can guide and draw him, as she does. They are in the Primum Mobile.

We are in the place that receives the heavenly motion from the Empyrean and transmits it to the planetary spheres. It is receiver and conductor of the light, life, and energy of God. It is the fastest moving of the revolving spheres. It is connected to the Seraphim, the divine intelligences who share God's love most directly. They are in the place where there is no other where, as Dante puts it. It is simultaneously the center and the circumference. These living powers pass on its life force.

The description raises the intriguing challenge of how to imagine this relationship because if the Primum Mobile contains all the planetary spheres, right down to earth and into hell, it is itself contained by the Empyrean, which is also outside of it. God's dwelling circles all creation in love and light, filling all creation with it, and is also a circle unto itself.

The image is sometimes referred to as a hypersphere, the fourth dimension of the Empyrean sustaining the three dimensions of the visible heavens. The comparison is to the four-dimensional space of modern physics, and the way time might be said to encircle space, generating the sense of moving through time in space. Similarly, Dante is saying, there is the sense of moving through time, though we are really in eternity. He is drawing on insights that reach back to Plato, who had identified time as the "moving image of eternity." It captures much of what Dante sees in the ninth sphere.

Their arrival in this pristine place prompts Beatrice to rail against the greed on earth that despoils the desire for goodness. Like the child that reaches out in love for the delights that surround it, so human beings might too, and receive the loveliness of heaven. But before beards have formed on faces, Beatrice cries, human beings have forgotten about the cosmos around them, and the higher domains within which it exists, and have become interested only in the worlds they believe they control and make. Not that you, Dante, will be surprised, she adds. There is nothing of human life that you have not seen. People have neglected how to connect with the heavens.

She makes her last point by referring to the medieval calendar. It had not solved the problem of how to adjust the years to keep up with the revolution of the heavens, the reason now that there are leap years and leap seconds. Beatrice's point is that the calendar offers periodic reminders of distance and disconnection. It becomes uncoupled from its stellar reference points, much as human beings do from God.

It means that people don't know that heaven always has more in store. They miss that a new ray will shine down, she predicts, in another reference to Dante, I'd say. From this high point of reflection, Dante can absorb that his desire and love will not only bring him satisfaction. It will foster a purpose, to carry what the Seraphim know to human hearts. From this blossom, good fruit will come. It will be true to the divine source and restore heavenly awareness, in those with eyes to see and ears to hear.

I think Beatrice is alluding to the fact that we readers, pondering Dante's poem, absorbing his insights, longing for the delights he knew, are that good fruit. We are the proof of his vision, given that we have followed him thus far.

Dante gains sight of the still center, the spark of being and ever-present origin.

PARADISO 28
Imparadised

D ANTE HAS LEFT THE VISIBLE HEAVENLY SPHERES
and is in the zone that makes direct contact with the Empyrean,
the Primum Mobile. It is as much a spiritual as physical space: like
"2 + 2 = 4" written on a page, the reality is in what is symbolized, in what
it means. Beatrice has outlined the desperate state of humankind, born of
losing touch with life's meaning, which is known when earth is perceived
as a manifestation of heaven. Listening to her, Dante understands clearly,
which is itself to be "imparadised," as he calls it. He is in paradise by virtue
of the clarity of her mind and the awareness she awakens in him.

Her vision draws him. He responds to its allure freely. He describes it
as like seeing the reflection of a candle in a mirror, before turning around
to see if the candle is there, and, finding it, seeing that the mirror spoke
truly. Her eyes are the mirror for the candle of divine love and he himself
is close to turning around and seeing that love directly.

He looks at her and, in her eyes, he sees an intense, infinitesimally small
point of astonishing, brilliant light. He has gazed at her eyes many times
before, to acclimatize to a livelier heaven or to snatch a glimpse of subtler
truths, as he did when he saw the two images of the griffin flipping between

the human aspect and the divine, like a gestalt duck-rabbit. But this dot of incandescence is steady. It is nothing less than a reflection of the light of God in God's self.

It is more than a light. It is the light of lights. Eyes exposed to it directly shut at its concentration. The earth that he has seen as vanishingly small from the distance of the Primum Mobile would look like a moon, if set alongside it, he says. Today, comparisons with black holes come to mind, the physical entities with gravity of such strength that light can't escape them. What Dante sees in Beatrice's eyes is the spiritual opposite. A black hole is its negation. This is the infinite source from which the light of creation pours, and upon which the light of creation depends.

Circling the mind-blowing singularity are concentric coronas, looking like halos around a light source seen through mist. They are rings of fire, whirling around the center at speeds greater than he has experienced so far in the spheres of the heavens. The first and closest is fastest, the second tracks that speed, as the third does the second, the fourth the third, all the way up to the ninth, which moves with the least swiftness, though still with a lovely alacrity.

The pattern is the opposite of the visible spheres that, with the still earth at the center, had sped up as the arcs widened, to the high speeds of the Primum Mobile, sustained by the Seraphim. What he is seeing is the reverse form: the closer to the center, the greater the dynamism. Beatrice explains that because the central light is being itself, the twirl of the coronas becomes swifter as they come closer to the source they love.

Dante is bewildered. He knows that freedom and space increase with proximity to the divine, as well as swiftness and movement. But what he is seeing appears to show a constriction, akin to a weight spinning on a string that accelerates as the string shortens, and so with less room for maneuver.

Beatrice confirms that the point of light and haloes are difficult to understand, at first. His mind is like fingers struggling to untie a knot that is so tight it is unclear where to begin. So, she suggests the mental flip she has invited him to consider before.

Instead of thinking in terms of quantities, which implies that more space equals more freedom equals more joy equals great good, think in terms of relationships and qualities. Then, it is intensity that counts: more focus equals more freedom equals more joy equals great good. That is what he is seeing.

She doesn't say so, but I think this mirrors the truth of love. The more it infuses the individual with its distinctive quality, the more of life the individual can embrace. The one attitude can accept anything. Or it is like seeing into the essence of something, and thereby making sense of the whole. An example is the small number of natural laws that can account for a vast range of natural behaviors, because lawfulness is a singular principle that usefully describes much of nature. In theological terms, this is the meaning of simplicity: the common unity present in a diverse multiplicity. It explains the focus of the spiritual quest, when the whole of life comes to be experienced as reflections of the one desire for God, leading along various paths, but in the same direction.

Beatrice unpacks the ramifications of this insight by explaining how the smallest crown he sees spinning closest to God relates to the largest spinning sphere in the visible universe, namely the *Primum Mobile*, where they are currently. The second relates to the expansive, though not quite so spacious, sphere of the fixed stars; the third to the heaven of Saturn; and so on, down to the narrow confines of earth. The notion of the hypersphere comes to the modern mind once more, and the awareness felt intuitively of an inner dynamism implicit in the three visible dimensions of space, which we call time. The physicist, Carlo Rovelli, has explained how Dante's imagination could seemingly anticipate Einstein's insights by six centuries. In short, it is because it was not constrained. "For Dante, just as for Aristotle, space is only the structure of the relations between things, and that structure may adopt peculiar shapes," he has written (*There Are Places in the World Where Rules Are Less Important Than Kindness* [London: Allen Lane, 2020], 36).

Dante sees what Beatrice means. Her words are like a fresh wind that clears the air bringing good visibility to the day, he says. He understands, truth shines, and more appears to him, as happens in heaven.

Scintillating sparks shower from the coronas of fire that encircle the source. They are like embers leaping from molten metal in a furnace. As he looks, the number of them grows, augmenting by the thousand. He thinks of the exponential growth arising from doubling the number of grains placed on successive squares of a chess board. Before long, the sparks have become too many to count.

The explosion of activity arises with his perception that intensity makes for more vitality, not less; relationship is what is truly spacious. He is seeing the angels of these domains, the living creatures who love the light. Reality is not about abstractions, or patterns, or dynamics, or force. It is alive, through and through.

Its quality is felt, rather than measured. He enjoys experiencing it, with multidimensional perception. Intuition is enhanced by his senses, not limited by them. Imagination is clarified by his reason, not dismissed by it as fanciful. Intelligence is about resonance, receptivity, and insight, not closed systems of self-referential logic that shut out the living, relating world. His mind is drawn by the aesthetics and playfulness of the heavens, which he doesn't pin down, but appreciates. Its energy is gripping. What he sees satisfies his desire with desire, like a crescendo that never stops. As is the case with great literature or music, which gives more as it is relished more, he is led into more nuance, more brilliance, more secrets.

Thought itself comes alive. Ideas are not electrical pulses buzzing across neural networks, though they may correlate with synaptic firings. Concepts are not just clever constructions. They have a life of their own. They come into our minds, much as words come to our lips, from a wider consciousness that speaks through us as much as being spoken by us. Angels are called living intelligences for this reason. They are the Virtues, Powers, and Principalities that guide the forces at work in the world. When genuine angel seers perceive angels, my guess is that this is what they are seeing. They have a spiritual synesthesia, like being aware of the sound of shapes or the color of numbers. They detect what Barfield called "the inside of the whole world." It's alive.

Dante hears a loud hosanna. The angels are singing to the light of lights that is their eternal home, their perpetual *ubi*, or whereness, as he puts it. Beatrice calls the nine circles by their names. The first and second are the Seraphim and Cherubim, who are most like God. The Thrones come next, close to it too. This first triad delight because they see, enjoy because they know, love because the understanding of God fills them to the brim.

It fills the angels who come next, as well, though in a different way. The second triad are in the bliss of an eternal, overflowing spring, Beatrice suggests. The Dominions pass divine knowledge to the wider circles of movement, first to the Virtues, who are angels of the great cosmic qualities like faith, hope, and love; and then to the Powers, who keep the cosmos in its dancing order.

The third triad dance divine life in the realms of experience with which human beings are most usually conscious. The Principalities inform the souls of regions and countries, Archangels bring messages from on high, and Angels attend to the lives of individuals.

They form a hierarchy, each playing a part in a cascading chain of being. They are not restricted in their place as if graded or oppressed, but delight in transmitting the light from the blazing source across a refulgent universe. They all know the fullness of the music, like players in a celestial orchestra.

They excel in their own way and savor the whole. The outpouring from God flows through them and sharing that extravagance is their freedom.

There is an interesting detail in Beatrice's description of the ranks in the heavenly hierarchy because Dante is implicitly correcting the order from the one he gave in his earlier work, *The Convivio*. There he had followed the insight of Gregory the Great, who had the Principalities in the second triad and the Virtues in the third. The order Beatrice gives corresponds with that of Dionysius the Areopagite, who had written about the orders of angels and, in fact, coined the word "hierarchy" to do so. It is a correction that has meaning. Dante can change his mind because his love and desire to know are better informed by the vision and intellectual perception this journey is bringing. Beatrice remarks that when Gregory died, he saw his mistake as well, and laughed. Errors are good in heaven because, when acknowledged, they are simultaneously the occasion to see more.

The canto ends with another reflection on the often-cloudy perception of mortals. Don't worry about contradictions, even squabbles, Beatrice implies, for all that religious people clearly can and do indulge them. Worry, instead, about how much of the truth you have glimpsed. Imitate Dante, whose desire to know God, as opposed to correct others, led him to these sights. Followed through, they will carry you to the heart and source of reality.

The unity of the eternal and temporal is explained by Beatrice.

PARADISO 29
Eternity

ANTO 29 OPENS WITH ONE OF DANTE'S EXTRAOR-
dinary astronomical visions. Imagine the dawn on the vernal equinox, he writes, when the sun is rising on one side of the sky and
the full moon is setting on the opposite horizon. It is the moment when
the day is born from the night.

The children of Latona, as he calls them, Apollo and Diana, the sun and
the moon, are each crowned by a constellation of stars. The sun is set against
the backdrop of Aries, the moon against the backdrop of Libra.

Next, in your mind's eye, look up. At the pinnacle of the great dome
of stars, set like a jewel on the summit of a tiara, is the zenith. It can be
imagined as the pivot upon which the scales of the sky hinge. Only, for an
instant, on the equinox, the sun and moon are in balance. They are equally
visible and seemingly stationary, before the sun appears and the day begins,
as the moon slips below the horizon.

Dante's point is that for such a magical moment, Beatrice's eyes were
fixed on the divine point that Dante's eyes cannot yet bear. Her face radiates.

She tells Dante what he longs to hear. She is looking at the source in which every place we would call where, and every moment we would call when, coincides. She enjoys a timeless moment, set in eternity.

Adding to the allusion is the way Dante constructs the opening twelve lines of the canto. The opening and closing words of the tercets are the same: "*quando*," or "when." The middle word in the tercet is "*emisperio*," or "hemisphere." The poem mirrors the cosmic balance Dante invites us to see.

The further implication is that the temporal and the eternal coincide. They are not opposites or complementary but intertwined. Beatrice holds sight of the eternal, Dante invokes the temporal with his astronomical moment, and sees how one is infused with the other. Metaphysics doesn't come after physics, as the word "meta" originally meant. Metaphysics embraces physics, as physics expresses aspects of what is meta. We catch it in moments of balance, when our vision expands across dimensions and we see in depth. It is the sense Blake had when he held infinity in the finite palm of his hand, and eternity for the period of an hour.

The canto as a whole is a meditation on the relationship between the eternal and the temporal. It begins with the divine perspective, *sub specie aeternitatis*, which Beatrice perceives. She describes how God created, not to increase goodness, which is already infinite, but to reflect that goodness in the multiple beings of creation. Each can proclaim "I am," she says, and so echo the divine I AM.

The story of creation unfolds in her account, like a great swoop from eternity, across time, and then back to eternity. The heavens and earth are formed. The beings who inhabit the spheres appear. Humanity falls. Civilizations disintegrate in petty squabbles. Then, surprisingly, she realizes that the fighting and quarrels are a digression.

She uses that word in the canto, implying that fallen life is a digression. It is important because when these events, that can seem so preoccupying, are reframed as a temporary detour, the mind's eye is freed. It can look up once more and return to celestial goodness and love that was unchanged all along.

It is almost as if the fall didn't happen, though it did, and marvelously became the occasion for the return. The phrase "*felix culpa*," or fortunate sin, catches this understanding of the fall, though it can only be understood in this happy way when creation and incarnation are seen to be God's central, continual act. The coincidence of God and humanity is the temporal mirroring of the eternal creativity. If the fall is seen as a fault, a disruption to God's plan, then the focus shifts to the Crucifixion, interpreted as a necessary intervention to redeem the situation and get humanity back on track. It is an understanding that I take Dante to have rejected because it cannot account for the bigger truth: that the divine I AM is the unstoppable fount and unperturbable foundation.

It's reflected in the fact that we, human beings, can talk about having an identity. That doesn't make sense biologically, because the human body continually replenishes itself. It doesn't make sense psychologically, because people change, sometimes dramatically through trauma or illness. It doesn't make sense philosophically, because identity is impossible analytically to pin down. And yet, we think of ourselves as integrated individuals, the same person when we die as when we were born. And the intuition is right. We came from God and we are returning to God, changing in the sense of actualizing our potential, and not, in our essential nature, disintegrating due to the vagaries of time.

In spiritual and wisdom traditions, this is the recognition of the participatory nature of our "I am-ness." Also called returning to the center or seeing with the "private divine face" by Sufis, it knows that the deepest truths are found in subjectivity, not objectivity. There is a part of you and I that doesn't change, as the objective conditions of life around us shift all the time. Constancy is in the interiority that shines all around.

It is the difference between experiencing within the sphere of the earth and the sphere of the Primum Mobile, with its unmediated line of vision to God. It's the difference between feeling all is transient and perceiving a relationship between time and eternity. It is asymmetrical, because without eternity, there would be no time.

Beatrice explains how this is so. Before the creation of the cosmos, there was no after or before, because there was no time: it is not as if God were idle until the divine bow shot a threefold arrow into life, she continues. The three arrows correspond to the three domains of existence that Dante sees. One is pure matter, the realm of earth. The second is pure form, the realm in which the angels sing. The third is a mix of matter and form, the realms through which Dante has been travelling as the heavens of the planetary spheres.

It can be envisaged as a cosmos of potential and perfection. Matter carries potential, which is perfected when shaped by form. Form injects the love of perfection and desire for the divine.

Then, Dante adds a correction to an earlier Christian source, for the second time in as many cantos. Much as Gregory the Great had spotted his mistake about the ordering of the heavenly hierarchies, so Saint Jerome must have laughed at his oversight in suggesting that the angels were created before humanity. Beatrice explains that this could not have happened because it would mean the angels were idle in the period before the worlds of matter and form were made. But they cannot be idle, any more than the sun cannot shine. Conversely, the Dominions do not work at passing divine knowledge across the cosmos; the Virtues do not work at sustaining cosmic qualities; and the Powers do not work at maintaining the cosmic order. It is simply their nature and joy. They exist with these qualities of existence to perfection, in the sense of every aspect of their potential being actualized. Their excellence is why they know delight.

It explains the manner in which Lucifer fell immediately after the creation: Beatrice says you could not have counted from one to twenty before it happened. The tragedy for Lucifer is that, had he practiced his art, he would have loved it. He would have learned what human beings learn in time: that there is greater joy in being carried by love, and sensing it being born inside you, than there is in trying to possess it. That kills love because it uncouples love from its infinite wellspring. And sources cut off from the eternal fountain freeze and run dry.

Beatrice explains that, as a result, Lucifer feels crushed by the weight of the universe. He is trapped in a monstrous depression. The levity of existence cannot reach him. He knows only separation and nothing of the circulating mingling of the angels with the intelligence to rejoice in the infinite quality of goodness. Unlike him, they stay lambent, like a stained-glass window designed to catch the sun, knowing that there will always be more light to enjoy in the ways that they can refract and reflect it. Their worth is the extent that they do so, a value that, in heaven, is permanently set to maximum.

This prompts another amendment from Beatrice about a theological misunderstanding of angels. They share understanding and will with human beings, which is to say sight and love. However, they do not have memory, as some say. Her point is that memory is a product of experiencing time. It is an attempt to hold onto the past and so enrich the present. However, in eternity, there is no past. Each moment, if there were moments, is fully present. Memory gives way to complete cognizance. There is nothing to be reminded of.

It's an interesting reflection because one of the marks of enlightenment among humans is sometimes described as time diaphaneity. The enlightened soul appears to time travel because all instances of time are immediately present to them. The effects of the past are known. Past lives are said to be now. Similarly, the recovery of memory is a mark of healing from trauma.

When a memory is known, it is present. It no longer has to be forgotten to protect the individual from its damaging effects.

Beatrice becomes ferocious in her reflections. She is in the section of her account of creation contemplating the digressive disintegration of humanity after the fall. She points out two key troubles. One would nowadays be called narcissism: the attempt to command, charm, or intimidate people so as to secure what you want. It is fatal when, unchecked, it convinces practitioners that they have godlike powers of persuasion and they fall in love with themselves.

A second trouble is the skepticism that attempts to explain away signs of divinity in the world. Beatrice highlights an example from Christianity. She says that the darkening of the daylight for the hours after Jesus's death, as described in the Gospels of Matthew and Luke, is not to be understood as an eclipse of the sun that happened to occur at the same time. The darkening was a spiritual perception that the spiritually attuned perceived. And we need that spiritual perception.

Parallel skeptical examples that do the rounds today would be explaining the Resurrection as trauma induced hallucination, or the feeding of the five thousand as a spontaneous outbreak of sharing. To reduce these stories in this way is a disaster because it blinds the eyes that might see farther and blocks the ears that might hear more. It keeps people in the flatland of earth, divorced from heaven.

"Jesus said, preach truth, not preach garbage," Beatrice asserts, adding that those who do so are being dictated their lines by devils.

Then she stops. Enough of this digression, she says. And she returns to the eternal view. She and Dante are in the *Primum Mobile*. They are standing in the light of God. They are on the cusp of eternity. They can see how the one light is mirrored in myriad ways through the generous cascade of creation. The multiple reflections from within all beings distribute the one light. As a crystal in the sun will sparkle in a blaze of color, so the divine light divides itself — although, in so doing, it only celebrates more fully its unity.

Dante enters the Empyrean and the direct experience of divine light.

PARADISO 30
Empyrean

I N ASTRONOMY, DISTANCE MEASURES TIME. WHEN Dante opens canto 30, remarking that noon is 6000 miles away, he is mapping the circumference of the earth onto the circumference of a twenty-four-hour clock. Between sunrise and noon, the earth revolves a quarter of its circumference, which is a distance of about 5000 miles, given the complete circumference is about 20,000 miles. Add in another 1000 miles, to make 6000, and the time he is describing is an hour before sunrise.

Aurora is just beginning to spread her golden fingertips across the night sky. It is the blue hour before dawn. But why does Dante ask us to contemplate the hour via distance? This is one of his imaginative exercises that opens the mind to the felt experience of the canto.

Dante and Beatrice are in the Empyrean. They have spontaneously left the *Primum Mobile*, and the eternal light diving itself across the cosmos, and remaining one within its center, is simultaneously the circumference containing everything. Space and time collapse in this zone. All is present, proximate, and pellucid to God. 6000 miles? Seven hours? It makes no difference.

The Empyrean reminds him of the hour when night fuses with day because the dazzling light of lights is commanding the scene. It is, he intuits, self-contained. Outside of it there is literally nothing, not even an outside. And as he perceives more of its infinite brilliance, the angels of the nine hierarchies are eclipsed, like early morning stars absorbed into the growing light.

He is forced to take refuge in Beatrice's eyes while his capacity to appreciate their intensity strengthens. Sight has an outer and inner aspect. Outwardly, additional light means seeing more, be that in terms of distance, nuance, or clarity. But to gain that benefit, inward adjustments must be made. The ability to focus, organize, and understand the accumulating information must grow in tandem with the added light. It is a bit like receiving the first pictures of an alien planet. It may take decades for scientists to understand what they are looking at. Interpreting the image requires imagination and tenacity, as well as analysis. Dante must draw on resources of inspiration, desire, and understanding to see the Empyrean. The experience will change him — transhumanize him, to recall his neologism. Nothing will look the same because he will not be the same hereafter. He will be permanently conscious of more than someone who had never seen the sight.

Even his body is altering. In this domain, which is simultaneously outside of the cosmos while containing the cosmos, the stuff of which we are made manifests potentials that are rarely seen on earth. Matter transforms as it more fully expresses the form, or living vigor, that shapes it. It is like splotches of oil paint that, when applied to a canvas, morph into the sun and sky. The potential within the paint is actualized by the artist. Dante is in the final stages of becoming all that he might be as a human. He is becoming one with the divine, or rather, able to see what was true all along.

As he rests in Beatrice's beauty, her radiance grows, and words fail him. He reflects that if all the effort he has made, throughout his life, since the first moment he clapped eyes on her walking the streets of Florence, were combined together, they would not be up to the task. Other poets must see whether they can capture beauty in ways he has not managed. The time for that arduous labor is behind him.

Words are intermediaries. They transpose perceptions from one mind to another, much as musical notation carries the music from the composer to the player, and a drawing conveys the image from the artist to the viewer. But some emotions and experiences are best left to silence. The effort to capture them reaches a point when it becomes counterproductive. It is a bit like the phrase "I love you." Its very ordinariness means that it can disappear into the shared moment when lovers say it to one another. If one lover decided to quote some Shakespeare instead, the other might well tell him to shoosh. Before they kissed.

Dante sees beauty itself in Beatrice. That is why there are no words. Though I think a bit of him wants to try to find more words because he takes seven tercets, twenty-one lines, to let go his genius and habit. To see it all, he has to abandon the entirety of his life's work. It must be left behind, sacrificed to the supreme vision. That is not easy, for all that, paradoxically, he could not have reached this moment without a lifetime's effort.

It is a terrific spiritual truth. Fullness comes with emptying, awareness in a cloud of unknowing, life with death. Detachment connects.

Luckily for us, Dante has a few more words still left for the Empyrean because he has not yet absorbed its fullness. Beatrice speaks of its light, love, and ecstasy, repeating these words in poetry that transfers the pulse of the animate qualities. The light is comprehended and loved. The love is good and ecstatic. The ecstasy is transcendent and delicious.

The movement is trinitarian. Light precipitates love precipitates ecstasy, as ecstasy springs from love springs from light. This is the being, consciousness, and bliss of the Vedantic texts: *sat-chit-ananda*.

Beatrice explains that they will see the angels and saints united in one. And suddenly, a light envelops Dante. The light is grace, the ray of God about which Peter Damian had spoken. It will enable him to embrace whatever brightness confronts him. He is like a candle being prepared to carry the flame.

His journey has completed his knowledge of himself and so he is able to offer himself completely and consciously. He is launched into a series of visions that fill the rest of the canto. They are preparations for the direct, unmediated knowledge to come.

The first is of a stream of brilliance like a river. Scintillating lights fly from it, rising onto the banks, which are covered by ruby-like flowers. They too blaze. Beatrice explains that he must drink of the lustrous river and, by taking it into himself, the vision will change into a more perfect image. He must intermingle with its spirit and, by becoming completely porous to it, perceive more of it.

He longs to lean down. He feels like a child who has awoken late and must feed. Its mother obliges, which is to say the river fills him.

As it does, it changes. Its linear flow diverts into a circle. This is an image of completion. Seeing it, he says, was a bit like the moment in a masked ball when the partygoers remove their headgear. Their true identities are revealed, and he sees the nature of the beings around him that had previously looked like scintillations and ruby flowers.

They are angels and saints. Moreover, he sees them in their spiritual bodies, not only as splendid sparks. His eyes are "bettered," he tells us. What Benedict advised is coming true and Dante celebrates by repeatedly using the phrase "I saw." "I saw" the courts of heaven. "I saw" by the tremendous grace of God. "I saw" things that words might be just about powerful enough to transmit in part. The glory within him and the glory about him is one glory.

There is a heavenly light, he continues, which shines to empower the souls and angels to see the light as it shines upon them. They shine in response, welcoming the enabling shining.

It is like the reflection of a mountain in a perfectly tranquil lake. If you look, it becomes unclear whether the mountain delights in its reflection or whether the reflection delights in its source. The two become one, amplifying their mutual existence: the mountain because its majesty is shared and the reflection because it loves the majesty.

The abundance of God is the same. It is not that the angels and saints increase God's goodness. They elaborate God's goodness, like an endless set of musical variations that explore what is implicit in the theme.

The vision of the circular flow shifts once more. As if becoming mountainous, covered in expanses of meadow replete with flowers and grass, which are the myriad beings who are present, it develops tier upon tier, and morphs into what looks like an amphitheater, with seats for the souls, who look down to the central light. The shifting doesn't stop because immediately the amphitheater becomes like a rose, the tiers becoming petals, the brilliant stage the heart of the bud.

It is vast, though Dante can see across its breadth and height with unbroken ease. The far is as near as the near. The number present and the quality of their bliss no longer blinds or confuses him. He realizes that in the Empyrean, there is no need for quantities through which we experience nature, like space and time, past and present, near and far, because the living power and intelligence of the angels transmits it all directly, without impediment, with relish.

An echo of this simultaneity goes on in our minds with its stream of consciousness. Where am I now, where was I yesterday, who did I see then, who is next door? Mentally, we travel through the world with little or no effort, though skill is required to control the flood of thoughts. In the Empyrean, Dante discovers he has that ability faultlessly. What he sees is distinct though without difference, like a wave on the swell of the sea, a pattern in a fractal expanse and, supremely so, the three in the oneness of God.

A momentous canto draws to a momentous close by recording Beatrice's last words. Ever his guide, she points out that while many of the seats of the celestial amphitheater-rose are full, a few are still empty. She is not counting the saved, like a numbers-obsessed prophet. This is a qualitative zone, so the implication is that many kinds of people are here, and more types are to come. There is always room for more in the infinity of heaven, without heaven being any less full.

She highlights one seat, which will be for Henry VII. He is the type of the good leader, a man who became emperor during Dante's exile and whom Dante hoped might end the Italian wars. He didn't, and actually turned into a high-minded tyrant when power came to his hands. At best, he was a well-intentioned king whose reign was a failure. Only here, that is a detail. What matters is what his soul became. Beatrice speaks of this seat both to stress that utopias do not exist on earth, which can only ever partially reflect the perfection of heaven — though it does do that — and to console Dante that suffering on earth, not infrequently caused by leaders trying to create political utopias, is redeemed in heaven. Life on earth is a preparation for the return, not an attempt indefinitely to lengthen the stay away.

Beatrice also seizes the moment for a final judgment of the Church. Henry failed because of pontifical machinations. Pope Clement V undermined the king's attempts to do good. The prelate is like a child who has a nurse and pushes care away. The pope is possessed by that perversion of love, cupidity. Beatrice sees his destination in making her judgment. He will join Boniface VIII, face down, in the cylinders of hell, she says, with the flames that might have shone with heavenly brilliance, dancing an agony on the soles of his feet.

This is no doubt true. But why does Beatrice choose to add, at the last, to the already ample amount of anti-ecclesiastical invective? It is hard to digest after the feast of divine life.

Some commentators put it down to Dante's personal animus against the popes who ruined his life, though I don't think that can be right because Dante has raged against, lamented for, and openly embraced the ups and downs of his life. The process has been a crucial part of his journey.

I think a clue is given by Beatrice's previous long speech, which ranged across the great span of eternity, time, and the return to eternity. She had called the fall and human wickedness a digression, and I suspect she is judging the compulsive politicking of the Church a digression too.

She is saying that the Church can be ugly. It can cause distress. It can persecute people in the name of the one who was crucified. It then sips its own lifeblood, sapping its spirit. And ultimately, the preoccupations that lead it to behave in such ways are an utter waste of time. They only risk its ruination. Everything returns to God because nothing really leaves God. There is no outside. There is nothing not encompassed. The most distant souls in the cosmic diversity are still part of the multiplicity of one. That is the extent of the divine. Beatrice returns to the fallen popes one last time to place them in the anagogic vision.

Dante enjoys paradise as a white rose and heavenly amphitheater.

PARADISO 31

Grace

ARADISE STRETCHES BEFORE DANTE. IT IS LIKE
a white rose, tended by a host of angel-bees. They bring spiritual
honey to the souls on the petals, sourced from the glory that shines
as a sun at the zenith.

It is a good metaphor. A rose evokes beauty of form and clarity of purpose. It looks desirable and evokes love. It is patterned and free, elegant
and layered. It is a glowing climax in the life of a plant.

Dante sees an amphitheater in paradise's expanse as well. This image
expresses the sense that the whole of life is here. All the players and specta-
tors gather around a common focus, which is a representation of life going
on outside of the arena. Dante is aware of both, as there is a light that fills
the amphitheater above and outside it, as much as within it.

The angels riding the beaming waves of light from the source have red
faces, golden wings, and white bodies. They enjoy the colors of triumph and
glory. They are so many in number that if they were swarming bees, the mass
of bodies would cover any flower around which they were gathered. But in
heaven, they block out nothing. There is only one light, so the angelic covering actually illuminates further the already incandescent. Their presence
amplifies the light in which they fly, so Dante feels he sees it all the more.

There is joyful, generous activity. There is harmonious, free unity. There is plurality and plenitude. Dante sings in praise of the triune light. There is one star blazing and thrilling all other lights.

The sight brings to his mind the constellation of the Great Bear, Ursa Major, that is tracked around the sky by Ursa Minor, the Little Bear. Thinking of the heavens being traversed brings pilgrimage to his mind, particularly the moment of arriving at a destination which is more magnificent than anything seen before, such as the Lateran Palace in Rome, one of the greatest in his day. Or there is the pilgrim who walks to see the handkerchief of Veronica, the famous relic that was said to carry the impression of Jesus's face. She was said to have used it to mop his bloody brow on the way to the Cross.

My guess is that these images come to Dante's mind because he is at his destination. He has tracked the great stellar presences like a younger star. He seeks the divine face.

But the images are also prophetic. The Great Bear and Little Bear, a mother and child, resonate in his mind because he is realizing that Mary is key to the last part of his journey, the forerunner of contemplatives whose bodies shine with light as her belly filled with Jesus. She bore the child.

Dante's love, which began with a greedy infatuation that organized his mind around whom he longed to hold, and then transformed into the love that is a vehicle upon which to ride to greater heights, develops further. He can take love back into himself, not as a possession but as a flow from perfection, thereby enabling participation with perfection. Mary knew God primarily because God was conceived within her. God was part of her. She contemplated the divine in her own person, in her womb, in her body and soul. There is one final shift Dante will make.

Then, almost out of habit, after he completes his survey of paradise, musing on these things, he turns to meet Beatrice's eyes. And she is not there. She is gone. In her stead is an elder, dressed in celestial robes. He will guide Dante through the last steps: Dante must complete the journey without Beatrice because that completion can only come when he is complete within himself.

The elder is Saint Bernard. To Dante, he was the greatest exponent of the contemplative love known by Mary, so he can communicate the last mysteries to Dante freely. He was also the preacher of the second crusade, which is a complication for us, knowing what those militarized pilgrimages entailed, although as was seen with Justinian's aggrandizing zeal, and Henry VII's failed efforts, what matters in heaven is the passion which fosters desire for the divine, while acknowledging how confused it became on earth. Bernard felt that Christianity had severed the links with its spiritual origins, symbolized on earth by Jerusalem. He hoped that the reconquest of the holy city would re-energize lost souls.

He appears like a tender-hearted father to Dante, radiating the devotion known by the blest. Dante asks where Beatrice is. Bernard replies that he is at Dante's side at her request, because she has taken her place in the great white rose. Dante can see her if he raises his eyes to the elevated tiers. There Beatrice sits, as her capacity for God allows.

He sees her. She is crowned with eternal light. She is far off, though it is also as if there is no distance between them. She has stepped beyond him, although there is no distance in the Empyrean. And Dante sings in praise and thanks. She gave him hope and strength, endured entering hell, and shared her excellence so that he could awaken to grace. She showed him the path to freedom. He prays that she will remember him so that, when he dies, he may retrace the track once again.

Beatrice looks down, and smiles, before turning back to the eternal light.

Bernard tells him to fly, with his eyes, through the heavenly garden. Its splendors will prepare him for the supreme majesty, assisted in particular by the example and transmission of Mary. He moves through the petals and recalls the pilgrim who reaches Veronica's handkerchief. That person might have wondered whether Jesus's face really did match the image. Bernard picks up Dante's thought and tells him that he will not reach the consummation of his quest until he looks up at Mary, in the highest seat, reserved for the Queen of Heaven. She did not see the imprint of Christ. She knew him as a mother knows a child, intimately and directly.

Dante raises his eyes toward her. It is like watching the sunrise, alongside which the other lights of the rose look like fading sunsets. It is like glimpsing a mountaintop and seeing its blazing summit catching the light. She is the brightness of the stellar zenith, a flaming flag of peace. The saints on either side of her appear dimmed in comparison. Her radiance is surrounded by a thousand angels, each beaming distinctly their glow and love.

He does not try to reach for further words to describe the bliss. His descriptions are properly coming to a halt. We readers must leap in our imaginations to enjoy the sight. We must know it in our minds, not just as a reflection in a poem on a page.

Bernard joins his gaze to Dante's, focused on the fire that fires him. Dante feels Bernard's devotion. It increases his own ardor. Their love is not in competition. It is not possessive. Joining together, for it is already one, it grows.

Bernard takes Dante on a tour of paradise.

PARADISO 32

Gathering

ANTO 32 CAN BE READ FOUR TIMES, EACH ITER-
ation raising a reader's sights higher. A first reading inevitably
tends toward the literal, as the outline of the tour of heaven Dante
describes in the canto is absorbed. The second becomes more allegorical,
as the reader ponders what the details Dante portrays might mean. The
third grows tropological, as we ask whether we can sense anything of Dante's transports of delight? The fourth tips us toward the anagogic, as the
penultimate canto in the great Divine Comedy might and must. It is at the
threshold of the extraordinary end.

Literally, Bernard takes Dante on an expedition around paradise. They
see the tiers of the mystical rose that is also a heavenly amphitheater. The
seats are filled with lots of saints, lots of lives, lots of love. Dante appreciates
the unity of the multiplicity, sharing the one light, though a reader might
ask why souls are assigned this particular seat and not that one. Why is
she here and not there?

For example, while a Christian would expect to see Mary in the best seat, he might not expect to spot Eve seated beside her. The temptress, the fallen and banished one, the mother of cursed humanity. What are we being invited to contemplate in this celebration of Adam's helpmate? Has the standard story been entirely re-written?

A tussle begins in our minds, prompting the allegorical take. Eve next to Mary might mean that the beginning and the end are being represented. After all, the fall was the *felix culpa*, the happy fault. Eve's act becomes Mary's "Yes." The rush to know God led to the path by which to know God: the teachings of Mary's son and the fulfilment of humanity. This makes more sense of Eve's presence, as Christianity is not a gnostic faith. It does not teach that humanity is trapped in a prison of materiality, awaiting rescue and escape. It teaches that humanity is trapped in the ignorance of misunderstanding, wrestling with the restoration of sight and a return to communion with God, which Eve enjoyed at the start. She was Adam's over-reaching guide, but also made from his rib, created for glory. Her glorious presence beside Mary witnesses to a story culminating in the freedom to know God, with the knowledge of good and evil.

Bernard's tour is notable for the many other female saints they encounter. The first five he highlights for Dante are women, from the Hebrew Bible as well as the New Testament. It makes sense. The story is of creation and incarnation, not sacrifice and substitution. The latter, which may stress the Cross above the incarnation, feels more masculine. It makes men like the centurion wonder who Jesus was. The former, which puts birth center stage, feels more feminine. It leads Mary to ponder these things in her heart.

Dante sees women as he thinks of the account he has heard. God's creating is an emanation. God's Incarnation triggers new life. Upon reflection, it is no surprise that this vision of liberation looks female, as Dante sees in their radiant faces.

This is the manifestation of divine action, though it raises doubts, even here. In fact, especially here, in the Empyrean, having left Beatrice, seemingly near completion, there are questions. Dante himself stresses the fact by using the word for doubt three times in the canto. And that might be no surprise, once more. Desire is the beginning and end of this path. It prompts his inquiry, it fosters the yearning for fresh dimensions, and it sustains his openness to infinity and drinking from the eternal fountain. Paradise is tropological in its nature.

Doubt is often about something specific, which nags and bothers. As might be expected in the man whom we have got to know, Dante's doubt is about justice, his particular pressing concern. Bernard is showing him many figures, from the Hebrew period, from before Moses, from the Christian period, from the pagan world. These are very different periods of time, which is to say, very different epochs of human consciousness. Dante knows that everyone is saved, I think. So, his question now is more nuanced: how is everyone saved in their own way? Doesn't the universality of this great vision produce additional injustices?

The doubt is compounded when he sees the souls of children who died before they were able consciously to accept grace, as adults. Many of Dante's contemporaries would have already been surprised that Dante encounters the unbaptized in heaven, not limbo. But elevating them creates a theological difficulty. It appears to support two standards for salvation and suggests the possibility of many more. The infants unconsciously received grace. Adults have to do so consciously. So, what are the implications of this difference?

It is a tremendous question. It continues the stretching of Dante's imagination, which is the dynamic of paradise. It keeps us in a vision that is not static. Seven hundred years after Dante, fewer might worry about the postmortem status of unbaptized innocents. Today, people might ask how different perceptions of divine life can be reconciled. If Dante's force of flight is toward a Christianity beyond Christianity, how might we talk about this vision with no bounds?

To my mind, Dante is aware of the evolutionary shape implicit in the Christian story. It doesn't just speak of change. It changes as well. Bernard talks to him about different phases of time, which carry spiritual as well as historical novelty. There is the period from the creation of Eden to the Mosaic law. That ran to the time of Christ, which tipped into another dispensation. Dante is interested in the future as well as the past. He allows for readers to continue addressing the questions he himself asked, seven hundred years on.

The Divine Comedy itself can be read as a structure to characterize a parallel, inner pattern. It can be understood to represent different positions along a spectrum of human interiority. In the Inferno, souls were trapped in their individuality. They were so entangled by the enticements or difficulties from the specifics of their lives that they became unable to see the divine light present, through, and around it. They became locked in their concerns, and in the lowest reaches, frozen by an addiction to near death.

The souls on Mount Purgatory are in a second position. They are conscious of how their individuality has trapped them and they want out. They explore the nature of their vices, the why of their mistakes and misfortunes. They have hope and take responsibility for the way their lives turned out, including the aspects that were beyond their control. And it expands their souls. They become more than they are, and so grow into the light. It takes time. It is not a magical transformation, which would mean losing yourself. Descent combines with ascent so that nothing is lost, and there are no fragments. I think this is a key purpose of time: it ensures that everything returns consciously, intentionally to eternity.

Dante has implicitly described that third position in The Paradiso. The fullness of life is enjoyed by everyone, in the particularity of the humanity that they enjoy. Faces radiate, bodies are transhumanized, individuality reflects the boundless singularity of God. People are free because their own desire has led them to the brimming satisfaction of their hearts and minds.

They are at one with themselves, with those around them, and with being itself. An echo of this state of mind can be felt on earth, when in the presence of a person who is comfortable in his own skin. He radiates quiet joy because he is fully himself and porous. He has, as it were, got over himself and so can be more than himself.

In paradise, Dante experiences this transparency with growing intensity. In the Empyrean, looking at Mary, he sees rains of bliss falling down her face. The wisdom in her mind combines with the living intelligences of the angels. Thoughts are alive in this domain as creatures, flying through the heights, mingling with souls. They hold Dante spellbound. "Hail Mary, full of grace!" the angels sing. It is a precise description and exclamation. Redounding around the sacred court, the joy compounds in her, as it is celebrated by the heavenly host.

Dante sees an angel who gazes at Mary with extra devotion, if the notion of extra any longer makes any sense. Its gaze flames with love. Bernard identifies it as Gabriel, the archangel who is not only close to God but was close to the moment God became man on earth. The celestial being's confidence is of one who has witnessed it all.

The sight leads to Bernard escorting Dante on another swoop of heaven. He greets more individuals. Saint Peter. John the Baptist. Anne, the mother of Mary. And he sees Lucia, who had carried him a way up Mount Purgatory, and assisted in the chain of hope that had led to Virgil intercepting him in the dark wood. The beginning and the end of Dante's return is present.

But they are a beginning and end that presage more. Bernard tells Dante that there is a final step to take. Dante must not trust in his own wings, full and beautiful though they have become, but must step into what he

433

doesn't know to resonate with the inexhaustible depths of eternity. There is a final step into a perpetual mode of realization.

The cycle of openness, reception, and expansion will continue with a prayer for grace from Mary — a remark from Bernard with which canto 32 abruptly stops. The hiatus is full of meaning. It enacts what the prayer is for: a final jump into the unified sight, the conscious meeting of the human and divine, the end of The Divine Comedy.

Dante participates in the love that moves the sun and other stars.

PARADISO 33
Beyond

AINT BERNARD HAS ADVISED DANTE OF THE
need for a prayer, and he is offering it, as canto 33 opens. It is for
grace, and it enacts the nature of that grace, thereby receiving it
as well as requesting it. It is a good prayer.

Saint Bernard expresses the impossible paradoxes of who Mary was. He
describes her as the daughter to her son. She is a virgin mother. This is a
maternity that is more than human: a maternity that can nurture God in
human form, in a womb that was itself made by God. Enigmas pile up as
Bernard prays.

He talks of Dante, the man who has travelled all this way, seen all these
things, and longs for the mist of his mortality to be dispelled. Bernard
longs for Dante to see immortal mysteries directly and with his own eyes.
He says he longs for it more than he has longed for anything else, which
seems unlikely, except in infinite realms, every thought and feeling can

carry full intensity because everything is fully realized. Infinite love gives infinity to all. Bernard's prayer shares that extravagance.

I think the most important moment comes when he stops. Mary remains silent. She has not spoken yet and will not do so. She doesn't even smile, though Bernard and Dante don't doubt that she has heard him.

It turns out that the prayer is a preparation, and my understanding of the moment Bernard stops draws on an essay about detachment by Meister Eckhart, the Dominican who was a contemporary of Dante. Among other things, he was a contemplative who understood detachment, and his exemplar for what he regards as the highest virtue is Mary. Eckhart notes how she is celebrated for many things, as Bernard has just demonstrated. She is hailed for her humility. She is praised for the love she has for her son. And yet, Eckhart explains, her detachment was more precious than anything else. It is not, of course, that she was aloof or impassive. She was engaged and dispassionate.

It is an invaluable quality because it is unlike humility, love, longing. They are powered by human concerns, to be less or to know more, as the human soul reaches toward the divine. They are, therefore, colored by human perceptions and needs.

Detachment, though, is empty. It is a potential space. Into that womb can descend the complete vision of God, unimpeded. God can wholly and perfectly fill it.

To my mind, Mary shows her detachment in response to Bernard. She doesn't speak or smile. She doesn't shine more brightly as she turns her eyes back to the divine light. She is identified with God. God is already completely, visibly expressed within her. Dante can appreciate this final nuance in her "reply" to the prayer. He is ready.

Bernard turns to Dante, to tell him to look toward the eternal source as well. But Dante is already looking. He knows.

It is a remarkable moment because the canto simultaneously contains several references to the efforts Dante is still making. He strains toward God. He yearns for the vision. But I think what is going on is that he is remembering all that he has been through, as Bernard had reminded him in the second part of his prayer, so as to let it all go. He needed his passion to arrive at this moment, and now it must cease. Feeling his interiority is prior to his self-emptying. The striving is to prepare for it falling away. This is probably, partly, a matter of exhaustion, but more importantly, of perception.

You might put it like this. The kind of intelligence that Dante shared with Virgil in hell was practical. It was about problem-solving and decision-making, not unlike what is called artificial intelligence today. The type of intelligence they shared on Mount Purgatory differed. It was emotional. It can explore experience and feeling, and discern, via intuition and sense-making. It connects with others. But there is a third type of intelligence which has become increasingly important in paradise. Spiritual intelligence arises with a growing awareness of the essence of all things and then it tips into detachment. It seeks to know the ground of being, not the symptoms or problems of living. It is the steady source of intuition, the unchanging intuition within understanding, the condition of knowledge. It is the secret core that knows I am, and rests in the divine I AM.

It can sound obscure but is actually continually present. For example, if you have a conversation about beauty, you may or may not agree with your interlocutors about whether this or that object is beautiful, or whether this or that action was. There will likely be some agreement, some dis-agreement. But implicitly, you agree that there is something worth talking about — beauty — which means there are not only candidates that might be rightly called beautiful, but there is that which beautifies. It underlies beauty, is oddly beyond beauty, though it is beauty's wellspring. Spiritual intelligence perceives that.

The same can be said about what is good, not good, and so on. The point is that human beings keep talking about goodness, intuiting it is a real excellence in the world. As they do about truth and other qualities. Indeed, people will give their lives for these things, without being able precisely to say why. They simply know they speak of a part of existence without which there would be no existence worth having. That is why people are prepared to die for it. That is the detachment of spiritual intelligence in action.

Spiritual intelligence perceives that the most important and basic convic-tions are silent. It might venture that they belong in not knowing — the fount of existence that is beyond existence — hence valuing pregnant emptiness.

Dante expresses his awareness of Mary's detachment with three similes. Looking at her engenders the impression of snow that sublimates in the sun's warmth: it simply disappears, with no trace or puddle. Looking at her is like the leaves upon which the sybil writes her prophecies that are lost to the wind: they are dispersed. Looking at her is like waking up from a dream: it was intense and seemingly real, though upon waking up, the images slip away. This is pure consciousness, ready to know itself by giving up itself in rivers of abundance.

Dante praises the light of lights that is far beyond mortal understanding. He asks that some impression of this awareness will be felt through the words of his poem. It is a negative request, because the subtlety is known in the space the words create, not what they say. If Dante is successful, the perception will slip through his lines successfully.

This explains what Dante says next because he stresses that this high moment, focused on the living ray, was hard. He might have turned away from it. Imagine that! In the one hundredth canto, he might have told us he lost the plot.

But, to my mind, the confession speaks of the authenticity of what Dante is trying to describe. He is speaking of another insight known by spiritual intelligence. It recalls the tragedy of Lucifer, the seraph capable of the supreme light who fell. The infinite can feel like it is too much, so there is a temptation either to turn from it, as Dante senses, or to attempt to envelop and control it, as Lucifer tried.

The hard moment is another reflection on the replete nature of emptiness. He is stood before a change that is almost impossibly counterintuitive for a man used to doing. He must stay with the taste for being.

He does. He is strengthened by the quality of presence that does not hold back the infinite. He stays still as the consciousness of God wells up. And it does. There is a light, Dante exclaims, that desires that we share in it through being absorbed by it.

He knows how the many pages upon which creation is written are bound together along a single spine, he continues in another simile. He knows how form and matter, the pure and the partial, the necessary and the contingent hold together. An echo of the awareness he had then returns, as he writes the final lines of his poem, he tells us. His heart still leaps with the joy of what he knew in that moment, insofar as he can recall it.

My sense is that recalling the experience of God might be likened to the presence in the air during the hour before the dawn, when the sun is sure to rise and the golden light is certain to touch the sky. Blake called it "Eternity's sunrise." Or it is like the experience of being aware of being aware, and sensing that your gaze casts a light into the world, that is mirrored by the awareness that fills the world. Our awareness does not neutrally detect like a physicist's meter, it animates because it is animated. This is why someone's eyes can shine, a smile can beam, a face light up. It is why a person can be said to be sunny, energetic, radiant. That is a reflection of God.

Dante uses a fascinating analogy to describe this state of mind, in which he knows of something sure, because of being aware of what he has forgotten. He refers to Jason for the last time, to the retrieving of the golden fleece, and how the sea god, Neptune, was astonished when he saw the first ship, the Argo, riding across the waves. The deity had never observed anything like it. The sight above his head was so bizarre that he wrestled for centuries not to forget what he had seen as the boat passed by. The sight was so unexpected that he almost didn't see it, though it was there, and so he had to repeatedly, actively try to keep it in his mind.

Dante explains that the sight of God was, by comparison, so much more astonishing that he could not keep the memory for an instant, though he lives with its vivid, certain after-effects.

This is another big indicator of the nature of spiritual intelligence, and how different it is from its cousins, on which we mundanely rely. Building the Argo was not primarily about the development of new technologies, but the emergence of a new consciousness — one that could imagine sailing across the sea to unknown lands, inhabited by gods and monsters that would confuse and confound. Navigation too is an inner skill as much as an outer technique. The new consciousness is what really caught Neptune by surprise. He struggled to adjust to the presence of it, much as Dante wrestles with recalling the light of lights — though he perfectly well knows the light of lights is in the world, as Neptune knew that there were now ships.

I wonder if such forgetting happens to us very often in every day, because we are continually stepping into the next moment of novelty. Life is a continual procession of cusps or crests over which we might see with new eyes though we almost always keep seeing in familiar ways. And when we do have intimations inviting us to detect more — perhaps because we feel the wonder of the instant, or experience it as a dissociation or synchronicity, or as if another dimension is present — we spontaneously step back, rather than drop into the fresh consciousness. It is too frightening or startling or unexpected, though it can be prepared for in meditation or by practices like active imagination. It is part of the appeal of entheogenic drugs. Dante says keep at it. Keep waiting. Keep setting out on the boat of consciousness to follow the currents that lead not to more, but to the all. If we do, we are not far from him at the end of The Divine Comedy.

He feels himself changing further. He has let go of everything in order to receive everything. His detachment is perfected.

First of all, he sees a vision of the Trinity. It looks like three circles that are co-extensive and occupy the same space, though are also differentiated, as if by a difference of color. Double rainbows come to his mind, refracting light into one another, and flaming between them as well.

These are weak analogies, he exclaims, as he writes the words on the page that we read. Indeed, the word "weak" itself fails to capture the distance between the analogy and the image. He is compounding the paradoxes again, underlining how the failure of words can actually be a moment for the intuition of his readers to step in. Can we go there, and stay in his wake as he nears his destination?

He sees the eternal light is a self that is completely contained, without outside, simultaneously containing itself. It is known, knowing, and knower. It encircles itself, reflects itself, dives into itself.

And then, he sees something further. Within God is the presence of humanity. He sees himself in the light. It is the origin of the sense that, within us, is a divine spark or flame which is our very life.

It would be called nondual consciousness today. Uncoupled from identification with transient experiences, and returning to the first or primary experiencing, the presence of God is known as a steady presence containing the human mind. "My eye and God's eye is one eye, and one sight, and one knowledge, and one love," Meister Eckhart remarked. Dante perceives the divine I AM that is the condition of possibility for the multitude of shining "I ams" that walked the streets of Renaissance Florence and walk upon the earth today.

Dante knows himself to be within divine life. He sees it, for all that it appears impossible. He references trying to square circles, allowing himself a final few lines of failure that hope to transmit finally, fully seeing it all.

A prodigious flash of insight strikes him, and the wish is granted. He knows himself to be spinning like a perfectly balanced wheel.

He shares the truth of being, which is his being. God was his love all along, not the object of it, there being no objects in God. His intelligence and sight are the intelligence and sight of God. He moves as the love that moves the sun and the other stars.

And his extraordinary poem ends. The ceasing of words is its completion. To say more would distract from the truth. Our life and God's life is one life.

INDEX OF NAMES

ABOUT THE AUTHOR

MARK VERNON is a writer and psychotherapist who lives in London. His journalism has been published on both sides of the Atlantic, and his books — on subjects from love and friendship to the history of Christianity — have found readers from around the globe. He has a PhD in Ancient Greek philosophy, and degrees in theology and physics. He works with the research group Perspectiva, which champions the place of soul in society, and the International Society for Science and Religion, which is currently investigating spiritual intelligence.